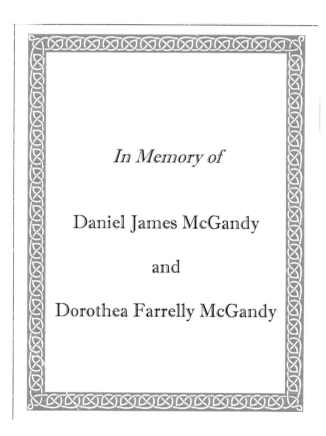

*In Memory of*

Daniel James McGandy

and

Dorothea Farrelly McGandy

# MURDER MOST RUSSIAN

# MURDER MOST RUSSIAN

## TRUE CRIME AND PUNISHMENT IN LATE IMPERIAL RUSSIA

### LOUISE McREYNOLDS

CORNELL UNIVERSITY PRESS

*Ithaca & London*

Copyright © 2013 by Cornell University

First published 2013 by Cornell University Press

Printed in the United States of America

Library of Congress Cataloging-in-Publication Data

McReynolds, Louise, 1952–
   Murder most Russian : true crime and punishment in late imperial Russia /
Louise McReynolds.
      p. cm.
   Includes bibliographical references and index.
   ISBN 978-0-8014-5145-4 (cloth : alk. paper)
1. Murder—Russia—History.   2. Trials (Murder)—Russia—History.   3. Sociological jurisprudence—Russia—History.   4. Detective and mystery stories, Russian—History and criticism.   5. Murder in mass media.   I. Title.
   HV6535.R9M36   2013
   364.152'3094709034—dc23          2012025097

Cornell University Press strives to use environmentally responsible suppliers and materials to the fullest extent possible in the publishing of its books. Such materials include vegetable-based, low-VOC inks and acid-free papers that are recycled, totally chlorine-free, or partly composed of nonwood fibers. For further information, visit our website at www.cornellpress.cornell.edu.

Cloth printing   10 9 8 7 6 5 4 3 2 1

*To my sister Betsy,
my best friend*

# CONTENTS

Acknowledgments      IX

Note on Dates and Names      XI

Introduction      1

1 Law and Order      15

2 Criminology: Social Crime, Individual Criminal      47

3 The Jurors      79

4 Murder as One of the Middlebrow Arts      113

5 Russia's Postrevolutionary Modern Men      141

6 The "Diva of Death": Maria Tarnovskaia and the Degenerate Slavic Soul      171

7 Crime Fiction Steps into Action      201

8 True Crime and the Troubled Gendering of Modernity      235

Conclusion      265

Index      271

# ACKNOWLEDGMENTS

The debts that I have collected writing this book will be a pleasure to repay. Don Raleigh has always been there for me, critiquing the drafts in ways that improve my scholarship and sharing the easy with the hard times, life lived to its fullest. Joan Neuberger bounces around ideas and laughs that help to keep me sharp. In St. Petersburg, Tania Pavlenko and Tania Chernetskaia enrich my life more than they can imagine, and I appreciate conversations with Liuda Katenina, even though they must now be long distance. I am particularly beholden to the friends who took time from their own work to read and comment on mine: Marko Dumančić, Robert Edelman, Beth Holmgren, Lynn Mally, Mark Steinberg, and Robert Weinberg. Though I remain responsible for the end product, their input made it a much better book. The line between colleague and friend is too narrow to be drawn, and I deeply appreciate the many ways that the following have been there for me: Boris Anan'ich, Laurie Bernstein, Steve Bittner, Pam Chew, Boris Kolonitskii, Dan Orlovsky, Ethan Pollock, Mark Sidell, Nancy Brave Solomon, and Bonnie Teel. My sister Rebecca was always so generous with her murder mysteries before she went digital, but we still share so much else. My sister Alice and I have enjoyed many a murder at the movies together. And I mourn the loss of those who began this project with me but departed before I could see it through: Alexander Fursenko, Janie Roden, Richard Stites, and Reggie Zelnik.

I am especially grateful for the institutional support that gave me the time to research and to write. I begin with the Fulbright-Hays Committee, which funded six months in Russia, and add the International Research and Exchanges Board (IREX), the Kennan Institute, and the University Research Council at the University of North Carolina, which provided for shorter trips. A year at the Institute for Advance Study at Princeton gave me the time to read through my copious materials, and a semester at UNC's Institute for the Arts and Humanities allowed me to begin writing. Generous funding from the John S. Guggenheim Foundation and the National Endowment for the Humanities gave me a year to complete the writing and revisions. In St. Petersburg, I have long depended on the professionalism of staff at the Saltykov-Shchedrin Library, complemented by the help I received from Nadia Zilper at the Davis Library in Chapel Hill. I thank Fred Stipe in particular for his help with the illustrations, and Jacqueline Solis for her detective work ferreting out sources. At Cornell University Press, I thank Mary Petrusewicz for her careful copyediting, Karen Laun for the skill with which she guided this book through production, and am again grateful to be working with John Ackerman, whose sense of humor remains as sharp as his editing pen.

My deepest appreciation lies with my sister Betsy. Our road together to murder began in West Hollywood on Poinsettia Drive, during those lazy summer evenings with burgers on the grill, margaritas in the blender, and *Police Woman* on channel 9. We still laugh about watching *Dragnet* in Oakland, sitting on the floor because my couch had no springs. Our brush with true crime came while cheering for the Knicks in the 1994 NBA finals, coverage interrupted by the police chase of O.J. Simpson in that infamous white Bronco. We have enjoyed so much together, from Caesar's Palace to St. Petersburg, that a catalog of our misadventures would read longer than this book. To quote our mutual friend Tania, "Betsy is a remarkable person. You are fortunate to have her in your life." I am indeed.

# Note on Dates and Names

Unless otherwise noted, all dates are given according to the Julian calendar, which in the nineteenth century was twelve days behind the Gregorian calendar used in the West, and thirteen days behind in the twentieth century. In transliterating Russian titles, quotations, and names, I have used a modified version of the Library of Congress system by conforming the old orthography to modern usage. In addition, when giving the first names of individuals, I have omitted diacritical signs and the additional "i," and have also Anglicized versions of well-known names and places.

Some material presented in chapter 4 appeared first in "Who Cares Who Killed Ivan Ivanovich?: Detective Fiction in Late Imperial Russia," *Russian History* 36, no. 3 (2009); and material from chapter 5 appeared in "Ubiitsa v gorode: Narrativy urbanizatsii," in *Kul'tury gorodov Rossiiskoi Imperii,* ed. Mark Steiner and Boris Kolonitskii (St. Petersburg: Evropeiskii dom, 2009).

# MURDER MOST RUSSIAN

# INTRODUCTION

"One day perhaps the leading intellects of Russia and of Europe will study the psychology of Russian crime, for the topic is worth it. But this study will come later, at leisure, when all the tragic topsy-turvydom of today is behind us."
— The procurator in *The Brothers Karamazov*, 1866

The man delivering water heard only a dog bark when he knocked at a first-floor apartment in the Iakovlev house in Gusev Lane on June 4, 1867. The blinds were drawn, suggesting that all were still asleep. This surprised the *dvornik* (janitor), because the people who lived there tended to be early risers. He roused the owner of the building, who brought a locksmith. Ultimately they got in through an open *fortuchka*, a small window in the back. The scene inside shocked every sensibility: In the bedroom, next to each other, lay the bloodied corpses of Colonel Vasilii Ashmarenkov and Elena Grigor'eva, "the lady passing as his wife." Their heads were bashed in, and her legs tangled in the sheets as though she had tried to get up. Moans drew them to the adjacent room, where the scarcely breathing body of gymnasium student Sergei Petrov lay under the divan. The boy would not survive. The body of servant Agrafena Babaeva, her skull smashed, lay face down across the doorway between the hall and the living room. The investigation turned up blood-encrusted hand irons and a log with traces of blood and dog hair. One dresser drawer had been emptied, but silver icons still hung on the walls. Government bonds lay stashed in the oven, but no cash. The absence of signs of forced entry pointed toward the attacker as someone familiar with the apartment's inhabitants. Only Sergei's tortured dog would pull through.[1]

Law enforcement officials looked no further than the courtyard for suspects. They arrested Iakim Fedorov, the *dvornik*, Anna Andreeva, a widow who lived on the premises, and Maria Korneeva, a washerwoman who had been at the house the day before the murders. The evidence against these three was flimsy: the investigation had turned up an overcoat belonging to Grigor'eva in Andreeva's room, Korneeva's shoes in the victims' apartment,

---

1. The information about the case comes primarily from the stenographic account of the trial, "Ubiistvo v Gusevom pereulke," *Russkie sudebnye oratory v izvestnykh ugolovnykh protsessov*, 7 vols. (Moscow, A. F. Skorov, 1895), I: 1–50.

and blood stains on various items in the possession of all the accused. Korneeva claimed to have drunk to excess at the Peking *traktir* (tavern) on the night in question, accounting for the blood on her sleeve from the spill she took when staggering home. Alibis did not hold up, and the suspects gave contradictory testimony.

Arrested within days of the crime, these wretched three were still languishing in jail eight months later when an additional suspect popped up. Grigor'eva's nephew had come to clean out the apartment, and found a bloody shirt stuffed in a steam pipe. A tag identified it as belonging to Daria Sokolova, a soldier's wife from Orlov Province, who had worked for Ashmarenkov some years back. The police sent an official to investigate, and he found items of Ashmarenkov's jewelry locked in a box. Details of the arrest then become murky. Sokolova had reputedly told the investigator that she had spent the night with her former employer because she had missed the train back to Orlov. She subsequently confessed to having awakened with an inexplicable desire to kill them all. Once in Petersburg, she recanted that version, insisting that the investigator had promised her exoneration if she would return and tell this story to "a general." What she got was newly appointed chief of detectives I. D. Putilin, to whom she admitted being in the apartment that night. In the revised account, she hid under the divan, listening to the voices of killers she could not identify. No evidence connected Sokolova to the others accused, but they stood trial together, formally charged with premeditated murder for purposes of theft.

Hardly the first ghastly murder to be perpetrated in St. Petersburg, the "Bloody Affair in Gusev Lane" provided a test case for exploring how Russians would adapt to the reform of their legal system in 1864. As one of the so-called Great Reforms launched by Tsar Alexander II (1855–1881) following his nation's disastrous defeat in the Crimean War (1853–1856), the new courts revolutionized justice. The impetus to reform the legal system was the widespread corruption that haunted all legitimate attempts by the autocracy to win the public's confidence about its ability to maintain law and order. The first step was to create an independent judiciary with trials now open to the public. Structurally, the new Code of Criminal Procedure transformed the inquisitorial system into an adversarial one. Before 1864, judges had levied tremendous power because they held exclusive right over the collection and interpretation of evidence. The judge in the adversarial courtroom, in obvious contrast, mediated between prosecution and defense. Guaranteed the right to an attorney who would represent their interests, those accused now rested their fates with jurors.

The jury, in the sense of fellow countrymen levying judgment, was not limited to the twelve who served, because so many other Russians followed the major trials in the newspapers. As Jonathan Grossman pointed out, press coverage worked "to inculcate a new forensic subjectivity . . . crime and trial reports constructed the newspaper reader as an answerable member of a law-bound state."[2] Weighing in on guilt by evaluating the evidence and the circumstances, Russians used the reformed legal system to pave a path from subjecthood toward citizenship. Both identities involve a personal connection to the larger polity, but the citizen enjoys a sense of participation and has rights, not simply duties.

2. Jonathan Grossman, *The Art of Alibi: English Law Courts and the Novel* (Baltimore: The Johns Hopkins University Press, 2002), 33.

A skirmish about how this mattered at court broke out in the 1870s when Minister of Education Dmitrii Tolstoi protested, in vain, that his penmanship teachers had a right to payment when subpoenaed to give expert testimony on handwriting; Minister of Justice K. I. Pahlen insisted such service was their civic duty.[3] Through the new courts, Russians could, and did with increasing assuredness, take active part in firming their own boundaries of law and order.

In this book I use the multiple aspects of sensational murders, previewed by the horror in Gusev Lane, as a means to explore how Russians engaged with the modern world that they witnessed unfolding around them as the reforms moved from official decree to daily life. The term "modernity" has become so heavily freighted that its utility has diminished, but as Carol Gluck pointed out, the term is not "dispensable in history-writing" because of the many commonalities shared in experiencing modernity as a condition.[4] Realized first in Western Europe, modernity seemed to hold the promise of progress because it imagined that human reason could apply science to solve social problems as it raised living standards. Liberal democracy would then allocate those solutions more equitably than had the rigid system of social estates. Modernity offered many people a palpable hope implicit in breaking with the past, but this rupture also produced instability, insecurity, and confusion. Whether celebrating the scientific progress that opened possibilities for individual mobility, or bemoaning the loss of community that left the individual isolated, all understood that the relation of self to both society and institutions had been made different by the combined effects of industrial, political, and social revolutions.

Russia's Great Reforms put the tsarist empire on that path to better living through instrumental reason, but the caveat that the autocracy maintain its position as the primary allocator of the benefits of modernity underscored the historical specificity of how Russians experienced it.[5] Russia's new legal system, designed to mediate objectively among competing claims, proved better at showcasing the many competitions that arose over how to manage the repercussions of reform. The theatricality of the adversarial courtroom made it a place where modernity could be performed by all involved in the pursuit of justice. Charles Baudelaire's oft-quoted appraisal of the modern as the flip side of reason, "the transient, the fleeting, the contingent," characterizes a Russian murder trial better than does the reformers' ideal of objective mediation of material evidence.

Murder is as old as Cain, though, so what does it have to do with modernity? One facet of self-consciously modern governments, in response to the Enlightenment, was to cease disfiguring criminals with the "mark of Cain" and to rely instead on a rationalized set of punishments for crimes. Articulated most cogently in 1764 by Cesare Beccaria in *On Crimes and Punishments*, the faith in the possibility of deterring rational man

3. Rossiiskii gosudarstvennyi istoricheskii arkhiv [Russian State Historical Archive] (hereafter RGIA) St. Petersburg, f. 1405, op. 64, d. 7491.

4. Carol Gluck, "The End of Elsewhere: Writing Modernity Now," *American Historical Review* 116, no. 3 (2011): 676.

5. Frederick Cooper argues to "keep one's focus on how such concepts [of modernity] were used in historical situations." In *Colonialism in Question: Theory, Knowledge, History* (Berkeley: University of California Press, 2005), 149. Mark Steinberg points out that "urban Russians were painfully aware that it was 'modernity' they were experiencing." In *Petersburg Fin de Siècle* (New Haven: Yale University Press, 2011), 3.

from committing irrational crimes inspired judicial reform throughout Europe and the Americas. Positivism reigned, with its faith that scientific methods could be applied to human institutions. Russia's "thick" journals, distinctive media that suffered harassment by a suspicious censorship, spawned the empire's critical intelligentsia by circulating ideas invested heavily in positivism as the best path to progress. Several of the most famous names associated with the reformed legal system contributed to these monthly periodicals.

I analyze the breaking of laws, however, not the writing of them. Lawmakers considered jurisprudence a science, but lawbreakers knew it to be an art. In 1888, the man slicing up prostitutes in East London's Whitechapel district personified the failure of rational deterrence. Calling himself "Jack the Ripper" in letters he posted to newspapers, the killer intuited the mounting significance of the sensational.[6] Indeed, sensationalism marked modernity in several ways, beginning with the technology that allowed for increasingly swift and inexpensive circulation of shocking information and visuals. Of equal importance, though, was the psychological impact of sensationalism, its capacity to stimulate emotional responses. Just as some killers took lives in response to their own heightened emotions, their audiences reacted in personal ways that registered changing attitudes toward the complexities of life itself. Jack kept the whole town talking. The world, really.

Publicity about the crime placed murder squarely in the public sphere, recognized first as the material spaces of the crime scene and the courtroom, and second as the social imaginary that interpreted it. From the outset, the nightmare in Gusev Lane served to champion the reformed censorship. Before 1865, the necessity to submit newspapers for prepublication scrutiny had undercut the timeliness of news itself. Once this censorship was lifted, a mass-circulation press could flourish, provided that it could attract readers. And what could be more enticing than the horrific murders of the sleeping residents in that apartment just off Liteinyi Prospect, near the center of St. Petersburg? The story was especially important to the fledgling *Peterburgskii listok* (Petersburg Sheet), founded in 1864 as a "boulevard" newspaper, that is, a paper published to serve the interests of its immediate urban readership. The initial editorial had promised that "we will speak exclusively about life in Petersburg . . . life that boils like a whirlpool,"[7] a nice characterization of what had happened in Gusev Lane. Crime reporting drew readers directly into the social narrative written by so heinous an act, providing the intimate details that connected victims to readers, such as in the autopsy confirmation that the servant Babaeva was "a girl of good behavior," and that although "the colonel was known to get upset with her [Grigor'eva] when he drank, they lived happily."[8] Pioneering in the technology of illustration, the editors published a layout of the apartment, showing readers where the bodies had lain.[9]

The editors of *Golos* (The Voice), a nationally circulated newspaper with respectable liberal credentials, recognized a second underlying theme. They knew that their readers would be alarmed by the brutality of the crime, but would also be chary of the police

---

6. *The Times* of London, October 4, 1888, reprints his letter to "Dear Boss" signed "Jack the Ripper."

7. *Peterburgskii listok* (hereafter *Pl*), 15 March 1864, no. 1.

8. *Pl*, 10 June 1867, no. 83.

9. Ibid.

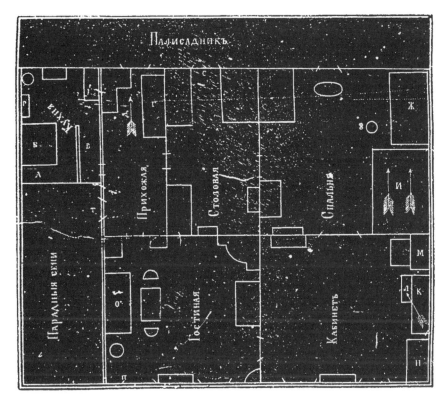

Fig. I. The layout of the Ashmarenkov apartment.

investigation and treatment of suspects. "All sorts of people run into our office with questions, wanting to know if the investigation has turned up anything new," they reported on the intensity of alarm. Aware, however, that although "the public's impatience is understandable, as this crime is unusual in both the number of victims and degree of savagery," they reminded readers that "it is simple to arrest someone, but we must bear in mind that all citizens must be respected, and to deprive them of liberty, even for a short time as a precautionary measure, can only occur in good conscience and when it has been proven necessary."[10]

The trial did not open until January 22, 1869, one of the first widely publicized cases to be tried by a jury. A slightly abbreviated stenographic account was published in *Sudebnyi vestnik* (The Judicial Herald), the official register for the new courts, from which private papers could republish information.[11] The audience at court cheered the acquittal of the three defendants from the neighborhood. Sokolova, found innocent of murder, was

10. *Golos*, 16 June 1867, no. 184.

11. Press coverage of judicial proceedings had been forbidden as late as 1857 because Minister of Justice V. N. Panin worried that news from the courtroom might become "the embryo of social disorders and of a subversive spirit." David Keily, "*The Brothers Karamazov* and the Fate of Russian Truth: Shifts in the Construction and Interpretation of Narrative after the Judicial Reform of 1864" (PhD diss., Harvard University, 1996), 28.

convicted for not informing the authorities of what she had witnessed in hiding. This verdict rekindled the stories of her being tortured into confession.[12] Her sentence of twelve years at hard labor raised the ire of her defense attorney, who argued that this punishment did not fit the crime of which she had been found guilty.[13]

The location in Gusev Lane emphasized the extent to which the crime was a city phenomenon, a critical component of the process of urbanization that followed in the wake of the reforms. The boulevard press used sensational crime to create what Mark Seltzer termed the "pathological public sphere," a new sort of publicly shared space that depended on representations of crime to strike a bond among diverse readers.[14] In 1876 the editors of *Peterburgskii listok* (The Petersburg Sheet) vowed to improve readers' access to the reenactment of crimes: "we have adopted a rule to send our reporters to the more sensational trials so that the reader can enjoy a lively story, not a dry stenographic account."[15] Pushing their weight around in 1884, two days after a particularly heinous murder, they announced that "we do not want to interfere with justice, but we have the name of the criminal: I. I. Mironovich."[16] When Mironovich was convicted, his lawyer got the verdict overturned in part because of such prejudicial reporting.[17] As the jurist Sergei Gogel' noted, "murder was a goldmine for the press."[18]

The multiple discourses sparked by murder, from the commission of the crime to the sentencing of the accused, lay the groundwork for what I hope to accomplish in this book: a portrayal of how Russian society adjusted to the seismic shifts set in motion by the Great Reforms. Less concerned with what "really happened," like incident analysts my interest lies in "what these incidents meant to the people who experienced them."[19] Like the ubiquitous American television series *Law and Order*, each chapter opens with a murder, a specific premeditated death that lays out the theme to be addressed. In the same vein, each chapter considers the contemporaneous context, the pressing interests of the time and place, and uses the murder and its aftermath to discuss a variety of relevant issues. The diversity of the

12. *Golos* supplemented news with a report on rumors of abuse from *Sudebnyi vestnik* on 25 January 1869, no. 25.

13. *Golos*, 29 January 1869, no. 29. Her lawyer was incorrect, in that according to article 14 of the *Ulozhenie o nakazaniiakh ugolovnykh i ispravitel'nykh* (Codex of Criminal and Correctional Punishments) "hiding" a crime was tantamount to committing it.

14. More than a quenching of the crowd's thirst for blood, Seltzer connects media representations with a "bond of togetherness" based on shared trauma. *True Crime: Observations on Violence and Modernity* (New York: Routledge, 2007), 40, 57. Historians of the U.S. press have long credited the coverage of the trial of Richard Robinson, a bank clerk accused of taking a hatchet to the pretty prostitute Helen Jewett, to establish the penny press as a novel form of urban communication. See, for example, David Anthony, "The Helen Jewett Panic: Tabloids, Men, and the Sensational Public Sphere in Antebellum New York," *American Literature* 69, no. 3 (1997): 487–514.

15. Keily, "*Brothers Karamazov*," 99.

16. *Pl*, 30 August 1883, no. 198.

17. N. P. Karabchevskii, *Okolo pravosudiia: Stat'i, soobshcheniia, i sudebnye ocherki* (St. Petersburg: Trud, 1902), 114.

18. Sergei Gogel', *Sud prisiazhnykh i ekspertisa v Rossii* (Kovno: Tip. Gub. Uprav., 1894), 89.

19. Robert Darnton, "It Happened One Night," *New York Review of Books*, June 24, 2004, 1. http://www.nybooks.com/articles/17224 (accessed August 26, 2008).

sources themselves contribute to the discursive tone: newspaper reports; lawyers' speeches; polemical journal articles; "true crime" periodicals; the multiple venues of crime fiction, including movies; killers' confessions; and the occasional archive that provides information beyond the already well-studied position of the state on the legal reforms.[20]

The autocracy, in fact, often made a better villain than the accused. Whereas the American TV show depends on the prosecutor's office to restore order, it is the defense that prevails in most murder trials included in this study, even when the killer still holds the smoking gun. In tsarist Russia, where the state intruded so bluntly into private lives, it was more often the defense that protected the social order, as is evident in the number of acquittals that hovered just below 40 percent. The attorneys who defended those acquitted in the Gusev Lane case turned the prosecution's case inside out by highlighting the clumsy and abusive tactics of the preliminary investigation, publicizing in open court the inadequacies of law enforcement.

The perceived primacy of the defense spoke to the major historiographical issue addressed in studies of Russia's legal system, that is, its failure to establish a rule-of-law state. "The court reform was the most thoroughgoing of all the Great Reforms," observed Richard Wortman. But the new courts "were also limited by the continued predominance of administrative authorities and the growing suspicion of judges and lawyers of the newly established Russian bar."[21] Laura Engelstein saw the judicial reform as a Potemkin village, arguing that Alexander II "appropriated the institutional appurtenances of a rule-of-law state (legal codes, independent judiciary, trial by jury), while continuing to exercise absolute sovereignty through the mechanisms of a virtually unimpeded administrative state."[22] Ekaterina Pravilova has detailed the administration's continued ability to bypass the independent judiciary when government personnel abused their authority.[23] Moreover, from 1884 the autocracy maintained a separate office, reorganized in 1895 as the Imperial Chancellery for Receipt of Petitions, designed to give the people the sense that they had direct access to the tsar, where he could resolve for them what the courts could not.[24] The successive tsars placed themselves above the legal code, and they pressured the bureaucrats who administered their realm to follow their example.[25]

---

20. Sadly, none of the most intriguing of St. Petersburg's sensational murders can be found in the City Archive, which retains only scraps in the *fond* of the detective division. The one complete murder file, an 1896 murder of a girl by a family friend, includes a variety of statements that deepen the regret that so much is lost. Tsentral'nyi gosudarstvennyi arkhiv Sankt-peterburga [Central State Archive of St. Petersburg] (hereafter TsGIA SPb), f. 965, op. I, d. 1037.

21. Richard Wortman, "Russian Monarchy and the Rule of Law: New Considerations of the Court Reform of 1864," *Kritika: Explorations in Russian and Eurasian History* 6, no. I (2005): 153.

22. Laura Engelstein, "Combined Underdevelopment: Discipline and the Law in Imperial and Soviet Russia," *American Historical Review* 98, no. 2 (1993): 343.

23. E. A. Pravilova, *Zakonnost' i prava lichnosti: Administrativnaia iustitsiia v Rossii, vtoraia polovina XIX v.–oktiabr' 1917* (St. Petersburg: SZAGS, 2000).

24. Barbara Engel discusses this chancellery's "public relations dimension as well as its symbolic significance" in *Breaking the Ties That Bound: The Politics of Marital Strife in Late Imperial Russia* (Ithaca: Cornell University Press, 2011), 20–21.

25. For example, Alexander III instituted a series of extraordinary measures after his father's assassination in 1881, granting extrajudicial powers to fight sedition, defined very broadly.

My interest lies in how reactions to murder played into the shifting relations between the autocracy and the public in postreform Russia. The former proved unwilling to surrender fully its discretionary exercise of power, but the latter happily asserted its own sense of justice in criminal trials. Indeed, the jury was simply the most democratic institution in tsarist Russia. The legal code's restrictions on who could serve reflected the state's desire for sober, Orthodox, property-owning males. The jury was, however, composed of all social estates, and depended on its members working together in judgment of other Russians. An immediate issue before the jurors in the Gusev Lane trial was: what would be the limits of social integration? The accused were illiterate peasants, and their contradictory alibis, coupled with the alcohol that had fogged recollections, made them less than ideal citizens. But before we cast the jurors who acquitted them as Populists sympathetic to peasants, we must heed the report from *Golos* that "they prayed three times before reaching a verdict."[26]

Even more remarkable, particularly in the provinces, was the reality that yesterday's serfs could decide the fates of their former masters. Selection to serve provided but one means of participation. Those who crowded the courtrooms or read the news happily weighed in their opinions. Furthermore, the gendered facet did not prevent women from flooding the courtroom and making their opinions known in various ways, from collecting funds for particularly sympathetic defendants, to tossing flowers at especially handsome ones. Perhaps Russia's women drew the long straw; jury duty proved so onerous that many men tried to escape it.

The open, adversarial courtroom introduced two emergent professions to the public, the defense attorney, or *zashchitnik*, and the forensic specialist. Originally intended as the guarantor that the accused's statutory rights would be protected, defense attorneys moved quickly beyond mere issues of exculpatory evidence, mastering instead a new judicial genre, the scripting of competing narratives of the incident in question. *Zashchitniki* grasped just as quickly the value of performance, aided by their reviews in the press.[27] The tales they spun for jurors drew from the experts, who in their testimony brought to court information about the many changes that science was undergoing throughout the century. What began as an exploration of official ineptitude, a predominant flaw in the inquisitorial system, gradually transmogrified into a question of personal culpability. Rethinking the etiology of crime, experts shifted the focus from the action to the person, from the crime to the criminal. This movement was part and parcel of the scientific discoveries that created new fields of inquiry, including psychiatry, sociology, and anthropology, each of which developed a dimension in forensics.

The experts called to court opened the world of the blood spatter to audiences that reached millions through print and rumor. Before the Great Reforms, a washerwoman such as Korneeva would not have enjoyed the possibility of a university professor verifying in public her account of the blood on her sleeve. By century's end, the professor would

---

26. *Golos*, 26 January 1869, no. 26.

27. The editors of boulevard newspaper *Peterburgskaia gazeta* (hereafter *Pg*) complimented *zashchitnik* Ordin for his articulate defense of Sokolova, but as for Fedorov's lawyer, "most sincerely, with hand over heart, we advise him to decline from ever giving speeches. Not only does he lack eloquence, he cannot even speak properly." *Pg*, 25 January 1869, no. 12.

be measuring her ears to explain her actions as symptomatic of her hereditary degeneracy. Arguably the most far-reaching aspect of the open court, the explanations for murderous actions provided a primary source for the popularization of psychiatry with the introduction of the insanity plea. As defense and prosecution alike turned increasingly to experts, they drew attention to the evolution of the modern subjective individual.

Subjectivity, however, evolved within the larger cultural framework shared by most Russians, the Orthodox Christianity that urged forgiveness and mercy.[28] The accused's confession mattered because Russia's Orthodox culture and its language differentiate between *ispoved'*, a religiously inspired confession that implies remorse, and *soznanie*, a straightforward admission of having committed the action. The two kinds of confession served different cultural as well as discursive functions.[29] Orthodox theologian Vasily Zenkovsky put forth that "the Russian view of criminals . . . is not one of indifference or castigation, but of hope for the possibility of their moral resurrection and renovation."[30] Even the law code counseled jurors to be guided first by their conscience. The comparatively high acquittal rates prompted criticisms that religiosity had overwhelmed legality. When debating the viability of juries, some reformers worried that they would regard "criminals as nothing but *neschastnye*,"[31] a word that lacks a direct English translation because it implies both "unfortunate" and "unlucky." The notion that luck played a role underscored the sense that jurors could have found themselves in positions analogous to those of the defendants.[32] The restrictions on personal autonomy that many Russians felt living under the autocracy regularly evoked empathy with those whom the state was threatening with the harsh punishment of exile and hard labor, regardless of what they had done.

Acquitting even the admittedly guilty posed a challenge to the fundamental basis of the rule of law. The most notorious such trial occurred in 1878, when jurors exonerated would-be revolutionary Vera Zasulich for the nonfatal shooting of F. F. Trepov, the governor-general of St. Petersburg. Technically, the jurors acted within their legal

28. Theologian of Eastern Orthodoxy Metropolitan Kallistos (Ware) explains, "'mercy' [is] a term that signifies *love in action*, love working to bring about forgiveness, liberation, and wholeness. To have mercy is to acquit the other of the guilt which by his own efforts he cannot wipe away, to release him from the debts he himself cannot pay, to make him whole again from the sickness from which he cannot unaided find any cure." Bishop Kallistos Ware, *The Orthodox Way*, rev. ed. (Crestwood, NY: St. Vladimir's Press, 1995), 69.

29. Michel Foucault characterized confession as "a ritual of discourse in which the speaking subject is also the subject of the statement; it is also a ritual that unfolds within a power relationship, for one does not confess without the presence (or virtual presence) of a partner who serves a corroborative function to the confession." *The History of Sexuality*, vol. I, *An Introduction*, trans. Robert Hurley (New York: Pantheon, 1978), 61–62. Peter Brooks distinguishes between "referential" (to truth) and "performative" (to explain the self) confessions, citing confessions by Dostoevsky's characters Raskolnikov and the Karamazov brothers to illustrate his argument. *Troubling Confessions: Speaking Guilt in Law and Literature* (Chicago: University of Chicago Press, 2000), 96.

30. Vasily Zenkovsky, "The Spirit of Russian Orthodoxy," *Russian Review* 22, no. I (1963): 49.

31. Samuel Kucherov is quoting D. N. Bludov, the chair of the editing commission that drafted the legal reform. Samuel Kucherov, *Courts, Lawyers, and Trials under the Last Three Tsars* (New York: Praeger, 1953), 54. So did liberal jurist V. D. Spasovich, *Sochineniia*, 10 vols. (St. Petersburg: Rymovich, 1890), 3: 269.

32. A former juror noted, unsurprisingly, that people in his pool commented on this. *Zametki prisiazhnogo zasedatelia* (St. Petersburg: Obshchest. pol'za, 1884), 9.

responsibility; she was on trial for attempted murder and they did not believe that she had shot Trepov with the desire to end his life. The Zasulich trial achieved symbolic status as an expression of public frustration with a heavy-handed and conservative administration, but it can also be measured as one among other murder trials that attested to the willingness of jurors to tip the scales of justice in favor of mercy. Hardly unique to Russia, the tension between local and official notions of justice stretched especially taut when the often arbitrary autocracy found itself defending the classic liberal position that objective law must transcend the subjective person.

For all the historical attention to the tsarist government and its legal codes, scant attention has been paid to those who enforced the laws. The secret police have attracted attention,[33] and the few historians who have studied the regular police force have focused on its institutional organization in the Ministry of Internal Affairs, one more bureaucracy that was understaffed, underfunded, administered by undereducated personnel, and therefore unable to perform adequately.[34] The judicial investigators, who served in the branch of law enforcement established in 1860 under the aegis of the Ministry of Justice, have found mention in histories yet remain anonymous. So have the urban detective divisions, personified by Putilin, who played heavily in the Gusev Lane affair. Investigators, aided by detectives, put together cases for the prosecution, and they enjoyed immediate contact with leading characters in every investigation. These men also figured prominently in the crime fiction that provided a cultural context for integrating the reforms into daily life. Therefore this study pays attention to those who pursued killers as well as those who prosecuted them.

Beginning in 1866, with Raskolnikov's butchering of two women in Fyodor Dostoevsky's eponymous novel about crime and punishment, Russian crime fiction customized a fictitious backdrop according to which factual crimes would, in part, be understood. Providing the comparatively safe haven of entertainment, crime fiction everywhere opened a door to the world behind the law code. Crime fiction's function as mediator between the true and the untrue empowered it to shape as well as to reflect cultural values associated with murder. The best-known example of this is Sherlock Holmes, who through his skills as a consulting detective became an icon of British pragmatism and imperial superiority. The protagonists in Russia's crime fiction, detective and killer alike, acted in ways that complemented performances in the adversarial courtroom, distinguished by the incompetence of the former and the sympathetic motives of the latter.

Although I explore the willful taking of lives for purely personal reasons, the most sensational murder of the post–Reform Era was political: the assassination of Tsar Alexander II in 1881. His heir, Alexander III (1881–1894), launched a conservative reaction

33. From Sidney Monas, *The Third Section: Police and Society in Russia under Nicholas I* (Cambridge: Harvard University Press, 1961) to Charles A. Ruud and Sergei A. Stepanov, *Fontanka 16: The Tsars' Secret Police* (Montreal: McGill-Queen's University Press, 1999).

34. For example, Robert J. Abbott, "Police Reform in Russia, 1858–1878," (PhD diss., Princeton University, 1971); John. P. LeDonne, "Police Reform in Russia: A Project of 1762," *Cahiers du monde russe* 32, no. 2 (1991): 249–74; Robert W. Thurston, "Police and People in Moscow, 1906–1914," *Russian Review* 39, no. 3 (1980): 320–38; and Neil Weissman, "Regular Police in Tsarist Russia, 1900–1914," *Russian Review* 44, no. 1 (1985): 45–68.

of counterreforms to stem the tide of liberalism that he held responsible for his father's violent death. This Alexander's own untimely death from nephritis in 1894 put the last Romanov on the throne, Nicholas II, whose inept politics led to a war with Japan and revolution in 1905, followed by even greater disaster in the Great War less than a decade later.

Two fundamentally political issues had been raised by the reformed courts and settled in favor of democracy by 1905: the acceptability of the insanity plea and the permanence of the jury to judge common killers, who were differentiated from political assassins. The first gave Russians a taste for interpreting the law and meting out justice, while the second allowed subjective behavior to triumph over the formalism of the law code. These two victories contributed to the mood that resulted in revolution in 1905, in the aftermath of which Russian society once again had to adapt to new sets of political and social rules, an enhanced modernity.

The violence that tipped off the revolution began on January 9, "Bloody Sunday," when government troops fired into a crowd of peaceful, working-class protestors. By October, the groundswell of opposition from all social estates brought the country to a standstill, forcing Nicholas to grant a quasi-constitution, his October Manifesto, which allowed for a representative electoral body, the State Duma. These concessions, however, neither ended the violence nor toppled the autocracy, which managed to regain sufficient composure by June 1907 to ensure the election of a conservative Duma. Nonetheless, much was different. Heightened political expectations combined with increased industrialization and urbanization that had psychological as well as physical impact. A contrast of illustrations of the bloody drama in Gusev Lane visualizes the change: a photograph of Sokolova from an 1869 book about the case juxtaposed next to a 1916 drawing of the murdered maid lying rather seductively in the doorway. The realism of a sinister peasant has been offset by the allure of her now-fictionalized victim, further sensationalized by her bloody handprints on the door. Times had changed attitudes.

The first four chapters chart the evolution and entrenchment of the legal reforms as Russians came to terms with what could be accomplished when accused killers pleaded their cases in court. The next four pick up after the country had calmed down and begun to take stock of the recent violence. In 1914, the outbreak of the Great War once again affected perspectives on premeditated death, and therefore I concentrate on the years between revolution and war. The war pushed sensational murders off the front page, but not off the silver screen, so I include movies about murder until 1917. Chapters 5 and 6 present case studies that depict a postrevolutionary urban Russia more professional, self-confidant, and striving to assume the burden of citizenship in the modern world. Chapters 7 and 8 concatenate a number of murders, fictional and then factual, to piece together a kaleidoscopic view of that society in transition. Gender plays an increasingly significant role, both as a cause and effect of change. Men who murdered their female partners captured a distinctive moment in time, epitomizing Russia's struggle between past and future. These deaths opened the conversation with the vulnerability of women, but then spoke just as eloquently to the impotence of the Russian male as the autocracy foundered. Instead of reading these killings as foreshadowings of the Bolshevik debacle to come, though, I see them as their audiences did, as junctures in a historical road that pointed in several directions.

УБІЙСТВО
въ
ГУСЕВОМЪ ПЕРЕУЛКѢ,
ПО СВѢДѢНІЯМЪ
С.-ПЕТЕРБУРГСКОЙ
СЫСКНОЙ ПОЛИЦІИ.

ДАРЬЯ СОКОЛОВА.

С. ПЕТЕРБУРГЪ.
1868.

Fig. 2. Daria Sokolova, found guilty
in the Gusev Lane affair.

Fig. 3. Agrafena Babaeva, the
murdered maid in Gusev Lane.

By stipulating my murders as "most Russian," I consciously invoke the cultural specifics of the crime, its commission, and its prosecution. As historian Joy Wiltenburg has reasoned, "the representation of crime operates semi-independently of the crime itself," and what matters are the "varying cultural uses" to which these representations are put.[35] Articulating their Russianness requires that they be contrasted with others, and applying a comparative frame helps to structure two important lines of interpretation. First, it locates Russia within the broad schemata of science and philosophy that were sweeping the West and to which Russian professionals also contributed. Psychiatry and sociology clashed with religious notions of free will, and also with political institutions over issues of professionalism and social control. The high acquittal rates of Russian jurors were not capricious; in every society where this institution renders justice, citizens judge one another on the basis of local norms.

Local cultures included the imaginative alongside the real. Crime reframed fictional genres, not simply in subject matter but also in strategies of reading. Edward Bulwer-Lytton's moralizing Newgate novels of the 1830s taught readers a different approach to murder than did Edgar Allen Poe's introduction of ratiocinative detective C. August Dupin in "The Murders in the Rue Morgue" (1841). French murderer Pierre François Lacenaire wrote memoirs that enjoyed international celebrity that lasted long after his execution in 1835. Dostoevsky numbered among the fans of both Poe and Lacenaire, but never as their imitator. The fictional detective developed such cachet that even a century later Europe's most radical, and influential, social theorists took him up to make larger philosophical points: Walter Benjamin, Michel Foucault, Mikhail Bakhtin, Roland Barthes, and Umberto Eco.[36]

My second mode of comparison situates Russia along a historical continuum. Though Hegel's philosophy long ago lost its power to explain history as progressive, during the decades under review many Europeans, not to mention Russians themselves, believed they were following a foreordained path toward a better future.[37] They evaluated Russia accordingly. Readers of the British publication *Chamber's Journal of Popular Literature, Science, and Arts*, for example, met the cast from Gusev Lane in 1870, Sokolova now dubbed an "evil presence." The accused were put forward to English readers as sinister examples of "what the Russian peasant *can* do."[38] One homicidal Russian sociopath initially found refuge in

35. Joy Wiltenburg, "True Crime: The Origins of Modern Sensationalism," *American Historical Review* 109, no. 5 (2004): 1377.

36. Carlo Salzani discusses Benjamin on this theme in "The City as Crime Scene: Walter Benjamin and the Traces of the Detective," *New German Critique*, no. 100 (2007): 165–87. Michel Foucault, *Discipline and Punish: The Birth of the Prison*, trans. Alan Sheridan, 2d ed. (1977; repr., New York: Vintage Books, 1995), 68–69. M. M. Bakhtin, *The Dialogic Imagination: Four Essays*, ed. Michael Holquist, trans. Caryl Emerson and Michael Holquist (Austin: University of Texas Press, 1981). Bakhtin discusses criminal fiction in "Forms of Time and the Chronotope." in Roland Barthes, *Critical Essays*, trans. Richard Howard (Evanston: Northwestern University Press, 1972), 189–90. Umberto Eco, *Il nome della rosa* (Milano: Bompiani, 1980); translated by William Weaver as *The Name of the Rose* (San Diego: Harcourt Brace Jovanovich, 1980).

37. In *Petersburg*, Steinberg argues the opposite, that many Russians lacked confidence that modernity was improving their lives.

38. "Glimpses of a Russian Prison," *Chamber's Journal of Popular Literature, Science, and Arts*, December 10, 1870, 797.

Paris in 1909 because the French police worried that the tsarist government was chasing him for political reasons, which made them hesitant to surrender him. In their turn, Russians proved themselves more sympathetic to the insanity plea than the British, and less tolerant of sexual revenge than the French. "True" crime quickened pulses from Moscow's swanky Strel'na restaurant to the rooftop café at Madison Square Garden.

Against the grand historical tapestry of Russian's struggle for democracy, that is, for popular participation in politics, common killers and their trials played meaningful roles in the shaping of public culture. The crime that cannot be undone, murder measures the sanctity and value of an individual life. It is in the discussions it sparks that makes murder so useful a category of historical analysis. By studying how Russians defined the crime and prosecuted the killers, we learn much about their cultural values, political norms, and social expectations. Furthermore, by stretching our analysis across five decades, we can map changes in attitudes toward the related issues that arise when a society pauses and considers the enormity of the taking of a human life.

# CHAPTER ONE

# LAW AND ORDER

"The main point of every criminal trial is to discover every detail of the absolute truth."
                                    —Notes from the men who reformed the legal code, 1864.

"What is law in the books is largely determined by history. What is law in action is chiefly determined by public opinion."
                                    —Roscoe Pound, Dean of Harvard Law School, 1930.

Drunken ne'er-do-well Alexei Volokhov was last seen about 2 a.m. on August 17, 1866, lurching along the streets of the Sadovskaia settlement not far from Moscow with another fellow in similar condition. Five days later his brother Terentyi found Alexei's corpse in the cellar of the latter's house, chopped in two, the upper half stuffed into a bag. The pieces of the torso lay partially covered with rocks under the muddy water that had flooded the space. Suspicion fell quickly upon his wife, Mavra, known to be unhappy in her marriage vocally. Their five-year-old son Grigorii told an investigator that he had seen his mother hacking his father, though the axe that he identified had no blade. Other than the boy's somewhat specious eyewitness testimony, the best evidence against her was circumstantial, based on the supposition that no one else but she would want him dead.[1]

The murder trial of Mavra Volokhova in Moscow in February 1867 would be one of the first to go before a jury, the macabre nature of the crime adding spice to the intrinsic interest of an open trial. The peasant woman found herself defended by a prince. Fresh from the law school at Moscow University, this only his second case, Prince A. I. Urusov is recognized as Russia's first influential defense attorney, or *zashchitnik*. He faced newly the minted assistant procurator M. F. Gromnitskii, both men educated in the culture of rule of law (*zakonnost'*) that had blossomed in the prereform atmosphere. The two debated before a jury. Without direct evidence, Gromnitskii had only probable cause, which

---

1. Much of the stenographic account of the trial was published in *Sudebnyi vestnik* (hereafter *Sv*), 15–17 February 1867, nos. 37–39, which was republished with additional materials in A. Liutetskii, ed., *Zamechatel'nye ugolovnye protsessy, razreshennye v Mosk. okruzh. sude s uchastiem prisiazh. zased.* (Moscow: A. I. Mamantov, 1867), 242–94. Urusov's defense speech has been republished often, including as the first supplement to the journal *Sudebnye dramy* (hereafter *Sd*), in 1898.

jurors interpreted as a continuation of the old, inquisitorial ways, when the prosecution operated in secret. *Zashchitnik* Urusov won them over with a fundamentally new approach when he raised the issue of "reasonable doubt." Urusov accomplished what had been unimaginable before the judiciary had been reformed in 1864: he scripted a narrative of both crime and criminal that contradicted the state's version. This chapter explores how trials for murder, beginning with the investigations of the crimes, gave depth and breadth to the judicial reforms.

### The Judicial Reform in Context

Tsar Alexander II (1855–1881) signed the declaration of independence for the Russian judiciary on November 20, 1864, with the promise to make justice "swift, righteous, and benevolent."[2] The system he replaced was so scandalously corrupt that even ministers of justice had resorted to bribery.[3] The most penetrating satirist of the era, Nikolai Gogol, created vivid images of wholesale judicial abasement, for example, in the judge who desires to have his bribes paid in greyhound puppies rather than geese, which honk too noisily in the hallways.[4] Playwright Alexander Sukhovo-Kobylin was the pre–Reform Era's most famous alleged murderer, charged in 1850 with the murder of his French mistress. Still in prison, before paying the hefty bribes that would secure his acquittal, Sukhovo-Kobylin mocked the system in *Krechinsky's Wedding* (1854), a play that today still retains its edge.[5] The parochialism saying "do not fear the court, fear the judge" summed up attitudes toward the legal system that stretched from the peasant *izba* (hut) to the Winter Palace.

Keenly aware that the legal system lacked both public confidence and the efficiency mandatory to achieve his goal of modernizing Russia, Alexander nonetheless continued to worry about an independent judiciary. Initially he entrusted D. N. Bludov, chairman of the State Council's Department of Laws, to reform rather than to reconstruct the legal system. Richard Wortman's skillful depiction of the many processes that led up to the judicial reforms need not be retold here.[6] Wortman fleshes out how a cadre of youthful Gromnitskiis and Urusovs became educated to appreciate "rule of law" as a philosophy capable of delivering justice. Coalescing around assistant minister of justice D. N. Zamiatnin, they persuaded the young tsar to support their project of sweeping reform. After several years of studying Western legal systems, the Russians borrowed more features from the French than any other. Adopting specific functions, however, must not be confused

2. Alexander was invoking the Old Testament prophet Isaiah, chapter 16, verse 5.

3. Sergei Kazantsev, "The Judicial Reform of 1864 and the Procuracy in Russia," in *Reforming Justice in Russia, 1864–1996: Power, Culture, and the Limits of Legal Order*, ed. Peter Solomon (New York: M. E. Sharpe, 1997), 51.

4. Nikolai Gogol, *The Inspector General* (1836) (Sioux Falls: NuVision Publications, 2007), 19–20.

5. V. M. Selezneva and E. O. Seleznevoi, eds., *Delo Sukhovo—Kobylina* (Moscow: Novoe Literaturnoe Obozrenie, 2002).

6. Richard Wortman, *The Development of a Russian Legal Consciousness* (Chicago: University of Chicago Press, 1976).

with the cultures of justice that the two countries developed in the nineteenth century. The Heidelberg jurist Karl Mittermaier (1787–1867), whose prolific writings connected the peculiarities of each country's history with its judicial system, exercised the single greatest influence on Russian legal theory in practice.[7]

How, though, had tsarist Russia developed a system so roundly despised and mistrusted? One paradox of Russian legal history lies in the inability of its most powerful autocrats to clean it up. The foundation of Russian legality dated back to the Law Code (*Ulozhenie*) of 1649, the most fundamental provision of which was the enserfment of the peasantry.[8] Peter the Great (r. 1682–1725) included legal issues among the many structures he borrowed from the West, but his notion of mitigating abuses of power meant beefing up the written proofs required by the inquisitorial court system then in operation. Never envisioning an adversarial courtroom, he coined the term *iabedniki*, "slanderers," for those who practiced law. His bitter distaste for lawyers prompted him to exclude them from criminal trials.[9] To establish some form of public law, he set up a procuracy in 1722 that, despite its Western varnish, extended rather than limited his autocratic prerogatives. The Ober-procurator oversaw the fulfillment of edicts issuing from both the tsar and the Senate, which made him second only to the tsar.[10]

Peter's most ambitious successor, Catherine the Great (r. 1762–1795), shared his antipathy for the venal and inefficient judicial system. She convened a legislative assembly in 1767, intended to rewrite much of the 1649 code on the basis of Enlightenment principles. Her instruction (*nakaz*) to the commission, however, came to naught, and was disbanded after two years of failed negotiations. Influenced by Cesare Beccaria's enlightened rationalism, Catherine responded to the failure of her assembly by expanding the procuracy into the provinces. Catherine's procuracy reflected the tension between center and periphery, as procurators responded first to the Ober-procurator in Petersburg, then to the local governor.[11]

Catherine's grandson, Alexander I (r. 1800–1825), redesigned the administrative system, replacing Peter's collegial system with ministries. His minister of justice assumed those "formidable" powers previously held by the Ober-procurator.[12] Aware that the succession of tsars and tsarinas had issued laws, mandates, and rescripts that often contradicted or overturned one another, Alexander appointed the extremely capable Mikhail Speranskii to begin the process of codifying the collection. Speranskii continued his work into the reign of Nicholas I (r. 1825–1855). The first Digest of Laws (*Svod zakonov*) was

7. I base this conclusion on the ubiquitous references to Mittermaier in Russian legal writings, which contrast to the relative paucity of citations from French jurists.

8. The codified legal system dates back to canon law introduced with the institution of Orthodoxy in 988; see Daniel H. Kaiser, *The Growth of the Law in Medieval Russia* (Princeton: Princeton University Press, 1980).

9. Peter followed in his father's footsteps; Alexei I had made it illegal to engage in legal representation. William E. Pomeranz, "Justice from Underground: The History of the Underground *Advokatura*," *Russian Review* 52, no. 3 (1993): 323.

10. Kazantsev, "Judicial Reform of 1864," 44–60; and Gordon B. Smith, *Reforming the Russian Legal System* (Cambridge: Cambridge University Press, 1996), 104.

11. Smith, *Reforming the Russian Legal System*, 105.

12. Wortman, *Development of a Russian Legal Consciousness*, 114.

published in fifteen volumes in 1835, and redacted in 1842 and 1857. Complementary to this, the Codex of Criminal and Correctional Punishments (*Ulozhenie o nakazaniiakh ugolovnykh i ispravitel'nykh*), which detailed punishments for specific crimes, appeared in 1845. The Statutes of Criminal Procedure (*Ustav ugolovnogo sudoproizvodstva*) promulgated in 1864 did not change laws or punishments, but rather restructured the ways in which crimes were investigated and prosecuted.

Circuit courts provided the first port of personal entry into the reformed system. Established initially only in the European provinces of Russia, the circuit court system included nine circuits that divided among themselves jurisdiction over 106 districts (*okruzhnyi sudy*). Circuit courts had civil and criminal departments that subdivided trials according to those judged by a jury or by crown (*koronnyi*) courts comprised of three estate representatives.[13] The personnel assigned to each circuit included a presiding judge supported by two members (*chleny*). The office of the procurator, also formally a part of the circuit court, would include prosecuting attorneys and judicial investigators. Circuit court decisions could be appealed to the fourteen Judicial Chambers (*Sudebnye palaty*), which functioned as a sort of grand jury and also tried some political crimes, though their competence here was ill defined.[14] The Governing Senate sat atop the legal system, the highest level of cassation. Although the Senate's decisions on cases appealed to it did not carry the force of law, the code mandated that the senators' explanations of their decisions be published and included in law school textbooks.[15]

The appeals process proved critical to the negotiation of justice between state and society. Gogol had complained that the "law is wooden; man feels that it contains something harsh and unbrotherly,"[16] but the use of juries and the possibilities for cassation endowed it with considerable flexibility. Technically, Russians enjoyed the privilege of double jeopardy and if acquitted could not be tried for the same crime, not even with new evidence.[17] However, cases could be appealed if either side could show that violations of the statute had occurred during the trial, which would result in a new trial with a different jury.[18] Violations were rarely difficult to prove. The code's article 746 held that "the defense, during the pleadings and debates preceding the verdict, shall refer only to legal statutes that assist in further defining the exact nature of the offense in question," but no successful defense attorney limited his speeches to the statutes. Retrying the case before a different jury, however, seldom resulted in a different decision.[19] Ironies abounded: if the judges

---

13. Samuel Kucherov, *Courts, Lawyers, and Trials under the Last Three Tsars* (New York: Praeger, 1953), 49, provides a useful table of the court structure.

14. *Ustav ugolovnogo sudoproizvodstva* (hereafter *UUS*), arts. 529–42, legislate relations between the Judicial Chambers and the procurators.

15. *UUS*, art. 933.

16. Nicholas Riasanovsky, *Nicholas I and Official Nationality in Russia, 1825–1855* (Berkeley: University of California Press, 1959), 98.

17. *UUS*, art. 21.

18. *UUS*, art. 855.

19. As the prominent defense attorney G. S. Aronson pointed out, juries would not adequately reflect the "public conscience" if different juries produced opposite verdicts. Quoted in N. V. Nikitin, *Prestupnyi mir i ego zashchitniki* (St. Petersburg: Trud, 1902), 158.

agreed that jurors had convicted an innocent party, instead of setting the accused free they called for a retrial with a new jury.[20]

Emancipating the serfs ipso facto subverted the Law Code of 1649, which mandated that at least parts of it would have to be rewritten. Regardless, the emancipation in and of itself did not provide a cause-and-effect rationale for why the new statutes took the shape that they did. Like the emancipation, the judicial reforms would not go fully into effect for two years, giving the ministries and local governments time to fill positions with qualified staff. The first jury trial was held in St. Petersburg on April 17, 1866, and six days later one was held in Moscow. Cities had to find space for courtrooms, or even places to build them. Enthusiasm ran high.[21] Now Russians charged with serious crimes were guaranteed the right to be tried in public, before a jury, and represented in court by an attorney. The well-meaning reformers had intended to replace personal decision making with procedural objectivity. What they had failed to recognize was that laws themselves were inflected by subjective culture, and murder itself proved quite malleable.

## Murder: The Crime

Yahweh kept it simple when he burned "thou shalt not kill" onto one of Moses's tablets. Local cultures, however, from villages to empires, have long recognized the deceptive simplicity that underlay this commandment. It might be a law of nature, and of some religions, that all humans are created equal, but such equality is rarely either politically or socially feasible. Tsarist Russia, like other countries administered by a law code, had a gradient for murder that took social concerns into consideration and was gauged according to the level of intentionality. What in the United States is measured by degree, in Russia had three points: an intentional killing that was plotted before being committed (*obdumannoe namerenie*); one in which the killer intended for his or her victim to die, but was not calculated so coldly (*umyshlennoe*); and one that happened in a burst of anger or passion (*v zapal'chivosti ili razdrazhenii*).[22] The severity of the punishment slid down the scale.

Nor were all victims created equal. Laws give insight into societies that codified them because of what they emphasize and how they differentiate among murders. Articles 1449–1471 of Russia's 1845 codex identified various forms and gradations of murder (*smertoubiistvo*), including those actions that might result in death but were not criminalized,

---

20. *UUS*, art. 818. Periodically, the opposite would be raised: could judges have the right to overturn convictions? The Ministry of Justice never seriously entertained this option, as the reformers had specified that any change to a jury's verdict must be "for the good, not the harm of the accused." *Sudebnye ustavy 20 noiabria 1864 goda, s izlozheniem razsuzhdenii, na koikh oni osnovany izdannie Gosudarstvennoiu Kantseliarieiu* (St. Petersburg: Tip. Vtorogo Otd. Sobstvennoi E. I. V. Kantseliarii, 1867), part 2, 309.

21. British envoy George Hume recalled the excitement in Kharkov for building the courthouse, and he received a ticket to the first trial, which ended in an acquittal. *Thirty-Five Years in Russia* (London: Simpkin, Marshall, Hamilton, Kent & Co., 1914), 136–37.

22. According to article 129 of the *Ulozhenie o nakazaniiakh ugolovnykh i ispravitel'nykh* (hereafter *UNUI*), the degree of punishment would be intensified by the level of education of the accused, although I did not find a single case where this was invoked.

such as self-defense. The importance of family and procreation to the social structure stands out, as the first and most severely prosecuted article forbade the intentional murder of a parent.[23] Pregnant woman were mentioned in six separate articles; the intentional murder of one was severely punished, but an unmarried woman who either killed or abandoned her newborn "from shame or fear" faced a comparatively light punishment.[24] Abortion, defined as "expulsion of the fetus," was punished more harshly if accomplished "without the knowledge or consent of the pregnant woman."[25] The persistence of canon law, with its religious precept for remorse, emerged in the five articles that punished for death as the result of brawling, which required church penance in addition to limited jail time.[26]

In 1873, the Ministry of Justice began compiling statistics on crimes, and calculated criminality according to the cases that came to court. Numbers offered the false security of scientific veracity, but nonetheless reveal patterns of prosecutorial interests.[27] The category of "murder" comprised approximately 5 percent of all crimes, but 40 percent of crimes heard by juries. The statistics included vital information about verdicts, the sex of defendants, and whether or not a jury decided the case.[28]

E. N. Tarnovskii, the chief statistician at the Ministry of Justice, oversaw the assembly of data. In his summary of the first twenty years, the patterns that he identified do not surprise: Russia's most common killer, as elsewhere, was the adult male. Females were charged with fewer than 10 percent of all murders, and their victims tended to be relatives, especially babies, aborted or otherwise.[29] Poison was everywhere a woman's weapon.[30] The numbers graph murder trials inching upward, only to explode after the 1905 Revolution. For example, excluding infanticide, 1,154 accused killers were brought to trial in 1880; 1,302 in 1890; 1,640 in 1900; up to 2,244 in 1904. After the revolution, the numbers more than doubled to 4,857 in 1907, rising to 7,531 in 1910.[31] These numbers refer

23. *UNUI*, art. 1449. Not only were the guilty exiled to hard labor for life (*bez sroka*), but "when they arrive at the place of work, under no circumstances can they be transferred to be among those who have reformed. Only infirmity can relieve them of working."

24. *UNUI*, art. 1452. Conviction resulted in "loss of rights and a minimum of fifteen years hard labor," whereas art. 1460 meant "loss of rights and up to two years in prison." A woman whose child was stillborn, and she hid it, received four to eight months in prison.

25. *UNUI*, arts. 1451, 1460–62.

26. *UNUI*, arts. 1464–68. No hard labor, and the longest possible jail time was two years.

27. The editors of *Arkhiv sudebnoi meditsiny* welcomed the ability to use statistics because they lacked the time and opportunity for the observations necessary for all medical answers. "Novye psikhiatricheskie issledovaniia" 4, no. 3 (1868): 55–57. Professor of law Ivan Foinitskii, though, recognized the fallibility of statistics, noting that information was collected only from crimes that went to trial. I. Ia. Foinitskii, "Sistemy razmeshcheniia tsifrovykh dannykh v tablitsakh ugolovnoi statistiki," *Sudebnyi zhurnal*, no. 7 (1873): 1–55. Foinitskii found another problem with the statistics: female criminality went underreported because women often instigate the crimes that men commit. Foinitskii, "Zhenshchina-prestupnitsa," *Severnyi vestnik*, nos. 2–3 (1893): 123–44, 111–40.

28. The highly detailed information was published annually by the Ministry of Justice, *Svod statisticheskikh svedenii po delam ugolovnym*, 1873–1913.

29. E. N. Tarnovskii, *Itogi russkoi ugolovnoi statistiki za 20 let (1874–1894 gg.)* (St. Petersburg: Senate Typography, 1899).

30. Every year for which statistics were kept, many more women than men stood trial death by poison, which merited its own statistical category.

31. These figures are from the *Svod statisticheskikh* for the respective years.

to trials, not the actual dead, and the ascent reflects multiple factors, including increased urban populations. Before suspected killers could be prosecuted, however, they had to be caught. Reforming the law had resulted in the need for new institutions to enforce it.

## Law: Investigating the Crime

Russia's police enjoyed perhaps less public confidence than did its judges. Charged to "maintain public welfare," a hopelessly broad assignment, numerous policemen exercised power arbitrarily. Salaried very poorly by the Ministry of Internal Affairs, many profited from their easy access to bribes. *Dvorniki*, such as the one charged in the Gusev Lane case, were at times commandeered to inform about the neighborhood.[32] Russia's national force was one of political police, established first under Nicholas I in 1826 as the Third Section of His Imperial Chancery. Alexander II supplanted the Third Section in 1871 with the corps of gendarmes.[33]

Central to the reform of the judiciary was the transfer of criminal investigations away from the police to the office of the judicial investigator (*sudebnyi sledovatel'*), established in 1860 but not fully operational until the new courts began convening in 1866.[34] Required to be educated in jurisprudence, the investigators were judicial personnel who often used this entry-level position to advance into the procurator's office.[35] They swore an oath of office and could not be fired without legal cause.

The overwhelming importance with which the reformers invested the judicial investigators can be gleaned from articles 249 through 542, which covered their competence. The reformers left notes on how they reached some of their decisions, commenting that they transferred the preliminary investigations from the police to the new procurator's office because they were specifically concerned with "eliminating arbitrariness,"[36] a nice euphemism for graft. Sharing the same educational background as the reformers, investigators would presumably share their respect for the law. Taking the lead in all investigations, these men also assumed authority in deciding questions of autopsy, expertise, and other matters of forensic medicine.[37] A stipulation that would acquire controversy with the advent of psychiatry required investigators to be able to recognize when a person was insane, and if so,

32. After the 1905 Revolution, the Department of Police supported the efforts by Petersburg *dvorniki* to organize an official *artel'* because "they are the first unit of safeguarding personal property and safety." *Vestnik politsii* (hereafter *Vp*), no. 20 (1908): 4.

33. A. A. Lopukhin, *Iz itogov sluzhdednogo opyta* (Moscow: V. M. Soblin, 1907), 15.

34. V. V. Shimonovskii, "Sudebnyi sledovatel' v poreformennoi Rossii," *Pravovedenie*, no. 3 (1973): 112.

35. A story in *Sv*, 15 March 1870, no. 71, spoke for better salaries and pensions in order to increase the investigators' job satisfaction. Gromnitskii made this career move; procurators began at 2,500 rubles and moved easily to 3,500. M. N. Gromnitskii, "Iz proshlogo. (Po lichnym vospominanniam)," *Russkaia mysl'*, no. 3 (March 1899): 84.

36. *Sudebnye ustavy 20 noiabria 1864 goda*, part 2, 111.

37. *UUS*, arts. 325–52. Rossiiskii gosudarstvennyi istoricheskii arkhiv, St. Petersburg [Russian State Historical Archive, St. Petersburg] (hereafter RGIA), f. 1405, op. 65, d. 3415, includes brief correspondence affirming this authority.

to conduct all interviews in the presence of someone from the local medical inspectorate.[38] Professionally oriented physicians welcomed these men, "young and educated in the sciences," qualities that made them superior to local doctors who "often sin against science, and limit their autopsies to superficial descriptions."[39]

Inspectors also had obligations to suspects. Foremost, they had to "examine without prejudice those circumstances that exculpate the accused as well as those that incriminate."[40] Additionally, once the investigator had charged a suspect, he had to seek out and verify evidence that could result in acquittal.[41] Justice must be swift; the lawmen would work Sundays and holidays if the situation demanded.[42] Searches were conducted in the presence of witnesses, and investigators had to account for all material evidence taken from its owner.[43] Anyone arrested by mistake had to be released with a protocol explaining the reason for the accusation, and all interrogated suspects had to know what they were being accused of.[44] Citizens could protest incompetent investigators.[45] And this they did.

The Russian population did not embrace the investigators with the hoped-for enthusiasm, nor did the officials always respect the public. An editorial in *Sudebnyi vestnik* reminded aggressive investigators that they needed official summonses to call witnesses.[46] Some citizens subjected to questioning filed slander charges against investigators, citing the law against false accusations.[47] Numerous cases against investigators for fabricating interviews, sloppy investigations, and overstepping their authority ended up on the Senate's docket of appeals, and the senators tended to side with the complainants.[48] One enterprising woman filed charges against an investigator who had refused her demand for an autopsy after she accused a neighbor of poisoning her chickens. She won her case, at the expense of his

---

38. *UUS*, art. 355. Local officials continued to challenge the investigators' authority with regard to the mental capacities of suspects. See correspondence for the 1870s in RGIA, f. 1405, op. 68, d. 2230; op. 73, d. 3652; and op. 77, d. 5970. In 1884, the year of Sarra Bekker's murder (see chapter 2), psychiatrists were complaining that judicial investigators needed training to recognize mental illness. A. A. Gosev, "K ucheniiu o brede samo-obvineniia u dush.-bol'nykh," *Arkhiv psikhiatrii* 4, no. 2 (1884): 54.

39. A. Askochenskii, "K sudebno-med. kazuistika," *Arkhiv sudebnoi meditsiny*, kn. 2 (1867): 13–41. This physician particularly welcomed removing the police from responsibility for the investigation. In another article, he argued that because the state treated doctors as bureaucrats, they behaved as such. "O sud.-med. ekspertize v Rossii," kn. 3 (1867): 1–32.

40. *UUS*, art. 265.

41. *UUS*, arts. 467, 477.

42. *UUS*, art. 295.

43. *UUS*, arts. 357–59, 367. The preferred witness was the owner of the house or quarters where the suspect lived; *UUS*, arts. 363, 376. Nighttime searches required special protocol.

44. *UUS*, arts. 402, 403.

45. *UUS*, arts. 491–509.

46. *Sv*, 24 August 1866, no. 27.

47. *Sv*, 7 October 1866, no. 56. The codified illegality of false accusations dated back to the Muscovite era. Nancy Shields Kollmann, *By Honor Bound: State and Society in Early Modern Russia* (Ithaca: Cornell University Press, 1999), 46–51.

48. Examples can be found in *Prigovory ugolovn. kassatsion. dep. pravil'stv. Senata* (St. Petersburg: Tip. Senata, 1873), 53–61; 81–84; 82–92; 92–97; 143–47. A general sued one poor investigator for insulting him by keeping his hands in his pockets during the interrogation, a slight to a man in uniform. *Sv*, 7 October 1866, no. 56.

heretofore promising career.[49] Several years later another investigator, having learned this lesson, ordered a postmortem examination on a chicken found dead of a shattered rectum in a case of a gendarme charged with *kurelozhestvo* (sex with chickens). Sobered up to find the dead foul next to him, the corporal could not remember any details. The absence of semen in the hen resulted in acquittal.[50]

More damaging to the investigators than public hostility was their postreform boss, Minister of Justice K. I. Pahlen. Despite having a law degree, Pahlen had made his career at the Ministry of Internal Affairs and in 1870 he acted upon his concerns about the independence that investigators enjoyed.[51] Removing the requirements of both a legal education and the oath of office, he undercut their professionalism. Pahlen established a new position of "judicial investigators in important cases," men not restricted in their activities to the circuit court to which they were assigned. This gave the minister of justice a group of investigators immediately responsible to him, overriding local procurators. In 1875 the ministry added an upgrade, the "investigator in especially important cases." The effects were multifold: more judicial investigators in place, but many were now seen more as bureaucrats (*chinovniki*) rather than specialists in law. More significant, they lost the promise of job security, which ensured their dependence upon those higher up.[52] Gromnitskii, who had begun his judicial career as an investigator, recalled the bitterness with which his colleagues met the changes.[53]

The investigator's legal obligation "to examine those circumstances that exculpate the accused as well as those that incriminate" put him in a bind. Law professor Ivan Foinitskii, who also served in the Senate's Criminal Cassation Department, commented on the paradox: "psychologically, as he pieces the evidence together, the investigator comes to believe in the guilt of the person he accuses."[54] V. P. Danevskii and I. G. Shcheglovitov, jurists leaning left and right, respectively, objected as "illogical" that one person be both the prosecution and defense in the same case.[55] Yet the reformers had placed their bets for cleaning out corruption in the belief that the "impartial actions of the investigator will secure respect for judges from both government and private persons."[56]

P. N. Obninskii, longtime presiding judge of the Moscow circuit court, sympathized with the task before judicial investigators: "they are given flour and told to imagine from this a wheat field."[57] He complained that jurors saw them as "predators" rather than

49. The Senate published its decisions annually: *Resheniia obshchogo sobraniia kassatsionnykh departamentov i obshchogo sobraniia pervogoi kassatsionnykh departamentov Pravitel'stvuiushchogo Senata*. This case appeared in no. 31, April 27, 1870.

50. *Sbornik sochinenii po sudebnoi meditsine* I (1872): 46.

51. *Sv* reported on the growing dissatisfaction with the institute's failures that contributed to Pahlen's changes, in 15 March 1871, no. 71. M. N. Gromnitskii recalled his new boss's objections to the institution. "Iz proshlogo," *Russkai mysl'*, no. 6 (June 1899): 30.

52. Shimonovskii, "Sudebnyi sledovatel'," 112.

53. Gromnitskii, "Iz proshlogo," no. 6: 10, and no. 12 (October and December, 1899): 60, 68.

54. I. Ia. Foinitskii, *Zashchita v ugolovnom protsesse kak sluzhenie obshchestvennoe* (St. Petersburg: Volf, 1885), 16.

55. Danevskii, quoted in Shimonovskii, "Sudebnyi sledovatel'," 113; and I. G. Shcheglovitov, "Prokurora na predvaritel'nom sledstvii," *Iuridicheskii vestnik* 26, kn. I (1887): 88.

56. *Sudebnye ustavy 20 noiabria 1864 goda*, part 2, 111.

57. P. N. Obninskii, "Oblast' issledovaniia v predvaritel'nykh i sudebnykhissleovaniiakh," in Obninskii, *Sbornik statei k iubuleiu sudebnoi reformy* (Moscow: Riabushinskii, 1914), 184.

disinterested professionals.[58] The ideal investigator walked on water: he was "educated," but also "conscientious," "independent," "self-reliant," and "knowledgeable in the human psyche," not to mention "honest" and "hardworking."[59] Readers of *Crime and Punishment* will recognize Porfiry Petrovich, the judicial investigator who realized that Raskolnikov was the killer but could never prove his case. Fictionalizing the intelligent and reflective type of investigator imagined by the statute, Petrovich attempted to cajole a confession psychologically rather than to beat it out physically.

Within a few years of taking the lead in investigating crimes, several of these new law enforcement officers published memoirs that skirted the boundary between fact and fiction: N. M. Sokolovskii, *Jail and Life: From the Notes of a Judicial Investigator*, was first serialized in Dostoevsky's journal *Vremia* (Time) in 1866. Other memoirs included P. I. Stepanov, *The Innocent and the Guilty: Notes from an Investigator* (1869); K. Popov, *The Guilty and the Innocent: Stories of a Judicial Investigator* (1871); and N. P. Timofeev, *Notes of an Investigator* (1872). Sokolovskii's and Timofeev's were both best-sellers in their year of publication.[60]

Setting a sympathetic tone, Sokolovskii opined that "I doubt that anyone has had to listen more often to tragic confessions (*ispovedy*), that anyone has had so many tears shed before him, [that anyone] has observed so much that makes one sick with sorrow."[61] Locating himself on the side of the accused, he wrote that

> someone who has committed evil, in all of its deformity stands before you . . . even keeping in mind that the most sacred personal rights have been violated, your hand is nonetheless shaking when it grabs the stone and readies to throw. The "accursed questions" arise. Who is guilty? An *idée fixe* spins in your head . . . society, with the clumsy way it poses and decides life's most vital questions? or the person, affected by physiological defects? or an inexorable fate? . . . You cannot give a straight answer.[62]

Timofeev echoed this sentiment:

> The psychological and moral aspects of every society leave their prints on the crimes committed by its members. . . . No one is born a criminal, but criminals are formed from life, . . . poverty, passions, and tribulations.[63]

One case that Timofeev recorded was particularly compelling for its tragic dimensions, and his conduct, more like a priest than a policeman, underscored the complexity that the role of confession played in the reformed legal system. Investigating the failed suicide of a peasant woman, he believed her to be concealing the true motive for her attempt, that poverty alone had not driven her. Piecing together the tragedy that was her

---

58. Ibid., 158, 164–65.

59. Quoted in Shimonovskii, "Sudebnyi sledovatel'," 114.

60. A.I. Reitblat compiled a list of the most widely read books annually, 1856–1895, in *Ot Bovy k Balmontu: I drugie raboty po istoricheskoi sotsiologii russkoi literatury* (Moscow: Novoe literaturnoe obozrenie, 2009), 193, 196.

61. N. M. Sokolovskii, *Ostrog i zhizn': Iz zapisok sledovatelia* (St. Petersburg: N. G. Ovsiannikov, 1866), 3.

62. Ibid., 11–12.

63. N. P. Timofeev, *Zapiski sledovatelia* (St. Petersburg: K. N. Plotnikov, 1872), 1.

life, he discovered that her father had raped her, then her brother did, and had fathered her children. The woman found peace when she confessed to Timofeev that she had murdered her depraved sibling.[64]

These stories appeared before Pahlen's reforms had achieved their full effect, before investigators "breathed the reactionary air."[65] Popov's are particularly interesting in their depictions of life in small provincial towns, where his arrival was more welcomed as a new face than feared as an officer of the state. Outstanding for their literariness, these stories differ markedly from those written twenty-five years later, which were "practical advice for discovering the guilty and understanding the psychology of the accused."[66] This first generation would inspire a wave of fictional exploits of investigators, which would set the tone for Russia's crime fiction (see chapter 4).

The investigators' handbooks show their workaday world. Emphasizing the writing of protocols that would assure efficient trials, these books expanded to include relevant laws and clarifications derived from how the Senate had interpreted them in appeals.[67] Statistics on the investigators' activities recorded for the years 1874–1894 charted a rise in the numbers of cases, from approximately 100 to 120 cases per year. Most of these were "resolved," which meant closed with or without an arrest. At least in the years 1889–1893, murder had the highest percentage, at 50 percent, of any crime to be resolved quickly, one way or the other.[68]

Significantly, the number of investigations that resulted in trial declined, from a high of eighty-six per one hundred in 1877 to only fifty-eight by 1894. This might suggest that investigators were growing less prone to rush into court without having first put together a credible case, although conviction rates did not rise accordingly.[69] Professionalism changed with the times. When the paranormal began to confront science in the second half of the century, one investigator from Simferopol recounted how someone appeared in his dream and helped him to identify a corpse.[70] N. K. Ogolovets added psychiatric analyses to his investigations by 1895.[71]

An incident from 1902 brought into focus the mistrust between public and law enforcement that continued to plague postreform Russia. Investigator P. F. Prusepp stood accused of the rape and murder of a young woman in the Northern Caucasus. He had charged the daughter of a local shoemaker with theft onboard a train and prostitution. She

64. *Pace* Peter Brooks: "confessor and confessant . . . engage in a fateful dialogue. The bond between them, like that of suspect and interrogator, patient and analyst, urges toward speech . . . confessions activate inextricable layers of shame, guilt, contempt, self-loathing, attempted propitiation, and expiation." *Troubling Confessions: Speaking Guilt in Law and Literature* (Chicago: University of Chicago Press, 2000), 6.

65. G. A. Dzhanshiev, "N. A. Butskovskii i sud prisiazhnykh," *Vestnik Evropy*, no. 12 (1889): 484.

66. N. K. Ogolevets, *Zapiski byvshogo sudebnogo sledovatelia* (Romny: Br. E. i N. Del'berg, 1895).

67. The most authoritative went through at least seven editions, written by the judicial investigator P. V. Makalinskii, *Prakticheskoe rukovodstvo dlia sudebnykh sledovatelei, sostoiashchykh pri okruzhnykh sudakh* (St, Petersburg: M. Merkushev, 1915). The author had been a member of the editing commission that drafted the reforms, and he was the judicial investigator in the Protopopov case of 1867 (see chapter 2).

68. Tarnovskii, *Itogi*, 3.

69. Ibid., 8.

70. N. I. Balabukha, "Iz protokolov sudebnykh sledovatelei" *Rebus* 8, no. 2 (1889): 20–21.

71. Ogolovets, *Zapiski byvshogo sudebnogo sledovatelia.*

died in his custody, killing herself by drinking carbolic acid.[72] The public outcry against Prusepp came from railroad workers, and also from local nobles led by Prince Mikhail Andronikov, who despised officials who abused their positions. E. E. Ukhtomskii, editor of the semi-official *Sankt-Peterburgskie vedomosti* (St. Petersburg Gazette) took up Andronikov's position. The Ministry of Justice tried to hush the scandal with a quick cover-up, but the aggrieved would not be silent. The ministry dispatched special investigator A. V. Burtsev to conduct a comprehensive inquiry.[73] Ultimately, Burtsev closed the case for lack of direct evidence against Prusepp.[74] But the official protocols included considerable testimony that "the judicial powers who conducted this investigation initially took every measure to hide the truth and shield the criminals."[75] The empire would soon be engulfed in revolution in part because of the failure of the government to police itself.

## The Police and the Procuracy

The procurator's office enjoyed control over the investigation, but it needed cooperation from a police force that often chafed at being subordinate to it.[76] If an investigator was not immediately available, the police had to begin questioning witnesses and collecting evidence, but everything had to be turned over once the proper official arrived.[77] Not just beat cops but also gendarmes and detectives reported to judicial investigators.[78] Mounting tension between the investigators at the Ministry of Justice and the police at the Ministry of Internal Affairs can be read between the lines of an 1867 editorial in the Ministry of Justice's *Sudebnyi vestnik* cautioning procurators to remember that their investigators needed permission to travel in districts not their own.[79] The Senate affirmed in 1872 that the investigators were to direct their requests for help to the local police headquarters, not to give orders to individual cops. A circular from the Ministry of Justice in 1878 addressed another irritant when it advised investigators not to order locals to complete assignments of "second-degree importance," such as delivering summonses.[80] Four years later the ministry sent an official inquiry to governors asking about conflicts between the two law enforcement agencies, but only a scattered few were reported.[81] Minister of Internal Affairs

72. Goading someone into suicide was a criminal offense, equitable with murder. Susan Morrissey, *Suicide and the Body Politic in Imperial Russia* (Cambridge: Cambridge University Press, 2006), 269.

73. Burtsev also investigated the second trial Tal'ma case (see chapter 3), when the wrong man had been exiled for the murder of his stepmother and her maid.

74. Burtsev serialized his memoirs in *Vp* beginning in 1907, but unfortunately failed to include discussions of the politics of investigation.

75. The Ministry of Justice published Burtsev's complete investigation, more than six hundred pages: *Prevaritel'noe sledstvie po delu Tat'iany Zolotovoi* (St. Petersburg: Senate Typography, 1903), 17.

76. *UUS*, arts. 250–61 spelled out the subordination of the police to the local investigators.

77. *UUS*, arts. 252–56, 260–61.

78. *UUS*, art. 261, which had thirteen supplements by 1913.

79. *Sv*, 11 January 1867, no. 8. The ministry published the paper in 1866–1877.

80. Reported in an article in *Vp*, no. 10 (1910): 260.

81. RGIA, f. 1363, op. 9, d. 29. That most governors reported no antagonisms probably painted a deceptively false harmony.

Dmitrii Tolstoi objected that his corps of gendarmes, who policed the growing number of railway lines, would be subordinate to the Ministry of Justice.[82]

However, an investigator new to the job in 1866, when stumped by a particularly savage slaying of an elderly brother and sister in the Moscow suburb of Mytishchi, turned to the local bailiff (*pristav*) N. Rebrov for help. Rebrov personified the old ways, and his name popped up at more than one of Moscow's early jury trials. The investigator needed to make an arrest, and Rebrov found two men whose background in petty crime, vodka, and confusion about their whereabouts on the night in question made them easy targets. These two never confessed, and they faced Gromnitskii following his unsuccessful prosecution of Mavra Volokhova. Proclaiming that "rarely does the prosecution find itself in such a strange situation," Gromnitskii nonetheless explained why he believed the accused to be guilty, despite the lack of evidence against them. Gromnitskii found himself arguing that "poverty is a vice," a proposition that flew in the face of common empathy. The defense made quick work of the bill of indictment, and the jury needed no time to acquit.[83]

Levying its power over corrupt cops gave the jury immediate credibility. The police needed some public confidence of their own. F. F. Trepov, famous for the shot that Vera Zasulich wounded him with in 1877, began his tenure as the police chief of St. Petersburg in 1866 with certain reformist ambitions. Appointed in the wake of an attempted assassination of Tsar Alexander II, Trepov's name became synonymous with repression. However, his directives also reveal a chief keen to the problems of public perception. For example, he ordered beat cops (*gorodovye*) to circulate in their neighborhoods, hoping to establish a constructive presence that would improve communications between people and police, as Robert Peel's "bobbies" had in London. In 1868 he established the capital's first department of detectives, appointing as chief Ivan Putilin, remembered for his role in locating Daria Sokolova in the Gusev Lane killings.[84]

A Ukrainian who spoke accented Russian, Putilin began his extraordinary career in Petersburg's Tolkuchii Market district in 1853. As he remembered it, his ambition had always been to clean up the corruption and arbitrary violence that made the police significantly more feared than respected. Putilin claimed a degree from St. Petersburg University, though a jurist with whom he worked remarked that his "education was shrouded in mystery." Putilin assumed his post as the court reforms were taking effect, and that he held his position until poor health forced his retirement in 1889 bespoke considerable success.[85]

Putilin received posthumous praise in 1907 from then-senator A. F. Koni, who had risen to iconic status as the presiding judge in Zasulich's trial. Koni had solidified his

82. RGIA, f. 1405, op. 68, d. 8126. Tolstoi fought this losing battle for years.

83. "Mytishchensko delo i dela Vavilova, Petrova i Kukhareva," *Russkie sudebnye oratory v izvestnykh ugolovnykh protsessakh* (Moscow: A. F. Skorov, 1899), 53.

84. A. Ikonnikov-Galitskii, *Khroniki peterburgskikh prestuplenii. Blistatel'nyi i prestupnyi: Kriminal'nyi Peterburg, 1861–1917* (St. Petersburg: Azbuka-klassika, 2007), 55–56. Trepov also improved sanitation with his support of street cleaning and plumbing.

85. Biographical information comes from the introduction to a collection of his stories, republished in post–Soviet Russia. *Ivan Putilin, Russkii Sherlok Kholms: Zapiski nachal'nika Sankt-Peterburgskogo syska* (Moscow: Eksmo Press, 2001), 4–10. A two-volume collection of his works had previously been published as *Russkii syshchik I. D. Putilin,* 2 vols. (Moscow: TERRA, Knizhnaia lavka—RTR, 1997). The quote is from *Russkii syshchik,* 1:264.

И. Д. Путилинъ.

Fig. 4. Petersburg chief of detectives I. D. Putilin.

liberal credentials when he counseled her jurors to vote their conscience, and then accepted their acquittal. Approval from him carried significant social weight. Recalling his years with Putilin when he worked in the procurator's office in the early 1870s, Koni pointed out that Putilin never hid the fact that before joining the detective bureau, "his life was often risky both legally and morally." Putilin had impressed Koni deeply when he caught the man who killed a bishop at the Alexander Nevskii Monastery from the blood evidence at the crime scene, retold later as "Murder at the Cloisters."[86] "He knew his world," noted Koni approvingly.[87]

The chief of detectives always kept on payroll *syshchiki*, paid informants from the "helpful poor," mindful of Sherlock Holmes's "Baker Street Irregulars." A word is in order about the term *syshchik*, which came to mean "detective." Loosely translated as "one who seeks out," the position dated back to 1745, when Tsarina Elizabeth I sent them to the provinces to aid local officials fight rampant banditry. These men quickly changed sides when they saw where the money lay.[88] Use of *syshchiki* could exacerbate the strains between

86. "Ubiistvo pod sen'iu sviatoi obitelia," in *Russkii Sherlok Kholms*, 265–78.

87. Koni's comments appeared first in the journal *Russkaia starina*, no. 12 (1907). They were reprinted in *Russkii syshchik*, 1:263–68.

88. I. D. Beliaev, *Lektsii po istorii russkogo zakonodatelstva* (Moscow: Tip. A. A. Kartseva, 1879), 595.

police and public. At a murder trial in Kazan' in 1873, the jury acquitted, in part because the police had refused to identify by name a *syshchik* who had supplied the information that led to the defendant's arrest. The prosecutor worried that naming names would scare off others from working with law enforcement. The jurors acquitted, refusing to accept that finding the truth depended upon hiding some part of it.[89] Likewise, the jurors who acquitted the drifters whom Rebrov had framed proved equally quick to convict his *syshchik* Artemii Vavilov, identified by the woman whose scalp he had opened with a chisel. The jury did not buy Vavilov's insistence that he had only been along with the others in a robbery gone sour because, as Rebrov's informant, he was obligated by law to catch them in the act. Vavilov stood charged with a second offense, slandering a policeman. His tales of torment in jail rang true, and the jury acquitted him on this count.[90]

The term *syshchik*, appropriated to mean "detective," carried a dual meaning for years. In a satirical journal from the 1905 Revolution, *syshchiki* continued to be identified as government thugs.[91] New slang for an informant became "setter," a hunting dog sniffing around and then pointing to the suspects.[92] But the continued dual use of the term *syshchik* spoke to the likewise dual appreciation of the police.

Catching killers as the result of a thorough investigation of the crime was only one of a detective's duties. In the Ministry of Internal Affairs, the director of police A. A. Lopukhin lost his position in 1905 when he failed to prevent the assassination of Grand Duke Sergei Alexandrovich, a favorite uncle of the tsar's.[93] Lopukhin, a former procurator of Moscow's Judicial Chambers, had for years wanted to professionalize the force, which would mean keeping them neutral from political pressure. The bitter irony that "the police were expected to defend the interests of the citizenry yet also to protect the government from that citizenry"[94] reminded of the political limitations on law enforcement's responsibility to serve and protect the public.

## Order: Prosecuting the Offenders

In their confidence that integrity and transparency would solve the problem of corruption that had plagued the inquisitorial court, the reformers had taken manifest care to protect defendants. Even Bludov had argued in 1858 that genuine reform of the criminal procedure depended on "providing the accused with reliable counsels."[95] The statute

89. *Delo o kolleszhkom asessora Nikolae L'vove Bel'skom i krestianin Kazanskogo uezda, der. Nizhnye Alty Tazetdine Khisamtutdinove, obvinaemykh v ubiistve i podzhoge* (Kazan': Gub. Tip., 1873), 236–37.

90. "Mytishchensko delo," 31–40.

91. *Bureval'*, no. 4 (May 1906): 3.

92. N. Sakharov, "Ubiistvo V. M. Karepinoi" (Iz zapisnoi knizhki sudebnogo sledovatelia)," *Sd* 3, kn. I (1899): 249–69. This story is about the murder of Dostoevsky's sister Varvara.

93. Lopukhin fared better than an ancestor who was tortured and had his tongue cut out in the 1740s. I. D. Beliaev, *Lektsii po istorii russkago zakonodatel'stva* (Moscow: Tip. A. A. Kartseva, 1879), 593.

94. Neil Weissman, "Regular Police in Tsarist Russia, 1900–1914," *Russian Review* 44, no. I (1985): 67.

95. Kucherov, *Courts*, 113. As chairman of the State Council Department of Laws, Bludov "could not conceive of a judiciary independent of the administrative hierarchy." Wortman, *Legal Consciousness*, 162.

envisioned the *zashchitnik* as an educated person who could ascertain that the accused's rights as spelled out in the code were being upheld. Now, "the procurator . . . and the defense enjoy exactly the same rights."[96] The judge had to "give the accused every possible means for acquittal."[97] The accused received a copy of the bill of indictment and the list of witnesses called to testify, to which he or she had a week to add names.[98] Objectivity reigned, given that "in his accusatory speech, the procurator must not present the case in a one-sided manner by drawing from it only the circumstances incriminating the defendant."[99] Furthermore, "if the prosecution is sufficiently impressed by the defense's vindication of the accused, then he is obligated to refute the original indictment, and his conscience must guide him to announce this to the court."[100] For his part, "the defense counsel shall explain all the circumstances and arguments that either refute or undermine the accusation brought against the defendant," but he "shall confine himself to topics bearing directly on the case."[101] The defendant got the last word, although the presiding judge then summed up the case to jurors before they retired to decide.

Orality was now paramount. All aspects of the trial had to be spoken: written documents were read out loud; witnesses who gave written testimony during the preliminary investigation were questioned again in court and cross-examined; the verdict was oral.[102] The accused as well as the *zashchitnik* could question witnesses, as could jurors.[103] The only person at court permitted to remain silent was the defendant, but that silence was not interpreted as guilt.[104] As an added protection, in conspicuous response to the inquisitorial system's notoriety for using violence to obtain confessions, the reformed statute mandated that even after an admission of guilt the accused got his or her day in open court.[105]

The accused did not, however, face a straightforward verdict of guilty or innocent. In a feature borrowed from the French criminal code, referred to as "splintering" (*droblenie*), the judge gave the jury a list of questions derived from the basic three: Had a crime been committed? Did the accused do it? If so, had the accused done so intentionally?[106] The third question left considerable room for debate. The Russian phrasing of it, *vmeneno emu v viny*, distinguished *vinost'* (guilty of committing the act) from *vmeniaemost'* (culpability for having committed it). Judges gave lists of questions that followed the logic of "if innocent of A, then guilty of B?," and so on, an indication of the reformers' conscious choice to give

---

96. *UUS*, art. 603.

97. *UUS*, art. 612.

98. *UUS*, arts. 556, 557, 570. The defendant and attorney could read and take notes from the preliminary investigation, but they had to remain under supervision in the court's chancellery.

99. *UUS*, art. 739.

100. *UUS*, art. 740.

101. *UUS*, arts. 744–45.

102. *UUS*, arts. 624–27.

103. *UUS*, arts. 720–24.

104. *UUS*, art. 684.

105. *UUS*, art. 680 allowed the defendant, after confessing, the opportunity to explain the circumstance of the crime.

106. *UUS*, art. 754 technically allowed for the three to be combined into a single question, but I did not find one case in which the three were combined.

the jury some leeway in order to avoid "formalistic, artificial, and potentially impersonal justice."[107]

The Russian courtroom opened an extraordinary space for victims to seek justice by allowing for a civil plaintiff to participate in criminal cases.[108] Those who had lost money as a result of the crime could receive compensation, should the accused be convicted, without filing suit in civil court.[109] Thus the state assumed authority for recompense, not just punishment.[110] As this legal stipulation developed in Russia, an aggrieved party could hire an attorney to reclaim lost honor as well as material goods. At the first murder trial held in St. Petersburg, of a man charged with beating his wife to death in a drunken stupor, the defense made the victim's shrewish personality and her own problems with the bottle the cause of her husband's violence.[111] It became common strategy for defense attorneys to paint victims as culpable in their own deaths, scripting the crime to show how they had provoked murderous action as a result of their own personality flaws. This resulted in the hiring of civil plaintiffs to defend the victim's reputation. In the murder trial of a man who had killed his mistress in 1889, a lawyer represented her two young children in order to salvage their mother's reputation for them. "If you find him guilty, you find her innocent," he counseled jurors.[112] They convicted, restoring honor to the victim's family.

The reformers' goal of using the open court to teach the public about the law had not anticipated its appeal as entertainment. The article that "observers will be allowed into court in numbers that correspond to the available space"[113] had led to ticketing, as in a theater, supervised by the presiding judge. Often the best show in town, trials led to scalping; tickets to the 1902 trial of the young man who had beaten to death his mother and two younger sisters cost as much as twenty-five rubles.[114] When modesty mandated, some of the testimony was delivered "behind closed doors," to the disappointment of the thrill-seeking public.[115] *Zashchitniki* recognized early on that they performed in a new sort of social spectacle, and many rose to the bar with no fewer skills than renowned thespians. We return to Prince Urusov, and his pathbreaking performance in defense of the peasant woman accused of chopping up her husband. Truly, no playwright could have scripted a more scintillating scenario.

107. Quoted in Girish Bhat, "Trial by Jury in the Reign of Alexander II: A Study in the Legal Culture of Late Imperial Russia, 1864–1881" (PhD diss., University of California–Berkeley, 1995), 158.

108. *UUS*, art. 7. Foinitskii referred to them as the "prodigal sons" of the legal system. In "O peresmotre sudebnykh reshenii," a booklet reprinted without other publishing information in 1896 from the *Zhurnal ministerstva iustitsii*, 7.

109. American history offers a memorable example of the strict separation of criminal and civil courts: In 1995, football icon O. J. Simpson went to trial for the murder of his ex-wife Nicole Brown and her friend Ronald Goldman. Acquitted in criminal court, Simpson was then convicted in civil court when the Goldman family filed a successful suit for "wrongful death."

110. I. Ia. Foinitskii, *Kurs ugolovnnogo sudoproizvodstva*, vol. 2, 4th ed. (St. Petersburg: Dvitotel', 1915), 80.

111. *Sv*, 7 October 1866, no. 56; and 8 November 1866, no. 81.

112. *Sudebnye dramy* (Moscow: A. A. Skorov, 1889), 62.

113. *UUS*, art. 620.

114. "Delo Kara," *Sd* 6, kn. 5 (May 1902): 147.

115. *UUS*, art. 621. Jurors heard all, and defendants and their attorneys were allowed a small coterie of witnesses behind those doors.

Procurator Gromnitskii boasted "a selfless faith in the infallibility of the court."[116] Yet he began his prosecution of Mavra with rumor, agreeing with the "local gossip" (*narodnyi golos*) that had declared her guilty "because it rarely makes mistakes."[117]

The primary evidence against her was the traces of blood that could still be detected on the apartment floor and walls, despite her having recently scoured the place.[118] Gromnitskii called professors of chemistry to the stand to explain what science could glean from the spatters.[119] Mavra rebutted that the blood had dripped from Alexei's nose as he had lain on the floor for three days after an intoxicated fight. She attributed her fastidious cleaning to her late husband's habit of vomiting when he habitually came home inebriated.[120] Not only could the experts not refute her statement, they could not even confirm that the blood was human.

Many statutes had guaranteed the defendant's rights, but none had given thought to personality. Mavra's jurors included three merchants, five bureaucrats, and four nobles, in addition to the crowd in the courtroom.[121] She made an attractive defendant, a peasant specimen for an urban audience. She and her in-laws did not disappoint, sparring on the witness stand as they had in the neighborhood. The legal scholar A. Liutetskii, an early enthusiast of the entertainment value of the adversarial court, introduced her to his readers:

> Exhausted from all that she has suffered, she still preserves her strength and self-respect. Automatically you think to yourself, this woman is capable of terrible vengeance, but she can also show the most heartfelt tenderness. Anger and meekness do constant battle within her . . . something in this peasant woman raises her conspicuously above her customary surroundings.[122]

The serious newspaper *Golos*, too, seemed smitten with Mavra: "Despite her obvious exhaustion and extreme pallor, she retained traces of beauty. Her appearance, voice, and the ingenuity with which she answered questions made a favorable impression on the jury and everyone in attendance."[123]

Urusov took notice. Having lost his first case in the provincial town of Bogorodsk, where he had not been able to save a drifter accused in an especially grisly murder of a

---

116. Quoted in Wortman, *Legal Consciousness*, 266.

117. "Delo Mavry Volokhovoi," *Russkie sudebnye oratory v izvestnykh ugolovnykh protsessov*, vol. 3 (Moscow: A. F. Skorov, 1899), 10.

118. *Sv*, 16 February 1867, no. 36.

119. The empire's top forensic specialist analyzed these experts' testimony. E. V. Pelikan, "Delo o krest'ianke Mavry Egorovoi Volokhovoi, rassmatrivavsheesia v moskovskom okruzhnom sude, s uchastiem prisiazhnykh zasedatelei," *Arkhiv sudebnoi meditsiny*, no. 2 (1867) 92–115.

120. "Delo Mavry Volokhovoi," 13; *Sv*, 16 February 1867, no. 36.

121. *Sv*, 15 February 1867, no. 35.

122. Liutetskii, ed., *Zamechatel'nye ugolovnye protsessy*, 263.

123. *Golos*, 15 February 1867, no. 46.

priest's cook, he realized that poking holes in the prosecution was not enough.[124] He had to draft a counternarrative of the case, one with fully formed characters. Playing up a particularity of the code, he further elicited empathy for this desperate housewife by painting her as deeply religious. Likely exaggerating the extent to which Russians of all confessions feared their God, the reformers had paid close attention to the taking of oaths. In liberal response to the empire's many religions, witnesses and jurors alike were sworn in by a representative of their faith.[125] Moreover, the law did not *require* witnesses to take a religious oath; the reformers sought to spare family members the temptation to perjure under oath, an act that threatened them with eternal damnation.[126]

Not swearing on a holy book, though, would undermine the veracity of the testimony. Urusov told jurors that he had advised Mavra against insisting that her husband's brothers testify under oath because that would diminish what they said against her. "But she answered me, 'they'll know that God is watching them and tell the truth,'" he confided as her show of faith.[127] The trial's transcript shows a less saintly Mavra. The most delightful rejoinders between her and her in-laws centered around whether or not Terentyi had bribed little Grigorii with gingerbread to encourage him to tell of having seen her whacking his father. Another sibling, Semen, denied any such sweet payoff. "He gave it to the boy in front of you!" Mavra protested. "You're just saying this because he's your older brother, and that's not good."[128]

Urusov dismissed the investigation, which could not connect his client to the crime. His closing words exceeded all leeway from the statute and echoed well beyond the Moscow courtroom:

> Before you is a woman who has been languishing for six months under terrible accusations. She lived unhappily with her husband for nine years, and an even more bitter ending awaits this moral person. . . . I do not ask you to take these mitigating circumstances into consideration. I expect a just verdict, and that will be an acquittal![129]

"This is a courtroom, not a theater!" The judge tried to quiet the applause that erupted when the jury fulfilled Urusov's expectations.[130] Urusov's speech became legendary because it announced that the *zashchitnik* had a very different role to play than the one imagined by the code. Juxtaposing Urusov's speech next to an unsuccessful one made by another

124. Gromnitskii had prosecuted this trial, to be bested by Urusov in the Volokhova case. L. Snegirev and S. A. Andreevskii, "Kniaz A. I. Urusov: Nekrolog," *Sd* 4, kn. 9 (1900): 9.

125. *UUS*, art. 711.

126. *UUS*, art. 717. In the debates when drawing up the code, the reformers concluded that "regardless of how decided they are to give unprejudiced testimony, the feeling of love that they have for the accused might force them against their will to suppress the demands of conscience. The law must not put anyone in a position that threatens them to commit perjury." *Sudebnye ustavy 20 noiabria 1864 goda*, part 2, 255.

127. "Delo Mavry Volokhovoi," 24.

128. Liutetskii, *Zamechatel'nye ugolovnye protsessy*, 263.

129. *Golos* reported Urusov's words enthusiastically from the trial, 17 February 1867, no. 48. An editorial in *Sv* already worried that "the defense's speech is not always strictly businesslike," because *zashchitniki* forget that like prosecutors, they are not supposed to be one-sided (15 January 1867, no. 12).

130. *Sv*, 17 February 1867, no. 37.

lawyer defending a woman of murder in 1868 illustrates the triumph of performance. One significant difference separates these two cases: Mavra Volokhova never confessed, and Aleksandra Rybakovskaia stood over the bleeding lover who had tossed her out, the gun still smoking in her hand. K. K. Arsen'ev, Rybakovskaia's attorney, was one of Russia's most articulate liberal voices in the 1860s. Concentrating on the evidence, he followed the statute's rules governing defense. His objective was to mitigate the circumstances of the crime in order to have her charged with carelessness with a gun rather than premeditated murder.[131]

Sticking to the facts, he rested his case on the sloppiness of the preliminary investigation. The policeman who had interviewed the victim at the hospital before his death had not written the proper protocols. Therefore, instead of reading the report officially into the record, the cop testified from his memory, which Arsen'ev doubted remained reliable. The *zashchitnik* presented medical charts showing the victim's fever and pulse as he lay dying, evidence that he was not "of sound mind and healthy memory" and therefore untrustworthy in recounting the details of the shooting.[132] More professionals new to the scene, weapons experts, testified that the shots could have been fired accidentally.[133]

Arsen'ev took logic to the extreme when he tried to turn Rybakovskaia into a rational actor. This woman had claimed to be a Moslem princess, faked tuberculosis by drinking bull's blood and throwing it up, and had lied about being a wet nurse so that she could take in a baby boy, who died under her care. Focusing on facticity, Arsen'ev argued that these incidents were legally irrelevant.[134] Not so to the jurors, who refused to believe that she was firing at a candle when she hit her lover. Rybakovskaia's biography of abuse, neglect, and poverty could have transformed her into a tragic heroine cast aside by the man she loved. The jury rejected Arsen'ev's plea to lessen the charge, and she got ten years of hard labor followed by Siberian exile *na vsegda* (forever).

A contrast between the careers of Urusov and Arsen'ev casts into relief much about how the legal profession developed from theory into practice. Urusov enjoyed family connections to the Naryshkin clan (that of Peter the Great's mother), and the presiding magistrate at the Moscow circuit court P. M. Shchepkin took the young lawyer into his home "as a relative."[135] Minister of Foreign Affairs V. M. Gorchakov was an uncle, and Alexander Pushkin, dead before Urusov's birth, had been a regular guest in the family

131. The details from this case are taken from "Delo Aleksandry Rybakovskoi, obviniaemoi v ubiistve," *Russkie sudebnye oratory*, 7 vols. (Moscow: A. F. Skorov, 1903), 7:273–324.

132. "Delo Aleksandry Rybakovskoi," 306. The procurator insisted that a Christian on his deathbed would tell the truth (295).

133. N. Shishkin supplied an extensive analysis of the bullets. *Sv*, 19 November 1868, no. 249.

134. Writing about this case later, Arsen'ev noted that a person's past might give grounds for amelioration, but not acquittal. *Predanie sudu i dal'neishii khod ugolovnoi dela do nachala sudebnoe sledstviia* (St. Petersburg: V. Dimakov, 1870), 74–75.

135. L. D. Liakhovetskii, *Kharakteristika izvestnykh russkikh sudebnykh oratorov* (St. Petersburg: M. Ia. Minkov, 1897), 271.

Fig. 5. The leading liberal, K. K. Arsen'ev.

home.[136] Very much a man of his era, Urusov was briefly suspended from the university for participating in student protests in the 1860s, *de rigeur* for those caught up in the reforming spirit that Alexander II had brought to the throne. He endured a second political penalty, a three-year exile to the Baltic provinces, for his spirited defense in 1873 of one of the participants in the Nechaev affair, the title character of which was a self-styled revolutionary who had persuaded members of his secret cell to murder one of their own. Urusov rehabilitated himself by working in the provincial chancellery and as the assistant procurator in both the Warsaw and St. Petersburg district courts. Awarded the Order of St. Vladimir, 4th class, in 1881 for service to the state, he returned to private practice. Like many of his colleagues, and such future state officials as Ober-procurator of the Senate N. A. Nekliudov, he flirted with oppositional politics but also worked at times for the government, still the primary source of power.

"Velvet baritone."[137] This described Urusov's timbre and style. His theatrical flourishes derived in part from his love for French literature, and in the absence of Russian

136. Biographical information comes from N. A. Troitskii, *Korifei rossiiskoi advokatury* (Moscow: Tsentrpoligraf, 2006), 81–82; and obituaries by Snegirov and Andreevskii, "Kniaz A. I. Urusov," 1–37.
137. Liakhovetskii, *Kharakteristika*, 273.

oratorical models he patterned himself after revolutionary statesman and lawyer Honoré Mirabeau.[138] A successful litigator, he "by nature thirsts for sharp polemics . . . he seeks passion, conflict, war. . . . If the case demands a detailed analysis of facts, Prince Urusov is not the appropriate advocate."[139] Characteristically, Urusov did not bother to acquaint himself with the details of the case until he was at court. Preferring to watch how it unfolded before him, he "loved emotional tirades, an angry tone of voice."[140] Twenty-five years after liberating Mavra, he was still appreciated for his "attractive base, lovely diction, and aristocratic manners . . . substituting serious thought and preparation with poise."[141] The public loved a polished performance.[142]

Arsen'ev personified the statute's ideal *zashchitnik*.[143] Having begun his career at the Ministry of Justice in 1855, he took a leave in 1863 to write for the most influential liberal thick journal of the day, *Otechestvennye zapiski* (Notes of the Fatherland). Arsen'ev moved to Bonn briefly to study philosophy at the university, returning in 1867 to join the newly formed St. Petersburg bar. Serving as the corporation's first chairman, Arsen'ev "more than any others served as a personal example . . . to establish the lawyer as a respectable type."[144] His speeches were "even, smooth, without affect, emotion, or spark, but logical and detailed. This orator gave the impression of seriousness, that every word had been thought out after a careful study of the case."[145] One of his most thankless tasks had been to defend Maksim Ivanov, the ringleader of a crew who had enticed a debauched nobleman to his apartment with the promise of a child-virgin for sale. Instead of sex, N. Kh. von Zon got strangled, chopped up, packed in a suitcase, and taken to the station for shipment to Moscow. Arsen'ev tried without luck to deflect suspicion from his client on the basis that the only witnesses to Ivanov's activities were also on trial for the crime.[146]

Arsen'ev noticed that the courtroom was not a mecca for legal truths, and defending Ivanov tested his mettle. In 1874 he returned to state service in the Senate, as assistant to the Ober-procurator of the Civil Cassation Department. He surrendered the Senate for political journalism in 1884, writing for the thick journal *Vestnik Evropy* (The Herald of

---

138. D. S. Mirsky, characterized Urusov as "one of the best critics of literature of his time" and credited him with introducing Gustave Flaubert and Charles Baudelaire to Russia. *A History of Russian Literature, Comprising a History of Russian Literature and Contemporary Russian Literature*, ed. and abrid. Francis J. Whitfield (New York: A. A. Knopf, 1949), 358–60.

139. Liakhovetskii, *Kharakteristiki*, 273.

140. Ibid., 275.

141. Peterburzhets, "Malenkaia khronika," *Novoe vremia* (hereafter *Nv*), 24 March 1895, no. 6849.

142. In 1886, the presiding judge at the Viatka circuit court asked the chairman of the Moscow Bar snidely if its members could be registered as an acting troupe. I. V. Gessen, *Advokatura, obshchestvo, i gosudarstvo, 1864–1914* (Moscow: Soviet pris. pover., 1914), 271.

143. Arsen'ev had argued otherwise, that attorneys must privilege law itself above all else. Quoted in E. V. Vas'kovskii in *Osnovnoi voprosy advokatskoi etiki* (St. Petersburg: M. Merkushev, 1895), 14.

144. Liakhovetskii, *Kharakteristiki*, 77.

145. Ibid., 79.

146. *Sv* covered the trial from 15 March 1870, no. 71, to 4 April 1870, no. 91. Future Nobel laureate Dmitrii Mendeleev analyzed the poison used.

Europe) after the censors had shut down *Otechestvennye zapiski*. He continued to write about the legal system but no longer practiced.

Arsen'ev's name is familiar to historians of Russia because of his place among the critical intelligentsia. Urusov, though, had the far more immediate effect on the evolution of its legal culture. He made the defense table the most prominent piece of furniture in the courtroom. Once the *zashchitnik* assumed cultural contours markedly different from those intended by the reforms, he showboated the persona of David against the goliath of the state. Code be damned. What mattered was justice. And winning the case.

## A Conscience for Hire

When Mavra Volokhova walked free, several members of the audience, including jurors, collected money for the pious widow. How, though, would the star performers be paid? Urusov had family money. Gromnitskii worked for the Ministry of Justice, so he received a state salary. In civil cases lawyers were remunerated according to a scale worked out with the Ministry of Justice, based upon percentages of monies involved in the suits. Criminal cases, though, had no such structure. Lawyers for these trials were either hired by the defendant or appointed by the court.[147] *Zashchitniki* defending in private criminal cases had to contribute a percentage of their fees into a fund from which monies would be distributed by the ministry to court-appointed lawyers. The issue of assignments created a real problem for the defense when attorneys found it difficult to muster commitment to such cases.[148] Moreover, finances came to play a sinister role in criminal cases when lawyers linked their fees to the verdict. This smacked of trying to sway jurors rather than seeking that elliptical truth.

As the new courts began weaving themselves into the fabric of Russian life, the defense began to look increasingly less like David and more like his gigantic adversary. A trial in the Riazan' circuit court in 1871 put local notables and high-powered *zashchitniki* on public display. Urusov defended Vera Dmitrieva, charged with theft, falsifying her identification, and attempting one of the criminal definitions of murder, "expulsion of the fetus." He was joined at the defense table by two of the other dominant figures that shaped criminal defense in tsarist Russia, V. D. Spasovich and F. N. Plevako. No dream team this, however, as each lawyer represented a different defendant. Plevako worked for the alleged father of Dmitrieva's child, Colonel N. N. Kostrubo-Karitskii, the former military commander of Riazan' Province. Spasovich represented the director of the Riazan' Medical Inspectorate, A. F. Diuzing, one of the doctors charged with conspiring in the attempted expulsion.[149]

147. *UUS*, arts. 565–68. Unlike in the United States, however, the affordability of representation was never mentioned. An enterprising defendant, "the student Danilov," exiled to hard labor for nine years, appealed unsuccessfully to the Senate that he had not received a fair trial because he had not trusted his lawyer, whom the judge had refused to replace. Liutetskii, *Zamechatel'nye ugolovnye protsessy*, 285.

148. P. V. Makalinskii, ed., *Prisiazhnaia advokatura* (St. Petersburg: N. A. Lebedev, 1889), 377.

149. Also on trial were a second doctor and a friend of Dmitrieva's who had helped her conceal the birth. Speeches from this trial are reprinted in many places. I am quoting from I. V. Potapchuk, ed., *Russkie sudebnye oratory v izvestnykh ugolovnykh protsessakh XIX veka* (Tula: Avtograf, 1997), 21–82.

Specifically, Diuzing had recommended an abortifacient, *ergot*, which had not worked. He had then suspiciously found a job in the city for a provincial doctor, also on trial, who had come to Riazan' and undertaken to aid Dmitrieva, well into her second trimester, to end her unwanted pregnancy. This sordid story had ended with the baby's corpse discarded on a local bridge.

Spasovich is among the best-known prerevolutionary jurists, perhaps even better known to literary scholars because of his many publications on Slavic, especially Polish, literature. From a prominent family (Spasowicz) in Minsk, his father was chief of staff at the Minsk Medical Inspectorate. His mother, from the line of a Lithuanian general and a well-educated Catholic, taught her children French and German. Spasovich enrolled in the law faculty at St. Petersburg University in 1845. Quickly ascendant, he defended two dissertations, the first in maritime law and the second on property relations in Poland. K. D. Kavelin, a professor of law and history at the university and convener of the most intellectually prestigious salon among liberals in the imperial capital, recommended Spasovich for a faculty position in criminal law. Despite no previous training in the subject, Spasovich lectured and wrote a textbook on criminal law that sparked intense criticism from the established law faculty for its "idiocies," but it had staying power because it demonstrated how "criminal laws develop from the demands of life."[150] Spasovich's participation in student demonstrations in the 1860s halted his ascent temporarily, and he, like Arsen'ev, wrote briefly for *Vestnik Evropy*. When the Petersburg bar association opened in 1866, Spasovich turned to private practice and became an active member.[151]

Plevako, like Urusov, graduated from the Moscow University Law School in 1864.[152] Nicknamed the "Muscovite with the golden tongue," this son of a serf and an ethnic Kalmyk soon became "well known not only in educated circles, but among all who read newspapers, and the masses of Russian people. In the city of Moscow he is as much an attraction as the tsar-bell or the tsar-cannon."[153] Appointed as a procurator to Moscow's Criminal Judicial Chambers, and then to its circuit court, Plevako resigned in 1870 to begin private practice. He is particularly interesting because, in telling contrast to other attorneys of note, he was deeply Orthodox and lacked the literary ambitions pursued by Urusov, Spasovich, and Arsen'ev, among others.[154] Plevako made use of his expansive

150. Quoted in the introduction to V. D. Spasovich, *Izbrannye trudy i rechi* (Tula: Avtograf, 2000), 8. The Ministry of Education forbade its use in classrooms, though the censorship did not prohibit it.

151. Biographical details can be found in Liakhovetskii, *Kharakteristika*, 230–42. The 1864 reforms allowed lawyers to organize themselves regionally into councils (*sovety*) in districts that had an appellate court. Only Moscow, St. Petersburg, and Kharkov lawyers had formed councils, which approximated Western bar associations.

152. Biographical information comes from obituaries published in *Nv*, 24 December 1908, no. 11778; and 26 December, no. 11780; and one in *Russkoe slovo* (hereafter *Rs*), 24 December 1908. Two volumes of his speeches were published, edited with biographical commentary by N. K. Murav'ev (Moscow: V. M. Sablin, 1910), 1:3–31. B. A. Podgornyi wrote a short biography, *Plevako* (Moscow: Vl. Vengerov, 1914).

153. L. D. Liakhovetskii, *Kharakteristiki izvestnykh russkikh sudebnykh oratorov* (SPB: Elektropechatnia, 1902), 5.

154. Plevako personified what Jane Burbank characterized as the "deceptively Western image of what lawyers were in Russia before 1917." Burbank, "Discipline and Punish in the Moscow Bar Association," *Russian Review* 54, no. I (1995), 48.

personality by serving as a longtime church elder and, when it became possible, a politician. When the 1905 Revolution brought about an electoral parliament, Plevako joined the conservative Octobrist Party and was elected to the Third Duma. Angina cut short his political career in 1908, and the crowds at his funeral rivaled those at Anton Chekhov's. Lev Tolstoy counted as an admirer.[155]

The case that pulled these three together began in July 1868, in provincial Tambov, when a local landowner reported the theft of thirty-eight thousand rubles worth of banknotes and government bonds. These notes had to be tendered in person, and several surfaced in November in a nearby town. The woman who cashed them in turned out to be his niece, Dmitrieva, using a false name. When her uncle discovered the identity of the thief, he withdrew the charges, explaining that she had taken the money "accidentally." This did not put off the procurator, who continued the investigation. When arrested, Dmitrieva implicated Karitskii, and in a crime more nefarious than theft. Identifying him as her longtime lover, Dmitrieva told of being impregnated, this her second time by him, and then abandoned after the two of them had robbed her uncle. Both Dmitrieva and Karitskii had spouses, although she had been separated from hers for four years. Now living with her parents, she met with the Karitskiis socially.

The core of procurator V. I. Petrov's case depended on Dmitrieva's testimony. She directed the money trail to Karitskii, blaming him for pressuring her into cashing the bonds, and also into ending her pregnancy. For his part, Karitskii simply denied everything, even a romance with Dmitrieva. Three local luminaries on trial, including a lovely heiress and the province's former chief military officer and medical examiner, sparked greater interest than peasants being intimidated by police. Each lawyer earned his fees, all securing acquittals by shifting the blame away from his client toward the others. Plevako noted accurately that Urusov's strategy depended on his "taking the rope from around [Dmitrieva's] neck, and putting put it around [Karitskii's]." Spasovich, defending Diuzing, whom Urusov had dubbed "the weapon," simply dismissed Dmitrieva's testimony as "slander."[156]

The contemporary reader will find no surprises in these legal strategies, but they say a great deal about how legal culture was evolving in autocratic Russia. Urusov's indifference toward the factual evidence of the case becomes apparent in his rambling, even amusing summation. He began by celebrating the equality of everyone before the law, because before 1864 no one of Karitskii's power and influence would have stood trial.[157] However, with someone like him protecting the city, "thank God Riazan' is not under siege!"[158] Urusov's best suit was bathos, served up in his demonization of Karitskii as "the father of those two who have been condemned to never know their mother's tenderness."[159] He finished with a tack that would become familiar, a direct appeal to the jurors' religious

155. The liberal *Rs* used the anniversary of his death to decry him as a "perverted talent" who had outlived his times (23 December 1909, no. 294).

156. Ibid., 45, 60.

157. Ibid., 44. Urusov's speech, 43–59.

158. Ibid., 51.

159. Ibid., 55.

sensibilities: "before you stands the pale image of this woman . . . who has endured many bodily and spiritual agonies . . . turn to her with Christian mercy and forgive her."[160]

This one of his first cases, Plevako had not yet developed the theatricality that would become his forte.[161] Ridiculing Urusov's style, he warned that, following the logic of his opponent, he would jump from "one subject to the next without any direct connection."[162] No hard evidence, in either the theft or the pregnancy, connected his client to either crime. Plevako put servants, privy to household secrets, on the stand, and they could not swear that Dmitrieva and Karitskii were lovers. Both doctors had placed Karitskii with Dmitrieva, but this did not guarantee that he had impregnated her. After his acquittal, the irate Karitskii published a book that broke down in detail how information from the preliminary investigation had been transmuted incorrectly into the bill of indictment. He repeatedly accused Urusov of slander.[163]

Spasovich eschewed histrionics: "starting slowing, awkwardly, even stammering, he disappointed those in the audience who had expected to be dazzled."[164] Not an improviser like Urusov, he wrote down his speeches in order to master the reasoning. Once warmed up, he persuaded the crowd to come with him. He began his defense of Diuzing with the first point of law: had a crime been committed? The dead baby on the bridge returned as an indeterminate piece of evidence because no one had proven precisely how the child had died.[165] He cleverly added that the law referred to "expulsion of the fetus," and the abortifacient given her by Diuzing had not resulted in that. But then Spasovich hedged the bet he had placed on framing every point within the code. "I hope," he concluded to the jurors, "that you will pray to God, who will help you to decide this very difficult question."[166] Cynical but successful.[167]

160. *Russkie sudebnye oratory*, 59. In a 1981 analysis of prerevolutionary judicial orators, the authors rather surprisingly praise their subjects for their "lack of false pathos." N. G. Mikhailovskaia and V. V. Odintsov, *Iskusstvo sudebnogo oratora* (Moscow: Iuridicheskaia literatura, 1981), 3.

161. The liberal lawyer V. A. Maklakov complained of Plevako's "verbosity, pomposity," also recalling a moment that he brought even the judges to tears. Gessen, *Advokatura*, 193.

162. *Russkie sudebnye oratory*, 62. Koni evaluated Urusov and Plevako very differently. He saw Urusov as the organized orator, and Plevako as less interested in the details. I do not know that either one argued a case before him, but reading their speeches I suspect that Koni allowed politics to cloud his judgment. A. F. Koni, *Otsy i deti sudebnoi reformy* (Moscow: I. D. Sytin, 1914), 285–86.

163. Polkovnik N. N. Kostrubo-Karitskii, *Iznanka na litso* (St. Petersburg: V. S. Ettinger, 1871).

164. Liakhovetskii, *Kharakteristika*, 235.

165. In fact, whether by accident or design, Spasovich misinformed the jurors about the relevant articles of the code, telling them incorrectly that it included a provision on the woman's participation. *Russkie sudebnye oratory*, 76.

166. Spasovich's speech is in *Russkie sudebnye oratory*, 75–81. N. P. Karabchevskii wrote in his memoirs of learning very early the importance of Orthodoxy when crafting his defenses. "Kak ia stal advokatom," in *Okolo pravosudiia: Stat'i, soobshcheniia i sudebnye ocherki* (St. Petersburg: Trud, 1902), 28–29.

167. In 1914, on the fiftieth anniversary of the legal reform, Plevako and Spasovich were linked to Arsen'ev as being particularly good lawyers because they "were not manipulative" (?!). *Sudebnye ustavy 20 noiabria 1864 g. za piat'desiat' let*, 2 vols. (St. Petersburg: Senatskaia Tip., 1914), 1:778–79.

If Urusov took the noose from Dmitrieva's neck and placed it around Karitskii's, the jurors removed it from all involved. Perhaps they ultimately agreed with Spasovich's basic point that no laws had been broken. Perhaps they were restrained by the differences in stature between the defendants and the dead infant. *Zashchitniki* in particular were carving out a considerably more powerful place for themselves than the statute had intended, and they were doing so by forcefully reminding jurors that it was they who determined justice. The law code lay wide open to interpretation; Gogol was mistaken to have called it "wooden."

The first loud cry against *zashchitniki* came from the liberal voice of Evgenii Markov, an established journalist at *Golos*, in an article from 1875, "The Sophists of the Nineteenth Century."[168] Markov damned *zashchitniki*, who "seem to sell their conviction and talents on the market."[169] In addition to accusations of the buying and selling of justice, critics of the legal profession worried that egoism would place winning a case above respecting the law. Spasovich returned to the scene of the philosophical crime in 1876 and became the emblem of lawyerly immorality when he defended Stanislav Kroneberg, a Warsaw-born nobleman accused of torturing his seven-year-old daughter. The presiding judge had appointed Spasovich, so no money soiled his hands at the jury's acquittal. Servants had turned Kroneberg in, and a medical examination found welts on the child's buttocks made with *spiztruten*, bundled sticks. The case quickly became a *cause célèbre*, its notoriety compounded by Spasovich's high standing in liberal circles. Defending a man who admitted to beating his child challenged the idealized spirit of the rule of law. Spasovich's primary critic, F. M. Dostoevsky, enjoyed even greater celebrity. Ever quick with a pen, the noted novelist dubbed the legal profession a "conscience for hire."[170]

Dostoevsky zeroed in with a novelist's acumen on Spasovich's concluding argument.[171] Like most others, Dostoevsky had read the stenographic account of the trial in *Golos* rather than hearing it in person. Beginning with the premise that a seven-year-old is by virtue of her age an innocent, Dostoevsky was appalled to read Spasovich portraying her as a lying, thieving, masturbating wretch who required corporal punishment. The *zashchitnik* had then manipulated the specifics of the legal code to prove that Kroneberg had not "tortured" his daughter as defined by law.[172] For Dostoevsky, "establishing a legal profession was an excellent thing but also a sad one."[173] Russians had to learn that the balance between rights, including the right to an acquittal despite the evidence, and the law, which must ensure public safety as well as personal equality, inevitably tilts back and forth.

168. Most of Markov's piece is reproduced in Gessen, *Advokatura*, 210–13.

169. Quoted in F. A. Vol'kenshtein and A. V. Bobrishchev-Pushkin, *Preniia storon v ugolovnom protsesse* (St. Petersburg: Trud, 1903), 4.

170. Fyodor Dostoevsky, *A Writer's Diary*, trans. and annot. Kenneth Lantz, intro. Gary Saul Morson (Evanston: Northwestern University Press, 1993), 361.

171. Ibid., 356–84.

172. Twenty years later, the differences between medical and legal definitions of torture remained contentious. "Khronika ugolovnogo suda: K voprosu o predelakh vrachebnoi expertisy na ugolovnykh delakh," *Zhurnal iuridicheskogo obshchestva*, kn. 9 (1896): 67–76.

173. Dostoevsky, *Writer's Diary*, 384.

Markov and Dostoevsky directed attention away from the fundamental of civil rights that underlay the right to a defense. Spasovich tried to have it both ways. He acknowledged, when others would not, that the structure of the adversarial courtroom meant that lawyers had to choose sides, and that being paid for their words "obligated lawyers to present a one-sided view." In this, he echoed the academic Foinitskii and the procurator Obninskii when they rued the difficulty investigators faced when trying to prove guilt and innocence simultaneously. Spasovich dexterously pulled a slight of integrity when he assured lawyers that they could separate their souls from their jobs: "he cannot for a minute forget that what is permitted to him in court, as a lawyer (*advokat*), is not permitted to him as a man (*chelovek*)."[174] By thus sweeping the moral dilemma under the rug, he sidestepped the complexities of the ethos of rule of law.

Their status as professionals required Russian lawyers to maintain a code of ethics, but their legal culture lacked the traditions that custom and common law had contributed to the development of barristers and solicitors in England, and also the Second Estate Nobles of the Robe that had produced *advocats* in France. If the Russian reader turns first to Gogol for a visceral sense of Russia's legal system, Charles Dickens provides the same service for England, embodied in the avaricious pettifoggers at the firm of Jarndyce and Jarndyce in *Bleak House* (1853). The historical role that lawyers played in the French Revolution contributed to the tsarist government's discomfiture about their independence.[175] Russia's bar associations, the institutional watchdog of its members' professional integrity, betrayed a hesitancy about both rule of law and civil rights when seeking to enhance their collective reputation, all in the name of an unnamable morality.[176] The Kharkov Bar, for example, ruled that "members must refuse to accept any case that does not correspond with the dignity of the legal profession." A member of the Moscow Bar was sanctioned for defending the madam of a brothel; only when he insisted that he believed in his client's innocence could his own be saved.[177]

Scapegoating the defense for accepting morally challenged cases hit a crescendo in 1879 when the St. Petersburg Bar expelled Professor of law A. V. Lokhvitskii. A former editor of *Sudebnyi vestnik*, his breach of professional etiquette had been to defend a man in a suit brought by a widow from whom his client had borrowed fifteen thousand rubles,

---

174. Gessen *Advokatura*, 224.

175. David Bell, " Lawyers into Demagogues: Chancellor Maupeou and the Transformation of Legal Practice in France, 1771–1789," *Past & Present*, no. 130 (1991): 107–41. Like Vladimir Lenin, the French revolutionary leader Maximilien Robespierre had trained in the law.

176. From 1875, Russia had a two-tiered system of legal professionals: lawyers belonging to the bar, *prisiazhie poverennye*, and private, *chastnye* lawyers, who paid an annual fee and registered with their local circuit court. Their credentials would be reviewed every three years. An editorial in *Nedelia*, 8 July 1873, no. 27, explains the plan. RGIA, f. 1405, op. 72, d. 3194, contains correspondence in the Ministry of Justice about the crying need for more lawyers, especially in the provinces, and local controls over who is allowed to represent litigants, because most who now serve are "solders discharged for drunkenness and bad behavior" (l. 15).

177. Gessen discusses these and other cases in "Boevye voprosy advokatskoi professii," in *Advokatura*, 312–33.

married her, and then evicted her from what had been her house.[178] Lokhvitskii appealed his disbarment to the Senate, which ordered him reinstated. He had broken no laws in executing his legal obligation to defend.[179]

Lokhvitskii's death in 1884 prompted obituaries that reopened the debate. Count G. A. Dzhanshiev, an 1874 graduate of the Moscow University Law School and columnist on judicial issues for the liberal newspaper *Russkie vedomosti* (The Russian News), rekindled the anger at the Senate's ruling. "The Senate affirmed that the defense attorney is simply a mediator between the court and the litigant . . . like a notary public," he complained.[180] Citing statutes that he believed empowered lawyers to decline cases that went against their convictions, Dzhanshiev critiqued the Senate for upholding "the letter rather than the spirit of the law." In response, another member of the bar, D. Neviadomskii, did not hide his irritation at those colleagues who had failed to recognize what a poor precedent they had set by their actions against Lokhvitskii's legal obligations.[181]

Dzhanshiev's posturing on the moral high ground raised another question that had been asked and answered in practice: what should defense attorneys do in cases of the admittedly guilty? When the reformers added the article that confession was to be but one piece of the evidence, they were reacting against the corrupted inquisitorial system, not imagining that some of the nation's best legal minds would be obtaining acquittals for confessed killers. Neviadomskii surveyed the opinions of Russia's leading jurists, and that of the ubiquitous Mittermaier. They all concurred, if reluctantly, that an attorney has the obligation to defend his client even should he know him or her to be guilty.[182] "The right to a defense is not just a private one," emphasized Neviadomskii, "it works in the interests of society."[183] Professor of law at Kharkov University L. E. Vladimirov voiced hesitation. Himself recruited to defend occasionally in the local circuit court, he favored revising the code to allow for the cross-examination of *zashchitniki* after their final arguments to jurors, a means of exposing those who had not bothered to prepare the case but trusted their performative skills.[184] One can only speculate how Urusov would have responded to this. Ironically, Urusov sat on the Moscow Bar that censured Vladimirov, a member of the Kharkov Bar, for defending a lieutenant colonel accused of rape.[185]

---

178. D. Neviadomskii blamed the press for stimulating reaction against Lokhovitskii. Neviadomskii, *Vechnye voprosy advokatury* (Moscow: M. I. Neuberger, 1886), 29. Kucherov discusses the details of the case in *Courts*, 163–68.

179. Gessen, *Advokatura*, 313, pointed out that the Senate had to set several such cases right before the law.

180. G. A. Dzhanshiev, "Vedenie nepravil'nykh del," reprinted in Dzhanshiev, *Sbornik statei* (Moscow: Zadruga, 1914), 475, 482, 484. Obniniskii's son Boris compiled these articles and Koni wrote the introduction.

181. Neviadomskii, *Vechnye voprosy advokatury*, 29, 38. As the author pointed out, there was no evidence that the accused had not initially loved the widow. Moreover, a woman having a fling with a man younger than some of her children was just as immoral as him seducing her.

182. Ibid., 54–55.

183. Ibid., 53.

184. L. E. Vladimirov, *Zashchititel'nyia rechi i publichnyia lektsii* (Moscow: A. A. Levenson, 1892), 357–63.

185. Gessen, *Advokatura*, 391.

Law professor Foinitskii reproved in 1885 that defending had become a "marketable commodity," but without acknowledging its function of protecting a civil right.[186] Strikingly, none of Russia's most eminent juridical theorists practiced as defense attorneys, the position that would allow them to protect ordinary Russians from the predatory state. Koni fashioned himself a reformer, but it can be argued that his gravitation toward state service also reflected a repugnance for the culture of defense. Obninskii, roundly respected from his many years of tenure in the Moscow procuracy,[187] worried in 1890 about "demoralization" among the ranks. Suffering nervous exhaustion, he opined that newest members of the legal profession had "forgotten the principles of public service," concerning themselves with fancy offices rather than social activism. From his twenty-five years of experience working with *zashchitniki*, he recalled how many he had helped when they had come into court unprepared. His chastisement of *zashchitniki*, that "the confluence of the highest degree of talent with the highest degree of lack of conscience always brings success to the defense," sounded clever, but did not address the basic issue: Obninskii represented a state that was rarely as sympathetic as the defendant whom he was prosecuting.[188] Moreover, his complaint that today "the infatuation with a pretty speech forces one away from looking for the truth" suggests an errant memory of time he spent in court with Urusov and Plevako. Like so many from his generation of reformers, he was disillusioned that today "society is completely different."[189]

A. V. Bobrishchev-Pushkin, scion of a legal family with practice on both sides in the courtroom, and a member of the generation that Obninskii had bemoaned, wrote perceptively in 1903 that "times have changed. The era of the Great Reforms, when everyone idealized justice and jurisprudence, is over."[190] Together with procurator F. A. Vol'kenshtein, he co-authored a study of prosecutors, whose speeches never seemed to meet with comparable enthusiasm from the public as those of the *zashchitniki*. Vol'kenshtein spoke for those who took upon themselves the prosecution of lawbreakers. He reminded of a point often lost in the public's antipathy for the government, that the procurator, "schooled in ideas of public safety," found it his obligation to protect society from the threat posed by the criminal. The defense, in contrast, took on "the face-to-face clash between the all-powerful government and the powerless individual."[191] Bobrishchev-Pushkin recognized the fallacy in the liberals' complaints that the procurator held the advantage in court because the judicial investigator controlled the collection of evidence and worked for him. Usurping the kinship that defense attorneys often built up with jurors as they pleaded more often

186. Foinitskii, *Zashchita*, 61. He called it a *torgovoi promysel*.

187. Koni praised his "speeches filled with humanity ... always striving for the truth rather than personal success at the expense of justice." A. F. Koni, "Predislovie" to Obninskii, *Sbornik statei*, 16.

188. Cited by E. V. Vas'kovskii in *Osnovnoi voprosy advokatskoi etiki* (St. Petersburg: M. Merkushev, 1895), 3. Obninskii had studied law under one of the foremost Westernizers, T. N. Granovskii.

189. P. N. Obninskii, "Otkuda idet demoralizatsiia nashei advotatury?" *Iuridicheskii vestnik* 6, no. 1 (1890): 25, 31, 43.

190. A. V. Bobrishchev-Pushkin, "Zashchitniki," *Pravo*, no. 8 (1903): 257–70.

191. Vol'kenshtein, *Preniia storon*, 9.

for mercy than for justice, Bobrishchev-Pushkin implored that because the "Slavic national character bears no malice toward its enemy, let the soldiers of the state going to battle against criminals be filled with simplicity and humanity, especially when the guilty has surrendered and is seeking mercy, not contempt."[192]

This brought the reformers' high ideals full circle. Their concerns about objectivity and facticity, necessary to find the truth about a crime, had surrendered to subjectivity and circumstance. The iniquity of individual lawyers, like so-called formalism of the legal code, surfaced as red herrings in complaints about the inadequacies of the new legal system. By 1902, defending the accused had become a "sacred occupation: it shines light on the crime and calls for mercy to the one who has fallen."[193] The handsome literary lawyer S. A. Andreevskii, who had resigned from the Petersburg procuracy rather than prosecute Zasulich in 1878, by 1903 was advising law school graduates that "the less the *zashchitnik* is a jurist by nature, the more valuable he is to the court." He recommended that they study psychology and belles lettres more than jurisprudence, so that they could better "protect the live subject from the dead codex."[194] The codex had not quite turned forty, but in its own way it was accomplishing what the men who wrote it set out to do: mediate justice publicly and collectively.

## Conclusion

Vol'kenshtein reasoned thoughtfully that "the adversarial debates constitute an act of primary social importance (because) they extract useful social lessons from crimes."[195] Among the many murder trials that gripped public attention in the first decades of reform, two stand out for the ways in which they involved society in the dispensation of justice. In Odessa in 1878, the acquittal of a man for the attempted murder of his brother met with satisfaction from both sides of the courtroom. Matvei Zasadkovich, sound and sober, had stabbed his brother Nikifor on a public street. Why? Matvei, married and with three children, had been exiled to Tobolsk three years earlier for insulting his parents, and Nikifor had signed all the legal documents that had sent his brother to Siberia. Matvei's family had remained at the family home in Kiev, thinking his exile only temporary. When Matvei petitioned to return and learned that his exile was permanent, he ran away in order to avenge himself upon his brother.

The fraternal discord derived from more than the older sibling's disrespect for their parents. Matvei had lent Nikifor, the only educated member of the family, three hundred rubles to finish his studies. The ungrateful younger brother now held a position in the

---

192. Ibid., 115.

193. Nikitin, *Prestupnyi mir*, n. p.

194. Troitskii, *Korifei*, 202–3. Andreevskii was D. S. Mirsky's favorite "literary lawyer" (*History of Russian Literature*, 69).

195. Vol'kenshtein, *Preniia storon*, 9–12.

philosophy department at the university, and Nikifor's dry, unemotional showing at court had generated sympathy for Matvei, who swore that he had not wanted to kill him. Like Zasulich's jurors in that same year, these men decided that Matvei had not intended to take his brother's life with his knife. Jurors and the audience collected money for Matvei. Even the judge stood up for him. When state officials asked that Matvei be held in custody for a return to Tobolsk, the judge denied them; the exile had been ordered in a Kiev court, but here in Odessa he was a free man.[196]

A generation later, Obninskii's fretting over demoralization among procurators found footing in one of Russia's most publicized trials, which took the accused to court three times before the Senate accepted the acquittal in 1900. The Skitskii brothers, Petr and Stepan, had been charged with killing their boss, A. Ia. Komarov, secretary of the local branch of the Holy Synod, in July 1897. The primary direct evidence against the brothers rested on the testimony of a woman who could say no more than she saw two men in the proximity of the area where the body was discovered, and that sausage and bread that the two might have eaten had been found nearby. Petr had fought with Komarov over a promotion, but the secretary's uncompromising stance against divorce on any basis had garnered for him many more dangerous enemies than a disgruntled employee and his alcoholic brother. The Synod levied the power of the autocracy, but it could not overcome the strength that public opinion had gained through the adversarial court. The grateful public of Poltava gathered outside the hotel rooms of the *zashchitniki*. Shouting "Hurrah!" about the acquittal, they were celebrating the successful transition of this Great Reform from ideals into reality.[197]

196. *Delo o lishennom vsekh osobykh prav i preimushchestv Matvee Aleksandrove Zasadkeviche, obvinnaemyi v pokushenii na ubiistvo* (Odessa: Trud, 1879).

197. *Delo o br. Skitskikh, obviniaemykh v ubiistve Komarova* (Poltava: L. Frishberg, 1900); and *Delo ob ubiistve sekretaria Poltavskoi dukhovnoi konsistorii A. Ia. Komarova* (Kharkov: P. D. Shidlovskii, 1899). Tried by a crown court rather than a jury, one of the three representatives was a village elder, a peasant who objected "that I do not consider that the accusation has been proven."

# CHAPTER TWO

# CRIMINOLOGY

## Social Crime, Individual Criminal

"Societies have the criminals they deserve."

—Alexandre Lacassagne, 1885

A correspondent for *Peterburgskaia gazeta* reported being "overcome with horror" at the sight of the body of thirteen-year-old Sarra Bekker, sprawled in a chair, her legs akimbo, lying in the pawn shop where she worked at 57 Nevskii Prospect.[1] With no sign of forced entry and valuables still in display cases, local authorities interpreted from the position of the body, wounds to the head, and the rag stuffed in her mouth that the killer had attempted to rape her. The atrocity of her murder brought the chief procurator of the judicial palace (and future minister of justice). N. V. Murav'ev to the crime scene. Suspicion fell quickly on the shop's owner, Sarra's boss I. I. Mironovich. Over the next two years he was arrested, released, rearrested, tried, convicted, appealed, and ultimately acquitted. In the audience for the first trial sat Minister of Justice D. N. Nabokov, Ober-procurator of the Senate Cassation Department; N. A. Nekliudov; and the conservative publicist Viktor Fuks. The author of a widely redacted textbook on criminal law and future senator N. S. Tagantsev had been in the jury pool; though his name was not called, he sat in on the proceedings. What attracted these legal luminaries to a story originally entitled "Just Another Murder"?

Mironovich protested his innocence throughout, and the prosecution had to make its case on the basis of circumstantial evidence. The investigation took an unexpectedly arresting turn when a month after the murder a young woman turned herself in to the police claiming to having killed Sarra while stealing jewelry for her lover, a married policeman. Explaining that her conscience would not permit her to sleep, Ekaterina Semenova was committed to a psychiatric hospital for observation, where the medical board found

---

1. "Eshche odno ubiistvo," *Peterburgskaia gazeta* (hereafter *Pg*), 28 August 1883, no. 236. The information about the investigation and trial comes from, in addition to the periodical press, *Ubiistvo Sarry Bekker* (Moscow: n. p., 1884), based on the news and the stenographic reports from the courtroom.

"long-term psychopathic characteristics."[2] Several weeks later she recanted her confession. She now told police that she was outside the pawnshop, heard a noise, and accepted goods from a man inside after she had threatened to call the *dvornik*. A gold watch chain and other items from the shop were found on her paramour, M. M. Bezak. In November 1884, Mironovich stood trial for murder alongside Semenova and Bezak, the latter two charged with knowledge of the crime but failure to report it. Semenova, the only one who admitted to a direct link to the crime, was also the only one acquitted.

The case depended on experts to supply the testimony that moved the evidentiary boundary from "direct" to "indirect." In 1869, Vladimir Snigirev, a member of the Medical Council, had described as "radical" the turn that criminal law had taken with the increase in weight that circumstantial evidence had begun to bear at trial.[3] Expert witnesses taking a public stance and subjected to cross-examination key-lighted a substantive difference between the inquisitorial and adversarial systems, the implications of which shaped more than simple justice. Expertise, too, could now be "circumstantial," in that knowledge did not have to come directly from the investigation itself. The specialists at the Mironovich trial came with impeccable academic credentials: I. M. Sorokin, chair of the Department of Forensics at the Military Medical Academy; the "father of Russian psychiatry" I. M. Balinskii, chair of the first department of psychiatry at the Medico-Surgical Academy[4]; and Balinskii's student O. A. Chechott, who had observed Semenova in the hospital of St. Nicholas the Miracle Worker.[5]

Sorokin reconstructed in the courtroom the sitting area in which Sarra had died; his explanation of rape as the motive depended on the placement and condition of her corpse.[6] Sarra's father, the civil plaintiff represented by Prince Urusov, accused Mironovich and posed himself in the position in which he had found her body on the bloodstained couch. Were this not sufficiently inflammatory, the two psychiatrists turned the stand into a tribune from which they popularized the condition of the psychopath ( *psikhopatka*). Though a witness for the prosecution, Balinskii secured Semenova's acquittal with the plea not to

2. *Eshche odno Ubiistvo*, 110.

3. Vl. Snigirev, "Sud.-med. issledovanie pritvornykh bol'nykh," *Arkhiv sudebnoi meditsiny*, kn. 3 (September 1869): 2.

4. Sorokin had produced the first textbook on forensics, *Uchebnik sudebnoi meditsiny* (St. Petersburg: Skoropechatnia, 1881). A decade later Balinskii opened the first psychiatric clinic in the imperial capital, and later pioneered in military psychiatry. V. Serbskii, "Nekrolog," *Zhurnal nevropatologii i psikhiatrii imeni S. S. Korsakova* 2, no. 3 (1903): 361–80.

5. Coincidentally, or presciently, the serial novel that had accompanied the investigation in *Pg* was "In Pursuit of Profit at Salpêtrière," a crime novel set in the famous French psychiatric clinic.

6. Sorokin's argument for rape rested on a fact mentioned in his autopsy, but not taken up by the press: Sarra had defecated, presumably in terror, which he said turned off her would-be rapist. *Delo o Mironoviche, Semenovoi, i Bezak v sudedno-meditsinskom otnoshenii* (St. Petersburg: Zhurnal *Meditsinskaia biblioteka*, 1885). Sorokin's creative scripting of the scenario remained a point of contention among forensic specialists for years. A journalist remembered Sorokin's testimony as "nonsense" ( *nevmeniaemost' ekspertizy*), *Novoe vremia* (hereafter *Nv*), 8 November 1887, no. 4201. Years later, another expert would recall Sorokin's demonstration as "fantasy." N. E. Greshishchev, "O sudebnomeditsinskoi ekspertize v dele ob ubiistve Komarova," *Vestnik obshchei gigenii, sudebnoi i prakticheskoi meditsiny* (hereafter *VOG*), no. 4 (1902): 488.

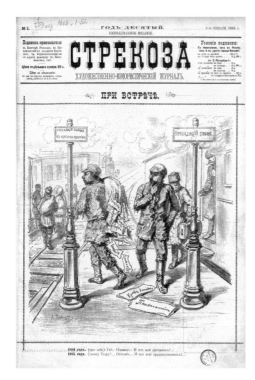

Fig. 6. The satirical journal *Strekoza* (Dragonfly), New Year's edition, 1885. Dropping the psychopath on the unwitting Russian public.

"brand such people . . . with the name 'criminal.' Have pity and compassion for them."[7] Far more intriguing was his description of the psychopathic personality:

> Capable of rational behavior, they can distinguish good from evil, but lack any moral comprehension. They think only about themselves, unconcerned about those around them except as they might be used to achieve their own aims. Other than the personal "I," the psychopath holds nothing sacred and is completely indifferent to the consequences of his actions.[8]

"Psychopaths" began to pop up in vaudevilles, ditties, and every form of popular culture. Popular writer Nikolai Leskov mused about the fatuous chattering that the trial had inspired in "Drowsy Recollections of the Sarra Bekker Affair."[9] The satirical journal *Strekoza* (Dragonfly) featured the psychopath in its New Year's edition for 1885 as something that

---

7. Quoted in *Pg*, 3 December 1884, no. 333. A gynecologist examined Semenova and discovered irregularities in her sexual organs.

8. *Nv*, 4 December 1884, no. 3151. The paper called his speech "sparkling," reporting that he "presented us with an image of the accused in such amazing clarity that we could penetrate the most secret corners of her soul."

9. "Dremotnye vospominannia na dela Sarry Bekker," *Nov'* 7, no. 2 (1885): 292–95.

Fig. 7. The lawyer N.P. Karabchevskii "had forgotten that one must still produce the evidence of the crime."

Fig. 8. N.P. Karabchevskii, the "singer from a fiery sun."

1884 had dropped on the Russian public.[10] Semenova's imitators left the public longing for the original.[11]

Mironovich hired rising star N. P. Karabchevskii as his *zashchitnik*. This "singer from a fiery sun"[12] attached his name to almost every murder trial that had legal implications beyond the verdict, including the two in which ethnic "others" were charged with the ritual murders of Christians: Votiak peasants in 1894, and Jewish clerk Mendel Beilis in 1913. Like Urusov, Karabchevskii had gotten into trouble during his years at the university, which had prevented him from receiving the mandatory certificate of trustworthiness that would have permitted him a job with the state. Insisting that he could not imagine himself incarcerating for the prosecution, Karabchevskii defended several notorious enemies of the state.[13] His client list included, in addition to Beilis, prominent Socialist revolutionary Ekaterina Breshko-Breshkovskaia, who joined other youthful quasi-revolutionaries and went into the countryside in 1874 to proselytize the peasantry for socialism; E. S. Sazonov, the assassin of Minister of Internal Affairs V. K. Plehve in 1904; and the industrialist and patron of the arts Savva Mamontov, who subsidized several Bolshevik publications.[14] Karabchevskii expanded on what Urusov had begun, solidifying the prominent role of the defense, prompting a colleague to mock the ego that had grown with each success:

> Karabchevskii allowed himself to ascend to the heights of heaven, and with no modesty quoted the Almighty, asking the defendant, "Cain, where is your brother Abel?" But he had forgotten that the Lord God had seen the fact of the crime, and the lawyer Karabchevskii still must produce the evidence of it.[15]

Karabchevskii made the headlines first when he defended the unpopular pawnbroker Mironovich. Losing the first trial, he appealed successfully to the Senate.[16] He scoffed at Sorokin's re-creation as a "coup de théâtre,"[17] and spoke of the "hypnotic" effect cast

10. The satires on the Semenova case were too plentiful to catalogue, making clear what a tight grip she had on the public imagination. In a 1905 spoof of the Jacques Offenbach operetta *La Belle Hélène*, which enjoyed great popularity in Russia, the heroine finds herself in a courtroom complete with *psikhopatki*. "Sud nad Prekrasnoi Elenoi," (St. Petersburg: n.p., 1905).

11. "Novaia psikhopatka," *Peterburgskii listok* (hereafter *Pl*), 14 March 1885, no. 70.

12. Vl. Ruadze, *Dva sudebnykh oratora: Ocherk* (St. Petersburg: Sel'skii vestnik, 1912), 11.

13. N. P. Karabchevskii, "Kak ia stal advokatom," in Karabchevskii, *Okolo pravosudiia: Stat'i, soobshcheniia, i sudebnye ocherki* (St. Petersburg: Trud, 1902), v–vi.

14. Karabchevskii could not keep Breshko-Breshkovskaia from Siberian exile, but he spared Sazanov the death penalty and secured an acquittal for Mamontov, accused of embezzlement. He remembered the young revolutionaries quite fondly in the memoirs he wrote in German exile, *Chto glaza moi vidieli*, 2 vols. (Berlin: Izd. Olgi Diakovoi i Ko., 1921), 2:31–32, 43.

15. "*A vse-taki ia ne vinovat!*": *Zapiska Grafini Ksaverii Roniker* (St. Petersburg: Tip. Obshchest. pol'zy, 1914), 229.

16. N. P. Karabchevskii. *Rechi: 1882–1912*, 2nd ed., supplemented with five speeches (St. Petersburg: Trud, 1902), 65–123. S. A. Andreevskii defended Mironovich at his second, unsensational trial. Without Semenova to entertain, few cared.

17. Karabchevskii, *Okolo pravosudiia*, 121.

in the waning evening light of the courtroom. For him, the doctor's hypothesis was "the most self-confident, and also the most circumstantial and least evidentiary expertise" that he had ever encountered. Sorokin's testimony "did not answer the strict demands of science, or facts, or the even stricter demands of judicial conscience."[18] Balinskii and Chechott found their very profession questioned: "I have taken courses in forensic medicine myself and know what an inexact science it is. Frankly, it is not a science in the sense of independent formulas, evidence, and hypotheses. . . . Psychiatry is a part of this branch."[19]

The lasting significance of poor Sarra's death derived from more than the sensational details. A.M. Bobrishchev-Pushkin, whose father had prosecuted the case, correctly observed that a course in jurisprudence could have been taught on this trial alone.[20] Karabchevskii himself, it must be noted, was challenging the inexactitude of psychiatry as a defense strategy, yet he happily put psychiatrists on the stand if that would help his clients. His objections in this case voiced concerns that others held, which is why he thought they would help Mironovich. Putting aside all those captivating performances at the Petersburg court, focusing instead on the nature of the experts, the trial raised a question that the verdict could not answer: what role would scientific expertise play in social reform? Balinskii had made an earnest appeal to treat deviant behavior differently.

Given the broad audience of the new courts, Sorokin, Balinskii, and Chechott were directing their interpretations to a larger public than the jurors. Significantly, the experts had moved beyond the materiality of blood analysis and into the subjective and mental. The Russian experts were following the same course as their Western counterparts, shifting from a focus on the social issue of criminality to the person of the criminal. This was part of a larger debate about human behavior that had cultural and political implications, the difference between voluntarism and determinism, between positivism's rational actor and social Darwinism's creature of heredity and environment. The persistence of an autocracy gave that debate its own peculiar political cast in Russia because of the way that the government could be held accountable for the environment that kept people from actualizing their selves, *svoe Ia* in Russian parlance. Semenova personified both sides of the debate: had she taken such a horrific action because she would always be denied the possibility of filling her empty life with satisfaction, or was she responding reflexively to circumstances with an utter lack of self-control? The liberal Positivist Arsen'ev, whose commitment to the rule of law was such that he stopped practicing it rather than compromise, had neither denied Rybakovskaia's volition nor reduced her actions to biology when defending her in the shooting death of her lover. But nor did he secure her freedom. Balinskii's testimony, in contrast, set Semenova free.[21]

18. Karabchevskii. *Rechi*, 126.

19. Ibid., 102.

20. A. M. Bobrishchev-Pushkin, *Empiricheskie zakony: Deiatel'nosti russkogo suda prisiazhnykh* (Moscow: A. I. Snegireva, 1896), 351.

21. Her lawyer, S. P. Margolin, did not plead her insane, but shifted the blame to Bezak, who had possession of the goods from Mironovich's shop. *Nv* condemned Margolin's speech as "so boring, so absent ideas, that I can only with difficulty give you an approximation of its contents." *Nv*, 5 December 1884, no. 3152.

# The Rise of the Expert Witness

In the nineteenth century, as historian Roger Smith pointed out, the "various so-called 'knowledge professions' articulated a newly systematic conception of social authority dependent on expertise rather than either tradition or economic power."[22] Law and medicine were two such professions, but their "knowledges" could both overlap and conflict with each other when staking claims to interpreting the evidence in court.[23] Peter the Great brought the two together in Russia with his Military Statute of 1716, which required doctors to perform autopsies in cases of violent deaths and to enter their reports into the legal record.[24] A medical council formed in 1803 set rules for forensic procedures that were codified in 1828. Physicians enjoyed a special status in the inquisitorial system because, in the hierarchy of testimony, their evidence was second only to that of the accused's confession. Moreover, forensic medicine was part of the curricula of law schools, where practicing doctors lectured to prospective attorneys. As historian Elisa Becker argued, doctors were inclined to support that inquisitorial system because its reliance on their specialized knowledge elevated their status.[25] The new code, though, lumped the physicians with other experts, "knowledgeable people" (*svedushchye liudi*) required to testify when summoned.[26]

Because of their legal obligation to participate in criminal investigations, physicians had been included in the editing commission that drew up the legal reforms. From their minority position, however, they found themselves, like the police, subordinate to the judicial investigator.[27] Nor was the investigator limited to giving orders to the local medical examiner (*sudebnyi vrach*); he could "invite" others to examine corpses.[28] The law required them to consult with a police doctor if the accused "does not have healthy reason" or "suffers intellectual derangement," but this was written before psychiatry began to rediagnose the symptoms and causes of mental illness.[29]

E. V. Pelikan, who as head of the medical department at the Ministry of the Interior was the empire's chief forensic expert, in 1865 sponsored the publication of the journal *Arkhiv*

---

22. Roger Smith, "Expertise and Causal Attribution in Deciding between Crime and Mental Disorder," *Social Studies of Science* 15, no. 1 (1985): 67.

23. Smith argues that "whereas medical expertise rests (ideally) on a body of systematic knowledge, the law's claim to authority depends on skills in deciding particular facts" (ibid., 70).

24. *UUS*, art. 154, which dates back to the origins of forensic medicine in Muscovy's *Aptekarskii prikaz*. Elisa Becker, "Medicine, Law, and the State: The Emergence of Forensic Psychiatry in Imperial Russia" (PhD diss., University of Pennsylvania, 2003). The Code of Forensic Medicine comprises volume 13 of the *Pol'noe sobranie zakonov rossiiskoi imperii* (hereafter *PSZ*).

25. Becker, "Medicine, Law, and the State," esp. 74–83. As she points out, there "were no ideological differences" between medicine and jurisprudence in the inquisitorial system (87).

26. *UUS*, 326, categorized experts as: "doctors, pharmacists, teachers, technicians, artists, craftsmen, pursers, and all persons whose work requires them to master a particular expertise." It specifically excluded female physicians.

27. *UUS*, art. 328, gave the investigator the authority to levy fines if experts did not respond to his summons. Art. 333 at least empowered physicians to "look for signs that the investigator had missed, so that the investigation can uncover the truth."

28. *UUS*, art. 338.

29. *Sudebnyi sledovatel'* (Moscow: Bakhmetev, 1868), 116–17.

*sudebnoi meditsiny i obshchestvennoi gigieny* (Archive of Forensic Medicine and Social Hygiene). This journal's editorial mission was to make concrete the implicit connections between judicial issues and the social concerns of doctors.[30] Moreover, *Arkhiv sudebnoi meditsiny* was widely respected, enjoying an audience well beyond the medical professionals to whom it was directed.[31] A. Askochenskii, a medical inspector in Tauride Province, reminded readers that many doctors who worked for the state were underpaid bureaucrats for whom autopsies provided a source of income, and he believed previously superficial examiners would profit from having professionals from the procurator's office directly involved.[32] Poltava medical examiner Khreptovich responded that the problem lay more in the cumbersome code that listed seventy-two questions for autopsies, a bureaucratic demand that produced very little useful medical information: "Are the eyebrows dark? Mouth open? Ears normal?"[33]

At issue was how to professionalize forensic standards such as judicial investigators were charged with accomplishing in law enforcement. Forensic doctors worked together with investigators in several highly publicized cases.[34] In 1867, in the "case of the student Danilov," a cold-blooded killer was identified in part by a cut on his left hand; the doctor at the crime scene had advised the investigator to look for this.[35] An instance of an investigator found shot through the mouth, a gun in his hand, required expertise in firearms, blood spatter, and the medical examiner, who demonstrated how a murder had been staged to look like suicide. This examiner urged his colleagues to conduct

> a strictly scientific evaluation of every phenomenon, a complete mastering of the event in every detail, an exact point of departure from the object, a careful sorting of the circumstances, a critical attitude toward various opinions, a steadfast logic, and, finally, the degree of conviction that is possible only from a complete familiarity with science.[36]

.

30. Radical journalist G. Z. Eliseev welcomed the journal because it "connected medicine so closely to social life." Daniel Philip Todes, "From Radicalism to Scientific Convention: Biological Psychology in Russia from Sechenov to Pavlov" (PhD diss., University of Pennsylvania, 1981), 155. The journal went through a series of name changes that point to reorientations in social medicine: *Arkhiv sudebnoi meditsiny* lasted until 1872, when it became the all-encompassing *Sbornik sochinenii po sudebnoi meditsine: Sudebnoi psikhiatrii, meditsinskoi politsii, obshchestvennoi gigiene, epidemiologii, meditsinskoi geografii i meditsinsoi statistike* until 1885, when it reverted to *Vestnik sudebnoi meditsiny i obshchestvennoi gigieny (VOG)*. In 1889, public hygiene won out over forensics, and the title that continued through 1917 was *Vestnik obshchei gigenii, sudebnoi i prakticheskoi meditsiny*.

31. Irina Paperno, *Suicide as a Cultural Institution in Dostoevsky's Russia* (Ithaca: Cornell University Press, 1997), 71, 87.

32. A. Askochenskii, "K sudedno-med. kazuistika," *Arkhiv sudebnoi meditsiny*, kn. 2 (1867): 13–41.

33. Dr. Khreptovich, "K sudedno-med. kazuistika," *Arkhiv sudebnoi meditsiny*, kn. 3 (September 1868): 2–17. N. I. Rozov continued these complaints in "O naruzhnom osmotre mertvykh tel, proizvedimom vrachami po trebovanii politsii," *Arkhiv sudebnoi meditsiny*, kn. 1 (1869): 81–83.

34. Contradictions arose at times because doctors had to follow the medical code, and judicial investigators the judicial code. V. Snigirev, "Ustav sud. med. 1857 i sud. ustavy 1864," *Arkhiv sudebnoi meditsiny*, kn. 2 (1867): 1–12.

35. Dr. K. Potekhin, "Perechen' ugolovnykh del s uchastiem vrachei-ekspertov," *Arkhiv sudebnoi meditsiny*, kn. 4 (1867): 105–38.

36. "Issledovanie prichin smerti G*** (Delo meditsinsokogo soveta o smerti sudsled. C-go uezda-oi Gubernii)," *Arkhiv sudebnoi meditsiny*, kn. 1 (March 1868): 106.

Physicians now had to answer questions aloud from all participants in a trial, including jurors.[37] They prepared by turning Westward. The translation of Adolf Schauenstein's *Textbook of Forensic Medicine* (1862) taught that "not only fundamental knowledge" mattered, but also "the ability to reveal that knowledge." Schauenstein exaggerated the deference from the bench when he stated that "the judge turned to the expert to form an opinion on that subject which he himself could not."[38] However, as Dr. K. Potekhin argued in *Arkhiv sudebnoi meditsiny*, the open, adversarial court made it easier for forensic experts to "find the truth,"[39] their claim to authority. Another contributor advised the substitution of Russian wherever possible for the Latin technical terms and, his eye still on jurors, suggested that experts show compassion because the prosecution, "by the very nature of its job, lacks this."[40] As had jurists, medical experts turned to Mittermaier, who counseled that now they had an audience to persuade: "in the most important criminal processes the opinion of the forensic physician decides the fate of the defendant, and not rarely is the jury's verdict based exclusively on trust in the authority of the forensic physician."[41] Balinskii took heed.

The numbers of experts interrogated by judicial investigators increased steadily, and they blossomed at court.[42] Blood was especially interesting, how it spattered, when it congealed, what it revealed.[43] The violent death of a peasant in Orlov in 1872 raised medical questions: had his blood vessel burst from the thrashing he had taken from his father-in-law, or had the sloppy doctor cut it during the autopsy? The barman explained that the blood found on the tavern floor where the victim was alleged to have been beaten had come instead from a customer with a sore tooth who had been spitting. Then the specialist Dr. Petrov cited French work in blood analysis that confirmed for jurors the guilt of the victim's jealous relatives, who had beaten him to death.[44]

At a trial in Kazan, in 1873, Professor of Medicine I. M. Gvozdev applied "the Vanden method," which allowed him to determine that not all the dark spots at the scene of the crime were the victim's blood. More engrossing, he denied that the wealthy widow had necessarily died from the brains spilling out of the blow to her skull, because a former patient of his had survived such a trauma. Another expert, Professor N. O. Kovalevskii, solved the riddle of whether or not the victim and the dogs with which she habitually slept had been given opium to sedate them; no, it was carbon monoxide from the fireplace that knocked them out.[45] Thus could science write narratives of crime formerly left to the plain eye and common knowledge.

37. *Sudebnye ustavy 20 noiabria 1864 goda*, part 2, 233. This became art. 633 in the *UUS*.

38. Becker, "Medicine, Law, and the State," 107, 117.

39. *Arkhiv sudebnoi meditsiny*, kn. 2 (1867): 71–91.

40. Dr. Shergandt, "Sud-psikh kazuistika," *Arkhiv sudebnoi meditsiny*, kn. 3 (1870): 56–73.

41. Becker, "Medicine, Law, and the State," 115.

42. E. N. Tarnovskii, *Itogi russkoi ugolovnoi statistiki za 20 let (1874–1894 gg.)* (St. Petersburg: Senate Typography, 1899), 9. In 1874–1878, judicial investigators interviewed on average 24,100 experts. That number had almost doubled to 45,368 in 1894.

43. Blood, like the brain, spilled at the forefront of the scientific revolution in medicine. Holly Tucker, *Blood Work: A Tale of Medicine and Murder in the Scientific Revolution* (New York: Norton, 2011).

44. *Protsess krest. M. G. Shabanova i drugikh: Ubiistvo* (Tula: D. A. Grushitskii, 1872).

45. *Delo o kolleszhkom asessora Nikolae L'vove Bel'skom i krestianin Kazanskogo uezda, der. Nizhnye Alty Tazetdine Khisam-tutdinove, obviniaemykh v ubiistve i podzhoge* (Kazan': Gub. Tip., 1873).

## The Individual Arises in the Courtroom

N. I. Krylov, professor of Roman law at Moscow University, proclaimed joyously to the graduating class of 1866 that "the open court, a mandatory prerogative for the self (*lichnost'*)— is open!"[46] Krylov himself later served as a foreman in a murder trial, and the point he was celebrating was that those accused of a crime would now have the opportunity to tell their story. Caught in the spirit of the reforms, in 1857 the jurist P. Kolosovskii noted the "degree of progress registered in the increased attention to subjectivity in our understanding of crime."[47] The new courts would open a public place for circulating information from the new social sciences devoted to uncovering the contours of the self: psychology, sociology, and anthropology, all of which contributed to the new science of crime and criminals, criminology.

"The emergence of criminology," as historian Ruth Harris described the analogous situation in France, "can only be understood as part of a process of constant interaction between different social groups and their diverging approaches to the problem of responsibility."[48] What, though, made responsibility an essential question in the nineteenth century? A by-product of Enlightenment thought and capitalist economics, responsibility emerged as essential to the modern ethos of free will: voluntarism. In critical response to this intrinsic connection between free will and free-market capitalism, sociology and socialism emerged to put forward instead that social circumstances shaped all aspects of a person's behavior. Interpretations of the self derived from contestations over the nature of free will, mired as that was in religion, philosophy, and the politics of behavior. In 1859 Charles Darwin pitched the battle from which there could be no turning back when *The Origin of Species* made the heretical connection of humans to apes that gave his work a shock value that superseded all others. Darwin's emphasis on the influence of environment on heredity marked the climax of an epistemic shift that had begun earlier, led by scientists and philosophers alike in seeking the sources of human volition.

In tsarist Russia, the symbiotic relationship between state and church had endowed free will with a particular conservative cast: having freely chosen their God, Russians had likewise chosen their autocracy.[49] Once science began closing the metaphysical distance between body and soul, it sparked political repercussions. When in 1863 I. M. Sechenov published "Reflexes of the Brain," radicals on the left jumped to appropriate his claim that "there is no physiological difference between voluntary and involuntary movements."[50] The nihilist and social Darwinist V. A. Zaitsev thrust Sechenov's clinical findings into the

---

46. Quoted in "Sudebnye oratory," *Sd* 6, kn. 2 (1900): 3.

47. P. Kosolovskii, *Ocherk istoricheskogo razvitiia prestuplenii protiv zhizni i zdorov'ia* (Moscow: T. T. Volkov, 1857), 153–54.

48. Ruth Harris, *Murders and Madness: Medicine, Law, and Society in the Fin de Siècle* (Oxford: Clarendon Press, 1989), 3.

49. As Daniel Todes quoted a member of the censorship committee, free will was "among the fundamental principles of Autocratic authority" ("From Radicalism," 20).

50. On Sechenov's "Reflexes," in addition to Todes, "From Radicalism," see Alexander Vucinich, *Science in Russian Culture* (Stanford: Stanford University Press, 1963), 119–29; David Joravsky, *Russian Psychology: A Critical History* (Cambridge, Mass.: Blackwell, 1989), 57–63, 93–99, 124–36; and Galina Kichigina, *The Imperial Laboratory: Experimental Physiology and Clinical Medicine in Post-Crimean Russia* (New York: Rodopi, 2009), 79–90 passim.

courtroom when he opined that "crime, like insanity, is a phenomenon completely dependent on the physiological conditions of the organism."[51] Sechenov himself never removed responsibility for criminal actions, but Zaitsev pulled him into the emerging "badness and madness"[52] debate that connected criminality with insanity in the belief that science could explain all forms of deviant human behavior.

Madness, however, had to be decoupled from badness. The mad had lost their ability to make their own decisions rationally, but had the bad? In his study of the bid by the "knowledge professions" to accrue social authority, Smith points out a central problem asked but not answered by this debate: "a coherent theory of responsibility appears unobtainable" because analyses of behavior "involve negotiations with physicalist and voluntarist vocabulary."[53] These two ways of talking about personal conduct exclude from each other more than they agree on, and professionals in different countries followed culturally specific courses in transitioning from the crime to the criminal. Lorraine Daston, for example, has described how British psychologists struggled to come to terms with the contradictions between these two modes of thought. The end result in pragmatic England was a "philosophical hostility to institutionalized psychology."[54] In France, the debates ended with the dominance of sociologists Émile Durkheim and Gabriel Tarde, himself a former *juge d'instruction* in the criminal courts, and their notion that a "delinquent is not, as a general rule, a sick being but a social case."[55] The Russian course would be complicated not solely by liberalism's constant conflict with autocracy over individual rights, but also by the dominant role that physiological explanations would come to play in Russian psychiatry.


## The Insanity Plea in Russia

The first legal case of a person whose behavior had been considered normal until the moment of the crime had been tried in England in 1843, when Daniel M'Naghten fatally shot prime minister Robert Peel's secretary, mistaking him for the politician, and was equally mistaken in his belief that Peel's Conservative Party wanted to kill him. The jury's acquittal stirred such a public uproar that the House of Lords formulated the (nonstatutory) "M'Naghten Rule," which reoriented the legal issue away from mental stability and required that jurors judge on the basis of whether or not the accused could distinguish right from wrong. This standard gave weight to rational action and free will, and generated criticism in *Arkhiv sudebnoi meditsiny* that the British had "outdated" views of culpability that "rushed (jurors) to judgment."[56] These new criteria for the defense of insanity, though, fit

---

51. Todes, "From Radicalism," 17.

52. Harris, *Murders*, 2.

53. Smith, "Expertise," 86.

54. Lorraine J. Daston, "British Responses to Psycho-Physiology, 1860–1900," *Isis* 69, no. 2 (1978): 207.

55. Robert A. Nye, "Heredity or Milieu: The Foundations of Modern European Criminological Theory," *Isis* 67, no. 3 (1976): 354.

56. Prof. Karl Mittermaier, "Novye psikhicheskie issledovanni," *Arkhiv sudebnoi meditsiny*, kn. 2 (1867): 45; and kn. 3 (1868): 54. See also L. E. Vladimirov, *O znachenii vrachei-ekspertov v ugolovnom sudoproizvodstve* (Kharkov: Tip. Universiteta, 1870), 3–4.

the evolving Victorian norms of personal responsibility characteristic of the age.[57] What, therefore, can we learn about Russia by exploring its use of the insanity plea?

Before the opening of the Russian courtroom, a structure had been codified in 1835 whereby government medical boards determined whether or not a person was mentally competent to be held responsible for murder.[58] These regulations derived from administrative practices of observation and interrogation before psychiatry was "conceptualized as a science of . . . the illness of an invisible essence."[59] The 1845 criminal code made provisions for "insanity from birth" (*sumaschestvie*) and "complete loss of memory" (*bespamiatstvo*). The reformed code of 1864 included legal options for a temporary loss of self-control, in a "fit of anger" (*zapal'chistvo*) or an "emotional outburst" (*affekt*), which distinguished the category of "premeditated murder" from "manslaughter," and did not remove culpability.[60] Only those who acted "in a complete loss of memory" would not be held responsible for their actions.[61]

Eager to reorient the discussion, *Arkhiv sudebnoi meditsiny* connected legal and social issues as a matter of editorial policy. Forensic psychiatrists inserted themselves into the courtroom immediately by challenging the competence of district doctors. A Dr. Sokolov wrote in 1867 about two instances of convictions, frustrated because the accused should surely have been declared mentally incompetent. One woman had been charged six times for murder since 1852; three courts had acquitted her on the basis of "*mania et melancholia attonita,*" yet the other three had found her culpable. In the other example, a soldier had "acted without motive or conscience," and after confessing his crime had requested exile "to either Siberia or Italy." Sokolov "proved" his case when he autopsied the man's brain and found the defects that proved insanity.[62] In 1868 Dr. P. Diukov bemoaned that the judicial chambers had refused his expert opinion about a defendant's sanity, only to have the autopsy uncover the irregularities in the skull that proved his diagnosis after the man had died in custody.[63]

The first case in which a *zashchitnik* pleaded mental illness involved assault rather than murder. On July 4, 1866, Nikolai Protopopov, a bureaucrat in the Department of Religious

57. Martin J. Wiener, "Murder and the Modern British Historian," *Albion* 36, no. 1 (2004): 1–11; and *Men of Blood: Violence, Manliness, and Criminal Justice in Victorian England* (New York: Cambridge University Press, 2004).

58. *Pravila otnositel'no svidetel'stvovaniia i ispitaniia tekh, koi v pripadkakh sumashestviia uchinili smertoubiistvo, ili posiagnuli na zhizn' drugogo ili sobstvennuiu.* Sostavlennye Med. sovetom dlia rukobodstva vracham i odobrennyia Gos. Sovietom (St. Petersburg: Med. Dep. MVD, 1827). The rules were revised in 1835 to include suicide.

59. Lia Iangoulova, "The *Osvidetel'stvovanie* and *Ispytanie* of Insanity," in *Madness and the Mad in Russian Culture,* ed. Angela Brintlinger and I. I. Vinitskii (Toronto: University of Toronto Press, 2007), 56.

60. *UUS* art.1455 lessened the hard labor to "from eight to twelve years," if murder was committed in a burst of anger (*v zapal'chivosti ili razdrazhenii*).

61. Articles 92 (section 3) and 96 of the 1845 criminal code. A. Liubavtskii collected information about the first trials in which mental illness was an issue, but these dealt with the perpetually rather than the momentarily insane. *Russkie ugolovnye protsessy,* vol. 3, *Kausistika dushevnykh boleznei* (St. Petersburg: Obshchestvennaia pol'za, 1867).

62. Dr. Sokolov, "Umopomeshatel'stvo, priniatoe za pritvorstvo, i prisuzhdenie k smertnoi kazni," *Arkhiv sudebnoi meditsiny,* kn. 1 (March 1867): 1–39.

63. Dr. P. Diukov, "Sluchai pomeshatel'stvo nepriznannogo St. Petersburg sudebnoi palatoi," *Arkhiv sudebnoi meditsiny,* no. 1 (1868): 106–22.

Affairs of Foreign Confessions, slapped the face of his superior when denied a promotion he felt he deserved.[64] At trial, Protopopov's lawyer summoned a Dr. Chekhov to testify, and requested that the accused be acquitted on the legal basis of *bespamiatstvo*, "complete loss of memory." When the jury obliged him, the procurator appealed immediately to the Senate. In this, the first year of the open court, much had yet to be decided. The reasons for his appeal exposed the procurator's anxieties about losing control over the expertise. He challenged the defendant's right to call his own specialist, Chekhov. The prosecution's doctor dismissed as indigestion what Chekhov called "melancholy," a legally accepted form of mental illness. The open court added the personal element when Protopopov's sister and two family friends testified to his anxiety and insomnia, the repercussions of an anonymous letter that he believed to be the cause of his losing the promotion.[65]

Appearing before the Senate's Cassation Department, *zashchitnik* K. F. Khartulari reminded Ober-procurator M. E. Kovalevskii that the latter's decision "will have profound judicial consequences." Khartulari focused on the authority of jurors to make the decision after listening to both sides, pleading for Kovalevskii to "set an example in our nation's budding legal practice."[66] Protopopov's jurors may have acquitted him because they admired his bravura in standing up to his boss, but the case as pleaded referred to his loss of volition rather than his assertion of it. For purposes of Russian judicial history, the Protopopov decision affirmed the right of jurors to decide questions of expertise, including mental capacity. The psychologist V. Smidovich counseled readers of *Arkhiv sudebnoi meditsiny* that experts did not always agree with each other, and their job was to provide jurors with professional information, not to make judgments.[67]

The code gave leeway because it differentiated between *vinost'* (guilty of committing the act) and *vmeniaemost'* (culpability for having committed it), which facilitated the option of being simultaneously at fault and not responsible. To be sure, all Western codes legalized this distinction between guilt and inability to control one's thoughts and actions; cultural differences emerge in how it was applied. One doctor tasked with examining Protopopov inadvertently raised a philosophical question when he refused because the defendant's "organism was not familiar to him."[68] His unwillingness to give a diagnosis of the mind because he was unfamiliar with the body speaks to the importance of physiology to developments in Russian psychology. It returns us to Sechenov's reliance on physiology, and the political brouhaha that had flared up before the adversarial courtroom had opened. The opposition to Sechenov had proved short-lived, in part because the Orthodox Church never took it up. Russians did not conflate one definition of *dusha*, "soul" in the religious sense, with another, the medical notion of "mental consciousness."[69] Faith and knowledge derived from different sources, the heart and the mind, respectively.[70] By 1873

---

64. The best discussion of it can be found in the appeal, "Delo po proteste prokurora," *Arkhiv sudebnoi meditsiny*, kn. 3 (September 1867): 106–31. See also Becker, "Medicine, Law, and the State," 325–37.

65. *UUS*, art. 578.

66. "Delo po proteste," 130–31.

67. V. Smidovich, "Sudebno-psikh. kazuistika," *Arkhiv sudebnoi meditsiny*, kn. 1 (1870): 79–103.

68. Both quotes are from Becker, "Medicine, Law, and the State," 329.

69. Sergei Gogel', *Sud prisiazhnykh i ekspertisa v Rossii* (Kovno: Tip. Gub. Uprav., 1894), 13.

70. Viktor Kandinskii, *Obshcheponiatnie psikhologicheskie etiudy* (Moscow: A. Lang, 1881), 9.

a *zashchitnik* had already explained the similarities between Christian and scientific limitations on freedom of action:

> In the Christian idea of crime and punishment, each person is guilty or not guilty, not on the basis of that which he has done, but on the basis of how much desire or will he had in committing the evil deed. Contemporary science has gone even farther: it has shown that . . . a person is influenced by all the circumstances that surround him, and that . . . anyone's past life must be taken into account when judging him.[71]

This left the jurors free to differentiate the sin from the sinner, as the psychiatrists did the crime from the criminal.

In 1874 Tagantsev, a liberal jurist whose friendship with Sechenov exemplified the compatibility of legal and medical views on physiology and behavior, wrote the first postreform textbook on criminal law, published in multiple editions until 1917. Even though he explained the legal differences between *vmeniaemost'* and *vinovnost'*, Tagantsev nonetheless used the terms interchangeably, underscoring Smith's point about the "unobtainability" of a coherent theory separating the two.[72] Culpability occurred only when the criminal "has the consciousness to realize what he has done, the consequences and values of his actions."[73] Tagantsev believed that psychiatry belonged in court, and he remained sensitive to the effects of social circumstances on criminal behavior. He held that "crime is the product of the character and temperament of the person, together with the circumstances in which he developed, which did not permit the development of the traits that would have let him lead a normal life."[74] These sentiments echoed those of his contemporary, the French sociologist Tarde, as both men sought to negotiate the individual into the social when analyzing deviant behavior. Tagantsev understood well the hold that sin exercised in defense narratives. "Confusing crime with immorality, or even worse, with sin," he wrote in 1887, "as the bitter lessons of history have shown, may empower the state to outlaw ideas, convictions, passions, as well as vices."[75] Sin never disappeared from the court, and neither did the notion that a criminal could atone internally for his actions without being punished externally by the state.

### Kharkov: The Epicenter at the Periphery

Perhaps because it lay distant from the two capitals, the "Little Russian" city of Kharkov became the center for serious attention to the controversial positions on matters of

71. *Delo o kolleszhkom asessore Nikolae L'vove Bel'skom*, 180.

72. Girish Bhat, "Trial by Jury in the Reign of Alexander II: A Study in the Legal Culture of Late Imperial Russia, 1864–1881" (PhD diss., University of California–Berkeley, 1995), notes the interchanging of the two terms, 200.

73. Quoted in P. G. Sushchinskii, "Ideia ugolovno-antropol. shkoly," *VOG*, no. 8 (1898): 533.

74. Quoted in Prof. N. A. Obolenskii, "Affekty i sudebnye otnosheniia," *Arkhiv* 24, no. 3 (1897): 32.

75. As Tagantsev continued, "Human justice thereby acquires 'unlawfully' the attributes of the Kingdom of God." Frances Nethercott, "The Concept of *Lichnost'* in Criminal Law Theory, 1860–1890s," *Studies in East European Thought* 61, nos. 2/3 (2009): 189–96 (194).

criminology. The only city other than Moscow and Petersburg to have a bar association before 1905, Kharkov was home to one of the most aggressive reformers of the legal system, S. I. Zarudnyi, and Koni had begun his procuratorial career there. Much of what made Russian criminology distinctive emerged first in this city, geographically Ukrainian but with a substantial ethnic Russian populace.[76] In 1869 L. E. Vladimirov defended at Kharkov University the first dissertation on forensic expertise, "On the Significance of the Physician-Experts in Criminal Jurisprudence."[77] A law professor at the university and a public figure in the city, Vladimirov became one of Russia's leading theorists in criminal proceedings.[78] A student of international psychiatry, but always keen to Russia's unique contributions to the field, he cited the influences of French psychiatrist Prosper Despine, British psychiatrist and philosopher Henry Maudsley, and Austro-German psychiatrist and sexologist Richard von Krafft-Ebing in developing authoritative theories of criminal behavior.

Vladimirov argued as early as 1877 that judicial investigators must "pay attention not only to the mental capacities of the accused and the circumstances of the crime, but also to the anthropological data of his life, and the organic reasons for his degeneration."[79] His membership in the local bar association meant that procurators could appoint him as a *zashchitnik*. Vladimirov's defense of a lieutenant charged with the murder of a reservist who had insulted him gave the lawyer the opportunity to present the notion of "temporary insanity" as a pathological disease. He put his colleague from the psychiatric faculty, P. I. Kovalevskii, on the stand, and the latter took his audience methodically through the three stages of "pathological *affekt* (emotional outburst that signaled complete loss of memory). A military tribunal, not a jury, decided this case, and it discharged the officer with a Siberian exile.[80]

When in 1884 Vladimirov invited Dmitrii Dril' to defend his dissertation before the combined law and medical faculties at Kharkov University, he was making a political statement about the reception of criminology in Russia. Dril', who would become one of Russia's most controversial psychiatrists because of his pursuits in sexual criminality and criminal anthropology, had originally submitted his thesis "On Juvenile Criminals" to the Moscow law faculty in 1884, where S. I. Barshev had rejected it. A legal positivist

76. P. I. Kovalevskii was snubbed when he proposed holding the first national congress of psychiatrists there in 1887. Laura Goering, "'Russian Nervousness': Neurasthenia and National Identity in Nineteenth-Century Russia," *Medical History* 47, no. 1 (2003): 32. Kharkov was also home to Russia's most famous psychiatric clinic, the Saburova Dacha.

77. L. E. Vladimirov, *O znachenii vrachei-ekspertov v ugolovnom sudoproizvodstve* (Kharkov: Tip. Universiteta, 1870). He quotes Mittermaier extensively.

78. Vladimirov wrote: *Kurs ugolovnago prava* (Moscow: Sytin, 1908); *Uchenie ob ugolovnykh dokazatel'stvakh*, 3rd ed. (ca. 1882; repr. St. Petersburg: Zakonovedenie, 1910); *Advocatus miles: Posobie dlia ugolovnoi zashchity* (St. Petersburg: Zakonovedenie, 1911).

79. Prof. L. E. Vladimirov, *Psikhicheskie osobennosti prestupnikov po noveishim issledovanniiam* (Moscow: M. Katkov, 1877), 64–65.

80. "Delo podporuchika Shmidta" was published separately as a booklet by the provincial government in 1887, and reprinted in L. E. Vladimirov, *Zashchititel'nyia rechi i publichnyia lektsii* (Moscow: A. A. Levenson, 1892), 60–93; see also *Russkie sudebnye oratory*, 7 vols. (St. Petersburg: A. F. Skorov, 1895), I: 101–18.

who did not accept medical explanations for deviant behavior, Barshev had authored the leading textbooks in criminal law from the 1840s. He endorsed "the standard view: crime is immoral, the criminal morally corrupt, and the role of punishment an act of moral justice in the name of preserving the legally ordered (*pravomernyi*) state."[81] Dean of the law school at Moscow University, he had opposed the participation of psychiatrists in legal matters because he put his faith in free will over their growing physiological explanations of behavior.[82] Dril' and Vladimirov were intellectually and politically compatible, both admirers of the French psychiatrist B. A. Morel, whose *Treatise on Physical, Intellectual, and Moral Degeneracies of the Human Species* (1857) had catapulted degeneracy theory into the mainstream.[83]

The historian Daniel Beer has written on the reception of degeneracy theory in Russia—"Morel's children," as he dubbed its advocates. Its main attraction lay in the variety of political and social opinions it triggered. The "widespread belief in the existence of degeneration as an empirically demonstrable medical, biological, or physical anthropological fact accommodated fierce disagreements over the *nature* of the disorder, its causes, trajectory, and possible responses to it."[84] Vladimirov and Dril', among others, were especially eager to mobilize degeneracy as a means to insert their professional opinions into politics, which they could showcase by taking it to court. Morel's views were accessible to the popular imagination because they were consonant with the Christian sentiment that "the sins of the father were visited upon the sons,"[85] or daughters, as it were: Semenova's father had been exiled to Arkhangelsk for corruption, and she had suffered syphilis, typhus, and a miscarriage.[86] She made an excellent case study for hereditary and environmental degeneracy. Years later she sprang back to life in a survey of forensic psychiatry written by Kovalevskii in 1898.[87] Returning to her old ways, stealing and lying, Semenova was hospitalized in 1886 after eating match heads in a suicide attempt. These doctors added anthropology to their analysis, noting that "her skull is fine, her face generally symmetrical," though she favored her right side.[88]

That aspect of Morel's theory that resonated most deeply with Russians, and that had implications for common killers, was his argument that alcoholism was a degenerative social pathology. Arguing that its destructive properties could be inherited, he denied that dipsomania was simply a personal failing. The Russian legal code did not hold that

81. Nethercott, "Concept of *Lichnost'*," 194.

82. Becker, "Medicine, Law, and the State," 65–67.

83. S. N. Shishkov, "Kratkii istoricheskii ocherk razvitiia sudebnoi psikhiatrii," in *Psikhiatriia: Uchebnik*, ed. A. S. Dmitriev and T. B. Klimenko (Moscow: Iurist, 1998): 16–32.

84. Daniel Beer, *Renovating Russia: The Human Sciences and the Fate of Liberal Modernity, 1880–1930* (Ithaca: Cornell University Press, 2008), 40–41.

85. Harris, *Murders*, 54–55.

86. Karabchevskii, *Rechi*, 110.

87. After her trial, an assistant lawyer and his wife had taken Semenova in, only to learn the hard way the difference between a *neschastnaia* and a "psychopath." She bullied with tantrums and refused to leave their apartment, telling a neighbor, "I need scandals, not money." Finally she succumbed to her landlords' bribery and left. P. I. Kovalevskii, "Sudebnaia psikhiatriia," *Arkhiv psikhiatrii* 32, no. 1 (1898): 27.

88. Ibid., 16.

intoxication relieved a defendant of culpability,[89] but when included as one page of a complex narrative, the acceptability of inebriation in the defense rested with the discretion of jurors.[90] The first murder case tried in the Petersburg circuit court put Peter Vereitinov before the bar for beating his wife to death. He, dead drunk, remembered nothing between drinking at the *traktir* and waking up to find his wife dead and blood and broken glass all around their apartment. His lawyer put a doctor on the stand to claim someone that intoxicated was not responsible for his actions. The jurors decided that he was guilty of such torture as to endanger her life, but not intentional murder.[91] A peasant who claimed to have been drunk when he beat his wife to death lost his case because after the assault he had fed their children, a rational action that cast doubt upon the amount he claimed to have imbibed.[92] *Zashchitniki* would start looking for alcoholic relatives to bolster a defense for hereditary degeneracy.

Atavism rather than heredity anchored the theory of the century's most polemical criminologist, Cesare Lombroso. A pioneer of criminal anthropology, Lombroso argued in *The Criminal Man* (1876) that criminals are "born" such and can be identified by their "atavistic" physical features. Borrowing from phrenology, he measured skulls and facial features, putting forth his highly controversial hypothesis that criminals are throwbacks to the premodern era, physically identifiable by their cranial calculations or the shape of their earlobes.[93] Theories that today appear at best misguided, if not fascistic or downright crackpot, grew from his deep commitment to the reform of criminal justice.[94] Although Lombroso's insistence on identifiable signs of atavism was not embraced by Russia's forensic psychiatrists, his idea that criminality was a subdiscipline of anthropology found a welcome reception among those seeking sociological interpretations of criminal behavior, including both Vladimirov and Dril'.[95] French anthropologist Paul Topinard coined the term "criminology" in 1889 in order to deny Lombroso's claim that what he was doing was anthropology, but that was a matter of semantics.[96] To be able to hold society accountable was to invite political, disguised as medical, intervention.

89. N. S. Tagantsev, *Kurs russkogo ugolovnogo prava,* 2 vols. (St. Petersburg: M. M. Spasliuvich, 1874), I: 123. However, one of the architects of the legal reform, Rovinskii, became so upset by the conviction of a peasant who killed in the state of drunkenness that he worked tirelessly to have the sentence reduced. M. N. Gromnitskii, "Iz proshlogo. (Po lichnym vospominanniam)," *Russkaia mysl',* no. 3 (March 1899): 81.

90. Dr. Bernard Ritter, "Op'ianenie v sud.-med. otnoshenii," *Arkhiv sudebnoi meditsiny,* kn. 4 (1870): 11–26.

91. *Sv,* 7 October 1866, no. 56; and 8 November 1866, no. 81.

92. N. Berg, "K sudebnoi kazuistike," *Arkhiv sudebnoi,* kn. 3 (September 1867): 33–39.

93. In their introduction to their translation of *The Female Criminal* (Durham: Duke University Press, 2004), Nicole Hahn Rafter and Mary Gibson credit Lombroso for being "a man whose work marked a turning point in conceiving of the body as a sign of human worth" (4).

94. As Stephen Jay Gould pointed out, despite the fact that Lombroso's biological model was "utterly invalid," his ideas had "enormous impact on (the) campaign for indeterminate sentencing and the concept of mitigating circumstances, which we have tended to view as humane and progressive." *The Mismeasure of Man* (New York: Norton, 1996), 171.

95. Although Dril' did not accept Lombroso's theory of atavism, he espoused the discipline of criminal anthropology because it regarded criminality as a "natural and social phenomenon." Quoted in P. G. Sushchinskii, "Ideia ugolovno-antropol. shkoly," *VOG,* no. 7 (1898): 504.

96. Nye, "Heredity or Milieu," 342.

Lombroso enjoyed a following in Russia as elsewhere because he was attempting to use science to explain deviance from the norms accepted as necessary for social stability.[97] The Russian physician Praskovia Tarnovskaia had supplied the Italian criminologist with the clinical information on prostitutes from which he wrote, with his son-in-law Guglielmo Ferrero, *The Female Offender, the Prostitute, and the Normal Woman* (1895).[98] The psychiatrist V. F. Chizh's positive review of this work put a different spin on Lombroso, worth citing here because it illustrates the extent to which psychiatrists were inserting themselves into sociopolitical issues. The Italian "did not confuse science with contemporary issues," that is, Lombroso demonstrated empirically that women are less intelligent than men because of the size and development of their brains, not because of their restricted access to higher education.[99] Chief of staff S. A. Beliakov of the Moscow Military Hospital was an important acolyte. Studying imprisoned murderers in 1884, he concluded that there are "similarities between the brains of primates and mammals, and the foreheads of criminals resemble those of predatory animals." Finding numerous parallels between criminals and the mentally ill, for example, the "asymmetry and traumatic wounding of the skull, the sharp slant of the brow," he agreed that "it is impossible not to recognize atavism in this evidence."[100] The jurist Tagantsev protested against this reductionist criminal anthropology and insisted "that the court cannot decide cases on the basis of whether or not the accused has a thief's nose or a bandit's eyes."[101]

Lombroso's name was sufficiently familiar that his death in 1909 was front-page news in the Russian press.[102] His attention to measurable physiognomy made criminals visual as identifiable "types." A newspaper description of Mironovich, for example, evokes Lombroso by suggesting the accused's guilt from his appearance: "His face is puffy, course, repulsive. His eyes are muddy, his disposition austere, and his speech vulgar and insolent. Slovenly, stingy, and suspicious, this is a person with vulgar, voluptuous passions."[103] The engagingly psychopathic Semenova, on the other hand, "has especially pretty eyes, large, dark, oblong, gazing expressively around . . . she shows no confusion or timidity."[104]

In 1883, the year of Sarra Bekker's murder, Kharkov psychiatrist Pavel Kovalevskii began to publish the first professional journal devoted to psychiatry, with physiology and forensics at the forefront: *Arkhiv psikhiatrii, neirologii i sudebnoi psikhopatologii* (The Archive of

97. P. A. Troitskii, "Itogi kefalometrii u prestupnikov," *Arkhiv psikhiatrii* 5, nos. 2–3 (1885): 6. Kovalevskii describes a sadist, whose wisdom teeth came in early, a biological signature of atavism. "Zapiski po sud. psikh.," *Arkhiv psikhiatrii* 32, no. 1 (1898): 10.

98. P. N. Tarnovskaia wrote on female criminals in *Zhenshchiny-ubiitsy* (St. Petersburg: Tip. Khud. Pechati, 1902). In 16 percent of her cases, women who poisoned their victims had a sloped brow (9).

99. V. F. Chizh, "Obzor sochinenii po ugolov. antropologii," *Arkhiv psikhiatrii* 24, no. 1 (1894): 97.

100. S. A. Beliakov, "Antropologicheskie issledovanie ubiits," *Arkhiv psikhiatrii* 4, no. 1 (1884): 19–48; and 4, no. 2 (1884): 12–52 (quote, 39). He cited P. I. Kovalevskii, *Sudebno-Psikhiatricheskie analizy* (1881) positively (in 1:39). Beliakov was also one of the few Russian criminologists who anticipated eugenics (in 2:51).

101. Quoted in Beliakov, "Antropologicheskie issledovanie," 19–48.

102. The street sheet *Gazeta kopeika* (The Kopeck Gazette) praised Lombroso for getting the criminally insane out of jails and into hospitals. The Italian criminologist would likely have shuddered, though, at the notion that he had "told them to go and sin no more!" *Gk*, 8 October 1909, no. 437.

103. *Pl*, 30 August 1883, no. 198.

104. *Nv*, 1 December 1884, no. 3148.

Psychiatry, Neurology, and Forensic Psychopathology). Stating that "our journal is a refuge for articles on pathology, criminology, and forensic psychopathology," he planted his research into the heart of the debate about voluntarism versus determinism:

> This journal is devoted to study, from the lowest organisms to the highest, the mental and moral activities of people. . . . Philosophical ideas about the soul belong in journals on those topics; it would be inappropriate for this journal to include theological articles. . . . Every thinking person cannot but agree with the argument that each individual is the product of the sphere in which he grew: he is a product of his parents, the nature surrounding him, other people, and environmental conditions.[105]

Thus did Kovalevskii affirm what had been developing in Russian psychiatry: the clear distinction between God and man, and the origins of a person's mental problems in his or her material conditions. His wife, Lidiia Kovalevskaia, participated in this journalistic venture, writing the occasional book review, but most important, by translating Jean-Martin Charcot's and other French psychiatric studies. Dril' and Russia's most influential psychiatrist, V. M. Bekhterev, sat on the editorial board. Bekhterev would keep the physiology of the brain front and center in Russian psychiatry.

Kovalevskii expanded his professional influence with his 1886 textbook *General Psychopathology*, which applied degeneration theory to postreform social problems. He argued for a new position in the procurator's office, the judicial psychiatrist, to work alongside investigators.[106] Kovalevskii's reputation landed him promotions to Warsaw and then to St. Petersburg itself.[107] The procurator of Petersburg's circuit court A. M. Bobrishchev-Pushkin supplied him with materials from the court for many of his psychiatric studies of criminals.[108] Rarely an expert witness in criminal trials, he circulated his ideas more broadly among popular audiences by giving lectures and writing self-help pamphlets that encouraged a healthy lifestyle to combat nervous disorders.[109] A fan of Teddy Roosevelt because of the American president's combined rigorous attention to nature and nationalism, Kovalevskii wrote travelogues of southern Russia and the Caucasus, which were important for their mineral waters.[110] More intriguing were the broadly circulated psychoanalytical sketches that he penned of historical personalities, including tsars Ivan the

---

105. Editorial statement, *Arkhiv psikhiatrii* I, no. 1 (1883): 2–3.

106. P. I. Kovalevskii summed up his main points of thought on criminology in *Bor'ba s prestupnost'iu putem vospitaniem* (St. Petersburg: Vol'f, 1909), 22, 28, 51.

107. Kovalevskii disliked living in the imperial capital. Champion of the healthy lifestyle, he wrote, "leave Petersburg for fifty years without renewing it with freshly arrived juices from the provinces and it will degenerate completely." Quoted in Goering, "'Russian Nervousness,'"43.

108. A. M. Bobrishchev-Pushkin, "Zapiski po sud. psikh.," *Arkhiv psikhiatrii* 31, no. 1 (1898): 77–113; and 32, no. 1 (1898): 1–70.

109. Susan Morrissey, "The Economy of Nerves: Health, Commercial Culture, and the Self in Late Imperial Russia," *Slavic Review* 69, no. 3 (2010): 658–59. Kovalevskii, *Vyrozhdenie i vozrozhdenie* (St. Petersburg: M. I. Akinfiev and B. I. Leont'ev) had gone through three editions by 1903.

110. P. I. Kovalevskii, *Ialta* (St. Petersburg: Arkhiv, 1898); and *Natsionalizm i natsional'noe vospitanie v Rossii*, 3rd ed., supplemented, 2 vols. (St. Petersburg: M. I. Akinfiev, 1912).

Terrible,[111] Peter the Great, Peter III, and Paul I, the latter two assassinated in part for the mental instability that made them unpopular rulers.[112] His most significant publication for popular consumption, *The Bible and Morality: The Bible and Science*, which reconciled Christian morality and science by supporting scientific discoveries while embracing Christian love, went through fourteen editions after 1907.[113] The local boulevard press naturally turned to this "famous scholar and psychiatrist" for quick commentary about sensation psychiatry, such as reports of a Jack the Ripper stalking the streets of Berlin.[114]

Kovalevskii personified the expert as public figure, showing how far expertise had moved beyond the confines of the courtroom. Two other Kharkov psychiatrists, through their highly publicized battles with each other in the 1890s, gave a live presence to the expanding social role of the expert witness. For our purposes, it makes no difference whether E. F. Bellin or his nemesis, F. A. Patenko, offered the correct scientific analysis of the evidence. What matters is how these two medical men took the issue of courtroom expertise to the public, and how their conflicting readings of the same materials were deeply imbedded in topical social and political issues.

Bellin, the city's chief medical examiner and a private docent at the university, took his analyses to the lecture circuit, much to the chagrin of professor of forensic medicine Patenko. The two locked horns first over a murder that occurred in Rostov in 1891 that featured a young widow accused of poisoning her husband.[115] Alexandra Maksimenko, from a wealthy merchant family, hired Plevako to defend her. Her deceased husband, Nikolai, had risen from the rank of clerk to the directorship of the family's shipping company. Nikolai had contracted typhus months earlier, but his doctor, Portugalov, had declared him solidly on the road to recovery on the day of his death. All night before he succumbed, Nikolai had suffered vomiting and severe stomach cramps. When the widow's family asked Portugalov for the death certificate necessary to bury Nikolai, the doctor balked. Puzzled by why a man he had just declared well had died so suddenly, Portugalov pressured for an autopsy. When this yielded no signs of violence, the doctor persuaded local medical examiner Mark Krasso to cut snippets from Nikolai's organs and send them out for chemical analysis. The discovery of arsenic in the organs prompted a murder

111. P. I. Kovalevskii, *Ioann Groznyi i ego dushevnoe sostoianie* (St. Petersburg: M.I. Akinfiev i I.V. Leontev, 1901). In a critique of Kovalevskii's profile of Ivan as "neurasthenic and paranoid," Sergei Gogel' responded that he was a man of the bloody times in which he lived, anticipating a debate that erupted decades later between Richard Hellie, who argued for Ivan's paranoia, and Michael Cherniavsky, who saw the tsar as a "Renaissance prince." Gogel', *Sud prisiazhnykh*, 34; Hellie, "What Happened? How Did He Get Away With It?," *Russian History* 14, nos. 1–4 (1987): 199–224; and Cherniavsky, "Ivan the Terrible as Renaissance Prince," *Slavic Review* 27, no. 2 (1968): 195–211.

112. P. I. Kovalevskii, *Imperator Petr III, Imperator Pavel I* (St. Petersburg: M.I. Akinfiev and I.V. Leontev, 1901); and *Petr velikii i ego genii* (St. Petersburg: M.I. Akinfiev and I. V. Leontev.

113. P. I. Kovalevskii, *Bibliia i nravstvennost': Bibliia i nauka*, 14th ed. (St. Petersburg: M. I. Akinfiev, 1916).

114. *Gk*, 6 February 1909, no. 34. I thank Joan Neuberger for this citation.

115. Facts of this case are from *Delo ob otravlenii potomstvennogo pochetnogo grazhdanina Maksimenko* (St. Petersburg: A. S. Suvorin, 1891) and from the coverage in the local paper of record, *Rostovskii na Danu listok*, which gave significant space to the disagreements among experts, 3 April 1891, no. 38 (Bellin), and 5 April 1891, no. 39 (Patenko).

investigation. Alexandra requested a second round of analysis from the already interred body. Arsenic, which produced the same abdominal symptoms as typhus, reappeared.[116]

Intrigues piled up quickly. Gossip appointed Aristarkh Reznikov, the handsome young clerk living in the Maksimenko home "like the master of the house (*khozianin*)," as Alexandra's lover and accomplice. She had reputedly given her victim a glass of seltzer that fateful evening, though the drink was no longer available by the time the police entered the case. Rumors placed Alexandra at an apothecary trying to purchase arsenic for rats that no one else had seen. Reznikov had accused Portugalov of trying to shake him down for three hundred rubles for the death certificate, and the doctor decidedly had his reputation to defend. Still, arsenic in the organs pointed to murder, so the prosecutorial finger pointed to those with means, motive, and opportunity. The Russian practice of splintering the questions delivered to jurors allowed them to weigh both science and subjectivity. The jury agreed that Maksimenko had been poisoned, but not that his widow and the young family friend had done it. The procurator appealed what appeared to him a contradictory verdict. Spasovich challenged this appeal in the Senate, which ultimately sent the case back for retrial on the usual basis of a minor legal technicality. The venue was moved to Kharkov, but the second jury concurred with the first: yes, he had been poisoned, but not by the accused.[117]

The Kharkov setting resulted in summonses to both Bellin and Patenko, neither of whom specialized in toxicology. Bellin's knowledge of poison appears solely in a publication on the deadly properties of castor beans.[118] Patenko's credentials lay in his professorial vision of the complexities of a comprehensive examination of all the medical evidence in context, much like Sorokin had provided at court in the Sarra Bekker case. Bellin was quick to argue the prosecutorial point that the amount of arsenic in the body had been administered with the intent to kill Maksimenko, although he bowed to the cross-examination and could not exclude typhus "absolutely" as the cause of death.[119]

The circumspect Patenko arranged the pieces of the puzzle into a coherent picture. Performing the autopsy, Krasso had disinfected the organs with sulema, a mercury-based corrosive sublimate with many of the chemical properties of arsenic. This could explain the chemical analysis, and no material evidence supported the rumors about an adulterous romance. Nikolai had eaten caviar at a neighbor's house that evening, which, if he were not completely cured of the typhus, could account for his nausea. Patenko's narrative could satisfy jurors hesitant to convict defendants who pleaded their innocence, and against whom no direct evidence had been entered. Bellin's fight with Patenko poured out into battling brochures.[120]

116. All agreed that the immediate cause of death was paralysis of the heart, but the forensic question was, what had brought this on? Arsenic or typhus?

117. Years later criminologist Sergei Gogel' cited this conflicting testimony over the poison in Maksimenko's organs as an important reason why expertise, like a confession, can only be one part of the evidence that jurors, not doctors, must decide (*Sud prisiazhnykh*, 13).

118. *O toksikologicheskikh osobennostiakh semian kleshcheviny v sviazi s neskol'kimi sluchaiami otravlenii* (Kharkov: P. I. Shmidt, 1888).

119. Bellin's testimony is in *Delo ob otravlenii*, 194–99.

120. F. Patenko, *K voprosu o sudebno-meditsinskom znachenii trupnykh iavlenii* (St. Petersburg: St. Petersburg Gub. Tip., 1891); and E. F. Bellin, *Sudebno-meditsinskoe znachenie omyleniia trupov* (St. Petersburg: P. O. Iablonskii, 1891).

Their next clash had national political implications, and was set off in 1896 when the local newspaper *Iuzhnyi krai* (Southern Region) praised Bellin as "one of the very few well-known Russian forensic doctors." The editors welcomed an article he had written, unsolicited by the court, denying that the ethnic Votiaks on trial had committed a ritual murder of a Russian vagabond.[121] The case had attracted considerable attention, and Patenko felt compelled to respond to Bellin's assertions.[122] Bellin saw himself as the authoritative source for the general public, specifying that he was writing for lay readers (*profany*).[123] Patenko responded to regain what he perceived to be the professional integrity lost when the dabbler Bellin inserted himself in matters beyond his competence.

The experts' quibbling over the Votiak case, "like rats or prizefighters,"[124] consisted of each taking apart the other's position piece by piece, even though both only had access to an autopsy report written two years earlier. Bellin hoped to prove that the accusations were preposterous, and Patenko wanted to show up Bellin's intervention in the case as foolish. Bellin got in a dig at the differences between the academic and practicing physicians, sniping that "if Patenko had my experiences with corpses," he would have concluded differently.[125] Patenko flirted with the prosecution's position, raising a question relevant to the narrative: why had the corpse been decapitated and disemboweled?[126] The case itself went to trial three times, ultimately ending in acquittals for the Votiaks.

A medical gadfly, Bellin died in poverty in 1902 because he had given his all to his city. A quick survey of his writings and lectures shows how he latched onto new ideas as quickly as they appeared, taking them public. Hypnosis, for example, had moved from obscure mesmerism to a potential threat for everything from murder to mass hysteria. Linked to spiritism, séances, and other forums at which persons willingly relinquished their free will, hypnotism by the 1880s threatened the unwilling surrender of volition.[127] *Arkhiv psikhiatrii* considered it sufficiently serious to comment on possible criminal abuses of it, and the Ministry of Internal Affairs outlawed public performances of hypnotism in 1890.[128] The "specialist" O. I. Fel'dman associated it with the newly invented phonograph in a lecture to the Russian Society for Experimental Psychology in 1895.[129] A natural topic for Bellin, he

121. The victim, Konon Matiunin, was epileptic, and had come to the village to collect alms in the manner of the holy fools that peopled Russian Orthodox culture. Robert Geraci, "Ethnic Minorities, Anthropology, and Russian National Identity on Trial: The Multan Case, 1892–1896," *Russian Review* 59, no. 4 (2000): 530–54.

122. F. Patenko, *Po povodu stat'i chastnyi: Prisiazhnii E. F. Bellin* (Kharkov: Tip. Gub. Upr., 1896).

123. E. F. Bellin, *Otvet g. proffesoru sudebnoi meditsini F. A. Patenko* (Kharkov: Adolfe Darre, 1896), 28.

124. Ian Burney, "A Poisoning of No Substance: The Trials of Medico-Legal Proof in Mid-Victorian England," *Journal of British Studies* 38, no. 1 (1999): 85.

125. Bellin, *Otvet g. proffesoru*, 12.

126. Patenko, *Po povodu*, 24.

127. On the "golden age" of hypnotism in the 1890s, see Jacqueline Friedlander, *Psychiatrists and Crisis in Russia, 1880–1917* (PhD diss., University of California–Berkeley, 2007), 130–202. Ia. A. Botkin and V. M. Bekhterev also published on hypnotism.

128. I. R. Pasternatskii, "Sluchai dushevnogo zabolevaniia vsledstvie zaniatii spiritismom," *Arkhiv psikhiatrii* 3, no. 2 (1884): 55–58; reviews in 19, no. 1 (1892): 116; and 19, no. 3 (1892): 141.

129. *Pl*, 9 April 1895, no. 95; and 27 September 1895, no. 113.

spoke on it to popular and professional audiences alike. "We live in a nervous century," he cautioned his anxious audience, urging them to bear in mind that hypnosis posed the latest threat to freedom of action.[130] Addressing the juridical faculty at Kharkov University, he emphasized the need to include hypnosis as a legal factor in the question of culpability. He advised the students that courts would soon to have to consider the consequences of hypnosis as a factor in various crimes.[131]

Bellin's name pops up in multiple contexts and sources. Reading his work in the light of twentieth-century criminology, he fluctuates between a poor man's Lombroso and a huckster. But fervently dedicated to the betterment of society, he kept fresh the issue of personal volition under threat from impersonal forces. He long studied suicide, that griev-ous action whose victims chose to surrender to the dark forces from which he hoped to save society.[132] As homosexuality became a topic of growing medical interest at century's end, Bellin spoke on it as hermaphroditism, seeing it as a biological and clinical issue.[133] His job with the city inspired his social activism, and his keen interest in sanitation of all sorts guided him to open a clinic for prostitutes.[134]

Bellin and Patenko make exemplary representatives of the changing civic status of the expert. The former intent on popularizing forensics, and the latter an academic called in on numerous significant trials,[135] their disagreements underscore how courtroom experts helped to midwife "the birth of the social" in Russia. A "new terrain," writes David Horn, "in which, in the course of the nineteenth century, a wide variety of problems came to be grouped together," this "social" included new institutions and their professional person-nel, embodied for our purposes by the experts testifying at court, who presented "a modern way of conceptualizing problems of society."[136] Modernity in this sense attempted to bal-ance the individual with the social, and to balance individual criminals with the influences of the society that had shaped them.

130. E. F. Bellin, *Gipnotism i prestuplenie* (Kharkov: Tip. Gubernskogo upravleniia, 1892), 84–86. He gave this lecture to raise money for a free reading room.

131. E. F. Bellin, "Gipnotism i ego znachenie v nauke prava i ugolovnom sudoproizvodstve," reprinted in *VOG*, no. 1 (1898) 77–89; no. 2 (1898): 136–54; and no. 3 (1898): 184–203. Bellin wrote of a merchant's daughter who had been hypnotized by a masseur to marry him and kill her millionaire father. Bekhterev testified at her defense (ibid., 78–79). In 1900, the man who killed the famed Petersburg oculist G. A. Donberg claimed that the victim had hypnotized his wife into a love affair. "Ubiistvo professora Donberga," in N. V. Nikitin, *Prestupnyi mir i ego zashchitniki* (St. Petersburg: Trud, 1902), 102.

132. E. F. Bellin, *Nervnye i dushevnye rasstroistva u ozhivlennykh poveshennykh i ikh ekvivalenty* (Kharkov: Zil'bergberg, 1896). He argued that because suicide was the result of mental illness, its victims should be permitted an Or-thodox funeral.

133. E. F. Bellin, *Sluchai lozhnogo muzhskogo germafroditizma* (Kharkov: Zil'bergberg, 1894); and *Sluchai zatruditel'nogo opredeleniia pola i grazhdanskikh prav: Muzhshina ili zhenshchina?* (Kharkov: Zil'bergberg, 1898).

134. Bellin's publications included the self-published *Ocherki obshchestvennogo zdravookhranenie* (Kharkov, 1883–1884); *Po voprosu nedostatochnosti vodosnabzheniia g. Khar'kova* (Kharkov: Kaplan I Biriukov, 1887); *Obshchestvenno-sanitarnye uchrezhdeniia germanskoi stolitsy* (St. Petersburg: A. Arnol'd, 1891); *K statistike prichin skoropostizhnoi smerti* (Kharkov: Zil'bergberg, 1893); and *Letnye kupal'ni Khar'kova* (Kharkov: n. p., 1893).

135. Patenko served as expert witness in the trial of the Skitskii brothers of Poltava, discussed in chapter 1.

136. David Horn, *Social Bodies: Science, Reproduction, and Italian Modernity* (Princeton: Princeton University Press, 1994), 11.

## Defense Strategies: Why I Killed

Karabchevskii had a favorite anecdote about the first judge he had to face as a young attorney. When another freshly coined lawyer pleaded "*affekt*" for his client, the judge told him to explain this to jurors. "It's when someone doesn't understand what he's saying and doing," he responded. "Yes," answered the judge, "just like this attorney."[137] The joke reflected the reality that although the experts provided the source of scientific truth, it was the attorneys who wrote their testimony into their versions of the crime. In the adversarial situation, both sides had to arrange convincing evidence, but their narrative thrusts took different philosophical directions. The prosecution would gravitate naturally toward voluntarism in order to show a motivated guilt. The defense, in contrast, would privilege determinism as a means of raising doubts about the accused's culpability. A highly publicized case from 1879 put these differences in action. Procurator Obninskii and *zashchitnik* Plevako sat across from each other in a Moscow courtroom at the trial of Praskov'ia Kachka, an eighteen-year-old noblewoman who had shot and killed the ex-lover who had cast her aside for her friend.

Obninskii entered the courtroom not unsympathetic to the young woman. This case opened a year after jurors had acquitted Vera Zasulich of the attempted murder of the governor-general of St. Petersburg; nor was he over confident that the jury would convict simply because she had shot her target. He built his prosecution on facts, logic, and psychiatry. The Moscow procuracy had kept Kachka under medical observation for better than a month, and both lawyers arrived at court steeped in psychiatric theory. Obninskii argued that she was not mentally ill, but had committed premeditated murder according to the rationale that "if I can't have him, no one can." He quoted the pioneering sexologist Krafft-Ebing that "there is not a single instance of derangement of intellectual activity that can be identified as an exclusive characteristic of the insane that is not also present in normal people." Marshaling international legal codes, he pointed out that medical specialists had not themselves agreed upon such concepts as "diseased logic" and "convulsive consciousness." He cited Kachka's supposedly favorite authors to attest to her "banal materialism": Immanuel Kant, John Stuart Mill, Herbert Spencer, and Karl Marx. Obninskii concluded that "since the government does not permit the death penalty for more serious crimes, how can a private individual be permitted to take this action?" Nevertheless, he rested his case by suggesting that a guilty verdict be moderated with leniency because she claimed to have purchased the pistol to use on herself.[138]

Enter the defense. Opening with a question already posed by the presiding judge, "does it follow that all of mental (*dushevnaia*) life is conditioned by the state of the brain?," Plevako raised Sechenov's ideas if not his name. He challenged the prosecution's assessment with a second opinion from a psychiatrist who had diagnosed Kachka as suffering from

---

137. Karabchevskii, "Kak ia stal advocatom," lxx.

138. Quotes are from "Delo Kachka," *Russkie sudebnye oratory*, vol. 3, 382, 378, 380, 387. Though I must agree with Plevako's counterpoint that "Marx's ideas about capital and labor went in one ear and out the other" (390).

Fig. 9. F. N. Plevako, the golden-tongued Muscovite.

*raptus melancholicus*, a medical condition identified by Maudsley in which a person would explode without warning into a paroxysm of violence.[139] Reading aloud from a psychiatric textbook, Plevako marveled to jurors that although the author "had never met (Kachka), he seemed to have torn a page from her life."[140]

Plevako began his defense with her conception. Not the product of a loving couple, but of "wild drinking and carnal passions," she had been carried in the womb by a mother "anxious and upset by domestic violence." He then situated Kachka in both religion and Russian history. Eschewing specific passages, he cited Canaan and Babylon as places where heredity had been accepted to explain antisocial behavior, and he invoked the spirit of twelfth-century grand prince Vladimir Monomakh to historicize the generosity of the Russia spirit.[141] Against this backdrop of Orthodox Rus', he put science in its place:

139. Maudsley developed this concept in *Responsibility in Mental Health*, which appeared first in 1874.

140. "Delo Kachka," 388.

141. *Strekoza* satirized Plevako: "He begins every speech with princes, the appanage system, the Tatar yoke, then adding spiritism, psychopathy, and homeopathy" (17 March 1885, no. 11: 2).

"I know that a crime must be punished and evil destroyed, but . . . tell me, is this an infection that must be eradicated, or an infected one that must be shown mercy?"[142]

Comparing her to Lazarus, dead to this world but capable of being reborn through faith, he sealed her fate with his closing exhortation that the only option to save her was to return her to the bosom of her family broadly conceived as Orthodox Russia: "This is a happy day for her . . . . The homeless wanderer[143] has at last found her mother, Russia, sitting before her in the form of representatives of public conscience. Open your arms, I give her to you!"[144] Plevako gave Kachka's jurors the opportunity to forgive her trespasses without denying that she had done wrong. When they acquitted, the crowd in the courtroom leapt up to applaud.

The jury did not simply decide in favor of the degenerate determinism in Plevako's defense over Obninskii's charge that she had exerted her free will. Extenuating circumstances would also have contributed to their decision. After all, Kachka had been jilted. Moreover, she was a female, and the chief of the psychiatric staff at the hospital where she was observed added that "when her sexual organs were developing, she did not have the proper education or guidance . . . and her reflective instincts became stimulated."[145] Such widely diagnosed female maladies put women in a double bind. On the one hand, depriving them of rational reactions kept them out of the public sphere, while liberating them in the private one to commit mayhem.[146] This posed a conundrum: to be charged with having killed under the influence of their natural feminine weaknesses robbed their act of its social significance as a response to unequal sexual relations. Still, the women walked away from prison.

Would Russian men be afforded the same murderous mental condition? V. V. Orlov, who in 1889 killed Pola Befani, a chorus girl at the Bolshoi, when she called off their affair, was not.[147] *Zashchitnik* Urusov unsuccessfully appealed Orlov's conviction to the Senate after the presiding judge had refused to let him call prominent the psychiatrist S. S. Korsakov to the stand.[148] The broader narrative of Orlov's crime, however, tamped down on sympathy for a single moment of impulsive insanity. The married Orlov had beaten his wife to the point that she was grateful when he acquired a mistress to abuse. Just prior to her murder, Befani had called the police for an injunction to stop his stalking her. What

142. "Delo Kachka," 393.

143. Pushkin and Dostoevsky both invoked "homeless wanderers" as a nationalist image. Hans Kohn, "Dostoevsky's Nationalism," *Journal of the History of Ideas* 6, no. 4 (1945): 392; and Andrzej Walicki, *A History of Russian Thought from the Enlightenment to Marxism* (Stanford: Stanford University Press, 1979), 523.

144. "Delo Kachka," 394.

145. Ibid., 367–68.

146. The American psychiatrist Isaac Ray also argued in 1866 "that the particular physiology of women made them particularly prone to insanity caused by male desertion or seduction." Robert M. Ireland, "Insanity and the Unwritten Law," *American Journal of Legal History* 32, no. 2 (1988): 162.

147. *Sudebnye dramy*, no. 4 (Moscow: A. F. Skorov, 1889). Snegirev reported that "no case has been so widely discussed, with the exception of the Mironovich case" (1). Urusov gave him a copy of his speech for publication.

148. Ibid, 53.

Urusov diagnosed as hereditary degeneracy, the prosecutor indicted as another contemporaneous malady, "egoism." Alcoholism in Orlov's family could not be blamed, because the father had not taken to the bottle until long after his son's birth, hence he had not passed along genetic defects.

In 1891 Plevako defended a similar case and could not secure an acquittal. A.M. Bartenev, a Russian officer stationed in Warsaw, shot the Polish actress who had refused to marry him. Like Befani, Maria Visnovskaia had feared her aggressive lover, and left notes to that effect found beside her corpse. When her autopsy revealed "changes in her sexual organs that allow us to say with great certainty that she suffered hysteria that could arouse abnormalities in her psyche,"[149] Plevako attempted to implicate her in her own death by painting her as an unbalanced actress who had desired this dramatic end to her life. Nor did Bartenev's alcohol consumption the day of the shooting persuade the judges that he had shot her "against his will."[150] Bartenev's conviction, however, is noteworthy for the changes psychiatrists would usher in so shortly thereafter.[151]

For reasons that will be discussed in chapter 4, by 1890 the defense that Vladimirov had deployed unsuccessfully to the military court, pathological *affekt*, had become an acceptable reason for male insanity. Urusov might well have been able to get Orlov off had Korsakov taken the stand, because the two of them secured an acquittal for Nikita Surin in 1894. The charge was arson rather than murder; Korsakov testified about both Surin's "neuropathological family" and his "physiological abnormalities."[152] Korsakov protégé N. N. Bazhenov took the stand for the reserve cavalry officer A. N. Shcherbachev in 1904 in the shooting death of a friend, whom he mistakenly believed was having an affair with his gypsy mistress. Shcherbachev relied on more than his "deeply degenerate heredity." When he was out on maneuvers, the gypsy mother of his two children had been seen in their hotel room with a Georgian prince, "wearing only her undergarments and brushing her hair in front of a mirror." Bazhenov had treated Shcherbachev for his nerves and told the court that his patient suffered "progressive paralysis." Shcherbachev's behavior the night that he shot his friend, who was in their hotel room with the gypsy, was deemed insane because he emptied his pistol, "firing at close range, without pausing." Only someone acting reflexively would continue to shoot after all the bullets had been spent.[153]

149. *Ubiistvo artistki Varshavskogo teatra Marii Visnovskoi: Podrobnyi sudebnyi otchet* (St. Petersburg: Suvorin, 1891), 159.

150. Bartenev's bill from the officer's club charged him for six shots vodka, *zakuski*, caviar, lunch, five half bottles of beer, one bottle of red wine and two shots of cognac. Ibid., 158.

151. Bartenev's conviction had reached the Senate's Cassation Department; his lawyers wanted his sentence ameliorated, according to the code, because he had acted in a state of "anger and aggravation." The Senate ruled that this code could be applied only in those cases where there is no interval between the agitation and the act; psychiatrists would soon be making the case that the interval was a symptom of pathological *affekt*. Discussed in *Vestnik politsii*, nos. 51–52 (24 December 1910): 1355.

152. "Delo Lui i Surina," *Russkie sudebnye oratory v izvestnykh protsessakh*, vol. 2 (Moscow: A. F. Skorov), 505.

153. "Ubiistvo," *Sd* 23, no. 11 (1904): 113–65.

## The Politics of the Shift from Crime to Criminal

A comparison of two analogous horrific murders, the first in 1868 and the second in 1902, will demonstrate how conceptions of criminality evolved in forensic psychiatry. Vitol'd Gorskii, a gymnasium student in Tambov who was tutoring children in exchange for room and board, shot and killed family members who had taken him in: the grandmother, wife, two boys aged five and ten, and the pregnant cook. Why? He was "feeling the weight of poverty in his own family." Gorskii had stolen the pistol, which jammed after the first shootings. He walked calmly to the local blacksmith, who fixed it, and then returned home to kill the kids. Provincial Tambov in 1868 was ill prepared for a trial of this awful magnitude. A member of the nobility, Gorskii could be tried by a military court. Local law enforcement supported this because the army had the option for the death penalty, which the Ministry of Justice did not. His defense attorney, who was also the local judicial investigator, asked for leniency because the killer was nineteen. Gorskii showed remorse before he was hanged, but the populace did not object to such punishment for this dreadful deed. His state of mind did not surface at trial.[154]

This popular sentiment differs substantively from attitudes toward Alexander Kara in Moscow, in 1902, after he beat his mother and two younger sisters to death for the most banal of motives: his mother had discovered that he had stolen money from her, so he killed her and then the girls, witnesses to his crime. Kara's father was a prominent brewer who, with his older sons, had traveled to Saratov to open another brewery when his youngest struck. Coincidentally, the oldest girl was friends with Plevako's daughter. Alexander was an easygoing young man who had fallen in love with a respectable young woman, but one who did not share the depths of his affection. To impress her, he had been pilfering cash and valuables from family members for the past year to buy gifts.

The crime was as incomprehensible as it was heinous: who would bludgeon innocent family members for trinkets to impress a girl? On the stand Alexander admitted that he thought about killing his parents for an inheritance, and had purchased strychnine and tested it on a neighborhood dog. The animal's agony tore at his heart, so he switched to an axe, which he had hidden in the shed. He held several alibis in reserve, all involving strange men in the house, but the investigator broke them all rather quickly. Like so many young Russians, Kara also kept a pistol for the purpose of suicide.[155] Remarkably, his father and brothers sent a letter of forgiveness read aloud in court. Alexander himself described his crime at length on the stand, speaking in a monotone and making no particular excuses for what he had done. His character witnesses said nothing negative about the good-natured killer.[156]

---

154. The murder and trial are covered in *Sv*, 8 May 1868, no. 97. Once the murder was reported in the semi-official *Moskovskie vedomosti* (Moscow News), *Golos* sent a special correspondent to cover it: 24 March, no. 84; 3 April, no. 92, etc. The provincial *Tambovskie vedomosti* (The Tambov News) covered the trial as "the open court in Tambov," 11 May, no. 19. *Golos* reported on the use of the military court to get him the death penalty, 14 May, no. 133.

155. A cartoon in *Strekoza*, no. 8 (1885): 6–7, pokes fun at a young man who bumbles through three unsuccessful suicide attempts.

156. The details are from "Delo Kara," *Sd*, kn. 5 (1902): 143–217.

Kara's defense attorney built his case exclusively upon degeneration theory. In addition to the requisite family members with mental or alcohol problems, Alexander's physiology entered into evidence.[157] A crooked chest and hunched shoulder were the physical abnormalities that helped to explain not only the murders but also two suicide attempts and the hallucinations he reported in jail. Moreover, the act of killing had aroused him sexually. The *zashchitnik* called for a psychiatric evaluation, which the judge refused. After almost two hours, the jurors returned with no verdict: "they, the representatives of public conscience, refused to pronounce a verdict, requesting that the case be returned for further investigation."[158] The jury demanded to know the state of Kara's mind, for which the public at court applauded them.

Snegirev published the transcript of Kara's trial in *Sudebnye dramy* (Court Dramas). He extolled the jurors for standing "on the same plane as the newest school of criminology, which demands, especially in such shockingly brutal actions as the Kara affair, that the investigation must include psychiatrists."[159] Snegirev was defending the process, not the young man: "let people of science say whether or not he is a sick man, a monster, or a hooligan." The presiding judge had told jurors that he should be drowned in a bag, like cats and other animals, to which Snegirev retorted, "Justice is not hurrying anywhere."[160] Besides, as A. A. Iakovlov noted, "The contemporary nervous man has attracted attention from all sides in society. He occupies a spot as a hero in our literature, experts interpret him at court, they write about him in journal articles and separate monographs, and give public lectures on him."[161]

The starkness in difference between the two trials illustrates the shift of the focus from crime to criminal. Writing in 1898, the criminologist P. G. Sushchinskii mapped that evolution through the relationship between the legal and medical professionals. He connected Tagantsev and responsibility with Bekhterev and the physiology of the brain.[162] Touching upon the crucial issue of cultural contingency, Sushchinskii pointed to the impossibility for medical science to resolve the question of the criminal personality because societies define crimes differently. "The primary question," he posed, "is not in the external crime, but in its subjectivity, in the personality of the criminal as both an individual and member of society."[163] Semenova, Mironovich, Kachka, and Kara all had to be accounted for in both spheres, first as individuals, then as participants in the social whole.

Sushchinskii was addressing an issue that the historian Daniel Pick has argued more cogently, that "theories of crime are inextricably connected with the particular political world

157. In a vaudeville sketch from 1902, a wife reports to the police that her husband is crazy. When the detective discovers that all the hereditary degeneracy is on her side of the family, he declares the husband sane, and allows the latter to wreak havoc in the station. L. Rakhat, *Sumashedshii* (Kiev: K. Ludkovskii, 1902).

158. "Delo Kara," 217.

159. Ibid.,144.

160. Ibid., 146.

161. A. A. Iakovlov, "Neskol'ko sluchaev neirastenii s preobladaniem iavlenii so storony psikhiki," *Arkhiv psikhiatrii* 9, no. I (1887): 2.

162. P. G. Sushchinskii, "Ideia ugolovno-antropol. shkoly," *VOG*, no. 7 (1898): 501–11; and no. 8: 530–47.

163. Ibid, no. 7: 505.

in which they emerge."[164] The historical and cultural specifics of turn-of-the-century Russia emerged in the defense of a peasant who had taken an axe to his alcoholic wife in 1898. *Zashchitnik* N. P. Shubinskii put this choice to jurors:

> Some people have moments of malice: anger, fury, bitter, violent. For others, sadness, shame, desperation. The latter is a sign of the clouding of the mind, a weakness of will. In my opinion, all of these characteristics are before you, and you must decide: is this a villain or merely a *neschastnyi*?[165]

Given the choice between characterizing killers as "unfortunate" rather than "villainous" allowed jurors to express a preference for seeking out external explanations, determinism over voluntarism.

## Conclusion

What do Russia's theories of crime, as applied by both sides in the adversarial court and interpreted by jurors, tell us about, to quote jurist-cum-sociologist Tagantsev, "the external circumstances and moral conditions that did not allow [accused killers] to develop traits necessary for normal life"?[166] Fast forward to a sensational case in 1910 and Karabchevskii, this time with Bekhterev, putting a new word in vogue: *psikhostenik* [psychotechnique].[167] Karabchevskii had been hired to defend the scion of an influential family in Kherson, Lev Skadovskii, the nephew of a state councilor. Lev had been shooting billiards with his boss, the governor, before shooting his wife that evening. He had no clear motive to kill his "guardian angel," but their fight that night ended with a bullet in her brain. Lev's brother, a local official, had tampered with the crime scene before the judicial investigator arrived, trying to pass the death off as suicide. The victim, Tania, was the daughter of the former director of the Kherson *gendarmes*. The prominence of both families accounted for the supernumeraries at the defense table. Lev had been in trouble before. In 1899, he had shot a waiter at a ball, and in 1903 he had been discharged from the army for shooting a student who had insulted his greatcoat "with a cancerous smile." The family had its typical share of degenerates, and Lev's father lamented that he had not

---

164. Daniel Pick, "The Faces of Anarchy: Lombroso and the Politics of Criminal Science in Post-Unification Italy," *History Workshop Journal* 20, no. 10 (1986): 61.

165. *Russkie sudebnye oratory*, 7 vols. (Moscow: A. F. Skorok and F. S. Butygin, 1902), 7: 408. Shubinskii concluded with the usual appeal: "If you let him go, you say 'let God judge him!'"

166. Quoted from Tagantsev in Prof. N. A. Obolenskii, "Affekty i sudebnye otnosheniia," *Arkhiv psikhiatrii* 24, no. 3 (1897): 32.

167. French psychologist Pierre Janet identified the concept of "psychotechnique" in 1894. J. Carroy and R. Plas, "How Pierre Janet Used Pathological Psychology to Save the Philosophical Self," *Journal of the History of the Behavioral Sciences*, 36, no. 3 (2000): 231–40. It later became classified in mainstream psychiatry as a neurosis.

gotten his son psychiatric help, as he had for his wife, who had been obsessed with "Jews and insects."[168]

Karabchevskii loses some of his liberal gloss by taking this case, and Bekhterev seems less of an objective scientist by serving up the latest psychosis for a rich boy who killed his young wife when "the devil pushed (his) hand." Speaking for four other expert psychiatrists, Bekhterev asserted that "the aggregate of the evidence shows he was abnormal, as was evident long before the murder." When pressed by the procurator, Bekhterev cited Lev Skadovskii's "high forehead and narrow ear canals" as evidence of hereditary degeneracy that led to this sorry incident. In one of his characteristically hypnotizing speeches, Karabchevskii thundered, "What does the prosecution want? Hard labor? Prison? That won't calm your conscience, or the conscience of society. This was not a crime, but an inexplicable horror." When the procurator countered with Kraft-Ebbing, Karabchevskii dismissed the eminent German for constantly revising his opinions. The jury, composed of doctors, teachers, bureaucrats, and railroad workers, acquiesced to Karabchevskii's rhetoric. Even though Bekhterev had called him a danger to society, Lev got to go home.[169]

Karabchevskii and Bekhterev were not simply cynical guns for hire, but opportunistic men who recognized the stress fractures in late tsarist society and used the weaknesses to their respective professional advantages. Yet given that both men enjoyed reputations as "liberals," it is important to bear in mind how their pressing for an exoneration of Lev Skadovskii muddied the waters of Russian liberalism: when would individuals assume responsibility for their actions? The best lesson learned from this trial comes from an editorial about it in *Russkoe slovo*. The columnist Sergei Iablonskii differentiated Russians from West Europeans, for whom "such a sentence would spark outrage, but thank god it inspires no indignation here." Stressing that Russians worry only about the possible conviction of an innocent person, he deployed Christian imagery: "we have put our hands in the wounds of this event." Doubting Thomases were persuaded by the psychiatrists, who have "enjoyed great success in the last few years."[170]

Iablonskii's religious images shrouded his political intent. He raised the specter of "the sick who not only walk freely among us but also reach the highest positions in service, who have our fate in their hands, and from whose excesses we cannot always be saved."[171] He had turned every Russian into an individual capable of a psychotic breakdown that could end badly for others, and had done so by underscoring the vulnerability of the good citizen, indistinguishable from the criminal one, before those who "have our fate in their hands." Thus did he voice the liberals' dilemma on the forensic question of free will: ideologically, it made sense to hold autocratic political culture responsible for the weak and

---

168. Information about the affair comes from the local coverage of the trial in *Iuzhnyi krai*, 7–9 April 1910, nos. 1162–64.

169. The official order to maintain separate facilities for the criminally insane was so expensive that in 1911 the Kharkov *zemstvo* stopped accepting these patients. *Russkoe slovo* (hereafter *Rs*), 8 September 1911, no. 207.

170. Serge Iablonskii, "Psikhostenik," *Rs*, 9 April 1910, no. 81. Iablonskii thought the term *psikhostenik* would become a widespread as the term *psikhopatka* had after the Mironovich trial in 1884.

171. Ibid.

degenerate psyche, thereby shifting the onus of self-control away from the individual. A problem materialized, though, when the violent and destructive actions of that psyche were acquitted in court. How to untangle oneself from the contradiction?

And to return to the murder that opened this chapter, who did kill poor Sarra Bekker? I must agree with *Novoe vremia*: "The secret remains a secret."[172]

172. *Nv*, 6 December 1884, no. 3153, in a front-page editorial; also quoted in *Pg*, 7 December 1884, no. 337.

# CHAPTER THREE

# THE JURORS

"We have a criminal jury system which is superior to any in the world; its efficiency is only marred by the difficulty of finding twelve men every day who don't
know anything and can't read."

—Mark Twain, 1873

"Our common people have common sense."

N. P. Timofeev, assistant procurator in the Moscow circuit court, 1882

On the evening of May 11, 1894, a student from St. Petersburg's Technological Institute
escorted a woman into room twenty-one of the Evropa Hotel, overlooking the Fontanka
canal. They dined quietly. In the morning, he rang for tea. Suddenly that afternoon, two
shots rang out, and a woman, bloodied, ran from the room crying out, "Help me! I've
committed a crime and wounded myself. Quickly, call a doctor and the police. I'll explain
everything to the doctor." Then she fell to the floor weeping, "I've killed him and myself!"
As the maid helped her to a chair, she moaned, "No one is to blame. Sooner or later,
this had to happen." Olga Palem had killed her longtime lover, Alexander Dovnar, and
wounded herself, the bullet piercing her lung. She confessed her crime to the police doctor
who attended her, claiming to have been responding spontaneously to a vile name he had
called her (the word was never spoken). She insisted that she had never meant to kill him.[1]

Palem's unusual biography, coupled with her social symbolism as a woman scorned,
guaranteed a piquancy that vaulted this story from a simple lover's quarrel to the front
page. A Jewish convert to Christianity, Palem had also claimed descent from a Moham-
medan of ancient Crimean royalty, whose family had given up Islam after her mother
had been kidnaped by a wealthy Jew. From an ordinary Jewish family in Simferopol, and
named Menia until her conversion, Olga had first met Dovnar in Odessa. At that time she
was romantically involved with the wealthy merchant Vasilii Kandinksii, who continued
to send her money even after she became intimate with Dovnar and the two had moved to
Petersburg for him to pursue his studies. Palem's relationship with Dovnar had long been

---

1. Details from the Palem case are from the generous press coverage and *Olga Palem: (Ubiistvo studenta Dovnara)*
(Moscow: Tip. A. I. Snegireva, 1895). Her quotes are from 1–2.

tempestuous; witnesses spoke of shouting matches and brandished knives. The source of the storm lay in her insistence that he marry her, which his mother strenuously opposed.

Dovnar's mother, in fact, was the civil plaintiff at Palem's murder trial; she joined the prosecution because a guilty verdict for Olga would salvage her son's reputation. The two women had been friendly in Odessa, but in 1893 "Sasha" was hospitalized for typhus and his mother moved to Petersburg to nurse him. Olga began competing with her over his care, a battle she was destined to lose. Upon release from the hospital, Dovnar evicted Palem from their apartment. They reached an official agreement that she could return to live with him if she would stop pressing for marriage, an order she refused to obey. She appealed to Dovnar's boss, minister of transportation Apollon Krivoshein, to the Populist priest John of Kronstadt, and tried to hire the prominent "literary lawyer" S. A. Andreevskii to force Dovnar to marry her; the embarrassed Andreevskii was subpoenaed to testify on her behalf.

Irritated by the rash of acquittals made possible by the defendants' pleading some form of mental collapse, the presiding judge had preempted the possibility for one here by simply declaring Olga sane. Nonetheless, he permitted considerable testimony about her mental state. The police doctor called to the scene described her as "highly agitated, psychically abnormal," and the physician who had attended her in prison described a childhood of nervous disorders, substantiated by letters from her parents read aloud in court. Her former lover Kandinskii, whose apartment had been searched by the Odessa police, sent written testimony. He deemed her a "psychopath," who had exhausted him with her jealous tirades and demands. Still, though, he cared, and continued to send money that Dovnar happily spent.[2] One of the alternate jurors had queried the prison doctor about the cause of her instability: "do not neurasthenia and hysteria develop on the grounds of some sort of organic inadequacies, for example, in this case, on the grounds of so-called female diseases?"[3] The case became such a *cause célèbre* that several psychiatrists, including the high-profile Bekhterev, petitioned the court to refute the opinion that she was mentally healthy.[4]

Karabchevskii took over her defense, and the objections he had raised to psychiatric testimony at Mironovich's trial evaporated when his client was the one with the deviant behavior. He requested that the jury be allowed to consider whether nor not she had shot "in a fit of insanity or complete loss of mind," which would have meant acquittal.[5] Having already ruled her sane, the judge denied his request. Karabchevskii then presented Palem as a moral woman for whom marriage was the appropriate objective of her relationship to Dovnar. Naive and poorly educated herself, she had been taken advantage of by university student Dovnar and his friends, who mocked her desires

2. *Olga Palem*, 38–39. *Novosti* reported on the couple's correspondence with Kandinskii, who also sent them books on "hygiene for newlyweds." Kandinskii signed his letters *Kot* (tomcat), which led to jokes about Dovnar as her *zaits* (rabbit). *Novosti*, 18 February 1895, no. 48. Kandinskii threatened to cut off the funds if she did not marry Dovnar as promised.

3. Ibid., 45.

4. In his appeal, Koni pointed out that the police doctors who had examined her were not psychiatrists. A. F. Koni, *Za poslednye gody* (St. Petersburg: A. S. Suvorin, 1898), 111–12.

5. N. P. Karabchevskii, *Rechi*, 1882–1914 (Petrograd: M. O. Vol'f, 1916), 279.

to be their equal through marriage.[6] The law code gave Palem the final say: "I am not guilty."[7] Four members of her jury, composed primarily of bureaucrats, plus a general and two professors from St. Petersburg University,[8] protested the judge's ruling that they could not consider her state of mind. They made a power play and acquitted her, to the satisfaction of the audience at court.[9]

Letting Olga Palem walk away from a murder that she had committed brought to a full boil the issue of lenient jurors that had been simmering for decades. The insanity plea bore only part of the weight of recriminations. The problem lay in a system that tolerated setting the guilty free. A. S. Suvorin,[10] publisher of the influential conservative daily *Novoe vremia* (New Times), inveighed, "Why this superfluous procedure? The interrogation of witnesses, reading of various documents, letters, long speeches . . . when the murderer is in the hands of the courts! The law should simply be applied to the action."[11] The press had subtly drawn sides earlier, when at the trial's opening personal tragedy struck two of the major players: Palem's father died, and so had procurator I. G. Shcheglovitov's wife, in childbirth. The liberal papers consoled the defendant, whereas conservatives solaced her prosecutor.[12]

The state found itself in a bind. In order to persuade the Senate to send Palem back for retrial, the prosecution had to argue that the judge had brought the case to trial too soon, and that the jury was correct that she should have been examined by psychiatrists. The legal issue might have been the mental stability of a pretty young killer, but the stakes went much deeper: who determined guilt, the judge or the jury? Thirty years had passed since the Senate had decided for the jury in the Protopopov case, but the reaction to the Palem trial suggested that its decision might be revisited. An ironical indication that this appeal had ramifications well beyond the Evropa Hotel, two of the foremost liberal legal minds of the era, Koni and Tagantsev, argued the prosecution's case before the Senate.[13] They

6. The contemporaneous rumor mill linked her to S. Iu. Witte, the current minister of finance, who was reputed to be acquainted with Kandinskii in Odessa when Witte was working there in the 1880s. Andzhei Ikonnikov-Galitskii, *Khroniki peterburgskikh prestuplenii: Blistatelnyi i prestupnyi kriminal'nyi Peterburg, 1861–1917* (Saint Petersburg: Azbuka-klassika, 2007), 140.

7. *Olga Palem*, 131.

8. Bobrishchev-Pushkin considered professors the worst possible jurors, "at the far reaches of common sense." A. M. Bobrishchev-Pushkin, *Empiricheskie zakony dieiatelnosti russkogo suda prisiazhnykh* (Moscow: Russkaia mysl', 1896).

9. *Peterburgskii listok* (hereafter *Pl*), sympathetic to Palem, reported in the 19 February1895, no. 48 issue that "the public shouted 'bravo,' she fell into a dead faint, and the judge ordered the courtroom cleared."

10. Ironically, Suvorin had lost his first wife to an unrequited lover who shot her before turning the gun on himself in a room in Petersburg's Belle Vue Hotel in 1873. *Novosti*, 21 September 1873; and *Nedelia*, 30 September 1873, no. 27.

11. Quoted in *Palem*, 2–3. The editors also rued, however, that Palem lacked "even a shadow of that especially articulate phrasing that sparkled from the psychopath Semenova in this same courtroom." *Nv*, 18 Feb. 1895, no. 6815.

12. *Novosti* wrote of Palem's father, 15 February 1895, no. 45, and *Nv* of Shcheglovitov's wife,15 February 1895, no. 6812.

13. *Novoe vremia* (hereafter *Nv*) noted ironically this was probably the first time the two had been in agreement. *Nv*, 22 March 1895, no. 6817.

secured her a second trial. The psychiatrists who observed her found her mentally unfit to stand trial. The new judge tossed out their opinion, but allowed the jury to consider her mental state. Ultimately, Olga served ten months in jail.[14]

This chapter traces the evolution of the jury system in Russia, beginning with the nearly unanimous support for it among those who reformed the judiciary. This reform, like others, encountered controversy once it moved from theory to practice, based largely on what Suvorin considered its failing: the guilty could go unpunished by the law. For the next thirty years, the state wrestled with the institution of the jury in a variety of ways, affecting which crimes juries could adjudicate and who could be sworn in to serve. Ultimately, the autocracy decided that it could not dispense with what functioned as an effective mediator between state and society. Olga Palem levied a greater impact on Russia's judicial system than its social history, despite her deadly desire to become a married woman.

## The Origins of the Russian Jury

M. N. Katkov, one of the most influential journalists of the Reform Era, had enthused at the opening of the first jury trial in 1866 that "the jury, the best guarantee of civil freedom, has been established in our country . . . and peasants are participating in it, these same peasants who were given their freedom only six years ago, and the success of the new courts exceeds the most sanguine hopes."[15] Katkov believed that juries would end bureaucratic arbitrariness and pronounce sentences on the basis of demonstrable actions. His politics, characterized by the historian Marc Raeff as "controlled liberalism," were grounded in a positivism that would not, however, survive the introduction of personal elements into the courtroom.[16] A decade later found Katkov vilifying the jury system as "street judgment."[17] Another initial supporter of the institution who quickly soured on it, K.P. Pobedonostsev, the archreactionary Oberprocurator of the Holy Synod, himself trained in law, decried the "herd of jurors . . . which possesses neither a conception of the duty of a judge, nor the capacity to master the complexity of facts requiring analysis and logical examination."[18]

In 1874 Katkov denounced the reformed courts as a "judicial republic," an exaggeration, to be sure, but one that captured the political essence of Russian citizens making decisions of legal consequence. Writing at the formative stage of the American republic, Thomas Jefferson and Alexis de Tocqueville had enshrined the jury as fundamental to republicanism. Jefferson had viewed it "as the only anchor, ever yet imagined by man, by which a government can be held to the principles of its constitution," while de Tocqueville

---

14. They found that she had shot "in a fit of anger," but the judge did not sentence her to hard labor for twelve to fifteen years as prescribed by article 1455 of the *UNUI*.

15. John Atwell, Jr., "The Jury System and Its Role in Russia's Legal, Social, and Political Development from 1857 to 1914" (PhD diss. Princeton, 1970), 54.

16. Marc Raeff, "A Reactionary Liberal: M. N. Katkov," *Russian Review* 11, no. 3 (1952): 158.

17. Samuel Kucherov, *Courts, Lawyers, and Trials under the Last Three Tsars* (New York: Praeger, 1953), 79.

18. Ibid., 57.

opined that it is "as direct and extreme a consequence of the sovereignty of the people as universal suffrage."[19] Tsarist Russia boasted neither a constitution nor universal suffrage, but Mark Twain's ironical epigraph about the difficulty of finding twelve ignorant men echoed Katkov's ire, an indication of how broadly based were the qualms about the vox populi empowered to levy discretionary justice.

Selecting twelve men to cast votes that decided the fate of other people was grounded in both the Bible and British common law. The *Guide to English Juries* (1682) held jurors akin to "the prophets were twelve to foretell the truth; the apostles twelve to preach the truth . . . the stones twelve that the heavenly Jerusalem is built on."[20] The institution had evolved from twelfth-century England as a public impediment to monarchial tyranny, and it had been adopted in revolutionary France for much the same sentiment. Intrinsic to the jury is its function as a representative of community interests prepared to defy those of the state when the two come into conflict. Through their verdicts, jurors assign meanings to crimes that reflect prevailing attitudes toward the law that has been breached.[21] Referred to across time and geography as the "public conscience," the jury provides unprecedented cultural access to local values because it levies justice according to local standards. Mittermaier integrated juries into the societies in which they render judgments: "there are grounds to recognize that the juries in every country have their own distinctive characteristics, and therefore it is impossible to talk about juries in general, but rather about English, French, or Belgian courts, for example."[22] Tellingly, Mittermaier interpreted acquittals as evidence that jurors often understood culpability better than "overzealous prosecutors and inexperienced doctors."[23] Always a fan of juries, he believed that their fundamental common sense could see through the self-interested platforms of both sides at an open, adversarial trial.

The resilience of the jury celebrated the limits of autocracy, pace Jefferson and Tocqueville. But in order to understand what role jurors played in the transformation of postreform Russia we need to know more about who they were and how they made their decisions. As one of the few institutions that allowed citizens to take active part in deciding questions with political implication, the jury helped to spark the 1905 Revolution. Indeed, in their first fifty years, juries decided approximately 7.5 million cases.[24] The line

---

19. John Hostettler, *The Criminal Jury Old and New: Jury Power from Early Times to the Present Day* (Winchester: Waterside Press, 2004), 13, 14. Tocqueville noted approvingly that jury service "rubs off that private selfishness which is the rust of society." Alexis de Tocqueville, *Democracy in America*, vol. 1 (New York: Colonial Press, 1899), 289.

20. Quoted in *Sud prisiazhnykh: Usloviia deistviia instituta prisiazhnykh i metod rasrabotki dokazatel'stv* (Kharkov: Tip. Universiteta, 1873), 56–57.

21. David Keily paraphrased J. L. Austin: "a verdict endorses and commands respect for one particular set of meanings." In David Keily, "*The Brothers Karamazov* and the Fate of Russian Truth: Shifts in the Construction and Interpretation of Narrative after the Judicial Reform of 1864," (PhD. diss., Slavic Languages and Literatures, Harvard University, 1996).

22. Bobrishchev-Pushkin, *Empiricheskie zakony*, 1. Mittermaier based this observation on straightforward analysis of 1,508 verdicts that he had witnessed in the course of his lengthy career; he weighed no one "national" justice superior to any other.

23. Prof. Karl Mittermaier, "Novye psikhicheskie issledovanni," *Arkhiv sudebnoi meditsiny*, kn. 2 (1867): 67.

24. A. F. Koni, *Otsy i deti sudebnoi reformy* (Moscow: I. D. Sytin, 1914), 27.

from jury pool to revolution is not direct, but it links with demands that participation in civil life be extended into other politicized realms. The insistence on partaking in the process, though, says nothing about objectives. Jurors reached verdicts, but what was their vision of justice? As legal scholar A. Liutetskii beamed at their advent in Russia, "The sentence is the legal conviction rather than the formality of an ordered truth. Open legal proceedings provide a rich source not only for studying the culture of a country as a fact, but also for thinking about the juridical views of the people."[25]

The decision by those rethinking the criminal code in 1864 to include trial by jury was remarkable. The reformers recognized that the institution was essential to creating a legal system capable of modernizing social and political relationships, but they were not blind to the chasm that separated their legal culture from that of their Western counterparts. England was the only nation in which juries enjoyed deep historical roots and had therefore evolved as a central aspect of the legal system; the colonial United States borrowed from the mother country, and then enshrined trial by jury for criminal offenses in its constitution in 1787. The French jury, born of its radical revolution, found itself modified in Napoleonic Code of 1808.[26] Prussia and some of the other German principalities had a history of permitting laymen to sit alongside professional judges in its *Schöffen* courts, which had antecedents in Roman law.[27] Napoleon's invasion ultimately brought his code to the German Confederation of 1815; the subsequent revolution of 1848 brought a constitution, and a law in 1849 brought jury courts into all Prussian dominions.[28]

Russia's reformers insisted that the institution of the jury had roots in their national history. Downplaying the connection to revolutionary France, they identified as dubious precedents the laymen who had fulfilled administrative duties in the judicial chancelleries, the *tseloval'niki* and *sudebnye muzhi*, mentioned in the *Sudebniki*, Russia's medieval law codes.[29] Kharkov University's L. E. Vladimirov, returning in 1873 from two years of studying Western European juries, echoed Mittermaier in his assertion that borrowed institutions such as this "will be reworked to find a harmony, and thus will make their own imprint."[30] Noting that "each country shall have those institutions that correspond to its character," he made the jury a central trait in newly reformed Russia, enthusing that it is "one of the shiniest decorations of our epoch."[31]

25. "Predislovie," *Zamechatelnye ugolovnye protsessy: Razreshennye v Mosk. okruzh. sude s uchastiem prisiazhnykh zasedatelei*, comp. A. Liutetskii (Moscow: A. I. Mamantov, 1867): 1–25.

26. The revision of the criminal code was not completed until 1810, and was implemented in 1811. William Savitt, "Villainous Verdicts?: Rethinking the Nineteenth-Century French Jury," *Columbia Law Review* 96, no. 4 (1996): 1019–61. James M. Donovan, "Justice Unblind: The Juries and the Criminal Classes in France, 1825–1914," *Journal of Social History* 15, no. 1 (1981), 89–107.

27. The German principalities represented the remains of the Holy Roman Empire.

28. William Forsyth, *History of Trial by Jury* (Jersey City : F. D. Linn & Co., 1875). 383–85, and Felix Herzog, "Philosophical and Social View of the Jury: Could It Have a Renaissance in Germany?," *International Review of Penal Law* 72, nos. 1–2 (2001): 553–57.

29. John P. LeDonne, *Absolutism and Ruling Class: The Formation of the Russian Political Order, 1700–1825* (Oxford: Oxford University Press, 1991), 33.

30. L. E. Vladimirov, *Sud prisiazhnykh* (Kharkov: Gub. Tip. 1873), 3.

31. Ibid., 194.

The procurator for Moscow Province D. A. Rovinskii was the member of Alexander II's reform commission most responsible for steering the jury through it.[32] Enormously frustrated with the corruption of the prereform court, Rovinskii introduced the notion of using juries in criminal cases in 1862, on the basis that the best medium for teaching citizens about the law was by allowing them to do something themselves about it.[33] Like those who considered the emancipation a worthwhile goal but objected that it was premature in 1861, the commission supervisor D. N. Bludov considered Rovinskii's suggestion untimely. As he read the situation, "the majority of our people are not only deprived of juridical knowledge, but lack the most elementary education; the notions of right, duty and law are so underdeveloped and unclear that the violations of the rights of others . . . is considered by many as a most normal act."[34]

Bludov then put forward the characterization that would lie at the heart of debates about jurors' attitudes toward the accused when he worried that "criminals are regarded as nothing but *neschastnye*," that is, unfortunate.[35] The liberal law professor Spasovich echoed his concerns that Russians were "so primitive politically that they empathize with convicts, looking upon them as *neschastnye*, and see the court a terrible place from which they must run."[36] Nevertheless, reformers of all coloration were determined to clean up the image that political theorist Herbert Spencer had painted of Russians in 1850, when he wrote that even if they had the jury "it would not work. They lack the substratum of honesty and truthfulness on which alone it can stand."[37]

Rovinskii ultimately brought Bludov and the other conservatives on the commission to his side, concurring with another Spencerian thought, that "it is not trial by jury that produces justice but it is the sentiment of justice that produces trial by jury."[38] Tsar Alexander II sanctioned the institution because it highlighted the image he had of himself as genuinely responsive to his people.[39] He believed himself to be strengthening his bond with them because "a government which does not reject useful reforms for the perfection of state administration and social order, cannot but find support among the well-intentioned part of the public in its prosecution of ill-intentioned malefactors."[40] A booklet informed prospective jurors of their "most holy and responsible obligations," supplying information about all the appropriate regulations. Warning that "enemies of the jury do not want to

32. The first call for the jury came from the notoriously liberal leader of the Tver nobility, A. M. Unkovsky. John W. Atwell, Jr., "The Russian Jury," *Slavonic and East European Review* 53, no. 130 (1975): 58.

33. Grigorii Dzhanshiev, *Sud nad sudom prisiazhnykh* (Moscow: Razsvet, 1896), 2. As Richard Wortman writes, "Rovinskii's integrity and desire to remove the abuses from the judicial administration made him a role model for Dzhanshiev and others." Richard Wortman, *The Development of a Russian Legal Consciousness* (Chicago: University of Chicago Press, 1976), 217.

34. Quoted in Kucherov, *Courts*, 54.

35. Ibid.

36. V. D. Spasovich, *Sochineniia*, 10 vols. (St. Petersburg: Rymovich, 1890), 3:269.

37. Quoted in Vladimirov, *Sud prisiazhnykh*, 19.

38. Quoted in Kucherov, *Courts*, 57.

39. Richard Wortman, "Rule by Sentiment: Alexander II's Journeys through the Russian Empire," *American Historical Review* 95, no. 3 (1990): 745–71.

40. Quoted in Wortman, *Development*, 261.

participate," it cautioned that juries hold someone's "entire fate in their verdict."[41] Critics who charged that the jury by its very nature "was incompatible with autocracy"[42] showed greater sense than the tsar, but these were the heady days of theory before the stark realities of practice had set in.

## The Twelve Who Served

The qualifications for jury duty made plain the official desire to engage the most responsible of men.[43] The Code of Criminal Procedure regulated their selection and service: male citizens of the empire between the ages of twenty-five and seventy who met minimum qualifications of income (five hundred rubles in the two capitals; two hundred elsewhere) or property ownership (270 acres, or immovable property valued at two thousand rubles in the two capitals, one thousand rubles in provincial centers, five hundred rubles in other towns). These turned out to be not especially arduous, as even clerks who "lived on the very edge of need" were eligible.[44] Twenty years later the critic Viktor Fuks sniffed about "our peculiar poverty qualification."[45] Moreover, the code stipulated that preference would be given to men already serving the national or local governments in some capacity other than the judiciary. In the provinces in particular, peasants qualified for jury duty by serving in their communal administrations.[46] Thus the Russian juror was selected not only on the basis of property but also on *sposobnost'*, or personal responsibility.[47] Members of groups whose absence from their post might harm society, including teachers, the clergy, and the military of all ranks, were relieved of jury duty. Jurors elected the foreman from among themselves, and because initially he was the only one required by law to be literate, critics saw this as a means for one man to exert untoward influence over the others.

Assembling a jury was weighted heavily in favor of ethnic and Orthodox Russians. Jews, for example, were restricted numerically according to their percentage of the local population. Even so, although Jews counted for half of the population in Kiev Province,

---

41. *Prosiazhennyi zasedatel': Knizhka dlia vsekh* (Moscow: A. A. Mamantov, 1870), 5, 7.

42. Atwell, "Russian Jury," 47.

43. The qualification for jury duty are elaborated in the *Uchrezhdenye sudebnykh ustanovlenii*, articles 81–109.

44. Alexander K. Afanas'ev, "Jurors and Jury Trials in Imperial Russia, 1866–1885," trans. Willard Sunderland, in *Russia's Great Reforms, 1855–1881*, ed. Ben Eklof, John Bushnell, and Larissa Zakharova (Bloomington: Indiana University Press, 1994), 215, 220.

45. Viktor Fuks, "Sud prisiazhnykh," *Russkii vestnik* 176, no. 3 (1885): 12.

46. More than three-fourths of peasant jurors did not meet the property requirements, but they did enjoy some practical experience in local affairs. Afanas'ev, "Jurors and Jury Trials," 225. In his novel *Peasant Jurors* (1874), the Populist author N. N. Zlatovratskii describes, probably realistically, how village leaders decide matter-of-factly to send the elderly father of a man who has been called because the son is needed for work at home.

47. Those excluded underscored the importance of responsibility: persons under criminal investigation, debtors, those without command of the Russian language, and those handicapped by mental or physical deficiencies that would impair their ability to judge. Perhaps the stipulation that affected the potential noble juror most was the exclusion for those "under guardianship because of extravagance (*rastochitel'nost'*)." *Ustav ugolovnogo sudoproizvodstva* (hereafter *UUS*), art. 82, pt. 4.

they constituted only 10 percent of the jurors.[48] Nor could a Jew serve as foreman. In provinces with large Moslem populations, this religious group comprised but a fraction of jurors.[49] In an important concession to religiosity, just as Orthodox priests administered the oaths to their flock, so did rabbis and mullahs swear in their congregations at court. Non–Orthodox Christians were also served by their own clergymen. Jury trials were not permitted in the Warsaw circuit court of the Congress Kingdom of Poland, a tacit acknowledgment that Poles would use the opportunity to defy the Russian state.[50] Such official skepticism was born out in the circuits in "Little Russia," present-day Ukraine, which consistently boasted the highest percentage of acquittals.[51]

Local government officials, whether in the governor's office or a *zemstvo*, the boards of local self-government, compiled lists annually from which prospective jurors' names were drawn. Provincial governors approved lists in their jurisdictions, and they had to explain their reasons in writing if they wanted any names excluded. The lists were mandated to include: for the two capitals, twelve hundred names on the primary list and two hundred on the reserves, with proportionally fewer names required in the other cities and regions of the empire, based on population.[52] Jurors were selected to serve the length of the court session, which lasted for days, depending on what lay in the docket. Thirty names were drawn from the list for every session, though not every juror served on every trial during the session to which he was appointed. Both prosecution and defense were given opportunities for peremptory challenge to recuse some persons from being seated. The prosecution was allowed the first six recusals, and the defense was then permitted to recuse as many jurors as it desired, so long as the number of names did not drop below eighteen. Mathematically, the defense could also recuse at least six, but it assumed that the lists really would include thirty names, which was not always so.[53] Twelve names were then drawn randomly from the list of eighteen, plus two alternates (*zapasnye*).[54] Stiff fines were assessed on those who did not report when called: ten to one hundred rubles for the first time, twenty to two hundred the second, and after 1887 a third nonappearance meant jail.[55]

48. Afanas'ev, "Jurors and Jury Trials," 223.

49. Afanas'ev, "Jurors and Jury Trials," 223. A. A. Demichev, *Istoriia Rossiiskogo suda prisiazhnykh (1864–1917 gg.)* (Nizhnii Novgorod: Nizhed. Gos. Ped. Universitet, 2002), 100, noted that in one primarily Tatar *uezd*, only 21 percent of jurors were Tatars.

50. Trials had to be conducted in both Russian and Polish, and were officiated by three Russian judges. The Duma passed legislation in 1912 to extend juries to the Warsaw circuit court.

51. E. N. Tarnovskii, *Itogi russkoi ugolovnoi statistiki za 20 let (1874–1894 gg.)* (St. Petersburg: Senate Typography, 1899), 77, simply states that "Odessa, Kiev, and Kharkov had the weakest repressiveness," the term used for convictions. Bobrishchev-Pushkin, *Empiricheskie zakony*, 89, remarks on this too.

52. Afanas'ev, "Jurors and Jury Trials," 216.

53. The Senate Cassation Department denied appeals made because the initial list had not included thirty names, although technically this denial violated the law. *Sistematicheskii svod reshenii kassatsionnykh departomentov Senata, 1866–1871* (St. Petersburg: V. S. Etinger, 1872).

54. The rules for service are in the *UUS*, articles 646–77.

55. *UUS*, art. 651. Americans were also fined for nonappearance, which critics assumed denigrated the quality by including those men who could not afford to pay. "The Changing Role of the Jury in the Nineteenth Century," *The Yale Law Journal* 74, no. 1 (1964): 191.

However much citizens of the empire embraced the concept of deciding among themselves issues of law and order and enjoyed sitting in courtrooms to watch the action, many fewer welcomed the opportunity to actually serve. One nobleman even harkened back to Peter III's so-called 1762 emancipation of the nobility from obligatory service to the state, contending that it freed him from this service, too.[56] Many claimed illness, but the code required them to provide a doctor's note.[57] Numerous suits against men refusing to serve were appealed all the way to the Senate.[58] One man who had served complained that when the police arrived to give him notice, his neighbors thought he was being arrested.[59] Another pleaded conscientious objection, that his conscience would not allow him to judge others.[60] In the early years of the reforms, newspapers published the names of those who preferred to pay the fine rather than show up at court. One such list of names of men who had not answered their summonses read like a who's who of the empire's most prominent families: Count Bobrinskii, Prince Dolgorukov, and Count Stroganov.[61]

Duty was onerous. The requirement for speedy justice packed all the trials, for the court had been convened in rapid succession and sessions often lasted late into the night. The procurator N. P. Timofeev, who had begun his legal career as a judicial investigator, commiserated with jurors and their "unbearable" working environment. He recalled one trial in which the jury room was so cold that the ink had frozen, so they could not write their verdict. Another room had recently been used for training dogs and had not been cleaned.[62] Those traveling to the center from outlying areas had problems finding food and paying for a place to sleep.[63] Until the law was changed in 1885, jurors had to spend the night at court to avoid being influenced by outside contacts. Sleeping in the courtroom, sometimes alongside the bloodied evidence, did not invite exuberance for performing one's civic responsibility. Fear of corruption had led to the proscription of any form of remuneration, an illogical move that increased the burden of jury duty.[64] Even one of the jury's most acerbic critics, Viktor Fuks, believed in remuneration because serving was "an obligation, not a right."[65] Perhaps surprisingly, in 1903 Bobrishchev-Pushkin noted that bribes had not been an issue for juries.[66]

56. Afanas'ev, "Jurors and Jury Trials," 223. Peter III, husband to Catherine the Great, ruled less than a year, but did manage to legislate this one significant act.

57. *UUS*, art. 388. *Sudebnyi vestnik* reported a man who tried to unsuccessfully to avoid his fine when he complained of a headache but had no doctor's excuse. *Sv*, 5 January 1867, no. 4.

58. *Prigovory ugolovn. kassatsion. dep. pravil'stv. Senata* (St. Petersburg: Tip. Senata, 1873), 154–61; 161–67; 167–77.

59. *Zametki prisiazhnogo zasedatelia* (St. Petersburg: Obshchest. pol'za, 1884), 5.

60. B. Nabokov, "Ob 'ukloniiushchikhsia' pris. Zased.-iakh," *Pravo*, 11 November 1901, no. 46.

61. *Glasnyi sud*, 1 October 1866, no. 1.

62. N. P. Timofeev, *Sud prisiazhnykh v Rossii: Sudebnye ocherki* (Moscow: A. I. Mamanotv, 1881), 117–20.

63. The Fourth Duma approved a project to subsidize travel, but this was not until 1913.

64. As James M. Donovan points out, French jurors did not receive recompense until 1908, when workers were allowed to serve. Before this it was assumed that jury duty did not impose a financial burden. "Magistrates and Juries in France, 1791–1952," *French Historical Studies* 22, no. 3 (1999): 406.

65. Fuks, "Sud prisiazhnykh," 23.

66. A.M. Bobrishchev-Pushkin, "Otvetstvennost' prisiahz. zas. po novomy ugol. ulozh.," *Pravo*, no. 30 (1903): 999–1003. From 1879–1892, only twenty jurors were convicted for bribery. Atwell, "Jury System," 86.

In 1875 the presiding judge of the Moscow circuit court, E. E. Liuminarskii, discomfited by what he considered a decline in the quality of jurors, requested the commission in charge of compiling the lists to improve the quality of verifiable information. In that year only 5 percent of males of the appropriate age were registered jurors, and this cannot be attributed solely to property and income qualifications.[67] A plea published in the newspapers for "all people entered into the list to inform us of your whereabouts" received only two responses.[68] In St. Petersburg, which could have been presumed to have no shortage of qualified candidates, the list of jurors for 1879 included five foreigners, twenty-three deceased, three insane, and eight deaf persons.[69] Koni, one of the institution's stoutest supporters, regretted that bureaucrats would fabricate *komandirovki* (official business trips) to keep their names off the roles.[70] Truancy in Kazan in 1883 reached 22 percent.[71] In a highly sensational murder trial in 1911, of the twenty-nine persons called, nine were excused and another five tried to beg off.[72]

Who, then, took the oath? Thirty viable candidates could not always be rounded up to form a pool. Personal information on jurors is scant and scattered, and very few wrote memoirs from their adventures on the bench.[73] The government set up a national commission in 1884 to collect statistical information from the annual registers. All that remains are partial lists from the previous year, 1883, and they suggest, unsurprisingly, that jurors reconstituted local demographics: in Petersburg, bureaucrats comprised more than half, and merchants better than 30 percent in Moscow.[74] Whereas peasants accounted for less than 10 percent of jurors in the two capitals, they topped 50 percent in the provinces.[75] Koni dubbed the jury a "social ocean" from which people were fished and then returned to the water to share their experiences.[76] Dzhanshiev, the jurist who objected strongly to defense attorneys' accepting cases that he believed dishonored the profession, served once. His description of those called with him mirrors that social sea: two wealthy locals preferred to pay the fine, and his pool included one retired state councilor, two retired colonels, two pedagogues, two engineers, two government inspectors, and the rest merchants, artisans, and a single peasant, "civilized, physically healthy, and surprisingly humanistic."[77]

Dzhanshiev's depiction of the peasant was less a condescension than a reaffirmation of the importance of jury duty to the assimilation of the peasantry into society, reconceived after the reforms as "all-estate," and he favored increasing their representation.

67. Afanas'ev, "Jurors and Jury Trials," 220.

68. Demichev, *Istoriia Rossiiskogo suda*, 82.

69. Ibid., 79.

70. Ibid., 95.

71. Afanas'ev, "Jurors and Jury Trials," 224.

72. *Sd*, nos. 7–8 (1912): 10.

73. I have found only five published sources, and none in archives.

74. Afanas'ev, "Jurors and Jury Trials," 219.

75. Ibid., 219, 221.

76. A. F. Koni, *Voprosy filosofii i psikhologii*, kn. 5 (published by the Moscow and St. Petersburg philosophical societies, 1902), 876.

77. G. A. Dzhanshiev, "Iz vospominanii prisiazhnogo zasedatelia," *Sbornik statei* (Moscow: Raduga, 1914), 440.

The historian Alexander Afanas'ev referred to the "nondemocratic character of the jury courts" in the two capitals because of the minuscule participation of peasants, but there is no evidence of estate-based voting differences.[78] News coverage of packed courtrooms, reports of applause that resounded when foremen read aloud verdicts, accentuated that those whose names were plucked from the urn did not simply represent the prejudices of property holders, but also represented Russia's "public conscience" at large. Pobedonostsev disdained the observer-participants as "a mixed crowd which attends the courts as though it were a show in the midst of a lazy and empty life."[79]

Being denied the opportunity to serve officially did not preclude women from offering their opinions. A virtual *soslovie* (social estate), the "court ladies" (*sudebnye damy*) were seated at every important trial and were never recalcitrant about sharing their views. The court ladies were known to collect funds for particularly sympathetic defendants, and to toss flowers to especially handsome ones. As one journalist characterized these "so-called Balzacian women, whose curiosity knows no bounds":[80]

> She is capable of spending the whole night on Liteinyi Prospect so that she can get into the courtroom the next morning. She devours them all with her eyes: every witness, the defense, the accused. When the questioning contains even the tiniest bit of intimacy, she turns it into gossip. . . . Many of them know most of the legal statutes by heart, feeling quite at home at court.[81]

In the vaudeville skit from 1885, a female character rued playfully that if women could sit on juries, they would judge men more harshly than they do one another.[82] In *The Brothers Karamazov*, Dostoevsky made half of those in attendance at Dmitrii's trial women who "longed for the acquittal of the interesting defendant" and almost threatened a riot when he was (wrongfully) convicted.[83]

The few who wrote about their experiences spoke of it in positive terms, with one exception. Writing in 1884, an ex-juror expressed aversion to "homeowners sitting alongside the *dvorniki*." He also found excessive leniency, asserting that "as a citizen I respect institutions and the laws and I have the right to demand that others do, too." Still, he did not want to return to the old judicial system.[84] Another ex-juror wrote in 1898 with hopes of inspiring others not to evade the summons, and he was even more ebullient than Dzhanshiev about the benefits of social mingling. He recalled one snob who had initially refused even to shake hands with those whom he considered beneath him on the social and

78. Afanas'ev, "Jurors and Jury Trials," 220.

79. Quoted in Kurcherov, *Courts*, 57.

80. *Nv*, 18 February 1895, no. 6815.

81. "Zigzagy," *Pl*, 19 February 1895, no. 48. The criminal courthouse was on Liteinyi Prospect. In England these women were vilified as "the ghouls of modern society." Mary S. Hartman, *Victorian Murderesses: A True History of Thirteen Respectable French and English Women Accused of Unspeakable Crimes* (New York: Schocken Books, 1977), 283.

82. A. N., *Ubiitsa-psikhopat* (Moscow: E. N. Razsokhina, 1886).

83. F. M. Dostoevsky, *The Brothers Karamazov*, book 12, part 2, "A Dangerous Witness."

84. *Zametki prisiazhnogo*, 18, 38. He surmised that "if we change a bad apartment for one that's even worse, have we accomplished our goal?" (70).

Fig. 10. Court ladies, those so-called "Balzacian women."

intellectual register. This attitude vanished quickly when everyone began sharing the intimacies of their lives with one another. His group ranged from the retired director of the St. Petersburg Opera to a religious sectarian, an Old Believer who consistently provided moral ballast to the proceedings. A petit-bourgeois (*meshchanin*) butcher earned everyone's respect for his careful note taking and thoughtful deliberations. The author was impressed with the forthrightness with which everyone discussed their opinions, giving the lie to critics who charged that foremen dominated.[85]

In another particularity of the code borrowed from France, juries were obligated to seek unanimity, but only a majority of votes was required for the verdict.[86] A tie went to the defendant. The liberal Vladimirov spoke strongly in favor of the need for a unanimous vote. He cited five centuries of the British system working well, and pointed out that when France moved from a simple majority to a requirement of a minimum of eight votes, acquittals rose rather than fell.[87] The issue of jury unanimity was contentious wherever juries decided. Jeremy Bentham, one of the dominant influences on Western legal reforms, argued in 1830 that "it is difficult to defend the justice or wisdom of the principle of unanimity," as

85. N. N. O., "Iz zametok prisiazhnogo zasedatelia," *Istoricheskii vestnik* 74 (1898): 186, 195.

86. Of the fifty United States, Oregon and Louisiana require only ten of twelve votes, although first-degree murder cases in Oregon and capital cases Louisiana require unanimity.

87. Vladimirov, *Sud prisiazhnykh*, 140–43.

it "most frequently leads to improper compromises among jurors."[88] Although the grounds are insufficient to decide conclusively, the considerable publicity stemming from trials never mentions confrontations among jurors. Even the crabby ex-juror had no faith in English unanimity because he believed dissenters would give in so as to leave the courtroom early.[89]

Dzhanshiev's recounting of his time on duty showed evident camaraderie punctuated with disagreements and discussions but no serious conflicts. One "merciless" merchant always voted to convict, but did not chafe that the others ignored him. The Old Believer argued consistently for mercy. The butcher who took notes discussed every case conscientiously and proved the most persuasive. Dzhanshiev recalled an episode in which a juror who had refused to acquit nonetheless contributed to the purse that the others collected for the young male defendant.[90] Suspicions that peasants would defer to their social betters did not hold up. Timofeev told how once the four propertied members of the jury elected the foreman, but the eight peasants overturned their choice.[91] No evidence supports the charge that the lack of unanimity turned jury trials into a "lottery."[92]

Statistics drawn from the circuit courts show remarkably symmetry in decision making.[93] The cultural glue that bound the diverse social backgrounds together was the Orthodox Christianity that the majority shared, coupled with the autocratic state that intruded into so many aspects of their lives. "Iron" Tsar Nicholas I had famously made Orthodoxy and autocracy two of the three planks in his official ideology, Russian ethnicity being the third. Jurors, however, used Orthodoxy to temper autocracy. The cultural as well as the philological difference that separated the two words for "confession," the religious *ispoved'* that asked for forgiveness, and *soznanie*, the admission of having committed the crime, resonated with jurors. Moreover, Russians used the word *repressivnost'*, "repressiveness," to measure the rate of convictions. Insinuating convictions to be repression, they took the linguistic turn and betrayed a politicized sympathy for the accused.

### The Public Conscience

The verdict delivered by Vera Zasulich's jury in 1878 has achieved canonical status in Russia's historiography because of how it fits into the master political narrative of an approaching and inexorable clash between the autocratic state and a democratizing society.[94] The dramatis personae in the Zasulich case guaranteed that this courtroom would

88. Ben B. Lindsey, "The Unanimity of Jury Verdicts," *Virginia Law Register* 5, no. 3 (1899): 140.

89. *Zametki prisiazhnogo*, 72.

90. Dzhanshiev, "Iz vospominanii," 443–53.

91. Timofeev, *Sud prisiazhnykh*, 203.

92. V. Ia. Fuks, *Sud i politsiia* (Moscow: Universit. Tip., 1889), 164, objected to the extreme openness of Russia's courtroom procedures, especially the permission for jurors to question experts and evidence.

93. Tarnovskii broke down some of the statistics after the first twenty of compiling numbers in the *Svod statisticheskikh svedenii po delam ugolovnym*, 1873–1913. Breaking the courts, not the districts, into five groups, he found wide swings, from 25 percent to 45 percent acquittals. Tarnovskii, *Itogi*, 75–77.

94. Louise McReynolds, "Witnessing for the Defense: The Adversarial Court and Narratives of Criminal Behavior in Nineteenth-Century Russia," *Slavic Review* 69, no. 3 (2010): 633.

stage a better show than could be performed at the imperial theater: a young woman who dabbled in revolutionary politics and a state official who had aroused her anger by his own illegal action—whipping a student, a "political convict," under arrest. The jurors counseled by presiding judge Koni to "follow their consciences" did so by acquitting her, agreeing that she had not intended to kill Fedor Trepov when she shot him. Since it had begun collecting statistics in 1873, the government was alarmed by the high proportion of acquittals.[95] Officials had hoped to reverse this trend with Zasulich's trial, banking that a conviction could be referenced as a demonstration of support for law and order, which the government could claim as its ideology. By setting free the girl who had pulled the trigger, the jurors affronted the state directly. It responded by removing the crime of assaulting government officials from the purview of juries.[96]

The autocracy's reaction against jury democracy exposed the limits of its embrace of the rule of law, but the issue was not so black-and-white as critics of the Russian state have painted it.[97] President of the French Republic Louis-Napoléon Bonaparte, for example, had taken a similar action in 1852.[98] The publicist Fuks, who had left a position in the chief administration of press affairs, became one of the most articulate critics of how the reformed system functioned. Not simply a reactionary in the mold of Katkov and Pobedonostsev, he had been a member of the commission that had put together the censorship reform in 1865. Writing for Katkov's *Russkii vestnik* (The Russian Herald), Fuks objected to the direction that the legal reforms had taken. He noted perceptively that the autocracy had misunderstood the nature of politics when it removed specifically political crimes from juries, "as though the jury had a political character only when the crime broke political laws, rather than in and of itself!"[99]

Fuks perceived correctly that the government was blinded by too literal a view of what constituted "politics." Zasulich's acquittal spoke to structural and procedural issues in Russia's jury system, as it also reflected the Russian popular legal culture that assumed a protective stance for those *neschastnye* harassed by the state. Russian jurors enjoyed significant latitude in determining the nature of guilt, because the authority to distinguish between being guilty of breaking the law (*vinost'*) and culpability (*vmeniaemost'*) empowered them to consider extenuating circumstances. Procedurally, the presiding judge was bound by the regulations that stressed his impartiality. This permitted him to explain legal issues

95. Demichev, *Istoriia Rossiiskogo suda*, 113, points out rising government concerns from 1874.

96. A law of May 9, 1878, moved crimes against state officials from juries, sending them now to judicial chambers with the participation of estate representatives. On August 9, 1878, these crimes were sent to military courts temporarily; on May 11, 1882, they were returned to judicial chambers, with some undecided cases to be overseen by juries. However, a law of July 7, 1889, took away from jurors those crimes that had been returned May 11, 1882.

97. This law, from 1878, affected fractionally more than 1 percent of cases that would have otherwise gone to juries. Demichev, *Istoriia Rossiiskogo suda*, 127.

98. Discussed in Donovan, "Magistrates," 400. Alexander III would have shuddered at a comparison with Louis-Napoléon Bonaparte, but both "distrusted juries when it came to trying politically motivated crimes against agents of the state."

99. Fuks, *Sud i politsiia*, 123. This included his two-part article on juries published first in *Russkii vestnik* 175 (1885): 617–59; and 176 (1885): 7–44.

to jurors, but forbade him from directing their verdicts. The wording of the oath that jurors took also allowed interpretive leeway. Swearing to "devote my full attention to the circumstances that both incriminate and vindicate the accused," they promised to "vote according to the evidence as it is presented in court and according to the conviction of my conscience." The oath concluded with jurors kissing the cross, or the Torah or the Koran, underscoring for them that they would answer for their decisions "before the law and before God on the day of his terrible judgment."[100]

Moreover, the Russian system of splintering the questions presented to jurors formed a sliding scale of culpability.[101] Zasulich's jurors, for example, had the following list: "Was her shooting premeditated? Did she shoot with the intent of depriving him of life? Did she do everything she could to ensure that her plan would succeed?"[102] These questions were drawn up after her defense attorney, P. A. Aleksandrov, had already asked jurors directly, "Who will stand up for the insulted honor of a defenseless political convict?"[103] In his summation, Koni admonished jurors that "if the facts are thrown aside, then every conclusion appears arbitrary and deprived of meaning."[104] But he also agreed that motives and character could be considered, and counseled that it was up to jurors to decide on the basis of evidence and conscience.[105] Aleksandrov had primed the defensive pump when he said that acquittals were often "an echo of divine justice, which takes into consideration not only the external side of an action, but its internal meaning as well—the real guilt of the accused."[106] This distinction between external action and internal meaning gave jurors a wide margin; conviction and acquittal were not synonymous with guilt and innocence.

Jury justice, however, gave pause to even Koni and other liberals when in 1884 the "public conscience" set free the children of Fedor Mel'nitskii, who were spending the money that their father had embezzled from the state orphanage in Moscow. The "Mel'nitskii Affair" became shorthand reference for the larger debate about jury leniency.[107] In 1881, Fedor, the orphanage's treasurer, had uncharacteristically taken the 337,000 rubles deposit in cash rather than the usual promissory note when transferring funds between banks. Walking from one bank to the next, Fedor claimed to have fainted, only to discover when he regained consciousness that his briefcase was missing. Not even the notoriously open-minded Russian jurors could swallow this, and they dispatched him to Tomsk Province in Siberia for four years. Soon thereafter his children were noticed making large purchases but could not explain their source of income. A police raid on New Year's Eve 1882

100. *UUS*, art. 713.

101. Ironically, the splintering was reformed in France to return more power to the judges.

102. Jay Bergman has shortened them thus in *Vera Zasulich: A Biography* (Stanford: Stanford University Press, 1983), 50.

103. Quoted in Kucherov, *Courts*, 220.

104. Quoted in Ana Siljak, *Angel of Vengeance: The "Girl Assassin," the Governor of St. Petersburg, and Russia's Revolutionary World* (New York: St. Martin's Press, 2008), 244.

105. Bergman, *Vera Zasulich*, 45.

106. Ibid., 49.

107. Dzhanshiev discusses the Ober-procurator Nekliudov's "overreaction" to the verdict in this case. In *Sud nad sudom*, 10.

uncovered more than 200,000 rubles in the eldest son's house. Where? Boris, a taxidermist, had stuffed many of the bills into birds.

If the jurors sentenced the father, why did they exonerate his children? Spasovich sat at the defense table, which helped to get an acquittal. On the stand, Fedor's progeny described him as a tyrant, bullying them into hiding the money. Moreover, they insisted that they only spent funds for self-improvement, including buying the taxidermy business. It was not clear how the daughter's purchase of Parisian fashions fit this bill. Anton Chekhov, then a reporter for *Peterburgskii listok*, captured public opinion about the children:

> Boris is young and has dedicated his whole life to natural science, even awarded a medal at a competition. . . . Varenka, the pharisee's daughter, is still a student [*gimnazistka*] . . . the others presented testimonials about their excellent behavior. These proper folks were guilty only of breaking off a piece of the state pie.[108]

Chekhov's last point hit the proverbial nail on its head: the "Mel'nichati" had not so much taken the bread out of orphans' mouths as they had helped themselves to government money. Ober-procurator N. A. Nekliudov called this "the last drop of prosecutorial patience" and procurator Voitenkov filed an immediate appeal with the Senate.[109]

Voitenkov's appeal laid bare what had become the favored prosecutorial ruse for subverting acquittals: he charged that several statutes had been violated in the oral presentation of documents. Spasovich exposed this legal reasoning for what it was, and accused the procurator of throwing up a smokescreen in order to overturn a verdict. He pointed out that "reference to these statutes in appeals has become like a branch, thick with leaves, producing such a shade that not a single ray of light can get through."[110] Insisting that in essence the institution of the jury was on trial, Spasovich also soberly recognized the potential danger: "this institution has grown up before our eyes, cared for by our hands; we have prayed for it, even honored it, and now we will possibly destroy it with our own hands."[111]

Like Koni, Spasovich realized that judging more by internal convictions than the facts of the crimes had generated significant dilemmas over the two decades of the jury's performance.[112] He might have been even more taken aback by the recollections of a juror from a "second Mel'nichati" case. This man told how his group had heard the case of a young man who claimed to have been exhausted one hot day and returned to his home to cool down with a briefcase filled with his firm's money, only to wake up from a short nap without the case. He lived with his wife and her mother, and when the jurors listened to

108. Quoted in "Gnezdo glukharia," *Sovershenno sekretno*, no. 6 (2007): 31.

109. I. V. Gessen *Advokatura, obshchestvo i gosudarstvo, 1864–1914* (Moscow: Soviet pris. pover., 1914), 255.

110. V.D. Spasovich, *Sudebnye rechi*, vol. 7 (St. Petersburg: K. Grendyshinskii, 1984), 68. He and Arsen'ev co-wrote a letter (with three other lawyers), published in *Novosti*, insisting on the right of any accused to a defense. They parried the blow that Nekliudov had dealt to juries by reminding that in his textbook on criminal law he had championed the role of the *zashchitnik*. Reprinted in Gessen, *Advokatura*, 257–61.

111. Spasovich, *Sudebnye rechi*, vol 7, 61.

112. Koni, *Voprosy filosofii*, 864–907.

the latter testify, they decided that she, the mother-in-law, had stolen the money: acquittal by solving the crime themselves.[113] Perry Mason would have been pleased.

### The Russian Jury in the Western Context

Throughout the nineteenth century, as the institution everywhere adapted to changing social and political circumstances, discord erupted over the scope of the jury's purview. The source of the dispute lay in whether or not jurors were supposed to judge only the facts of the case, based on the evidence, or whether they could they render judgments that had the effect of nullifying the laws themselves. The power of England's original jury lay in its ability to nullify a law by acquitting an admittedly guilty person, thereby balancing moral imperatives derived from community standards against the formality of the law code.[114] England's legal system, however, was nicknamed the "Bloody Code" because of the more than two hundred crimes punishable by death, and juries frequently hesitated to bring down the full weight of the law on what they considered merely venial transgressions.[115] Thus could juries take legal actions that affirmed their status as the conscience of their communities. In the nineteenth century, though, positivism, science, and Beccaria-inspired legal reforms combined to effect what juries would decide at court. Science, for example, increased the precision with which evidence could be analyzed, which enhanced the authority of professionals to explain facts. Electoral representation reduced the need for a jury to counterbalance monarchial privilege, because laws drawn up by elected legislators would not need public opinion to nullify them.

The American jurist Ben Lindsey commented in 1899 that "the jury system . . . undoubtedly had its origin in the attempt to separate judges of law and of fact."[116] He then drew attention to the tension that had developed from the rewriting of philosophical principles of common law into a formal statute.[117] The colonial United States, which had adopted English common law, accepted that juries were "the judges of both the law and the fact in a criminal case . . . not bound by the opinion of the court."[118] Upon independence, the United States gave its citizens a constitutional guarantee to "a speedy and public trial, by an impartial jury," with no mention of whether the jury decided law, fact, or both. In 1820, the delegates writing the constitution for the state of Massachusetts did not need

---

113. "Iz zapisnoi knizhki prisiazh. Zasedatelia," *Sd*, kn. 3 (1898): 139.

114. Irwin A. Horowitz and Thomas E. Willging, "Changing Views of Jury Power: The Nullification Debate, 1787–1988," *Law and Human Behavior* 15, no. 2 (1991): 165–82.

115. V. A. C. Gatrell traces the changes in *The Hanging Tree: Execution and the English People, 1770–1868* (New York: Oxford University Press, 1994).

116. Ben B. Lindsey, "The Unanimity of Jury Verdicts," *Virginia Law Register* 5, no. 3 (1899): 138.

117. Thomas Green locates the origins of this transition from law to fact in the political crises that rocked England in the middle of the seventeenth century. Common law had accepted that jurors could interpret the law, but once it became stipulated that they were "judges of the law as well as fact," the two categories were distinguished from each other. *Verdict According to Conscience* (Chicago: University of Chicago Press, 1985), 153–54.

118. Mark DeWolfe Howe, "Juries as Judges of Criminal Law," *Harvard Law Review* 52, no. 4 (1939): 589.

to articulate specifically that "the jury have the right of deciding on the law as well as the fact," because that was already "part of the common law of the country."[119]

During these same years, though, the law-finding power of juries was beginning to erode in Western nations. This happened incrementally and was attributable to multiple factors. Foremost was the professionalization of the judiciary, which, in concert with the growth of other professions, staked claims to expert knowledge beyond the competence of nonprofessionals. Jealous of their prestige, judges became frustrated with jurors who acquitted too easily, seemingly undercutting the stature of the law. The rulings of presiding judges reveal how they began restricting jurors to judge solely on the facts.[120] In his history of how this restriction evolved in the United States, Mark Howe points to the *United States v. Battiste* case of 1835 as the turning point. Supreme Court Justice Joseph Story instructed jurors that they had no "moral right to decide the law, according to their own notions or pleasure."[121] Over the next sixty years, Story's position gradually became as foundational as its antithesis had once been. In 1895 the Supreme Court decided in *Sparf and Hansen v. the United States* that jurors "cannot be allowed to increase the penalties or create laws of their own" and "cannot be allowed . . . to nullify the law."[122]

The Battiste and Zasulich rulings shared a salient commonality: both brought to their respective publics one of the pressing political issues of the day. Judge Story was an ardent abolitionist, best known in American history for his 1841 decision to free the mutinous slaves from the Spanish ship *Amistad* that had sailed into New England waters.[123] His vehemence against activist jurors can be attributed in part to his unwillingness to tolerate a potentially sympathetic verdict in the trial of a man charged with slave trading on the high seas.[124] Koni, no less than Story, used his legal position to advance his personal politics. When he reminded Zasulich's jurors that he lacked the right to direct their verdict, and then underscored the legality of jurors' using their conscience as a guide, he encouraged them to consider the circumstances that had prompted her shot. Koni knew that public opinion rested with Zasulich.

When in 1885 Fuks idealized Western European juries because they "judge not only by conscience but also by logic, reason, and the law,"[125] he was speaking indirectly to the issue of restricting them to weigh only the facts. Sympathy for the accused had become a pronounced feature of Russian juries, although it can be misleading, even analytically

119. "The Changing Role of the Jury in the Nineteenth Century," *Yale Law Journal* 74, no. 1 (1964): 175.

120. In 1670 the English court found that "the jury could not be fined for its refusal to follow the court's instruction," thereby giving legal foundation to common-law practice. Howe, "Juries as Judges," 583.

121. Quoted in Jeffrey Abramson, *We, the Jury: The Jury System and the Ideal of Democracy* (New York: Basic Books, 1994), 79.

122. Quoted in Franklin Strier, *Reconstructing Justice: An Agenda for Trial Reform* (Chicago: University of Chicago Press, 1996), 129–30. The *Sparf* ruling also increased the power of presiding judges by denying that they were obligated to instruct jurors of their rights.

123. Story inherited his political activism from his father, a participant in the Boston Tea Party.

124. On the effects of slavery on the American legal system, see William E. Nelson, "The Impact of the Antislavery Movement upon Styles of Judicial Reasoning in Nineteenth-Century America," *Harvard Law Review* 87, no. 3 (1974): 513–66.

125. Fuks, *Sud i politsiia*, 121.

dangerous, to look at the high percentage of acquittals without thinking more deeply about individual cases. Historian Girish Bhat has argued that Russia's juries tended to "moralize guilt," influenced as they were by a "widespread impulse toward mercy and conciliation."[126] Bhat located this "impulse" in the tendency of all participants in the Russian judiciary to adopt a mentality that permitted jurors to interpret the law, not just the facts of each case.[127] The Senate had chided jurors in 1885, and repeated this point at the appeal of the Palem case, that their "internal conviction" must be based upon "the aggregation of all the circumstances of the case," but it had no authority to overturn acquittals.[128]

The issue of "law finding" versus "fact finding" was not specified in the Russian statute or debated in detail as it was in English and American courts.[129] In his textbook on criminal law, I. Ia. Foinitskii dismissed the separation of fact from law as "impossible," in large measure because it weakened juries.[130] Fuks wrote sarcastically that Russia's reformers had set up an institution "that would frighten even the French."[131] Though he was overstating his case, the Russian jury in 1889 nonetheless resembled France's revolutionary one more than its post-Napoleonic version. At first, French juries acquitted violent crimes at a rate that surpassed the Russian, nearing 50 percent, which prompted reforms in 1810 and 1832.[132] In 1889, however, the French rate of jury acquittals was 27 percent, compared to 36 percent for Russia.[133] Conservative Frenchmen, like Fuks, bemoaned "scandalous acquittals" as evidence of "justice unblind" and "the shame of Marianne."[134]

Numbers, though, tell only part of the story; crimes that were forgiven write another chapter. Killers in France, for example, walked free from *crimes passionals*, crimes of passion, because local culture held that sexual excitation could be permitted to overwhelm the rational mind.[135] The Lyon lawyer Jean Appleton understood this culturally acceptable killing as a sign that "the impassioned murder" did not threaten social stability: "he shot his wife, so be it . . . he will not come to shoot mine!"[136]

126. Girish N. Bhat, "The Moralization of Guilt in Late Imperial Russian Trial by Jury: The Early Reform Era," *Law and History Review* 15, no. 1 (1997): 80.

127. Ibid., 81.

128. *Resheniia ug. Kassats. Dept. Prav. Senat.*, 1895, no. 17, 48–62.

129. Benjamin Hett points out that German juries were also limited to questions of fact after the turn of the twentieth century. *Death in the Tiergarten: Murder and Criminal Justice in the Kaiser's Berlin* (Cambridge: Harvard University Press, 2004), 214.

130. I. Ia. Foinitskii, *Kurs ogolovnogo sudoproizvodstva*, 2 vols. (St. Petersburg: V. Lesnikov), 2:448. First published in 1877, the textbook went through four editions until 1914.

131. Fuks, *Sud i politsiia*, 136.

132. Savitt, "Villainous Verdicts?," 1029.

133. Tarnovskii, *Itogi*, 88. The difference between acquittals in nonjury trials was even more pronounced: 28 percent in Russia, but only 7 in France. German and Austrian acquittals matched the French.

134. Savitt, "Villainous Verdicts?," 1019.

135. Katherine Taylor, *In the Theater of Criminal Justice* (Princeton: Princeton University Press, 1993), 37–38, 64–65 passim. Donovan, "Magistrates," 387, lists acquittals for those accused of violent crimes, if motivated by "considerations of honor, the protection of property, brawls between young people of different communes . . . even claims of self-defense against witches." See also "Crime in France," *New York Times*, August 19, 1921.

136. Donovan, "Justice Unblind," 95. Article 324 of the Napoleonic Code allowed men to be charged with a lesser crime than murder if they killed a wife or lover caught *in flagrante delicto*. Tagantsev criticized this French proclivity in *Lektsii po russkomu ugolovnomu pravu* (St. Petersburg: Tip. Spb. Tiurmy, 1894), 36–37.

Fuks worried that the Russian jury had adopted a personality of its own.[137] It had. As had the French, British, and American jury. Other countries had assassins and embezzlers, but none quite like Zasulich and the Mel'nichati. In provincial Tula, sixteen peasants stood trial for the murder and torture of a horse thief, which included plucking out his eyes. Their acquittal spoke eloquently to local culture.[138] In 1912, a colonel who had killed his wealthy wife claimed pathological *affekt*, but in self-defense he bragged that he "had cleaned the revolutionaries out of his regiment in 1905." His jury deemed him "a representative of the degenerate, impoverished nobility, who remain convinced that society is still not liberated from their tradition of slavery, and that his estate, and especially his epaulettes, give him license to do whatever he wants." They needed only a brief consultation to convict with no amelioration.[139]

Historian of the British legal system Martin Wiener observed that "courtroom understandings of criminal responsibility . . . were, of course, inseparable from movements in the wider culture."[140] In England, the Judgment of Death Act passed in 1823 revised the "Bloody Code" by designating only murder and treason as mandatory capital crimes. This complemented the evolving Victorian philosophy of holding people "sternly and unblinkingly, responsible for the consequences of their actions." Letter-of-the-law judges negotiated with "ordinary reasonable men" to develop the Victorian ideals of self-discipline in the courtroom.[141]

In the United States, the metaphorical closing of the western frontier by century's end[142] called for a repeal of the rough justice of "unwritten laws" that permitted men to murder in defense of "injury to domestic relations or family honor, imputations against female members of a family, and insults to the dignity of a man."[143] Coupled with the

137. Fuks, *Sud i politsiia*, 97.

138. *Vp*, 5 May 1909, no. 18.

139. "Delo Podpolkovnika Mordvinova," *Sd*, no. 5 (1912): 154–55.

140. Wiener, "Judges v. Jurors," 468. Martin J. Wiener, "Judges v. Jurors: Courtroom Tensions in Murder Trials and the Law of Criminal Responsibility in Nineteenth-Century England," *Law and History Review* 17, no. 3 (1991): 468.

141. Ibid., 477, 505.

142. See Frederick Jackson Turner, "The Significance of the Frontier in American History," delivered in 1893 at the World's Columbian Exposition in Chicago. The exposition provided cover for one of America's most proficient serial killers, H. H. Holmes, who found no sympathy from jurors and was executed for is crimes. Erik Larson, *The Devil in the White City: Murder, Magic, and Madness at the Fair that Changed America* (New York: Crown Publishers, 2003).

143. Roscoe Pound, *Criminal Justice in America* (New York: Henry Holt, 1930), 126. "The Changing Role of the Jury in the Nineteenth Century," *Yale Law Journal* 74, no. 1 (1964): 170–92, discusses aspects of this transition. Hendrik Hartog considers the "unwritten law" and the transformation from juries deciding questions of law rather than of fact as an indication of the ways that "the world was changing . . . husbands were losing control of their private domain." Hendrik Hartog, *Man and Wife in America: A History* (Cambridge: Harvard University Press, 2000), 237. See also Jeffrey S. Adler, "'It Is His First Offense: We Might as Well Let Him Go': Homicide and Criminal Justice in Chicago, 1875–1920," *Journal of Social History* 40, no. 1 (2006): 5–24. In 1861, before the jury trials had begun, P. Mulpov called for the right for men to be allowed to revenge themselves upon other men who had seduced their wives or daughters, positioning it in the importance of virginity. In practice, such an "unwritten law" did not become an issue in Russia. *Zhenshchina kak podsudimaia i prestupnitsa* (Moscow: Zhurnal Min. Iust.), 7–12.

Sparf decision, American courtroom justice was moving toward professionalization so much so that in 1915 Michigan law professor Edson Sunderland echoed Suvorin when he wondered, "Why then, has not the cumbersome law jury, with its tedious procedure, its loose organization, its irresponsible personnel, its blundering methods, and its unsatisfactory results, been long since discarded, in favor of an expert and well trained agency for sifting evidence and finding facts?"[144] Not all Americans, though, depended on juries, or on courts for that matter. Lynching remained a favored way to deal with racial issues well into the twentieth century.[145]

### The Quantity and Quality of Mercy in the Russian Courtroom

In autocratic Russia, God and tsar might have reserved for themselves the final authority to judge and to punish, but the jurors never hesitated to exercise their say. For all the work that trial lawyers did piecing together narratives of the crime, it was up to juries to interpret them and make the final decision. What influenced their decisions? One juror explained why of the thirty-five cases his group tried they acquitted twenty-six. He specified one acquittal based on the defense attorney's detailed challenges to the veracity of the evidence. Far more often, however, he and his colleagues disliked the "one-sided prosecution," which they knew to be in defiance of the statute. And he admitted to a gender bias on the occasion that they set free a particularly sympathetic defendant, despite the evidence against her.[146]

Two schools of thought emerged to account for the overly forgiving Russian jurors: that they were too religious, and that they mistrusted their laws. The view that their Orthodoxy instilled them with a compassion for *neschastnye* defendants that transformed the latter from perpetrators into victims, once they had shown remorse for their crimes, found reflection in the summations by the prosecution as well as the defense.[147] Indeed, it is nearly impossible to find a speech that does not include allusions to the New Testament, though the same can be said of other Christian countries.[148] What gave a peculiar Russian

144. Edson Sunderland, "The Inefficiency of the American Jury," *Michigan Law Review* 13, no. 4 (1915): 304.

145. The literature on this is so voluminous that I mention only three: Steven F. Messner, Robert D. Baller, and Matthew P. Zevenbergen, "The Legacy of Lynching and Southern Homicide," *American Sociological Review* 70, no. 4 (2005): 633–55; W. Fitzhugh Brundage, ed., *Under Sentence of Death: Lynching in the South* (Chapel Hill: University of North Carolina Press, 1998); and Michael J. Pfeifer, " 'Midnight Justice': Lynching and Law in the Pacific Northwest," *Pacific Northwest Quarterly* 94, no. 2 (2003): 83–92.

146. N. N. O., "Iz zametok,"199–208.

147. Harriet Murav plays out in fiction the battle between autocracy and lenient jurors: in terms of the former, the wrathful God of the Old Testament; in terms of the latter, the forgiving Christ of the New. *Russia's Legal Fictions* (Ann Arbor: University of Michigan Press, 1998), chapter 2.

148. In Arsenev's unsuccessful defense of Rybakovskaia, the prosecutor helped to secure a conviction by portraying her victim as a better Christian than she. "Delo Aleksandry Rybakovskoi, obviniaemoi v ubiistve," *Russkie sudebnye oratory* v. 7 (Moscow: A. F. Skorov, 1903), 295.

twist to this tendency to favor Christian mercy was that proponents of this school of thought played up what they considered a specifically cultural Russianness that rejected the formalism associated with the legal code, such as Gogol had decried, in favor of the personal element that allowed for atonement. The church's official organ, *Tserkhovnyi vestnik* (The Church Herald), upheld this tendency with an editorial that "the jury was and is one of the most powerful means for the strengthening in society of feelings of justice, love, and compassion for one's neighbors, as well as the propagation of religious principles in that region which was never synonymous with dry and dead formalism."[149] N. A. Nekliudov, the deeply irritated Ober-procurator of the Senate's Cassation Department, objected that jurors hewed too closely to the words of Christ: "Judge not, lest thee be judged!"[150]

The compassion of Russian jurors had a vitalizing social element. Beginning with Mavra Volokhova's murder trial in 1867, where the public not only applauded her acquittal but also collected money for her, because they agreed with the member of the audience that "hard labor is not for someone like her."[151] One ex-juror wrote proudly that during his tenure he and his colleagues collected money for everyone whom they acquitted.[152] In 1885, psychologist-criminologist N. Ia. Grot told the Odessa Juridical Society that the development of a juridical conscience reflected the maturation of society because it downplayed revenge.[153] Distinguishing between the "moral responsibility" of the juror and the "juridical culpability" of the accused, Grot explained the difference between the two to be fundamentally a social issue, an evaluation of how members of a society treat each other. Sharing his insights from having served as a jury foreman, Grot argued that as societies evolve and their members develop a sense of interconnectedness, a humanitarian conscience replaces an egotistical desire for retribution. A psychologist, Grot maintained that "the best people in the sciences have increasingly recognized that a criminal is a sick person, often the product of social evils." He continued, "In the need to extricate evil, society must carry in itself a part of the legal guilt for every crime and must treat and reform the criminals, redress their wrongs, save them from vice and return them, healthy, to society."[154] Grot was charging jurors in a very Christ-like manner to assume the guilt of the accused standing before them.

Jurors themselves denied a "special Russian sympathy." One ex-juror retorted that it was not the laws that he and his colleagues distrusted, but rather the state's capacity to administer them justly. Many credited juries with showing greater responsibility than the

149. Atwell, "Jury System," 200.

150. Quoted in I. V. Gessen, *Sudebnaia reforma* (St. Petersburg: F. Vaisberg and P. Gershunin, 1905), 164.

151. "Delo Mavry Volokhovi," in *Zamechatel'nye ugolovnye protsessy, razreshennye v Mosk. okruzh. sude s uchastiem prisiazh. zased*, ed. A. Liutetskii (Moscow: A. I. Mamantov, 1867), 28.

152. N. V. Nikitin, "Peterburgskii sud prisiazhnykh," *Otechestvennye zapiski* 196 (1871): 402.

153. N. Ia. Grot, *O nravstennoi otvetstvennosti i iuridicheskoi vmeniaemosti* (Odessa: Tip. Odesskogo vestnika, 1885), 13–14. Originally a philosopher, Grot moved to psychology because he believed in physiological explanations to all behavior, including moral actions.

154. Ibid., 28.

Fig. 11. Cain running to escape divine justice on the cover of *Sudebnye dramy*.

state for demanding solid evidence at trial. Several jurors in Volokhova's trial had complained to the presiding judge about the slipshod collection of evidence against her.[155] Another pacesetter from Kharkov, Vsevolod Danevskii, a professor of criminal law and director of criminal defense in the circuit court in the 1880s, examined the local judicial archives and uncovered the degree to which preliminary investigations were often inadequate to make a compelling case. In his opinion, the statistically high proportion of acquittals could be attributed to the careless work of the judicial investigators who, after Pahlen's "reform," had become simply bureaucrats in the Ministry of Justice.[156] Called later to jury duty, his experience confirmed his study. Procurator Timofeev, also a representative of the state, concurred.[157]

"Go into any court, listen to a few interrogations, put your ear to the door of any judicial investigator . . . and you will quickly become convinced that many accusations are made prematurely," cautioned the editors of *Sudebnye dramy*.[158] V. Nikitin criticized sloppy investigators from his days as a juror, complaining that "they are just trying to work their way up to the procurator's office."[159] The official statistician E. N. Tarnovskii compiled numbers to defend the judicial investigators, who he argued could not put together persuasive cases because of the constraints of too little time and too much territory.[160] In response, A. L. Levenstim argued that the numbers do not explain the cultural reasons why jurors tend to exonerate some crimes, such as those against the state, but condemn others, such horse theft. He believed that jurors took motives quite seriously when judging.[161] The longtime procurator N. Kobtsev reacted angrily against complaints about sloppy investigations, blaming instead the undisciplined defense attorneys who entertained jurors with their sleights of hand regarding the evidence.[162] However, the jurors had convicted, not acquitted, Mironovich for the murder of Sarra Bekker solely on the basis of indirect evidence.[163]

---

155. One of the assistant procurators, too, had not wanted this case brought to trial with the problematic evidence against the accused. "Delo Mavry Volokhovi," 5.

156. Vsevolod Danevskii, *Nashe predvaritel'noe sledstvie, ego nedostatki i reformy* (Moscow: A. A. Levenson, 1895). He found that more than one-third of all cases never even came to trial.

157. Timofeev, *Sud prisiazhnykh*, 394.

158. "Sudebnye oshibki," *Sd* I, no. I (1898): 5.

159. Nikitin, "Peterburgskii sud prisiazhnykh," 224.

160. E. N. Tarnovskii, "Otnoshenie chisla opravdannykh k chislu podsudimykh v Evrop. Rossii za 1889–1893," *ZhMIu*, no. 9 (1897): 169–89.

161. A. L. Levenstim, "Eshche neskol'ko slov ob opravd. prigovorakh prisiazhnykh," *ZhMIu*, no. 4 (1898): 199–208.

162. N. Kobtsev, "K voprosu o slaboi ugolovnoi repressi suda prisiazhnykh," *Zhurnal Iuridicheskogo obshchestva*, kn. 9 (1896): I–30.

163. An editorial in *Odesskii listok* (hereafter *Ol*) pinpointed the judicial significance of Mironovich's conviction: "Jurors often convict, to great applause, the obviously guilty killers. Now they have pronounced the fatal 'guilty' to someone not caught red-handed. If you criticize them for this, then you have begun down that slippery slope toward the abolition of 'internal conviction' and will return us to the old order." *Ol*, 11 December 1884, no. 273.

In 1899 the publishers of a series on *Russian Court Orators in Famous Criminal Trials* speci-fied that they were responding to a sentiment of "down with juries!" Their intent was to remind responsible citizens that they were needed to challenge in public the testimony gathered by state officials.[164] An ex-juror recalled that one trial on which he sat had been so poorly prepared that his fellow jurors provided better insight than had the investigator.[165] Another juror observed that "I am always surprised by the shocking absurdity of those who criticize jurors for having acquitted one who confessed. . . . You have to be in the courtroom, hear all and see all, and not as a curious viewer, but as a responsible participant in the case. Only then can you understand the jurors' motives."[166] In 1913 jurors were still defending the number of acquittals attributable to the weakness of the evidence.[167]

The public's attitude toward the judicial process itself reflected mistrust of the pros-ecutorial system, and not necessarily of the law. Fear of committing a "judicial mistake" was regularly invoked as an appeal for clemency, exemplified early by a booklet from 1874, "dedicated to jurors," warning them with examples from the British courts of convictions of the innocent.[168] In *The Brothers Karamazov*, Dostoevsky portentously entitled the chapter covering Dmitrii's trial for parricide "A Judicial Mistake," presaging the verdict, since readers would already know of Mitia's innocence. The popularly oriented journal *Sudebnye dramy* included a regular section of sensational mistakes, citing William Blackstone's axiom (incorrectly attributed to Catherine the Great) about the preference for ten guilty persons walking free rather than one being wrongly imprisoned.[169] In 1889 the journal published a three-volume supplement of *Judicial Mistakes in All Countries and Earlier Centuries*.[170] The *Ponomarev* case, circa 1890, became infamous because jurors had convicted a man later proven innocent. Dropping the name Ponomarev became a useful defense tactic because "the reading public is already familiar with the case."[171]

In a notorious case from 1895, Russian jurors did wrongly convict a man, Alexander Tal'ma, for the murder of his stepmother and her maid. The accused's half-brother testi-fied as his chief character witness, and he pleaded that the quarreling that others had seen between the two simply reflected bad tempers from people who in fact loved each other. The jury had not reached their verdict lightly, and the foreman sobbed so uncontrollably that another juror had to read aloud the conviction. Tal'ma had served five years on the prison island of Sakhalin before the real culprits were found, a father and son who worked

164. "Mytishchensko delo i dela Vavilova, Petrova i Kukhareva," *Russkie sudebnye oratory v izvestnykh ugolovnykh protsessakh* (Moscow: A. F. Skorov, 1899), 32.

165. N. N. O., "Iz zametok," 647–48.

166. Ibid., 649–60.

167. Sergei Ordinskii, "Sud'," *Obshchestvennoe nastroenie i glavnye sobytiia goda* (Moscow: Russkie vedomosti, 1913), 38–39. Snegirev, in commenting on the Senate's decision to retry Olga Palem because of the inadequate prelimi-nary investigation, noted that nothing had changed since Mavra Volokhova's 1867 trial. *Olga Palem*, 1.

168. N. Khodotov, *Zamechatel'nye ugolovnye dela Anglii* (Petrozavodsk: Gos. Tip., 1874).

169. *Sd* I, no. 1 (1898): 7, promised a regular feature on this.

170. *Sudebnye oshibki vsekh stran. Sudebnye oshibki prezhnykh vekov* (Moscow, 1898–1899).

171. *Delo ob otravlenii potomstvennogo pochetnogo grazhdanina Maksimenko* (St. Petersburg: A. S. Suvorin, 1891), 12. Spasovich cassated the prosecution's demand for a retrial, unsuccessfully (26–34).

for the stepmother and had stolen from her.[172] Although Tal'ma was released from Sakhalin, he had to remain under police observation on a legal technicality: the Senate ruled that he had indeed received a fair trial. Karabchevskii, Tagantsev, and Spasovich all involved themselves in trying to free Tal'ma, but the formality of the law proved sobering. The killers had been convicted of theft and of concealing their crimes, so no one else was found guilty of the murder. Without that, the Senate refused to retry Tal'ma, the only legal means that would have allowed acquittal.[173] The severity that the innocent Tal'ma suffered made a cautionary tale for jurors.

Concern also mounted that jurors developed a natural empathy toward the defendant because the prosecution enjoyed superiority over the defense in putting the case together. A premature worry that prosecutors wearing their uniforms (*mundiry*) at court would intimidate "simple people" on the jury proved groundless.[174] One ex-juror observed that "the defense attorney has in his hands a medium that the prosecutor lacks, that can achieve good results . . . the defense can find echoes of sympathy in the soul of the juror."[175] Another bemoaned that "sometimes the prosecutor forgets that the defendant is a human being."[176]

Prohibited by law until 1910 from knowing what punishment awaited the accused, many assumed that the state would be excessively harsh, and therefore they invoked with remarkable regularity their right to request that the sentence be ameliorated.[177] Jurists across the political spectrum agreed to the importance of information about punishment. Danevskii argued that Russian juries needed to be told what punishment awaited the accused because "they want to know the consequences of their actions." Even Nekliudov wanted reforms that would correspond the punishment more closely to the crime.[178] One ex-juror pointed out that at times those acquitted had already spent more time in prison awaiting trial than a guilty person might spend following conviction.[179]

Even those who favored the institution could spot problems with permissive jurors. M. Ratov, writing in 1899, expressed alarm when he looked at verdicts for husbands on trial for killing their wives. Specifically taking Dzhanshiev to task for saying that "juries do not have preconceived prejudices against the accused," Ratov marshaled journalistic evidence

172. The case was tried in the Penza circuit court. *Ubiistvo vdovy general-leitentanta P. G. Boldyrevoi i ee gornichnoi Savinoi* (Moscow: Tip. M. G. Volchaninov, 1895); "Delo Tal'my," *Sd* 8, kn. 1 (1901): 65–74; and 8, kn. 2 (1901): 298–314; and N. V. Nikitin, *Prestupnyi mir i ego zashchitniki* (St. Petersburg: Trud, 1902), 16–76. Gromnitskii prosecuted this case.

173. V. L. Binshtok wrote about the Russian borrowing from the French on this, and how it must be changed. *Russkaia mysl'*, kn. 3 (1899): 118–67. See also "Delo Tal'my," *Sd*, no. 3 (1901): 276.

174. *Golos*, 14 April 1868, no. 103.

175. "Zhilishche boga mesti" (Iz vospominanii prisiazhnogo zasedatelia), *Sd*, no. 1 (1901): 79.

176. N. N. O., "Iz zametok," 202.

177. *UUS*, art. 804. This was another formal and cultural borrowing from the French, whose concerns that the Napoleonic Penal Code was too harsh had led jurors to choose the option of granting "extenuating circumstances," which obligated the court to lessen the penalties. Donovan, "Magistrates," 384.

178. Vsevolod Danevskii, *O zakliuchitel'nom slove predsedatelia* (St. Petersburg: Senate Typography, 1896).

179. N. N. O., "Iz zametok," 643.

from around the country to argue that husbands who killed their wives got off more easily than did husband-killing wives. Ratov made a compelling argument that violence against women often resulted from excessive alcohol consumption by men. The problem lay in the code, which punished for death as the result of a beating much less harshly than it did for premeditated murder, and husbands were far more likely than wives to stand trial for beating deaths.[180]

Ratov's example of jury roughness toward wives, however, rested on the case of a woman who, with her lover, strangled her nonabusive husband while he slept and tossed his body into a river. Her sentence of life at hard labor merited no amelioration.[181] Young peasant beauty Anna Konovalova would have contradicted Ratov's point. In 1896, with her mother and several greedy friends, she strangled her drunk husband, packed his body in a trunk, and dumped it in a meadow. The friends subsequently blackmailed Anna, which made them profiteers. They landed in hard labor because they had gained financially from the killing. Anna and her mother secured acquittals by weeping to jurors about how they had knelt before the icon in the room where his corpse lay and prayed for his soul.[182]

Ratov identified a weakness in the code itself that belied Dzhanshiev's raw statistics, which quantified that women got off more lightly than men.[183] Timofeev's experience in court supported Dzhanshiev's data, and he found jurors considerably more sympathetic to peasant women, for whom murder was often a dire response to a forced and miserable marriage.[184] Neither side was scientifically sound, but both made excellent points. The first saw the inadequacies of the law, and the second, those of society. As the legal scholar Foinitskii argued, acquittals registered the disconnects between the law code and contemporary social norms.[185]

## Reforming Russia's Jury

By the time of the Palem trial in 1895, even the liberal Arsen'ev was lamenting that jurors were "mysterious strangers," as Turgenev had referred to serfs.[186] The frustrated

180. M. Ratov, *Zhenshchina pered sudom prisiazhnykh: (Mysli i fakty)* (Moscow: A. I. Mamontov, 1899).

181. Premeditated murder merited years at hard labor, but death as the result of a beating, just months in jail. *UNUI*, arts. 1454, 1465.

182. The defense included A.M. Bobrishchev-Pushkin and G. S. Aronson. Nikitin, "Anna Konovalova," *Prestupnyi mir*, 118–59. As Tagantsev pointed out, "jurors rarely even approve amelioration for murder for mercenary goals" (*Lektsii*, 36).

183. I. Ia. Foinitskii also weighed in on the gendering of crime, arguing that women were prosecuted less often than men; they were not indicted for inspiring men to commit crimes on their behalf. "Zhenshchina-prestupnitsa," *Sev'ernyi vestnik* 2 (1893): 123–44; and 3 (1893): 111–40.

184. Timofeev, *Sud prisiazhnykh*, 483–44.

185. He made this observation following the acquittal of Zasulich. I. Ia. Foinitskii, *Opravdatel'nye resheniia prisiazhnykh zasedatelei i mery k ikh sokrashcheniiu* (St. Petersburg: Tip. Prav. Senata, 1879), 64.

186. Quoted in Murav, *Russia's Legal Fictions*, 71. Koni, quoting Turgenev, made much the same observation, in reference to those jurors only recently emancipated from serfdom. Atwell, "Russian Jury," 49.

autocracy passed ten laws between 1878 and 1889 affecting juries.[187] Fuks expressed the conservative mistrust of the caliber of those who served: too many illiterates, and the income requirements were not sufficiently stringent to bring in men with an investment in "private safety and the legal order."[188] The current system "turned the judicial procedure into a social melodrama, the conclusion of which is not based on the evidence, but on the eloquence of lawyers." The result was not the "court of social conscience," but the "court of mob rule" (*samosud*).[189] Tsar Alexander III responded with a counterreformatory attempt to reaffirm nationalist and noble authority throughout the land: he doubled property and income qualifications and required all jurors to be able to read Russian. Two years later, the law of July 7, 1889 removed several crimes from the purview of juries, including some that had been returned in 1882 relating to the prosecution of officials.[190] Certain military ranks and state servitors were added to enlarge the pool, and those "in extreme need" would be excluded.[191] The statistics recorded an immediate slight drop in the percentage of acquittals, a decline that would not be sustained.[192] The men whom Alexander wanted in theory he could not trust in practice.[193] Acquittals played well for laughs in theatrical farces, but this tsar was not known for his sense of humor.

Fuks had written not simply to critique the jury, but also to argue that it was historically anathema to Russia.[194] Dzhanshiev felt compelled to respond, wanting to rehabilitate the generation of reformers whom he so admired but who had fallen victim to reaction. When Fuks charged those who had written the jury into the code of being "naive and unscientific," Dzhanshiev countered by showing how steeped they had been in the historical literature about juries.[195] He even ferreted out a quote from the Reform Era's reactionary minister of justice, V. N. Panin, who wrote that "only juries can be independent of the administration."[196] The problem was that Panin had envisioned twelve earnest noblemen weeding out corruption. No one had imagined the jury that had come to pass.

187. Demichev, *Istoriia Rossiiskogo suda*, 154. Crimes involving passport violations were removed from the purview of juries because, since they virtually never convicted anyone, trials wasted time. Nikitin reported that "even the most severe jurors acquitted" on all the passport cases" ("Peterburgskii sud prisiazhnykh," 386).

188. Fuks, *Sud i politsiia*, 140–41.

189. Ibid, 172.

190. Bobrishchev-Pushkin, *Empiricheskie zakony*, 50. Demichev, *Istoriia Rossiiskogo suda*, 129, emphasizes that this law was intended to separate the political from the criminal once and for all, but as Fuks had noted, the government had misidentified the nature of politics.

191. Atwell, "Jury System," 195.

192. Tarnovskii, *Itogi*, 69.

193. The city archive of St. Petersburg contains the lists drawn up in 1904–1912. Essentially, the chairman of the commission required bureaucracies and businesses to send lists of all employees who met the qualifications, and also to inform them when someone on the list had left employment or no longer qualified for other reasons. Tsentral'nyi gosudarstvennyi arkhiv goroda Sankt-peterburga [Central State Historical Archive of St. Petersburg] (hereafter TsGIA SPb), f. 941, op. I, d. I.

194. G. D., "N. A. Butskovskii i sud prisiazhnykh," *Vestnik Evropy*, no. 12 (1889): 476–507.

195. Ibid., 487–90. This included some rather specious information about juries during the reign of Ivan the Terrible (503).

196. Ibid., 502.

Minister of Justice N. A. Manasein, of the conservative postreform generation, convened a commission in 1890 to reassess the judicial reform, including the jury. He proposed a law that would allow the Senate to transfer a case to a new jury if the judges agreed unanimously that a guilty person had been acquitted, just as they could demand a new trial if they agreed that an innocent person had been wrongly convicted.[197] The Senators rebuffed Manasein because he provided no evidence that juries were not fulfilling their obligations at court.[198] The Russian Senate asserted the jury's right to take "into consideration circumstances pertaining to the personality of the accused, to the nature and consequences of their acts, (and) to conditions under which those acts were committed."[199] Manasein's successor, the equally conservative N. V. Murav'ev, kept the commission open, but on the crucial question of jury reform, eighteen of the twenty members voted to retain it in its present form.[200] Even the reactionary jurists who participated concluded that the jury system "is the most perfect form of court which may be imagined for the trial of the major share of important cases."[201]

## Jurors into Citizens

The jury "must be understood as a complex institution in which the force of evidence and shared community values contribute to the resolution of disputes."[202] Initial enthusiasm for it in 1864 had stemmed from the belief that it would facilitate the transformation of subjects into citizens, that is, from objects of the law into participants in applying it. L.E. Vladimirov argued in 1873 that "jurisprudence is not a science but rather rules of behavior, so if the jurors cannot understand a question of law (*pravo*), that is the best evidence that the law that generated the problem does not conform to social life."[203] Twenty-five years later he noted approvingly that "the Russian people recognize that the criminal is, above all, *neschastnyi*."[204] Liberal jurist Vladimir D. Nabokov, future minister of justice and father of the novelist, wrote in 1898 that any "law that would not rely upon the strength of morality, would in vain support itself by means of compulsion alone."[205] Bludov and Spasovich had been proven correct that jurors saw their choices as personal and moral, which made them also political, as Fuks had astutely broadened the

197. Following Semenova's trial, *Nv* had lamented that Russian judges were only allowed to overturn convictions, not acquittals. *Nv*, 3 November 1885, no. 3150.

198. Kucherov, *Courts*, 66–67.

199. Ibid.

200. Dzhanshiev, *Sud nad sudom*, 3–4.

201. Quoted in Kucherov, *Courts*, 82.

202. Savitt, "Villainous Verdicts?," 1021.

203. Vladimirov, *Sud prisiazhnykh*, 183.

204. L. E. Vladimirov, *Psikhologicheskoe issledovanie v ugolovnom sude* (Moscow: A. A. Levenson, 1901), v.

205. Quoted by Jane Burbank in "Legal Culture, Citizenship, and Peasant Jurisprudence: Perspectives from the Early Twentieth Century," in *Reforming Justice in Russia, 1864–1996: Power, Culture, and the Limits of Legal Order*, ed. Peter Solomon (New York: M. E. Sharpe, 1997), 92.

term. But so long as the autocracy kept with its narrow definition and cared only about keeping attacks on government personnel away from juries, the institution continued to function as it had from its origins in England: a means to protect the individual from the state.

In the 1890s, the conservative editors of *Moskovskii vestnik* (The Moscow Herald) noticed that the jury was becoming a less popular institution in Europe.[206] Just as the British and American courts were denying jurors the right to interpret the law, the French government had responded to "the shame of Marianne" with a "correctionalization" of their courts, which reclassified certain crimes to misdemeanors to move them away from sympathetic juries.[207] Moreover, in Germany *Schöffen* courts mixed lay persons with judges "in an effort to overcome the weakness of the jury system . . . in the latter half of the nineteenth century."[208] In Russia Danevskii used this opportunity to discuss historical differences in the evolution of juries. He agreed with his adversary Fuks that Russians, like the French from whom they borrowed so much, distrusted many of their laws. But Danevskii asserted this to accentuate how continuing mistrust was pushing the French government even further away from jurors in ways that emphasized the superiority of the greater Russian confidence in theirs.[209] French frustration with lenient juries had also increased the possibility of the presiding magistrate to influence jurors through the system of *échevinage*, in which the "judges and jury deliberated and voted together."[210] Fully aware that Russian judges, to wit, the presiding one in the Palem trial, did not shy away from trying to affect verdicts, Danevskii distinguished Russia from republican France by arguing that the two countries were moving in opposite directions. Russia ascended the moral high ground with jurors who admittedly voted against judges whom they considered prejudiced against the accused.[211]

Yet for all the hue and cry, and such publicized and controversial verdicts as those in the Zasulich, Mel'nichati, and Palem cases, a closer parsing of the statistics reveals a less lax jury than imagined by those speaking against it. Calculating the percentages from the statistics on criminality, from 1873 through 1913 juries absolved slightly more than one-third of the

206. Atwell, "Jury System," 97.

207. Ruth Harris, *Murder and Madness: Medicine, Law, and Society in the Fin de Siècle* (Oxford: Clarendon Press, 1989), 136–37, discusses the contemporary debates in France. See also, Donovan, "Magistrates," 379–420, and James W. Garner, "Criminal Procedure in France," *Yale Law Journal* 25, no. 4 (1916): 255–84.

208. Nancy Travis Wolfe, "Lay Judges in German Criminal Courts," *Proceedings of the American Philosophical Society* 138, no. 4 (1994): 498. See also Burt Estes Howard, "Trial by Jury in Germany," *Political Science Quarterly* 19, no. 4 (1904): 650–72.

209. Danevskii, *O zakliuchitel'nom slove predsedatelia*, 26. As early as 1871 K. K. Arsen'ev was praising the greater equity for the defendant in the Russian court than in the French. *Sudebnoe sledstvie: Sbornik prakticheskikh zametok* (St. Petersburg: V. Dimakov, 1871), 112–15.

210. Donovan points out that the history of the jury in France is one of antagonism between state and juries, even when liberal governments were in power ("Magistrates," 403).

211. Another critique of the changes in European juries that reflected well on the more democratic Russian juries: I. P. Zakrevskii, "Sud prisiazhnykh i vozmozhnaia reforma," *Zhurnal Ministerstva Iustitsii*, no. 12 (1895): 55–84.

men and half the women. Crown courts do not differentiate between the sexes, setting free approximately 25 percent of both.[212] However, if we limit our scope to adult males accused of premeditated murder, the percentages decline steadily, from 36 percent in 1880, to 16 percent in 1900, back up to 20 percent by 1910. The 50 percent rate of acquittal for women remained the same across these years.[213] The discourses about the jury make plain its success in helping Russians to navigate the changes ushered in by the Great Reforms. In his larger plea for jurists to recognize that 1903 was not 1864, procurator A. M. Bobrishchev-Pushkin called complaints about uncooperative jurors old-fashioned. Commenting that "the idea of the judge as a mechanism for blindly fulfilling the law has outlived its century," he cited Spencer's *Origins of Sociology* in his analysis of jury behavior. His observation that "the law is a social phenomenon, the product of interaction between social and psychological factors," gave jurors the license to change with the times.[214] Drawing on fourteen years of courtroom experience, Bobrishchev-Pushkin disagreed that acquittals posed a particular problem. Although he concurred that "judicial responsibility demands courage, strength of character, and a professionalism often lacking in jurors" who acquit murderers as *neschast-nye*, he concluded that jurors use common sense more often than not, "unswayed by the defendant's smile or the defense attorney's lack of principle." To those who would deny that Russian jurors had demonstrated the capacity for citizenship, "in the sense of being prepared to act, to judge the criminal, to subject him to punishment," he would remonstrate that "the jury court (reflects) the fruitful meeting of the written laws with the life views of members of society called to express them." Pronouncing the Russian institution "just and humane," Bobrishchev-Pushkin would reform it only by requiring that jurors explain how they reached their verdicts, which was reminiscent of Vladimirov's idea that defense attorneys submit to cross-examination.[215] Koni disagreed, arguing that forbidding jurors to discuss their deliberations in public is "the clearest recognition of their freedom."[216]

If Jefferson, Tocqueville, and even the young Katkov were correct, and the institution of the jury provides a foundation for a democratic government, it seems ironic that one of Russia's most celebrated reactionaries, I. G. Shcheglovitov, was writing in 1902 that "I would widen rather than narrow the competence of jurors." This prosecutor in the Palem trial, and the future minister of justice who put Mendel Beilis on trial for the ritual murder of a Christian boy, agreed that leniency "can be attributed to the imperfections in our criminal code and its lack of correspondence to the changing demands of our life."[217] Despite its occasional "dark sides," he echoed Koni that "we must defend this institution

212. Tarnovskii, *Itogi*, 74.

213. I took these figures from the annual *Svody* and did not include infanticide because the reasons for infanticide speak to a different set of social issues than the murder of an adult.

214. Bobrishchev-Pushkin, *Empiricheskie zakony*, 49, wanted to compare today's jurors with those from the first courts in order to "understand that life and culture have changed."

215. Quotes are from Bobrishchev-Pushkin, *Empiricheskie zakony*, 164, 41, 204, 35, 46, 564, 614, 17.

216. Koni, *Voprosy filosofii*, 871.

217. I. G. Shcheglovitov, *Sud prisiazhnykh pri deistvii novogo ugolovnogo ulozheniaa* (St. Petersburg: E. Evdokimov, 1902), 4, 26.

from changes which would injure its substance."[218] Shcheglovitov was accused of pressing for the substitution of presumably anti-Semitic peasants for intellectuals on the jury at the Beilis trial, but he did not persuade them to convict.[219]

## Conclusion

Karabchevskii and Shcheglovitov, the defense and prosecution at Olga Palem's trial, referenced that case when they faced each other again in 1904, the latter hearing his first appeal as the newly appointed Ober-procurator of the Senate's Cassation Department. Karabchevskii was appealing the case of a lawyer who had been dismissed by a circuit court judge for instructing the jury to acquit. As had happened in the Palem trial, when this judge overstepped his bounds he permitted a more important issue to be put before the Senate. The fired attorney had maintained that the jurors would be in the right to acquit because, even though his client admitted to stealing "from desperate need," to commit (*sovershit'*) a crime did not necessarily impute guilt (*vinost'*). Karabchevskii invoked the Senate's decision in the Palem case, arguing that it had agreed that jurors could ignore the directions of the judge if his advice contradicted their convictions. Shcheglovitov held a more circumspect view of the Palem decision, emphasizing that the Senate had also counseled that jurors could not deliver arbitrary verdicts, that "internal convictions" needed to be supported by evidence. But the new Ober-procurator concurred that "the institute of the jury is dear to all Russians," and he cited article 745 of the criminal code, that "the defense cannot be constrained by the court." In summation: to commit the act did not mean to be legally guilty of it. After this, the larger debate about the Russian jury simply faded from political discourse. The independent jury had survived intact.

Although 1895 enters Russian historiography as the year that the newly coronated Tsar Nicholas II told Russian liberals to put aside their "senseless dreams" of participating in politics, the jury system easily survived the threat posed by the acquittal of Olga Palem. Taking an active part themselves in interpreting laws and administering justice, Russian jurors, broadly conceived to include all who joined in the discourse of verdicts, gained confidence in their ability to participate in making policies. In order to render a judgment on someone else, the prospective juror had to see both himself and the object of his judgment behaving as individuals in a comprehensible set of circumstances. Russian jurors demonstrated repeatedly an antipathy toward the state, mollified by an empathy for its victims. They registered these sentiments in multiple ways, from contempt for prosecutors to accepting that the political restrictions on free will could also carry over into limits on the personal volition of the *neschastnye*. Jurors drew their legal values from multiple sources: the

218. Quoted in Kucherov, *Courts*, 84.
219. Ezekiel Leikin, *The Beilis Transcripts: The Anti-Semitic Trial That Shook the World* (Lanham, MD: Jason Arenson Press, 1993), 10. Kiev, however, also boasted numerous anti-Semitic intellectuals, including professor of psychology Ivan Sikorskii (father of Igor, who invented the helicopter), who testified for the prosecution about the nature of such Jewish rituals.

criminal code, personal experience, religion, and the political culture of autocracy.[220] They also turned to fiction as a medium through which to locate their place in the world around them. Crime fiction developed into an identifiable genre, evolving from Dostoevsky's *Crime and Punishment* (1866), which was written against the backdrop of the first jury trials. The evolution of this genre is the subject of the next chapter.

220. Post-Soviet Russia has also been characterized by seemingly lenient juries, and the elected government finds itself returning to the Soviet ways of relying on a group of three judges to decide cases. See, for example, Ellen Barry, "After Dismissal of Jury, Judges Convict Russian," *New York Times*, December 28, 2010.

# CHAPTER FOUR

# MURDER AS ONE OF THE MIDDLEBROW ARTS

"People begin to see that something more goes into the composition of a fine murder than two blockheads to kill and be killed—a knife, a purse, and a dark lane. Design, gentlemen, grouping, light and shade, poetry, sentiment, are now deemed indispensable to attempts of this nature."
—Thomas De Quincey, *Murder as One of the Fine Arts*, 1827

"Tolstoy and Dostoevsky cannot help but compete with the criminal code . . . they are professional accomplices to this collusion of sin and crime."
—Procurator F. A. Vol'kenshtein, 1903

There was not a moment to lose. He pulled the axe out, swung it up with both hands, hardly conscious of what he was doing, and almost mechanically, without putting any force behind it, let the butt-end fall on her head. His strength seemed to have deserted him, but as soon as the axe descended it all returned to him. The old woman was, as usual, bare-headed. Her thin fair hair, just turning grey, and thick with grease, was plaited into a rat's tail and fastened into a knot above her nape with a fragment of horn comb. Because she was so short the axe struck her full on the crown of her head. She cried out, but very feebly, and sank in a heap to the floor, still with enough strength left to raise both hands to her head. One of them still held 'the pledge.'[1] Then he struck her again and yet again, with all his strength, always with the blunt side of the axe, and always at the crown of her head. Blood poured out as if from an overturned glass and the body toppled over on its back. He stepped away as it fell, and then stooped to see the face: she was dead. Her wide-open eyes looked ready to dart out of their sockets, her forehead was wrinkled and her whole face convulsively distorted.

He laid the axe on the floor near the body and, taking care not to smear himself with blood, felt in her pocket, the right-hand pocket, from which she had taken her keys last time.[2]

1. This was the item that the killer had used, a "pledge" to pawn, to gain easy access into the old woman's apartment.

2. F. M. Dostoevsky, *Crime and Punishment*, trans. Jesse Coulson, 3rd ed. (New York: W. W. Norton, 1989), 65–66.

Aficionados of Russian literature will recognize this as Raskolnikov's first murder that day, and will know that he steals a few gold trinkets before turning his axe on his victim's hapless sister, who enters the apartment unaware. They will also appreciate how Dostoevsky made murder one of the fine arts, beginning with this, his first major novel, *Crime and Punishment*. Using murder more as a thematic than a plotting device, Dostoevsky informs readers early that the lead character has committed this heinous act, which allows the novel to develop around the killer's moral quandary rather than the deed itself.[3] A fine art, yes, but written to attract a middlebrow audience. *Crime and Punishment* began serialization in *Russkii vestnik* in 1866, against the backdrop of the opening of the new courts. Dostoevsky broadened his audience by discussing the new legal structure as a system of justice, not simply a political reform. As American literary critic Edmund Wilson learned to his chagrin in 1941 when he dismissed fictional murder as lowbrow entertainment, its rapt readers span the spectrum of social and intellectual categories.[4]

Investigating crime, including the search for its origins in the perpetrator's mind, suggests ways of representing the readers' social world. This chapter considers the fictional portrayals of murder as one means of understanding how Russian audiences adjusted to postreform society. Characters and themes return from previous chapters, including the judicial investigator unable to come up with compelling evidence, the seedy *zashchitnik*, and the congenial killer. Reinforcing stereotypes on the one hand, on the other they offered new media for exploring the social, political, and cultural issues raised by those who Russians who premeditated homicide.

A murder with no mystery, *Crime and Punishment* established what would become identifiable as the generic conventions of crime fiction in Russia. Richard Alewyn distinguished crime fiction from its better-known literary successor, detective fiction, in that the first "tells the story of a crime" and the second, "the solution of a crime."[5] The narrative structure of the two is essentially reversed, as are the central protagonists: the criminal acts in the first, the investigator reacts in the second. The two overlap in plot, but thematically they address different social concerns. Crime fiction takes up the ideological challenge of why individuals transgress the boundaries established by the society of which they are members. Detective fiction, on the other hand, evolved on a parallel course with the modernization of law enforcement, underscored by the increased use of science in investigations. It also speaks to the bourgeois instinct for law and order, because detective fiction concludes with the police at the door. The emphasis on the *why* rather than the *who*, the greater interest in the motive rather than in an identity that must be uncovered, would characterize Russia's fictional forays beyond the law, creating a distinctive genre unique to the culture.

---

3. Dostoevsky reversed the essence of De Quincey's argument; the English essayist believed that murder could only be aestheticized if the moral judgments were removed. The Russian novelist made morality central to the crime.

4. Edmund Wilson, "Who Cares Who Killed Roger Ackroyd?," reprinted in *Detective Fiction: A Collection of Critical Essays*, ed. Robert W. Winks (Englewood Cliffs, NJ: Prentice-Hall, 1980), 35–40. It turned out that thousands cared.

5. Richard Alewyn, "The Origin of the Detective Novel," in *The Poetics of Murder: Detective Fiction and Literary Theory*, ed. Glenn W. Most and William W. Stowe (San Diego: Harcourt Brace Jovanovich, 1983), 64.

## Crime Fiction as Local Culture

John Cawelti, a pioneer in the study of popular culture, has posited a "dialectic between formulaic literature and the culture that produces and enjoys it."[6] In order to secure the position of crime fiction as a window into the societies that produced it, I survey briefly some of the specific intersections between fiction and society. The first known works of crime fiction are the *kung-an* (court cases) that dated from China's Tang (618–906) and Sung Dynasties (960–1279). They appeared in various forms, from storytellers' prompt books to operas, before being "discovered" and translated into French in 1832.[7] The Chinese protagonists were judges, members of the government bureaucracy exemplified by Bao Zheng (999–1062), "a peculiar mixture between King Solomon and Sherlock Holmes."[8] The *kung-an* stories that featured Judge Bao were especially popular in the late Ming Dynasty (1368–1644), a reflection of the revival of the scholar-gentry as impartial mediators of justice. In the 1950s Dutch diplomat Robert van Gulik translated and re-created Ming arbiters for Western readers with the character Judge Dee.[9]

England's "Newgate novels," named for the London prison that housed convicted killers, helped British readers to negotiate the substantive changes to law enforcement and prosecution that began with the Judgment of Death Act of 1823, which all but overturned the "Bloody Code." In 1829, the Metropolitan Police Act put bobbies out to patrol the streets, a fresh approach intended to prevent crimes in the first place. The Newgate stories, exemplified by Edward Bulwer Lytton's *Eugene Aram* (1832), combined the biographies of criminals with the increasingly popular conventions of melodrama. Less about violence and more about the possibilities for those who had committed crimes to redeem themselves, the genre told cautionary tales. Newgate novels depended on a trial scene that would have the crime played out before the public, reinforcing the theatricality of the adversarial courtroom. William Thackeray condemned these stories for "creat[ing] a false sense of sympathy for the vicious,"[10] but no amount of empathy could spare the genre's murderers the gallows, their remorse be damned.

Wilkie Collins took the next literary step in Britain when his *Woman in White* (1859) added the gothic elements of mystery to crime fiction, using crime to uncover a network of personal problems to be resolved. Collins depended on happenstance as much as the sorting of facts to find a solution, building the literary link between Newgate morality and Sherlock Holmesian rationale. Holmes's comment to Dr. Watson, in the 1887 story

6. John G. Cawelti, *Adventure, Mystery, and Romance: Formula Stories as Art and Popular Culture* (Chicago: University of Chicago Press, 1976), 35.

7. Wolfgang Bauer, "The Tradition of the 'Criminal Cases of Master Pao' Pao-kung-an (Lung-T'u Kung-An)," *Oriens* 22/24 (1974): 433–49; and Patrick Hanan, "Judge Bao's Hundred Cases Reconstructed," *Harvard Journal of Asiatic Studies* 40, no. 2 (1980): 301–23.

8. Y. A. Ma, "The Textual Tradition of Ming Kung-an Fiction: A Study of The Lung-t'u Kung-an," *Harvard Journal of Asiatic Studies* 35 (1975): 190–220; and Ann Waltner, "From Casebook to Fiction: Kung-an in Late Imperial China," *Journal of the American Oriental Society* 110, no. 2 (1990): 281–89.

9. Gulik began with a translation of the eighteenth-century detective novel *Dee Goong An*, based on the stories of Ti Jen-chieh.

10. Jonathan Grossman, *The Art of Alibi: English Law Courts and the Novel* (Baltimore: The Johns Hopkins University Press, 2002), 61.

that introduced this redoubtable duo, connected the style of his detective work with the substance of the emergent Victorian male's culture of control: "There's the scarlet thread of murder running through the color-less skein of life, and our duty is to unravel it, and isolate it, and expose every inch of it."[11]

The less pragmatic French, especially following their 1789 revolution, developed a fascination for crime that kept the outlaw and law enforcement in competition for audience support that continues to this day.[12] The dualism was personified by Eugène François Vidocq (1775–1857), an ex-thief who in 1809 founded France's Sûreté, the detective branch of the police force. Vidocq later worked in private practice, vying for popular attention with Lacenaire, the elegant and amoral killer. The fictional incarnations of these two established the prototypes for French crime fiction: Ponson du Terrail's Rocambole, the appealing rogue and occasional killer who revolutionized the genre of the *roman feuilletons* in the French popular press during the Second Republic (1852–1870), and Émile Gaboriau's Monsieur Lecoq, the midcentury police detective who followed logical footsteps through a series of novels.[13] The readership of the *roman policier* and the *détectif* paralleled the rise of the bourgeoisie, plotted out in Gaboriau's first blockbuster, *L'affaire Lerouge* (1866). Secrets of the past are exposed by methods of the present: the modern villain sneaks out of a theater, takes a train to murder the widow Lerouge, and returns to his seat in time for the finale.[14]

Homicide in American fiction, as David Brion Davis has illustrated, charted the decline of Puritanism, with its view of the complete depravity of mankind, and bore witness to the rise of the frontier justice that "won" the West.[15] Collins and Gaboriau also had precedents in America, where in 1841 Edgar Allan Poe dispatched his fictional C. Auguste Dupin to the house in the Rue Morgue to investigate why the two women living there had been so brutally and inexplicably beaten to death. Stylized around the factual Vidocq, the fictional Dupin dismisses the former as "a good guesser," but one who "impaired his vision by holding the object too close." This might allow the police detective to see "perhaps, one or two points with unusual clearness," but forced him to lose "sight of the matter as a whole."[16] "Murders in the Rue Morgue" established the baseline of detective literature as the sifting through the evidence to find out "whodunit." In fine positivist fashion, it celebrated the power of reason.

Poe, a leading figure in American romanticism, also provided an alternative to relying on rationale. Dupin's colleague, the unnamed narrator of Poe's story, did not believe that simply figuring out what had happened could adequately explain the crime. Having

11. A. Conan Doyle, *A Study in Scarlet* (New York: Harper & Brothers, 1904), 45.

12. See, for example, the issue of *Yale French Studies* devoted to French Crime Fictions, no. 108 (2005), edited by Andrea Goulet and Susanna Lee.

13. Gaboriau introduced Lecoq in *L'affaire Lerouge* as a minor character, a former criminal who had then joined law enforcement, as Vidocq had.

14. David F. Bell discusses this in "Technologies of Speed, Technologies of Crime," *Yale French Studies*, no. 108 (2005): 9–12.

15. David Brion Davis, *Homicide in American Fiction, 1798–1860: A Study in Social Values* (Ithaca: Cornell University Press, 1957).

16. Edgar Allan Poe, *The Murders in the Rue Morgue* (New York: Worthington, 1887), 15.

determined analysis to be a "moral activity," he observed that "to calculate is not in itself to analyze."[17] In other words, Poe was also establishing a second baseline for a different generic fiction, one centered around the question, *why*. Focusing on *who* ultimately became reduced to a parlor game.[18] Asking *why*, on the other hand, forced the investigation away from the material evidence and into the personality of the killer. This made the investigation a moral activity rather than merely a fact-finding mission. Dostoevsky, a fan of Poe's, found *why* a significantly more compelling question than *who*. He laid the basis for the "whydunit" to dominate in Russian crime fiction.


## Crime Fiction Most Russian

Critics who revere the depth of Dostoevsky's psychological portraits question whether or not to consider *Crime and Punishment* crime fiction, or an *ugolovnyi roman*, to use the Russia term. Literary historian A. I. Reitblat, whose intellectual career spanned the collapse of the Soviet Union, stressed how Dostoevsky's fiction was the first to integrate the reformed justice system into contemporary life.[19] The plot tells what drives Raskolnikov to murder: the poverty his family endures, the bitter fate of a sister forced into marriage to a man she does not love, and the self-justification that he finds temporarily when he convinces himself that he murdered a principle, not a person. Believing himself to stand above the law, Raskolnikov invites readers to question the legal code and to participate vicariously as jurors, levying judgment on his actions. His internal justification hinges on the putative superiority of reason in the modern world. Only when he rejects reason for Christianity can he confess to his crime.

Dostoevsky's protagonist declines the opportunity to appeal for legal sympathy by refusing to explain to the court the extenuating circumstances that had prepossessed him to kill the women. Moreover, Raskolnikov ensured a knee-jerk solidarity with readers by making his first victim a pawnbroker, who, like Mironovich later, crawled into society as a parasite who sucked the lifeblood from the desperately poor. Dostoevsky keeps justice always in play, never fixed, certainly not in the temporal world. Punishment for a crime stands secondary to penance for a sin, and Raskolnikov asks forgiveness from God before surrendering to investigator Petrovich. Sentenced to eight years of hard labor, his ending is a happy one because he redeems his soul. His actions expose the concurrent strength and frailty of Russian jurisprudence, that the rationale of the law must be tempered by the faith that justice would conform to the multiplicity of circumstances that affected the individual criminal. Raskolnikov personifies the quintessential *neschastnyi*.

17. Terry J. Martin discusses this in "Detection, Imagination, and the Introduction to 'The Murders in the Rue Morgue,'" *Modern Language Studies* 19, no. 4 (1989): 31–45. Père Tabaret, the private investigator in *L'affaire Lerouge*, also expresses misgivings about arranging the facts into a satisfactory but incorrect narrative.

18. S. S. Van Dyne, creator of Philo Vance, published "Twenty Rules for Writing Detective Stories" in the September 1928 issue of *American Magazine*. See also Roger Caillois, "The Detective Novel as Game," in Most, *Poetics of Murder*, 1–12.

19. A. I. Reitblat, "'Russkii Gaborio' ili uchenik Dostoevskogo?," the introduction to A. A. Shkliarevskii, *Chto pobudilo k ubiistvu? (Rasskazy sledovatelia)* (Moscow: Khudozhestvennaia literatura, 1993), 10.

Murder had figured as a rarity in prereform literature because the crime and its aftermath would be played out so publicly. The authorless *The Butcher-Killer Uncovered by
an Apparition* (1863), for example, tapped into the creeping materialism made explicit by
I. M. Sechenov's work published that same year. It tells of an artist, narrating in the first
person, contemplating suicide because of his miserable living conditions. Then he paints
a crime scene of a murdered woman that he saw in a dream. Arrested because of his seemingly inside knowledge, he muses in prison that "they say it's better to be hanged innocent
than guilty. Perhaps for the soul, but not for the body!" In a second dream he sees the murderous butcher of the title, and paints him for the police, who capture the guilty man. The
hero ruminates metaphysically, "Is it true, that the immortal soul does not separate itself
from the body? During sleep it unfolds its rainbow wings and flies God knows where!"[20]
Dostoevsky enhanced the possibilities for murder to function as a trope to launch discussions of modern society and politics, helping to anchor postreform public attitudes toward
criminality. This savage action provides the climactic scene in *The Idiot* (1868), and proves
central to themes explored in two of his later novels, *The Devils* (1872) and especially
*The Brothers Karamazov* (1880).

True crime quickly became essential to crime fiction. In their daily crime logs and stenographic court reports, "newspapers began to inculcate a new forensic subjectivity . . . crime
and trial reports constructed the newspaper reader as an answerable member of a law-bound
state."[21] In St. Petersburg, the newspaper *Glasnyi sud* (Open Court) began publication in order to capitalize on the mounting curiosity about how crime would be addressed in the new
courts.[22] Anticipating that interest in 1866, A. Liubavtskii, a graduate of the St. Petersburg
University law school, published a collection of European criminal trials.[23] Promising to ed-
ucate Russians in the operations of the adversarial system, Liubavtskii called trials "superior
to novels," especially fascinating because they expose "the secrets of a person's inner life."[24]

Not about the new courts per se, *Crime and Punishment* makes plain the difficulty in
trying to separate crime fiction from crime fact. Dostoevsky had pitched the project to
Mikhail Katkov, the editor of *Russkii vestnik*, as an exploration into the mind of a murderer.[25] Hailed as a new form of realism, Dostoevsky's fiction was steeped in the facts of
life as it "boiled" around him, to quote the boulevard's *Petersburgskii listok*, which itself had
only recently begun publication. Dostoevsky's appreciation of mass communications had
led him to observe how "in every newspaper, you find reports of the most realistic as well
as the oddest facts."[26] These *faits divers*, the brief, sensational news blurbs that seized the

20. *Ubiitsa miasnik otkrytyi chudesom obrazom* (Moscow: M. Smirnov, 1863), 29, 36.

21. Grossman, *Art of Alibi*, 33.

22. Konstantine Klioutchkine, "The Rise Of 'Crime and Punishment' from the Air of the Media," *Slavic
Review* 61, no. 1 (2002): 97.

23. This genre dated back to 1734 when Francois Gayot de Pitival published *Causes célèbres et intéresantes*.

24. A. Liubavtskii, *Sbornik zamechatel'nikh ugolovnikh protesessov* (St. Petersburg: Obshchestvennaia pol'za,
1866), I, 3.

25. Claudia Verhoeven, *The Odd Man Karakozov: Imperial Russia, Modernity, and the Birth of Terrorism* (Ithaca:
Cornell University Press, 2009), 88. In his pitch, Dostoevsky told Katkov, "There is still much evidence in our
newspapers of the extraordinary instability of the notions that impel people to horrible deeds."

26. Klioutchkine, "Rise of 'Crime and Punishment,'" 99.

topics of the day, only to be replaced with a different one tomorrow, helped to develop a specifically urban mentality.

Literary scholar Konstantine Klioutchkine has advised students of *Crime and Punishment* that "efforts at disentangling the novel from the press are likely to lead to misunderstandings regarding the dynamic of their relationship."[27] In Dostoevsky's most free-handed journalistic venture, *A Writer's Diary*, published from 1873 until his death in 1881, he "suspend[ed] the boundary between realist fiction and journalism," assuming an authority that transcended a division between fact and fiction.[28] Sharing his views through this periodical medium, Dostoevsky also corresponded directly with readers about topical issues. Whether literary critics prefer to cite him for his "intertextuality,"[29] or praise his "dialogic imagination,"[30] Dostoevsky stands out for his constant engagement with a variety of texts and his ability to put them in dialogue with one another in ways that paralleled his own correspondence with his readers. Intertextuality can be visualized: imagine Dostoevsky sitting in his apartment reading *Golos* and spewing venom over Spasovich's argumentation in the Kroneberg trial, then recording in his widely circulated diary his indignation with a legal system corrupted by the self-righteous defense of an admittedly abusive parent.

*A Writer's Diary* provides especially valuable insight for understanding Dostoevsky's perspective on the legal system as a medium for administering justice. His personal politics matter to this analysis of crime fiction because of how they complicate the categories of "liberal" and "conservative" in late imperial Russia. Joseph Frank, Dostoevsky's preeminent biographer, pointed out that he has regularly been called "reactionary" for his support of autocracy, Orthodoxy, and ethnic Russianness in general. However, Dostoevsky's belief in continuing reform and his "harsh denunciations of existing social evils" show him not to be so "politically subservient as it has appeared to posterity."[31]

Dostoevsky's religious conception of justice, for example, put him at loggerheads with Ober-procurator Nekliudov, who distrusted the "judge not" attitudes of jurors. Dostoevsky offered more than his opinion when he intervened personally after the pregnant Ekaterina Kornilova threw her six-year-old stepdaughter out of a four-story window. The child survived, and the judge at her first trial sentenced Kornilova to three years of Siberian exile. After visiting her in jail, Dostoevsky worked to have her case retried by making sure that the affects of her pregnancy on her mental state would be entered into evidence. The second jury acquitted Kornilova because, in Dostoevsky's is words, "no crime had

---

27. Ibid., 100.

28. Harriet Murav, *Russia's Legal Fictions* (Ann Arbor: University of Michigan Press, 1998), 154.

29. Julia Kristeva coined the term "intertextuality" in 1966: the process by which "one or several sign-system(s) [becomes transposed] into another." Quoted in Toril Moi, ed., *The Kristeva Reader* (London: Blackwell, 1986), 111.

30. "What Dostoevsky's characters *say* constitutes an arena of never-ending struggle with others' words, in all realms of life and ideological creativity. For this reason these utterances may serve as excellent models of the most varied forms for transmitting and framing another's discourse." Mikhail Bakhtin, "Discourse on the Novel," *The Dialogic Imagination*, ed. Michael Holquist, trans. Michael Holquist and Caryl Emerson (Austin: University of Texas Press, 1982), 349.

31. Joseph Frank, *The Mantle of the Prophet, 1871–1881* (Princeton: Princeton University Press, 2002), 256.

been committed."[32] He further articulated his position when jurors exonerated Anastasia Kairova, who had slashed up her lover's wife, though without killing her. Confessing to be happy that Kairova walked free, he nonetheless expressed concerns about the process of acquittals because it offered a legal technicality that denied that she had done anything wrong. He wanted jurors to have Christ's option, to be able to "call a sin a sin" and then tell Kairova to "go forth and sin no more."[33] From Raskolnikov to Mitia Karamazov, when Dostoevsky's characters stood trial they turned to God and sought penance, even though society had forced them into the new courts and sentenced them according to its prescribed punishments.[34]

Popular novelists, Lisa Rodensky points out, have long "occupied a complicated position in social affairs, since his or her authority was unofficial yet undeniable."[35] Dostoevsky's influence was perceptible. The irate prosecutor in the Kornilova case complained that the "famous writer" had exerted undue influence over public opinion.[36] Dostoevsky's influence was also empirical, if one counts the number of times *zashchitniki* invoked Raskolnikov. Herein lies the key: defense attorneys, not prosecutors, referenced the cold-blooded butcher of two women to elicit sympathy for the accused. In a particularly heinous case from 1903, when a young man beat his neighbor's five-year-old son to death on impulse, his defense invoked Raskolnikov. This forced the prosecution to retort with a positive spin on Dostoevsky's protagonist, reminding the jurors that Raskolnikov had killed a pawnbroker, not a child.[37] Dostoevsky would agree with Gogol that the inflexibility of the law undermined its capacity to deliver justice, which both writers understood to be more personal and ambiguous than strict rationality permitted. Raskolnikov's contribution to the reform of the judiciary was to call into question from the very outset the applicability of the legal code to social justice.

The issue of Raskolnikov's motivation raised crucial debates, which connected to questions that criminologists were beginning to raise. As Rodensky illustrates, "criminal intent" developed as a juridical category in the nineteenth century and was adopted by novelists as a strategy for opening up to readers the interior lives of their characters.[38] Fictional protagonists, like defendants, had to explain their actions within the context of their lives. As law breakers they had to either admit to wrongdoing or bring attention to the unreasonable or inequitable laws. Russia's authors of crime fiction used two literary devices in particular, first-person narration and, more pointedly, the confession in both its religious and legal connotations, to establish intentionality.

32. Fyodor Dostoevsky, *A Writer's Diary*, trans. and annot. Kenneth Lantz, intro. Gary Saul Morson (Evanston, IL: Northwestern University Press, 1993), 641–47.

33. Ibid., 384, 474, 485.

34. M. V. Litovchenko argued that because Russia did not permit a person to be tried twice, should a guilty person be acquitted, he or she could still atone for the crime through personal penance. *Opravdanie suda* (Kiev: I. N. Kushnerev, 1903), 9–11.

35. Lisa Rodensky, *The Crime in Mind: Criminal Responsibility and the Victorian Novel* (New York: Oxford University Press, 2003), 4.

36. N. P. Karabchevskii, *Okolo pravosudiia: stat'i, soobshcheniia i sudebnye ocherki* (St. Petersburg: Trud, 1902), 399. The prosecutor made the unlikely charge that Dostoevsky would have voted differently had he sat on the jury.

37. "Delo Porozova," *Sd* 19, no. 12 (1903): 58–59.

38. Rodensky, *Crime in Mind*, 21.

Because of their concern with topicality, the reputations of the majority of Russian writers of crime fiction for the most part did not outlive the times that they illuminated so clearly. In his widely read *Confessions of a Criminal* (1877), D. A. Linev used the religious term *ispoved'* (confession). First-person narration makes an effective medium for establishing the social and political circumstances that force his young male protagonist to break numerous laws.[39] The quasi-hero begins his saga: "The court has pronounced me a criminal and sentenced me to harsh punishment . . . . I am dead to society, but I will write my confession in the hopes that it can be useful." The narrator, a converted Jew, seeks a career in the military, which is denied him after he is arrested for carrying a false passport, which he had used to try to help a friend. His story reads like a picaresque novel, as he partners up with a swindler and turns himself into a Georgian prince who travels around Europe on one of the many false passports he needs because the Russian police have retained his. He falls in love with two women, neither of whom he can marry because he is not the man that his papers attest him to be. One lovelorn lady takes poison, employing the rhetorical device of the suicide of an abandoned heroine made familiar to Russian readers by the sentimentalist Nikolai Karamzin's "Poor Liza" (1792). The second woman adopts a more modern persona, growing frigid and cynical by his rejection.[40]

Linev also builds the bridge across another literary convention, in *Confessions of a Criminal* and its sequels, *Around Jails: Notes of a Prisoner* (1878) and *In a Transit Prison* (1880). Taking readers on a fictional, though quasi-journalistic, journey through multiple prisons, he calls to mind Vsevolod Krestovskii's exposés of "The Slums of Petersburg" serialized in the journal *Epokha* (Epoch, 1864–1867), edited by Dostoevsky and his brother Mikhail. Krestovskii's slums included Haymarket haunts found in *Crime and Punishment*.[41] Twenty years later A. I. Svirskii would continue the genre with his even more graphic *In Prisons and Thieves' Dens*, "superb vignettes about the urban underworld."[42]

The former judicial investigators who published their professional encounters established the background from which writers of fiction borrowed and embellished. Alexander Shkliarevskii, christened the "Russian Gaboriau," began writing stories starring judicial investigators in the 1870s. A journalist on the provincial press, Shkliarevskii moved to Petersburg in 1869 with greater writing ambitions than his skills, and alcoholism, could support. His newspaper work included the serial novels found "below the fold" in the urban press, which read as embroidered narratives of sensational crimes.[43]

---

39. A. I. Reitblat, *Ot Bovy k Balmontu: I drugie raboty po istoricheskoi sotsiologii russkoi literatury* (Moscow: Novoe literaturnoe obozrenie, 2009), 199. Linev wrote *Po tiur'mam*, a best-seller in 1878, under the pseudonym D. A. Dalin (200).

40. D. A. Linev, *Ispoved' prestupnika: Ugolovnyi roman* (St. Petersburg: L. V. Fomin, 1877).

41. "Slums," modeled on Eugène Sue's "*Les Mystères de Paris*," published in the *Journal des Debats* twenty years earlier, also recalled Charles Dickens's journalistic exposés. The Moscow version was M. M. Maksimov's ten-part *Moskovskie tainy: Rasskaz syshchika*, published in at least two editions by P. Glushkov (1861).

42. Joan Neuberger, *Hooliganism: Crime, Culture, and Power in St. Petersburg, 1900–1914* (Berkeley: University of California Press, 1993), 190.

43. One specific example: In September 1873, *Novosti* was serializing Shkliarevskii's "Kto byl ubiitsa" in the same issues that it was reporting the murder of A. S. Suvorin's wife at the Belle Vue Hotel.

A plaintive appeal to Dostoevsky that "I am a writer, too!"[44] bespoke Shkliarevskii's disappointment at being an inferior talent. *Otechestvennye zapiski* (Notes of the Fatherland) condescended that "he will find a public that will read him not without satisfaction, and, at least, without harm to itself."[45] That he had no need to look beyond the quotidian adds relevance to his work because of how he made use of the *faits divers*. Shkliarevskii's work thus facilitated the emergence of a new kind of reader, one who savored him greedily.

One of Shkliarevskii's early novels, *The Exile's Confession*, echoed Linev's and included a judicial investigator as a minor character.[46] As Shkliarevskii developed the genre, he rotated nameless investigators in and out of his stories, eschewing a signature hero, such as Gaboriau's Lecoq. Moreover, his investigators often functioned as confessors, as Sokoloskii and Timofeev had described their roles in their memoirs. In "What Prompted the Murder?" Shkliarevskii presented the case as "the notes of a judicial investigator," writing in the first person to give readers access to the lawman's subjective musings about what is supposed to be an objective inquiry. The unnamed investigator is dispatched to the apartment of a retired cavalry colonel, V.K. Verkhovskii, found stabbed in his bedroom, the dagger still in his heart. The victim's wife insists rather improbably that her husband had committed suicide. Two other women live with the couple: one young, naive, and blond, the other an aging Frenchwoman. The investigator betrays his disdain for the "mademoiselle" in his keen powers of observation: "She decided to use the usual feminine subterfuge; suddenly she began to tremble, shaking hysterically, but was very careful when she lowered herself into a soft chair."[47]

His subjective personalization of the suspects becomes problematic when the investigator develops an emotional attachment to the victim's wife because she reminds him of his own mother. He wants to postpone interrogating her until she has rested, much to the annoyance of the police doctor who has accompanied him to the murder scene. His insistence that "we aren't just an investigator and a doctor, but also people. We will judge humanely" is rebuffed by the doctor's imperative that a delay will jeopardize the evidence, which has stacked up against the wife. She was heard having a loud argument with her husband the night of the murder, her face is bruised, and her husband was sexually involved with both of the other women in the house. A search turns up bloody clothes in both the wife's and the Frenchwoman's rooms. The latter insisted that she had gotten his blood on her clothes when she touched the body upon discovering it. Begging him, "Don't be a judicial investigator, be my advocate," she recounts her sordid relationship with the victim.[48]

44. A.I. Reitblat, "'Russkii Gaborio' ili uchenik Dostoevskogo?," in Shkliarevskii, *Chto pobudilo*, 11. Professor V.A. Manassein, a pioneer in studying addictions, took Shkliarevskii into his clinic for treatment, to no avail. Manassein famously recommended cocaine for seasickness. *America Druggist* 14 (1885): 215.

45. Quoted in David Keily, "*The Brothers Karamazov* and the Fate of Russian Truth: Shifts in the Construction and Interpretation of Narrative after the Judicial Reform of 1864," (PhD. diss., Slavic Languages and Literatures, Harvard University, 1996), 144.

46. A.A. Shkliarevskii, *Ispoved' ssyl'nogo* (St. Petersburg: V.V. Obolenskii, 1877).

47. Shkliarevskii, "Chto pobudilo k ubiistvu?," in *Chto pobudilo*, 29.

48. Ibid., 30, 33.

Shkliarevskii turns to the melodramatic devices of coincidence and the unstable family to resolve the case. A fourth character appears, the victim's illegitimate son. Listening to this young man's bathetic autobiography, the inspector developed "a decisive antipathy toward him. It seemed to me that he was painting, like an artist, the unhappiness of his life in especially dark colors with the objective of trying to impress me."[49] The investigator correctly surmised the young man's guilt; he had returned to the scene when he learned that his stepmother was under suspicion. The two had become close when the boy was abandoned by his biological mother, one in the long line of his father's mistresses. The wife had raised him in the countryside where the two escaped Verkhovskii's tyranny. The son had come to Petersburg on the night of the murder, where, wandering aimlessly, fate had drawn him to his father's address. His stepmother hid him under the bed when the colonel returned unexpectedly, and when his father began to attack her the son bolted from his hiding place and stabbed his violent parent. The investigator had no stomach to pressure his fantasy female, so he ignored the confession. With no direct evidence against the stepson, he allowed the case to lapse.

The way in which Shkliarevskii tied the loose ends together established what was thematically unique about Russia's crime fiction: the genre did not obligate the guilty to pay for their crimes. A postscript, written by someone else in the procurator's office, informed readers that the killer had escaped to America, the stepmother had joined a convent, and the investigator had died of cholera, adding that "he was a good man, but weak. He went too much by his feelings, which is not appropriate for a judicial investigator."[50] In another story, Shkliarevskii balanced this weak man with a protagonist determined to follow only the material evidence, as a British detective would. Paradoxically, the killer traps him rather than vice versa, as in British fiction. He loses his job when the female killer falsely accuses him of rape in order to escape arrest.[51]

Shkliarevskii structured "The Secret Investigation" as a series of imbricated personal stories and introduced an exotic new weapon, curare, a South American poison that paralyzes its victims.[52] His investigator shows enough talent to be promoted to assistant procurator, although his ability to solve the murder depends on an accidental acquaintance struck up with a provincial doctor while summering in the country. A few months earlier, the investigator had been called in on the death of a young woman so mystifying that the autopsy could not establish what had paralyzed her nervous system. One lazy afternoon on vacation, he recounted this to a newfound friend who, as happenstance would have it, had once been in love with the victim. More important, this doctor knew that curare had been used on her. Familiar with the poison from medical school, he had in a remarkable coincidence saved the same woman from a previous attempt on her life. Like the sanguinary son in "What Prompted the Murder?," a supernatural premonition had pulled the doctor to his beloved that night: "I found myself on the street, asking myself, where am I going and why?"[53]

49. Ibid., 62–63.
50. Ibid., 74.
51. Shkliarevskii, "Rasskaz sudebnogo sledovatelia," in *Chto pobudilo*, 75–134.
52. "Sekretnoe sledstvie," in Shkliarevskii, *Chto pobudilo*, 135–214.
53. Ibid., 153.

This new information did not inspire the investigator to cut short his holiday, though when he returned to Petersburg he felt a new sense of purpose. Poison is a woman's weapon,[54] and the killer turned out to be the victim's friend from boarding school who was in love with, and now engaged to, the husband of the woman she had killed. The murderess had an equally immoral mother, and the two had become involved with a loathsome cardsharper who had brought the poison back from Guinea. Upon arrest, she confessed, begging the investigator not to tell her beloved, which he promptly did anyway. Shkliarevskii plots a number of his stories around women using poison. All of them have been badly abused by men, though, so the author cannot simply be written off a misogynist. One of his venomous heroines is not punished by the court for adding the deadly drops to her tyrannical husband's water; far worse, she is forced into matrimony by the wicked doctor who planted the idea in her mind and "accidentally" left his phial on her table. The black widow does not survive long in this unhappy marriage. She had brought a young son with her, the child she bore from the lover she had hoped would join her after her husband's death. The boy dies a mysterious death, and his tormented mother withers away. Shkliarevskii intervenes authorially to raise a question to readers, perhaps the doctor had poisoned the lad? He does not answer it.[55] Again, the investigator does not catch the culprit.

None of Shkliarevskii's other killers matched the malice of the woman responsible for the unthinkable in "The Murder of a Baby."[56] With her latest lover, the town bailiff, she poisons her stepson, not yet two years old. Diabolical in her premeditation, she tries to pass his death off as a ritual murder by the local Jewish family, who are presumably in need of Christian blood for Passover. She has stolen a knife from the Jewish peddler and buried it in the chest of the already dead boy. The bailiff, after manhandling the Jewish family, ties them up in protective custody in his apartment and plants the child's corpse in their house. The judicial investigator does not believe in ritual murder and frees the family, but has no proof against the stepmother; neighbors had testified that they saw her holding the baby, his head covered with a blanket, hours after the time that the police doctor testified the child had died. The obtuse investigator needs more than a year to figure out that she had been holding a dead baby for display purposes. In a twist on the usual ending, a jury sends her to a much-deserved exile in Siberia. Here Shkliarevskii's fiction patterned the statistics on female poisoners, because although women were acquitted collectively of all crimes at a rate of approximately 50 percent, the acquittal rate could drop below 20 percent when the crime was poisoning.[57]

Crime novelist S. A. Panov also enjoyed a background in journalism, working as the courtroom correspondent for *Peterburgskii listok* and writing serial novels for the paper. The inspector-hero of his novel *Murder in the Mukhtolovaia Grove* (1876) stuck closer than his

54. The inspector worried that "a horrible poison in the hands of a woman does not portend just one death . . . there's no guarantee that she won't use it in the future!" (ibid., 160).

55. A. Shkliarevskii, "Neraskritoe prestuplenie," *Rasskazy iz ugolovnoi khroniki* (St. Petersburg: A. S. Suvorin, 1903), 170–216.

56. A. Shkliarevskii, "Ubiistvo rebenka," *Rasskazy iz ugolovnoi khroniki*, 217–302.

57. In 1880, for example, of the twenty-nine women tried for poisoning, only five were acquitted. From the *Svod statisticheskikh svedenii* for 1880.

counterparts to the material evidence and found the man who had killed the peasant whose hut he rented for recreational hunting. He exalted in his job:

> The law has armed the investigator with considerable power. Every lock will be opened at his initial appearance. . . . Jealously protecting his own knowledge, no expert can refuse him cooperation. . . . The investigator must build a pedestal on which the court can place the truth about the action that broke the law.[58]

The police doctor performing the autopsy likewise accentuated the professionalism of the new-style criminal investigation: "The doctor cut off the head and then scalped it, as adroit as a bloodthirsty, vengeful warrior. For the doctor, the scalp was a trophy for justice; for the Indian, a trophy for barbarism."[59] Logic and objective analysis proved the murderer to be the lover of the peasant's daughter. The killer was arrested, but the daughter, complicit in the parricide, revived the trope of feminine suicide and took her own life.

Panov's *Murder at the Ball* (1876), written in the first person by a particularly resourceful judicial investigator, multiplies the cast of characters and the dramatic scenes. During her coming-out ball, a local beauty is found in her bedroom with her throat slashed. The investigator follows the material evidence, even making plaster casts of footprints found outside the dead girl's window. Set in the countryside, this novella develops out of the relationships specific to provincial life, reminiscent of Popov's memoirs. The investigator, an outsider, works closely with a resident police officer, who fills him in on local gossip. Flirtations, seductions, and hopes for a more inspiring life had led one girl to kill her best friend because the latter had stolen her fiancé. After confessing, the guilty girl pines away in prison and dies before her trial. It turns out that she had a coconspirator, a young man who had procured the razor for her and then concealed it after the killing, who stands trial. The jury considered that he had acted from the lethal combination of ignorance and unrequited love, and acquitted him. Only the Jewish pawnbroker, who had accepted the jewelry stolen to mask the murder as theft, served jail time. Righteous justice is served when the homicidal girl's brother, not the law, kills his sister's faithless lover in a duel. The dead man's immoral actions had set the murder in motion, which made him the truly guilty party.[60]

Russia's fictional judicial investigators never quite made the generic leap from crime to detective fiction because their creators showed little interest in formulaic conventions of discovery, investigation, and capture. Ending the heyday of this type of protagonist from the 1870s, *Murder in the Puzyrevskye Baths* (1879), written by a lawyer from Saratov province, P. I. Telepnev, fascinates because of how it begins as a Western *détectif* but ends as a paradigmatic Russian *ugolovnyi roman*.[61] In the uncharacteristically macabre opening passage, an expensively dressed man and woman rent a private room in a public bath. He leaves alone, carrying a box. The suspicious attendant then discovers the body of the woman in the tub, minus her head. Enter the judicial investigator, who establishes an identity for the victim

58. S. Panov, *Ubiistvo v Mukhtolovoi roshche: Rasskaz sudebnogo sledovatelia* (St. Petersburg: A. A. Sokolov, 1876), 18.

59. Ibid., 26.

60. S. A. Panov, *Tri suda: Ubiistvo vo vremia bala. Rasskaz sudebnogo sledovatelia* (St. Petersburg: Skariatin, 1876).

61. P. I. Telepnev, *Ubiistvo v Pyzyrevskikh baniakh: Rasskaz iz ugolovnoi letopisi* (Saratov: Ishchenko, 1879).

from a series of interviews he conducts about missing girls. Once he knows the identity of the victim, he pieces together a narrative of motivation involving an ex-lover who was now engaged to a wealthy widow, and who therefore was trying to conceal his relationship with the victim. At the moment of arrest, the accused shoots himself.

Lo and behold, the woman thought to be the victim returns to the city, knowing nothing about what had happened. Innocent of the murder, the suspect had nonetheless been guilty of dishonesty, so it seemed appropriate that he took his own life. Ten years pass, and the investigator runs into the purported victim by chance at the opera. When queried about whether he had ever found out to whom the head had belonged, or who had removed it, the author responded, "Well, dear reader, I have no answers to these questions. Whether it was the incompetence of the investigator or some other reason, I don't know. The bloody deed about which I wrote was turned over to the will of God."[62]

In 1892 Alexandra Sokolova, a prolific contributor to mass-oriented journals who often wrote as "Blue Domino," resurrected the genre of "notes from a judicial investigator" in *The Song Is Sung*. Added to the familiar themes and characters is the noticeably new vocabulary of the "court of conscience," evidence of the widespread discussion about juries. Set "in the first days of the new law code, when Russian society could not adjust to the open court," Sokolova recalls the honeymoon period before Pahlen's changes would have been felt by both the investigators and the society they served. As the code commanded him, her investigator-protagonist sets out "not to acquit the guilty or accuse the innocent." Sent to the provinces, he is met by a prominent count "with a hundred-year-old bottle of Tokai," mindful of Popov's recollections of bored locals happy to see a fresh face. Those living at the count's estate include his young second wife, their six-year-old son, the son's tutor, and Isabella, his beautiful daughter from a first marriage. The tutor predicts that he will die on the estate and, sure enough, his murder is the investigator's first case. The count, though, moves the body and disturbs other clues. His actions puzzle because "he had never broken the rules in the old days, so why now?"[63]

Isabella explains "why now" in her confession to the murder, which is necessary because the investigator could not solve the case with the compromised evidence. The tutor and her stepmother were having an affair, "but this was not feminine revenge for the family honor." Isabella grasps the investigator's hands and, as his throat tightens, she tells him that "one must confess to the commission of the crime, but one can take the motive to the grave and answer only to God." The new order, though, disagrees: "the court of conscience needs more than the fact of the crime, it calls for the motive!" As he takes her to jail he reminds her that she has not yet been convicted, that the jury could legitimize her action if it understood why. She accepts her guilt by drinking poison in the prison hospital. Her baby brother falls ill soon thereafter, and they lie buried together in the sepulcher on the estate.[64] Their deaths reify an essential convention of Russian crime fiction: the victim whose death prompts the investigation is never the only one to suffer. Not even the answer *who* could resolve the reasons *why*.

62. Ibid., 187. Wilkie Collins also used this narrative device of addressing his readers at the end of *The Woman in White* and *The Moonstone* (1868).

63. A.I. Sokolova, *Spetaia pesnia* (Moscow: V.A. Prosin, 1892), I, 21.

64. Ibid., 141, 150.

Alexander Sokolov was another columnist for *Petersburgskii listok* who also wrote novels for the paper and published others separately. The protagonist in his novel *Dark Deed* (1895), Boris, charms his way into his wealthy aunt's household and, in a ruse borrowed from *L'affaire Lerouge*, uses train travel to establish his alibi. He and his coconspirator check into a hotel in Moscow when the aunt is in Petersburg. Boris takes the night train and strangles the aunt and her faithful servant, while his friend leaves two pairs of boots outside their room for the staff to clean. And in the end, "no one ever confessed to the murder, and remorse never came."[65] Although Russians happily consumed Gaboriau in translation,[66] their native novelists followed Dostoevsky, one another, and courtroom professionals, from the investigators to *zashchitniki* composing their own criminal narratives. Sokolov's malevolent offender walks away from his "dark deed" because the Russian genre had never required that the law catch and punish him.

## Murder 'Neath the Proscenium Arch

The theater provided another cultural setting for fictionalizing crime. A staging of Gaboriau's *L'affaire Lerouge* in 1873 could not satisfy Russian theatergoers because a detective piecing together minutiae did not make for ripping good entertainment.[67] Although the story itself contained numerous family secrets and intrigues, the translators concentrated on what was novel about Gaboriau's story, how amateur detective Père Tabaret solved the murder of the Widow Lerouge. Panov's novella *Murder at the Ball* moved more easily to the Russian stage, with its familiar theme and characters.[68] The highpoint of Panov's action, Anna slitting the throat of her childhood friend, Elena, occurs offstage. Nor does the audience witness the trial of Nikolai Kachalov, the young man implicated by the stolen jewelry. Drama comes when the local doctor tells Anna that she cannot allow Nikolai, "who loved her above all else," to pay for her crime. The actress who plays Anna gets a lengthy confession scene; the investigator is but a minor character in the theatrical version. Anna's brother, resigned in the novella to a third party's description of his actions, gets to rush to center stage and announce that he has killed the man for whom his sister had murdered her friend. He pulls out a revolver and Anna collapses. Curtain.

The transfer of *Murder at the Ball* from page to stage emphasized the implicit melodramatic motifs that characterized the crime when played out under the proscenium arch in the theater. When Fuks voiced his annoyance about the transformation of "the judicial procedure into a social melodrama," he disdained the role of performance in both media.[69]

---

65. A. A. Sokolov, *Temnoe delo* (St. Petersburg: V. V. Komarov, 1895), 134.

66. Gaboriau's works counted among the most checked out from public libraries. Reitblat, *Ot Bovy*, 299.

67. Keily, "*Brothers Karamazov* and Fate of Russian Truth," 128, quotes at length *Pl's* critique. By 1952 Agatha Christie had mastered the theatrical detective play, and *Mousetrap* became history's longest running play, still in performance at London's St. Martin's Theatre.

68. *Ubiistvo vo vremia bala*, trans. A. Laur (St. Petersburg: Litografiia Kurochkina, 1877). This play was performed at Petersburg's Bouffe and Moscow's Hermitage, two popular venues.

69. French critics likewise objected to melodramas that romanticized criminals. See James Donovan, "Magistrates and Juries in France, 1791–1952," *French Historical Studies* 22, no. 3 (1999): 406.

Fig. 12. Jealousy prompts the murder.

Premeditated murder had great theatrical potential, dramatizing as it did the happenings at the circuit court. Murder as melodrama adapted these conventions easily to the aesthetics of performative excess, not unlike *zashchitniki* Plevako and Urusov. Moreover, as Laura Mulvey contends, melodrama has distinct value as a cultural indicator because it "symptomizes the history of its own time."[70] Applying the melodramatic mode to crime fiction aided its authors in exploring the ambiguities of postreform society. Certain generic conventions that structured the novels would be repeated on stage: inept investigators, and death for the guilty rather than prison. Either criminals took their own lives, or a higher power struck them down as the curtain dropped.

Foreign locales proved popular when Russianized. The Russian adaptation of Adolphe Belot's 1868 *Drama on the Rue de la Paix*, a novel he also adapted for the stage, changes the plot and theme enough to make it Russian. Belot, a well-known second-tier novelist in France with a connection to Émile Zola, specialized in boulevard fiction.[71] His *Drama* becomes *Murder on the Rue de la Paix* (1873) in Russian. Belot's story took place against the backdrop of the French Revolution, and the killer-protagonist dies as a casualty of street fighting in Paris. The Russian version provides instead a peaceful contemporary Parisian setting, a Gaboriauesque emphasis on detection, but satisfies with a Russian denouement.[72] A minor character dreams of writing detective novels, a self-conscious nod to the current fashion, but as the corpses pile up he decides instead to pen historical stories.[73] The action stays simple: a wealthy man is murdered and the chief suspect, someone who owed him money, turns out to be guilty. Between the first and the last scene, the victim's wife has fallen in love with his killer. When exposed by the investigator at his trial, the guilty man turns a knife on himself, and the widow prostrates herself over his body, grieving now for him.[74] The detective turned up the murderer, but to what avail?

In *The Murder of Young Miss Al'dzhern in New Orleans* (1878), the title character is strangled by the jealous and greedy foreman of her family estate. He pays local ruffians to toss her body to the alligators in the Mississippi and tries to pass her death off as a suicide by drowning.[75] "I am an American, so I take revenge!," he announces, suggesting that his Western nationality explains why he showed no remorse at his trial. The girl's true love, an investigator from the New Orleans procurator's office, solves the case, though two years too late. As ever, the judicial investigator fails to protect the public.

70. Laura Mulvey, "'It Will Be a Magnificent Obsession': The Melodrama's Role in the Development of Contemporary Film Theory," in *Melodrama: Stage. Picture. Screen*, ed. Jacky Bratton, Jim Cook, and Christine Gledhill (London: BFI Books, 1994), 122.

71. Adolphe Belot's *Succès de scandale Mademoiselle Giraud, ma femme*, published in 1870 with a preface by Zola, told the story of a man who discovers that his wife is a lesbian, although that word is not used. After her death he surreptitiously murders her female lover.

72. The guilty Noël Gerdy commits suicide as the police pound on his door, but stays alive long enough to sign a confession that will free the innocent Albert, an act of criminal altruism not found in Russian crime fiction.

73. This reflects the literary turn to historical novels in the 1880s in Russia, when those titles dominate in newspaper serials as well as library catalogues.

74. Adolf Belo, *Ubiistvo v ulitse Mira* (St. Petersburg: Mozer, 1873). The two also fall in love in Belot's version, but the wife never discovers that he killed her husband.

75. V.M. Tsilliakus fon-Veisenfel'd, *Ubiistvo devitsi Al'dzhern v Novom Orleane* (Tiflis: I. Martirosian, 1878), 23.

The most elaborate foreign setting for a melodramatic murder, however, was *The Murder of Coverly* (1881), based on the real-life case of Arthur Orton, who in 1865 claimed to be Roger, the long-lost heir to the Tichborne baronetcy in Hampshire, England. The elements of the case lent themselves beautifully to the genre. Roger had disappeared with all passengers when his ship, en route from Rio de Janeiro to New York, sank in 1854. His mother, French, Catholic, and unwelcome in Hampshire, had refused to believe him dead. When a lawyer contacted her from Australia a decade later she was eager to embrace the claimant, even though he bore no resemblance to her son. Orton was eventually found guilty of fraud in 1872, his lengthy trial having grabbed international headlines. Indeed, Shkliarevskii had created a "Russian Tichborne," a tale of murder to assume someone else's identity, followed years later by a second killing to hide the first.[76] *Sudebnye dramy* included a book on the Tichborne case in their "library" in 1904. Himself no more than a corpulent imposter, Orton stole a man's identity but did not take his life. Named Gordon in the Russian cast, he kills Coverly/Tichborne in Australia and assumes his identity to claim his inheritance. Gordon falls victim to a stage trick: seeing hallucinations of the man whom he murdered, he falls down dead.[77]

Staging murder in the provinces provided another popular setting, a means of connecting the country through crime and courts. Females dominated as victims and often as villains, reflecting in part that portion of the audience for whom the theater provided an acceptable place to appear in public. In the play *The Female Criminal, or Scenes from Life* (1879), a happily married wife and mother falls for a visiting dandy. Their affair can be anticipated early on, but the ending is more problematic. Despite her husband's forgiveness, she tosses the baby she had conceived with the gigolo down a well, and then shoots herself. In *The Court of Conscience* (1886), yet another woman poisons a friend from boarding school, although this time it was her victim's son rather than husband whom the murderess desired.[78] Haunted by the ghost of the woman she killed, she confesses to the husband before collapsing to death.

Like Alexandra Sokolova, the prolific Kapitolina Nazar'eva, included crime fiction in her broad *oeuvre*. Her drama *Uneasy Happiness* (1889) anticipated the Senate's decision that "having committed the act is not synonymous with guilt." The heroine, on the run from an abusive husband, had not murdered the woman whose identity she had assumed when she took the passport from her dead body. Her crime was bigamy when she married again, this time for happiness. Nazar'eva staged the last act as her trial, a play within a play, giving the theater audience the opportunity to cheer when the foreman reads the verdict, "She did it, but she is not guilty!"[79]

True crime provides the plot for *The Merchant Osipov's Murderous Daughter* (1894), based on court reports from a trial in Nizhnii Novgorod. A poignant melodrama of the violent clash between the old ways and the new, a merchant has promised his daughter in marriage

76. Shkliarevskii, "Russkii Tishborn," in *Chto pobudilo*, 215–280.

77. N. Kirpev, *Ubiistvo Koverlei* (Moscow: Razsokhin, 1881).

78. Published by a provincial periodical, this drama in four acts attests to the widespread popularity of the genre. *Sud sovesti* (Ekaterinburg: *Ekaterinburgskaia nedelia*, 1886).

79. Kapitolina Nazareva, *Trevozhnoe schast'e* (St. Petersburg: V. A. Bazarov, 1889). This four-act drama played at the imperial theaters. A particularly gossipy court lady enjoys a minor role.

to a man like himself. She loves a young clerk instead, who suffocates by accident when she stuffs him into a narrow closet, hiding him from her father. The *dvornik* who helps her to dispose of the corpse then blackmails her with a marriage proposal, which leads to his death at her hand. Her father weeps at her incarceration, unhappy because he has raised a terrible sinner.[80]

These melodramas of murder recalled the multiple admonitions from the bench that "this is not a theater!" The conventions of the genre coincided with the criminologists' shift from the crime to the criminal because the authors constructed a context of individual despair. The vulnerability of women made standard fare. Victims of a patriarchal society, women could rage violently against it. Both courtroom and theatrical stage provided them a place to perform their struggles and penances. The "court ladies" could sit comfortably in their loges at the local theater, drying their eyes. Semenova might have toured the provinces playing Anna in *Murder at the Ball*, so artful had been her court performance.

Playwrights were somewhat less generous than juries, who offered acquittals rather than suicide. Death by their own hand, however, gave these women control at the final curtain. The opportunity to declare remorse and then anticipate the possibility for a better life in the hereafter also offered wonderful material for that final scene. Against the laws of both church and state, as historian Susan Morrissey has argued, suicide provided keen insights into Russia's social and cultural changes. In the second half of the nineteenth century charges were brought with increasing frequency against those accused of instigating a person to take his or her own life. Such "individual instances of cruelty [were conceived of] as expressions of broader social and political problems . . . now characterized as despotism,"[81] and reflected some of the larger sociological issues being raised at court. Both Kachka and Palem had purchased pistols with the intention of taking their own lives, defeated as they had been by unequal gender relations. Murder and self-murder alike dramatized the intersection between private life and public expectations, which played melodramatically as well in court as on stage.

### Fictionalizing the Russian Jury

The "conscience of society." The "social ocean." This was Alexander III's vision of the conservative, propertied class. The merchant who refused to acquit anyone and the professor who enjoyed cross-examining the experts. Suvorin's bane and Arsen'ev's "mysterious strangers." Mediators between the criminal and society via the reformed courts, and reliant upon the investigator's collection of evidence, juries and their portrayal must be included in a discussion Russia's crime fiction. Fictional juries were as fraught with controversial politics as their factual counterparts, but they enjoyed less independence because they had to behave according to their creators' views. In many ways their personnel and actions on the page reflect on the debates that swirled around the institution of the jury.

80. P. I. Felonoz, *Ubiitsa-kupecheskaia doch' Osipova* (Moscow: n. p., 1894).

81. Susan Morrissey, *Suicide and the Body Politic in Imperial Russia* (Cambridge: Cambridge University Press, 2006), 269.

The journalist-novelist Sokolov serialized "The Jury Trial" in *Peterburgskii listok* in 1873. Also published separately, the story had appeared in three editions by 1888.[82] Most of the story concentrates on the life of Serafima and leads up to her trial for the death of her illegitimate child. Sokolov wrote in journalese, interjecting his story with asides to readers. After describing Serafima in glowing terms, he apologized that "the reader today has a difficult time making peace with such a heroine, but what could I do? I have many such modest, good, and childishly naive heroines in reserve."[83] Orphaned while at boarding school, she becomes a governess in the house of a general's widow, who has a mountain of debts and a handsome son, Nikolai. Sokolov pokes fun at the predictability of his plot, reminding readers of the fabrication while at the same time protesting that "the general's widow was so secretive that even I, the author, did not know what she was up to."[84] Kicked out after Nikolai impregnates her, Serafima cannot bear to part with their daughter, but neither can she find a job to support them. In desperation, she leaves her baby on a doorstep, from which the child falls and dies. The prosecution's insistence that she had killed her baby sounds heartless to the reader who has followed Serafima's tragedy. Her defense attorney has fallen in love with her, although she does not recognize him from years gone by, when she was still a governess and he a tutor in Nikolai's household. When the foreman reads aloud "not guilty!, the courtroom resounded with the hysterical shudders of the accused."[85] In another drama of the same title from 1877, the foreman turned out to be the true killer. He confesses from the bench when he realizes that the accused is refusing to defend himself in order to spare the foreman's daughter, whom he believes to be guilty.[86]

Shkliarevskii, too, steps into the debate about the jury, in a story that he entitles "The Jurors' Incorrect (*nepravil'nyi*) Verdict." Russian readers would have noted that he did not call it "a judicial mistake (*oshibka*)." The twelve men play no direct role until the very end when they deliver their decision, the acquittal of the woman who had confessed, in both the legal and religious connotations of the word, to having stolen a gold watch from the judicial investigator for whom she worked occasionally as a scribe. The story tells of two childhood friends from boarding school, both of whom make terrible matches in their marriages and end up in poverty in St. Petersburg. The one who stole the watch, Margarita, had needed money for the pregnant Kaleria, whose child was stillborn. "My God!," protested one man about the verdict, "it's clear that she's a thief," sounding as a refrain the title that the jurors had erred. Her magnanimous victim, happy with the decision, asserts that it was not a "mistake" when he responds, "yes, but there are many kinds of thieves!"[87]

The debates about jurors' leniency made the fictional jury an ideal site for writers to air their personal opinions of the institution. In *Peasant Jurors*, the Populist writer

82. A. A. Sokolov, *Na sude prisiazhnykh: Roman v trekh knigakh* (St. Petersburg: A. A. Sokolov, 1873).

83. Ibid., 9.

84. Ibid., 28.

85. Ibid., 129.

86. Iosef Korisenevskii, *Sud prisiazhnykh* (Kharkov: A. I. Kukolevskii, 1887).

87. A. A. Shkliarevskii, "Nepravil'nyi verdikt prisiazhnykh," *Rasskazy iz ugolovnoi khroniki* (St. Petersburg: A. S. Suvorin, 1903), 1–56.

N.N. Zlatovratskii displayed his own politics on his characters' ragged sleeves.[88] One of the most popular books of 1875, the novel highlighted the simplicity and religiosity of the Russian village.[89] When the men are called to serve in the provincial center, they brave snow, wolves, and nights crammed together in a flophouse in order to perform their civic duty. Taking pride in their appearance, they grease their hair, comb their beards, and visit the local church before appearing at court, where a merchant's son and a seminarian join them for duty. Zlatovratskii peppers their conversations with exhortations that "God judges everyone," and distinguishes between peasants (narod) and "cultured people" on the basis of their understanding of "sin and unhappiness," as the peasants viewed crime. He specified that the narod saw the "pain of a flesh-and-blood person," as opposed to the "abstract idea of the law."[90]

Zlatovratskii, however, betrays the pessimism of Russian Socialists when he directs his peasants to reach verdicts that contradicted how juries tended to deliver justice in provincial circuit courts. On the one hand, his jurors acquit an accused teenaged arsonist whose mother had met them before the trial and begged for mercy, weeping about his innocence.[91] The peasants then convict a bigamist who had married a second wife on the basis of what he insisted was faulty information about the legality of his first marriage. Zlatovratskii adds a telling touch when one of his peasants reflects on his own temptation in the past to falsify marriage documents, and he votes to convict in order to assuage his own guilty conscience. As cynical as Nekliudov, who sat at the opposite end of the political spectrum, Zlatovratskii explained how they reached their verdicts:

> They study all sides, spend a lot of time thinking about it, and then get tired and throw out all their long, preparatory investigations and pronounce a decision that is sometimes the complete opposite of the preliminary results of their investigation, but fits their spiritual mood.[92]

Zlatovratskii's position here accentuates the unwillingness of the left to accept the reformed legal system because they "reviled the law as an instrument of coercion."[93]

Dostoevsky's use of juries gives greater insight into his overall mistrust of the adversarial courtroom, evidenced already in his distaste for zashchitniki and his dissatisfaction with the acquittal as a legal means for abdicating responsibility for having, in essence, sinned. He did not bother to turn over Raskolnikov's fate to a jury, possibly because he was writing as the new courts were opening and he had not formed an opinion on it. In his final novel, however, The Brothers Karamazov, he portentously entitles book four, Dmitrii

88. N.N. Zlatovratskii, Krest'iane-prisiazhnye (1874), Izbrannye proizvedeniia (Moscow: OGIZ, 1974), 11–132.

89. Reitblat, Ot Bovy, 191.

90. Zlatovratskii, Krest'iane-prisiazhnye, 22.

91. Ibid., 76. Peasants did not trust the government to protect them from vengeful arsonists. Cathy A. Frierson, All Russia is Burning!: A Cultural History of Fire and Arson in Late Imperial Russia (Seattle: University of Washington Press, 2002), 163.

92. Zlatovratskii, Krest'iane-prisiazhnye, 13–14.

93. Laura Engelstein, "Combined Underdevelopment: Discipline and the Law in Imperial and Soviet Russia," American Historical Review 98, no. 2 (1993), 346.

Karamazov's trial, "A Judicial Mistake."[94] This signals that Mitia will be convicted of a crime that readers already know he did not commit.

In these twelve chapters Dostoevsky exposes what he considers the inadequacies of legal-code justice, with particular contempt for the adversarial procedure that turns the crime itself into someone else's fiction. The twelve who judged Mitia included four petty officials of insignificant rank, two merchants, and six peasant-artisans, men who "spent their leisure over cards, and of course had never read a book."[95] Reputedly, the author had based his *zashchitnik* on Spasovich, and he borrowed from the courtroom media that constructed the narratives of crimes and criminals: the bill of indictment and the opposing counsel's closing arguments. Hired from Petersburg by the Karamazov family, this Fetiukovich exhibited many of Spasovoich's characteristics, including his bearing, a speaking style that eschewed emotionalism, and the incessant logic with which he broke down the procurator Ippolit Kirillovich's summation.

Fetiukovich's closing argument, however, came from Dostoevsky's sensibilities, not the Western-oriented Spasovich. Fetiukovich echoes Dostoevsky's thoughts on Kairova's acquittal: "And I swear, that by finding him guilty you will only make it easier for him, you will ease his conscience, he will curse the blood he has shed and not regret it. At the same time you will destroy in him the possibility of becoming a new man." He challenges the jurors "to punish him . . . with the most awful punishment that could be imagined. . . . overwhelm him with your mercy!" Was the Western-oriented Spasovich amused or aghast to read his fictional double's words that "the Russian court does not exist for punishment only, but also for the salvation of the criminal! Let other nations think of retribution and the letter of the law, we will cling to the spirit and the meaning—the salvation and the reformation of the lost"?[96]

For the hour that Mitia's jurors are out, Dostoevsky teases with snippets of conversation, including Fetiukovich's conceit that "there are invisible threads binding the counsel for the defense with the jury. . . . Our cause is won."[97] Having entitled this chapter "The Peasants Stand Firm," the question is why they would convict, given the absence of material evidence against Dmitrii, and his protestation of innocence. Peasants jurors in cases of true crime demonstrated a propensity to acquit under these circumstances. Dostoevsky completes his personal subversion of the legal system by writing in a *deus ex machina*, an escape from the prison hospital for his innocent defendant.

The other Russian literary titan from the second half of the nineteenth century, Lev Tolstoy, also fictionalized the adversarial courtroom as a literary tactic to express his deep antipathy toward the legal reforms. In Tolstoy's first major contribution to crime fiction, *The Kreutzer Sonata* (1889), the trial is long over when the story begins. Pozdnyshev,

94. Part 4, book 12 is titled "Sudebnaia oshibka." The literal translation "A Judicial Mistake," is sometimes translated as "A Miscarriage of Justice," which contradicts Dostoevsky's intent. Justice was not "miscarried"; the jurors mistakenly believed him guilty.

95. F. M. Dostoevsky, *The Brothers Karamazov*, trans. Constance Garnett (New York: Macmillan, 1922), 712.

96. Ibid., 807–8.

97. Ibid., 812. The only novel that I have found specifically about lawyers is N. E. Geintse, *V tine advokatury* (St. Petersburg: V. V. Komarov, 1898). One "slimy" character "had the preconceived notion that he could get around any statute in the code" (420).

the central figure in this highly polemical work, was acquitted of the murder of his wife, a crime to which he had confessed. The point of Tolstoy's story and the reason for its controversy lie in Pozdnyshev's fixation on carnality, even in marriage, which drove him to stab his wife, whom he mistakenly believed was having an affair with a violinist. He fantasized about the two of them together, incited to adultery when playing the Beethoven sonata of the title. The story opens with him on train, discussing sex and sexual equality with his fellow passengers.

Tolstoy, however, strikes a false note when Pozdnyshev informs the passengers that "the verdict was rendered that I was a deceived husband, that I had killed in defense of my sullied honor (that is the way they put it in their language), and thus I was acquitted."[98] In France and the United States, for example, both codified laws and "unwritten" ones exempted murder if it involved an adulterous spouse, but Russia had no such tradition.[99] Tolstoy manipulated this fact in order to stir up Pozdnyshev's indignation so that he could reveal his character's compulsive personality. When Pozdnyshev explains that "if the pretext had not been jealousy, some other could have been found,"[100] he is admitting that he would have taken violent action against his wife in any case because of his sexual obsessions. Tolstoy misuses the jury when making his statement about carnality in marriage. He would pay for this judicial error.

In his last novel, *Resurrection* (1899), Tolstoy portrays the reformed legal system as a failed institution, emblematic of how postreform society had lost its soul. Chapter titles such as "The Absurdity of Law—Reflections of a Juryman" and "The Astonishing Institution Called Criminal Law" make plain his contempt.[101] Tolstoy's prosecutor addresses the jury with what he "considered to be the last words of scientific wisdom. There was heredity and congenital crime, Lombroso and Tarde, evolution and the struggle for existence, hypnotism and suggestive affect, Charcot and decadence."[102] Dripping even more venom from his pen than had Dostoevsky, Tolstoy directs his fictional jury to commit a judicial error out of confusion and indifference; at least the "peasants who stood firm" against Dmitrii Karamazov believed him to be guilty. These jurors simply forget to address the qualification of "without the intent of causing death" to the question of whether or not the accused was guilty of giving the poison to her victim.

Tolstoy himself had once refused jury duty, but he does not permit his protagonist Prince Dmitrii Nekhliudov to remove his name from the official list, so the prince must serve when called. His fellow jurors, all of them whiners, include a merchant, a Jewish

98. L.N. Tolstoy, *The Kreutzer Sonata and Other Stories*, trans. Benjamin Tucker (New York: J.S. Ogilvie, 1890), 112.

99. The wife did not enjoy the husband's license to kill. For France, see Harris, *Murders and Madness*, 289. For the United States, see Robert M. Ireland, "The Libertine Must Die: Sexual Dishonor and the Unwritten Law in the Nineteenth-Century United States," *Journal of Social History* 23, no. 1 (1989): 27–44.

100. Tolstoy, *Kreutzer Sonata*, 144.

101. Ibid., book 1, chapter 34, and book 2, chapter 30. *Resurrection* was serialized first in the mass-oriented journal *Niva*, whose readership would have included those most likely to be called to serve as jurors.

102. L. N. Tolstoy, *Voskresenie* (Moscow: I.D. Sytin, 1915), 51. Lombroso enjoyed a visit with Tolstoy at the latter's estate, *Iasnaia poliana*, in 1897. Irina Sirotkina, *Diagnosing Literary Genius: A Cultural History of Psychiatry in Russia, 1880–1930* (Baltimore: The Johns Hopkins University Press, 2002), 78–79.

shopkeeper, and the former tutor of his sister's children. Only belatedly does Nekhliudov recognize one of the defendants, Katia Maslova, whom he had seduced and abandoned years ago when she became pregnant. Now a prostitute, Katia is one of three on trial for a murder she did not commit. Guilty only of taking the 40 rubles that was owed her for services performed, Katia finds herself condemned to fifteen years hard labor because the jurors were not paying attention. Nekhliudov spends the remainder of the novel trying to correct the judicial error. When he is finally able to have her sentence reduced, Maslova no longer cares because she has found personal satisfaction living with the political prisoners in Siberia. Having followed Katia into exile, Nekhliudov turns to the New Testament for atonement.

## Crime Fiction into Criminological Fact

Tolstoy's "undeniable" influence on Russian politics and society had risen well beyond the point of only semi-official by the time of his death in 1910. *The Kreutzer Sonata*, forbidden at first by censors because it shocked the pious Tsar Alexander III, became one of his most popular works and was filmed twice, in 1911 and again in 1914. The sensational plot explains the appeal, but Tolstoy, even if inadvertently, tapped into a topic on the front burner of psychiatric expertise: the legality of *affekt* as a diagnosis that diminished culpability. This had particular resonance for male murderers, who could not reference a uterus to explain their behavior. *The Kreutzer Sonata* appeared against the background of two important murder trials that raised this issue. In one, the judge had denied Urusov the opportunity to call a psychiatrist to the stand in his defense of the man who had shot a chorus girl at the Bolshoi. At the other, in Kharkov, Vladimirov had put Kovalevskii on the stand to explain the stages of *affekt* in order to assert his client's instability as a medical condition. Neither attorney had secured an acquittal. That Russia's psychiatrists happily welcomed Tolstoy's protagonist into their clinics says a great deal about the author's standing with the public.

Private-docent Ia. A. Botkin, or "Uncle Iakov," a celebrity psychiatrist in the fashion of Bellin and Patenko, gave a lecture on Pozdnyshev to the forensic psychopathology faculty of Moscow University in 1893. Unconcerned that Tolstoy "has contempt for medicine," Botkin presented Pozdnyshev as the perfect patient to demonstrate the critical difference between physiological and pathological *affekt*. The difference mattered mightily because although someone convicted of a crime in the throes of a physiological outburst could legally receive an ameliorated sentence, only pathological *affekt* gave grounds for acquittal.[103] Botkin carefully guided readers through all of Pozdnyshev's moods and actions before, during, and after he plunges the knife into his wife. By keeping his audience in Pozdnyshev's mind throughout the process, Tolstoy had accomplished the impossible for psychiatrists, who could observe the accused only after he had committed the crime. Ironically, Botkin read

103. In my extensive reading about this topic, I did not find an explanation of why the courts made such a substantive legal difference between two conditions that doctors had trouble separating. I presume that a diagnosis of "pathological" allowed for an acquittal because pathology indicated disease in a way that "physiological" did not.

Pozdnyshev's behavior following the stabbing as scientific evidence of physiological *affekt*. However, the point he hoped to make was that Tolstoy had provided the proof that this type of *affekt*, too, proved diminished capacity because someone in the throes of it lost all self-control. Botkin insisted that a jury would have acquitted Pozdnyshev.[104]

Botkin's reasoning prompted an immediate response in Kovalevskii's *Arkhiv psikhiatrii* from one of his students, Dr. A. A. Petrov. More detailed in his breakdown of the story, Petrov "proved" that Pozdnyshev acted in a state of pathological *affekt*. Moreover, he cited a variety of psychiatric opinions, including the Lombroso protégé Enrico Morselli, to support his idea that Pozdnyshev was suffering neurasthenia, paranoia, and the onset of preliminary psychosis. Having practiced onanism in his youth, which Theodor Meynart had demonstrated leads to physical degeneration, Pozdnyshev had "agitated vascular centers, which resulted in the narrowing of arteries which prevented them from nourishing the nerves." Stabbing his wife was as reflexive as jerking his knee when it is tapped by a doctor.[105] Five years later psychiatrists were still citing Pozdnyshev, Botkin, and Petrov in the quest to distinguish between the two types of *affekt* and the legality of the difference.[106]

Pozdnyshev played a significant role in the psychiatric literature because he gave the experts a figure familiar to an ever-expanding group of Russians, not just readers of either Tolstoy or professional medical journals. "*Kreutzer Sonata*" became shorthand for murder in a jealous rage, an example of fiction building a bridge to fact.[107] Pozdnyshev never enjoyed Raskolnikov's popularity among defense attorneys, but as a favorite among forensic psychiatrists he helped them to sell the insanity plea for men. A prototype highlighting the benefits of intertextual explorations, the psychiatrists' Pozdnyshev could be acquitted on the basis of his pathologically based mental instability rather than for avenging his sullied honor. To Tolstoy's presumed chagrin, the condition of pathological *affekt*, which forensic psychiatrists diagnosed from his fictional Pozdnyshev, became a mainstay in legal defenses. For example, A. I. Vysochin was being treating for impotence in 1904 when he killed his wife, who had cuckolded him.[108] Although no psychiatrist testified, his *zashchitnik* invoked Pozdnyshev and claimed pathological *affekt*.[109] Acquittal. Thus did the novelist whose "authority was unofficial yet undeniable" influence the etiology and diagnosis of a disease.

In *Resurrection*, Tolstoy had portrayed the Orthodox Church as spiritually and morally bankrupt as the adversarial courtroom. The novel had deep political resonance because it contributed to the Holy Synod's decision to excommunicate Tolstoy in 1901, an action that neither lessened his popular appeal nor drove Russians away from their church. His death in November 1910 in a railroad station outside of provincial Astapovo, where

104. Dr. Ia. A. Botkin, *Prestupnyi affekt, kak uslovie nevmen* (Moscow: D. A. Bonch-Burevich, 1893), 26. Sirotkina discusses other psychiatrists preoccupied with Tolstoy in *Diagnosing Literary Genius*, chapter 3, "Tolstoi and the Beginning of Psychotherapy in Russia."

105. Dr. A. A. Petrov, "Affekt i prestuplenie," *Arkhiv psikhiatrii* 23, no. 2 (1894): 20–52.

106. S. S. Bykovskii, "Iavlenie patologicheskogo affekta," *VOG*, no. 11 (1898): 906–19.

107. *Severnyi vestnik*'s coverage of the 1891 trial of Bartenev for the murder of the Polish actress Visnovskaia compared him to Pozdnyshev, though this was immediately prior to the broader acceptance of pathological *affekt*. *Sv*, no. 3 (1891): 53–70.

108. The treatment for impotence was strychnine powder dissolved in phosphoric acid.

109. "Istoriia odnogo braka," *Sd* 22, no. 8 (1904): 145–236.

he had collapsed after having embarked on a religious pilgrimage, prompted futile appeals even among clergy to lift the excommunication so that he could be buried on hallowed ground.[110] Tolstoy's rejection of the reformed court and jurors quite likely prompted some readers to recognize their own cynical experiences in his. Others, though, like the psychiatrists who adopted his Pozdnyshev, fully aware that the author would not approve, would have used his rich characters and Christian morals as they saw fit.[111]

## Conclusion

By the turn of the twentieth century, the effects of the reforms and the government's push toward industrialization could be felt throughout urban Russia. The reading public had expanded greatly, but numbers alone mattered less than the reality that the new generation had never known serfdom or the inquisitorial process. Even seasoned readers had developed different interests, expectations, and life experiences. Crime fiction began changing perceptively, moving away from moral melodramas toward shorter stories that emphasized violence. Several popular trials were revised from stenographic and newspaper accounts into semi-fictionalized stories by author N. V. Nikitin in *The Criminal World and Its Defenders*.[112] Broadsheets of crimes, popular in the West a century earlier, appeared in Russia around 1900. Woodcuts illustrated "A Terrible Crime: The Father Who Froze His Children to Death" and "A Beastly Crime: The Daughter Cursed by Her Mother Chops Her Up with an Axe." In the West, the criminal broadsheets had circulated as a form of morality tale, the killer brought to justice in the end, often allowed to repent.[113] The few such sheets available from Russian culture, in contrast, drew sensational attention to the vodka and violence of the peasant household.

Murder stories were also serialized in five-kopeck installments that were less wordy and had characters who expended greater energy than the previous investigators tailing suspects. *Murder on Sadovaia Street* (1903), the main thoroughfare in the central market area of St. Petersburg, billed as an *ugolovnyi roman*, promised ten installments about a ruthless circus performer who kills women for their jewelry.[114] *Jealousy Prompts the Murder* (1903) spun suicide pessimistically. A wealthy aristocrat marries the local beauty, well aware that she loves an impoverished bureaucrat. First he kills her true love in a duel. He then buys

110. And a motion picture, *The Last Station*, dir. Michael Hoffman, Sony Pictures (2009). See also, William Nickell, *The Death of Tolstoy: Russia on the Eve, Astapovo Station, 1910* (Ithaca: Cornell University Press, 2010).

111. Pål Kolstø, "The Demonized Double: The Image of Lev Tolstoi in Russian Orthodox Polemics," *Slavic Review* 65, no. 2 (2006): 304–24.

112. N. V. Nikitin, *Prestupnyi mir i ego zashchitniki* (St. Petersburg: Trud, 1902).

113. For the United States, see Karen Halttunen, *Murder Most Foul: The Killer and the American Gothic Imagination* (Cambridge: Harvard University Press, 1998); and Daniel Cohen, *Pillars of Salt, Monuments of Grace: New England Crime Literature and the Origins of American Popular Culture, 1674–1860* (Amherst: University of Massachusetts Press, 2006). For early modern Germany, see Joy Wiltenburg, "True Crime: The Origins of Modern Sensationalism," *American Historical Review* 109, no. 5 (2004).

114. Vl. D-n, *Ubiistvo na Sadovoi* (St. Petersburg: El. Porokhovshchikovaia, 1903). I found only the first five.

Fig. 13. She chopped her own mother with an axe.
Fig. 14. The horrific crime of the father who froze his children.
Fig. 15. The woman buried alive gives birth.

two guns, using one on his wife and the other on himself, staging the scene as a shootout to escape the stigma of suicide.[115]

Shkliarevskii's crime fiction, like Dostoevsky's, aided readers coming to terms with re-formed law enforcement. The themes that emerge from Sokolov to Sokolova, from Linev to Tolstoy, echo corresponding messages: the facts by themselves do not explain the crime because they cannot account for the criminal's motive, and justice in all its complexity cannot be determined by the code alone. D.A. Miller has famously adopted a Foucauld-ian approach to detective fiction by arguing that readers internalize the policing functions of the novel, re-creating the law-and-order atmosphere of the modern liberal state.[116] To internalize the actions of Russia's fictional judicial investigators is to reject the desire to re-store the present order. Additionally, narrative structures as well as themes parallel factual trials: the confession as a mode of explanation superior to the investigation; the melodra-matic privileging of happenstance over logic; and antipathy toward the state, registered in its failures to capture killers, much less to prosecute them successfully. Cawelti's dialectic between literary genres and the cultures that consume them plays out most concretely in the psychiatrists' appropriation of Pozdnyshev, followed by the courts' acceptance of pathological *affekt*. The dialectic held in more subtle ways, too, reinforcing the significance of sensational murder as an entry into the world of those who killed or were killed, and of those who cobbled together explanations of how *that* could have happened *here*.

115. *Ubiistvo iz za revnosti* (Kiev: T.A. Gubanov, 1903).

116. D.A. Miller, *The Novel and the Police* (Berkeley: University of California Press, 1988).

# CHAPTER FIVE

# Russia's Postrevolutionary Modern Men

> "Evil is not something superhuman, it's something less than human."
> —Agatha Christie, *The Pale Horse*

"The body of a man was found in his apartment this morning, brutally stabbed, his head cut off and scalped. Discovered in the bed where he had suffered so horribly, the dagger used to stab him was lying next to his head, a terrible sight: the skull was visible where the skin had been torn away, his eyelids were sliced, and his lips, nose, and ears had been cut off. Blood had collected in a pool. . . . A puzzle. Under what circumstances had this Fedorov been so badly disfigured? Was this even Fedorov? The most likely answer to the riddle is that this was an act of diabolical vengeance. But for what? Jealousy? Political betrayal? Undoubtedly, though, revenge of some sort."[1]

"Boulevard" newspaper *Peterburgskaia gazeta* broke this story on October 5, 1909. The motive for this shocking crime had nothing to do with vengeance. The corpse did not turn out to be that of Stepan Fedorov, the name on the passport of the man who had rented the apartment in a building in Leshtukov Lane on the Fontanka Canal, just off Nevskii Prospect and across from the Suvorin Theater in the heart of St. Petersburg. The first to be christened "the greatest criminal of the twentieth century,"[2] this perpetrator merited that moniker because of his very modern motive and plotting, despite the fact that he had committed the crime in the most barbarian fashion.

Not just a villain, this story had a hero too, chief of detectives V. G. Filippov, who on October 9 announced with confidence that "all the threads of the crime are in our hands."[3] Filippov gathered evidence to solve the riddle of how engineer Andrei Gilevich had advertised for a secretary in order to hire a man who resembled himself, then had taken out

---

1. *Peterburgskaia gazeta* (hereafter *Pg*), 5 October 1909, no. 273.
2. *Pg*, 18 December 1909, no. 347.
3. *Pg*, 9 October 1909, no. 277.

a hundred-thousand-ruble insurance policy on his own life.[4] Gilevich's younger brother Konstantin, a law student in Petersburg, aroused immediate suspicion when he insisted that the badly disfigured remains were those of his missing brother Andrei, and demanded a death certificate in order to collect on the policy. This alerted Filippov to the probability that Andrei had assumed his victim's identity. The uncle of a student who had inexplicably left for the Continent showed Filippov postcards that he doubted his nephew had written. This helped the detective to track the pseudonymous killer to Paris. He dispatched special agent (*osoboe poruchenie*) M. G. Kuntsevich to the French capital to trap the suspect in a sting operation. This perp, though, escaped courtroom justice by popping a cyanide capsule while under the not-so-watchful eye of the French police. The killer's corpse was returned to Petersburg, his brain to be autopsied for clues that might account for his unspeakable actions. Filippov took less than three months to fit the pieces into place and capture the culprit, a feat that spoke well of his high degree of professionalism.[5]

The Gilevich affair, however, told much more than this murderous plot of hide and seek. It had begun in 1905, when the levels of violence had made "pools of blood" commonplace, the revolution exposing the incompetence of the Russian police to maintain law and order.[6] The originally peaceful demonstrations had turned violent most visibly in Moscow in December, when workers erected barricades in the Presnia district and were subdued with force by government forces. *Russkoe slovo* (The Russian Word), its circulation halted temporarily when rioters torched the publishing plant, then printed photos of the destruction.[7] Violence continued throughout 1906, featured in every newspaper's events of the day section. Sensational *faits divers* had been a staple, but now reports of suicides gave way to bombers, and drunken brawls to shakedowns of shopkeepers and other armed assaults. Often, the familiar chronicles from the courthouse were now from the military courts exercising summary judgments against those charged with resistance to state authorities. September 9, 1906 was "an exceptional day in Warsaw," one newspaper reported, "there was no bloodshed and no robbery."[8] Even when terrorists targeted politicians, the collateral damage was significant. In an attempt on the life of prime minister P. A. Stolypin in August 1906, for example, the minister was spared but a daughter was seriously wounded and at least two dozen others lay dead. The state used violence to pacify violence, so when Stolypin executed his coup d'état on June 7, 1907, the political and social stability that he instituted as a result would not erase the memories.

---

4. In 1867 the editors of *Arkhiv sudebnoi meditsiny* translated an article from English on the growing importance of insurance policies in criminal investigations. "O zastrakhovanii zhizni" 3, no. 3 (1867): 40–64.

5. I followed the case by reading a wide variety of newspapers from Petersburg, Moscow, and Odessa. At least one author pieced the stories together, treating rumor as fact, and published a three-kopeck booklet, sold before Gilevich had been apprehended. G. A. Rigin, *Ubiistvo v Leshtukovom pereulke v S.-Peterburge* (Kiev: K. I. Milevskii, 1909). I footnote only direct quotes, or significant stories carried only in a single source.

6. *Russkoe slovo* made the direct connection between Gilevich's actions and "that which we have survived of late," *Rs*, 16 December 1909, no. 288.

7. The New Year's edition of *Iskri* (Sparks), the weekly illustrated supplement to the daily, published pictures of the devastation, including a corpse in the street and naked bodies cowering in police custody.

8. Abraham Ascher, *The Revolution of 1905* (Stanford: Stanford University Press, 2004), 167.

Fig. 16. Chief of Detectives V. P. Filippov in his office.

The spike in the numbers of accused killers brought to trial following the revolution speaks to the increased aggression, and of a civilian population bearing more arms. In 1907, when a man emptied his pistol into a woman in a public park, a crowd brandishing their own weapons quickly surrounded him, thinking him an "expropriator."[9] In fact, the gunman had been elected to the First Duma in 1906, the quasi-parliament established by the quasi-constitution, the October Manifesto. By the summer of 1907, however, a Third Duma had already been convened, the first two prorogued by Nicholas II because he found them too radical in their demands for further political and civil rights. Ambitions were abbreviated, but times had changed.

In a nation with nerves still on edge, the Gilevich case evolved to trace the contours of postrevolutionary urban life and politics. It developed two narratives, which overlapped at critical junctures: one about how to live in the modern city, and the other about Russia's pressing need to modernize its law enforcement. This chapter follows both narratives as it presents the challenges faced by massive urbanization, against the background of political uncertainty, because neither the autocracy nor the Duma enjoyed widespread public confidence. Technology plays a major role, physically as the science that improved lives and

9. *Ubiistvo K. G. Zheleznovoi* (Moscow: *Sudebnye dramy*, 1911), 56–57.

psychologically as the liberator unleashing and circulating ideas. I have interspersed the narratives with each other because the tales that they tell are interdependent.

## "Tracing" the Modern

Gilevich's crime and the unraveling of his avaricious scheme by Filippov adhere so closely to Walter Benjamin's theory about the importance of the detective to the emergence of modernity that the German social observer could have cited this case to argue his points. Although Benjamin was writing in the 1930s, after war and revolution had decimated Gilevich's Petersburg, many Russians in these years "would have recognized Benjamin's metaphors."[10] Drawing the connection between a person's interior self and the interior of the physical space he inhabits, Benjamin focused on the "traces" of identity left behind for the detective to pursue.[11] A devoted student of Baudelaire's writings about, and visions of, modernity, Benjamin also looked to individual behavior in the city as a means of explaining modern experience. The city was not new, but mass transportation, communications, and lighting had affected how its residents would live in it. Benjamin celebrated Baudelaire's *flâneur*, the man who strolled the city's streets, as modernity's hero. Again like the French poet, he looked to Edgar Allan Poe, the creator of the modern detective, as "one of the greatest technicians of modern literature."[12]

Filippov and Gilevich filled the roles of Poe's detective and Baudelaire's *flâneur* because both the crime itself and the solving of it depended on a mastery of modernity, not only its technologies but also the ways in which it remade social identities. In addition, the extensive coverage of the investigation made Gilevich's a distinctively urban crime, not St. Petersburg per se, but in the complex of communications, transportation, and interaction that turned the city itself into an object for sociological study at the turn of the twentieth century.[13] The Russian city, positioned by Daniel Brower "between tradition and modernity," required many different sorts of interactions—social, cultural, and political—after the 1905 Revolution.[14] Following the Gilevich story instructed many Russians in the perils, and benefits, of modern urban life.

To make a case in point, Benjamin's observation that the *flâneur* "will find every bed hazardous" echoed eerily of Gilevich.[15] He also brought attention to the scene of the crime

10. Mark Steinberg, "Melancholy and Modernity: Emotions and Social Life in Russia between the Revolutions," *Journal of Social History* 41, no. 4 (2008): 829.

11. As Benjamin wrote, "To dwell means to leave traces. . . . Enter the detective story, which pursues these traces." Walter Benjamin, *The Writer of Modern Life: Essays on Charles Baudelaire*, ed. Michael W. Jennings, trans. Howard Eiland (Cambridge: Harvard University Press, 2006), 39.

12. Benjamin, *Writer of Modern Life*, 74.

13. Pioneer urban sociologist Robert Park characterized the city, as "a concept and a structure . . . a psychophysical mechanism." In "The City: Suggestions for the Investigation of Human Behavior in the City Environment," *American Journal of Sociology* 20, no. 5 (1915): 577–78.

14. Daniel Brower, *The Russian City between Tradition and Modernity, 1850–1900* (Berkeley: University of California Press, 1990).

15. Carlo Salzani, "The City as Crime Scene: Walter Benjamin and the Traces of the Detective," *New German Critique*, no. 100 (2007): 168.

as a culturally specific location, the "bourgeois interior." The rooms that Gilevich rented as "Fedorov" marked him as bourgeois; he had the income to pay ninety-five rubles monthly, including a servant, for the privacy necessary to do the deed.[16] Benjamin's suggestion that the bourgeois "transforms his interior, the space that belongs to him and surrounds him, into an extension of himself"[17] found concrete expression in the clothes in Fedorov's closet, measured by a forensic tailor to prove that they did not fit the corpse. Filippov traced the suit back to Gilevich through the labels that showed them purchased at a fashionable Moscow men's store. Young professionals such as this engineer were often transients, renting furnished rooms, ever able to move around neighborhoods and between cities. The rooms Gilevich rented had entered urban lore as a sinister bourgeois interior, bewitched first by the suicide of the previous occupant's wife, then by the gruesome dismembering that frightened away prospective renters.[18]

Gilevich's private rooms differed appreciably from public places such as the Evropa Hotel, where Olga Palem had shot her lover in a hotel room. In July 1909, even as Gilevich was setting his plan in motion, a young man from a prominent family in Vladimir strangled and then slashed the second of his two prostitute victims in the Danube Hotel on Petersburg's Ligovskii Prospect. Behaving like the villain in crime fiction, he had brought her in at 2 a.m., left by himself the next morning, and told the desk clerk to waken her later. When no one responded to the clerk's knock, the police broke down the door and found her "swimming in a pool of blood."[19] Upon arrest, Radkevich claimed that hearing the popular waltz "Above the Waves" aroused in him an uncontrollable passion for women.[20]

Such spontaneous acts by disturbed individuals filled the newspapers daily. A month after Gilevich's crime, in a small hotel also in Leshtukov Lane, a couple paid the hourly rate for a room and ended their stay with two bullets from her Smith and Wesson in his chest.[21] This sort of crime got little traction in the press because tomorrow would bring an analogous incident. The Gilevich affair reverberated broadly because it tapped into so many insecurities. Holmesian in the cleverness of both hero-detective and villain, it made a better read than serial crime fiction as it helped readers to experience the day-to-day according to modern rhythms.


## Modernizing the Police

The violence begun in 1905 that continued well into 1907 had exposed the gross incapacity of the police to protect life and property. The collapse in authority during the

16. Jurgen Habermas placed the bourgeois private sphere in a dialectical relationship with its public one: "the more the city as a whole has transformed into a barely penetrable jungle, the more (the bourgeois) withdraws into his sphere of privacy." *The Structural Transformation of the Public Sphere: An Inquiry into a Category of Bourgeois Society* (Cambridge: MIT Press, 1991), 159.

17. Daniel F. Bell, "Reading Corpses: Interpretive Violence," *SubStance* 27. no. 2 (1998): 98. Benjamin also traced the notion of the bourgeois interior back to Poe.

18. Rigin, *Ubiistvo*, 4. The landlady complained about curious spectators milling about but refusing to rent.

19. As reported in *Birzhevye vedomosti*, 26 July 1909, no. 11229; and *Gk*, 26 July 1909, no. 363.

20. *Vestnik politsii* (hereafter *Vp*), no. 39 (1909): 840–41.

21. *Peterburgskii listok* (hereafter *Pl*), 4 December 1909, no. 333.

revolutionary years had allowed for the widespread circulation of satirical journals, which circumvented the censors with particularly sharp invectives for all law enforcement personnel.[22] Prime Minister Stolypin, nicknamed "the strongman of the autocracy" for the rigor with which he had put down the revolution in Saratov Province when he served as governor, entertained a second sobriquet, in that "Stolypin's neckties" referred to the hangman's noose deployed in the summary executions authorized to restore order.[23] The weary public could turn a blind eye when the result was stability, but how would they respond to law enforcement after order had been restored? Former director of police A. A. Lopukhin directed attention to the changed political circumstances that would require a different role for the police, now tasked with defending the new civil and political rights enumerated in the October Manifesto.

One of the points for which Lopukhin argued was the separation of the investigation of crimes from the maintenance of public order. Criticizing the Ministry of Internal Affairs as a "dusty, bureaucratic mechanism" that stifled initiative, he hoped for a complete overhaul of law enforcement.[24] Certainly miserable wages and high turnover distinguished the police as the "stepchild" of the Ministry of Internal Affairs.[25] The personnel attracted to such employment were exposed regularly in the popular *Sudebnye dramy* when their acts of brutality and corruption landed them in court. In Odessa, for example, several constables had organized into a gang as ruthless as the ones they were supposed to arrest.[26] Civic populations recognized the need for protection, as members of one *zemstvo*, the board of local self-government, voted to increase taxes in order to hire more police in "the battle with terror" in 1905.[27] Yet the physical attacks that beat cops suffered during the revolutionary years made plain the fluctuating levels of public confidence and the crucial requirement for institutional respect.[28]

In a public relations gesture, the Ministry of Internal Affairs in 1907 launched *Vestnik politsii* (The Police Gazette), a weekly designed primarily to redress the problem of rampant public mistrust. Originally intended for police subscribers to boost their morale, this newspaper in its first years had such a broad readership that Singer sewing machines counted among its many non-police-oriented advertisements. *Vestnik* also featured crime fiction and had a supplemental "library" that offered subscribers translations of popular literary

22. I cite but a single example, from *Bortsy*, no. 1 (1906): 5. "A schoolroom riddle: What forms do reptiles take?" "Slithering, subaquatic, and walking on two legs." "Huh? Two legs?" "Yes, *syshchiki.*"

23. Stolypin challenged the liberal politician who introduced this depiction, F. I. Rodichev, to a duel that never took place. Abraham Ascher, *P. A. Stolypin: The Search for Stability in Late Imperial Russia* (Stanford: Stanford University Press, 2001), 219.

24. A. A. Lopukhin, *Iz itogov sluzhdebnogo opyta* (Moscow: V. M. Soblin, 1907), 7, 10–11, 68.

25. Neil Weissman, "Regular Police in Tsarist Russia, 1900–1914," *Russian Review* 44, no. 1 (1985): 51.

26. Roshanna P. Sylvester, *Tales of Old Odessa: Crime and Civility in a City of Thieves* (DeKalb: Northern Illinois University Press, 2005), 23. Russia showed no "exceptionalism" on this score; the New York Senate's Lexow Committee uncovered considerable graft and extortion by policemen in 1894–1895.

27. *Vp*, no. 18 (1908): 18–19.

28. Robert Thurston reported seventy-six attacks on Moscow police in 1906–1907, numbers that curtailed dramatically in subsequent years. *Liberal City, Conservative State: Moscow and Russia's Urban Crisis, 1906–1914* (New York: Oxford University Press, 1987), 94.

detectives Gaston Leroux and Sherlock Holmes.[29] One of *Vestnik*'s appeals lay in the particularly graphic photographs it published. In the Gilevich case, for example, the newspapers reprinted the same woodcut rendering of the victim's head in a jar of formaldehyde. *Vestnik* published shots of the head itself, the bed, and the knives used to cut the victim up. This intriguingly sensational aspect was balanced by the use of photos for purposes of fighting crime, including pictures of "most wanted" criminals and missing persons. At least one young man was found when someone recognized his photo in *Vestnik*.[30]

In mid-1909 the Department of Police assumed publication of *Vestnik politsii* and dropped the arresting photos and supplemental library. Gone, too, were most commercial advertisements. Editors focused instead on the point made in their inaugural editorial about the police's "new path of service to both society and the state." Bemoaning that although "no one has more obligations than the police . . . when people come home at night, they take the serenity for granted," they also admitted to having more than a few poorly trained and ignorant constables. Public support posed a constant problem. One writer noted that in Russian paintings, the arrested *neschastnye* inevitably appear more sympathetic than the uniformed police beside them.[31] Nor did the government value its personnel. Private witnesses ordered to appear in circuit courts outside their districts received subsidies for travel, but police officers had to pay their own way when summoned.[32] What the editors wanted was the opportunity to earn esteem, and their demands for substantive reforms focused on professionalization.

The core of the new professionalism would lie in the expansion of detective bureaus, adapted according to Lopukhin's argument that investigating crimes must be separated from maintaining order. The two capitals had detective divisions in their police departments, as did Odessa before 1908.[33] Petersburg's Putilin had marked the transition to the sort of department that paid more attention to crime than to politics. S. I. Inikhov, assistant to the chief in Petersburg from 1899 until his death in 1906, asserted that he "served society, not the administration." A member of the hereditary nobility in Moscow Province, Inikhov had studied Eastern languages at the Lazarevskii Institute until financial circumstances forced him to take a paying job, beginning as a bailiff "when Lecoq and Holmes were still in the foggy future."[34] Two issues that emerge from Inikhov's brief memoirs

29. Subscribers complained when the paper stopped offering this "library of criminal novels" in 1909. *Vp*, no. 29 (1909): 626. Leroux, best known as the author of *Le fantôme de l'opéra* (1910), wrote mysteries solved by amateur detective and journalist Joseph Rouletabille. Leroux's *Le mystère de la chambre jaune* (1907), pioneered the detective genre motif of the locked room, which challenges the reader to uncover how the culprit could have exited such a crime scene.

30. The young man had switched passports with someone in a dosshouse, and his mother generously rewarded the person who found him. *Vp*, no. 4 (1909): 77.

31. *Vp*, no. 9 (1910): 216–17.

32. *Vp*, no. 11 (1908): 15–16; and no. 22 (1908): 9. Police doctors also had to pay their own way, whereas private doctors would have their expenses paid.

33. Minister of the Interior V. K. Pleve pleaded successfully for more money from Minister of Finance S. Iu. Witte to fund the Odessa division in 1903, as crime and public disturbances were on the rise. Provincial governors also requested funding, which was not met until after 1905. Russkii Gosudarstvennyi Istoricheskii Arkhiv (Russian State Historical Archive) (hereafter RGIA), f. 565, op. 6, d. 22809.

34. I. K. Markuze,"Iz praktiki syshchika," *Istoricheskii vestnik* 107, no. 3 (1907): 939–40.

Fig. 17. Woodcut illustration of the victim's head in the Gilevich case.

Fig. 18. Photo of the victim's head in the Gilevich case.

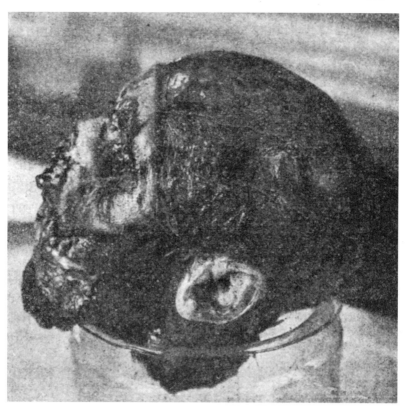

draw attention to the modernization of the police: first, his support for psychiatric evaluations in criminology, and second, the increased use of photography.

Filippov had begun his career as a judicial investigator in provincial Orenburg before becoming the imperial capital's chief of detectives. He shared common objectives with the editors of *Vestnik politsii*, and they gave him flattering coverage. So did the urban papers *Peterburgskaia gazeta* and *Peterburgskii listok*, whose petit-bourgeois readership would be heavily invested in law and order on their city's streets.[35] *Vestnik* foregrounded the problems and the hopes of law enforcement at the end of Russia's old regime. Keenly sensitive to the public's "organic fear" of strengthening the police, editors argued instead that the force would be substantively different and therefore a sign of the same sort of cultural advancement that characterized police functions in Western Europe.[36] Bemoaning that "a sense of citizenship was simply too weakly developed among Russians,"[37] they realized that their relationship to the public had not changed sufficiently since the 1872 trial when the prosecution had refused to name the informants in a murder trial because state officials could not rely on the upright citizenry for cooperation. The slogan "Not the public for the police, but the police for the public!"[38] intended well but rang hollow until the police force would, in fact, serve and protect.

*Vestnik's* ideological slant could be read in its repeated commitments to defend God, tsar, and motherland. Poignant photos of funerals of police killed in the line of duty, especially from 1906, addressed morale as they also reminded readers that officers formed the line that, theoretically, protected them from malfeasance. These photographs capture the crowds at what were fundamentally politicized demonstrations, visual evidence that many policemen were esteemed in their communities. A related issue surfaces in news about crimes, stories in which *Vestnik* intermingled political revolutionaries with common thugs. This perception was not always myopic, and a significant portion of the urban population shared it.[39] Kursk assistant procurator V. P. Girchenko, an early enthusiast of forensic photography, regretted that it had not been widespread during the revolution; police could have captured with a camera the faces of those workers bearing arms, as well as revolutionaries in the crowds.[40] Like Lopukhin, *Vestnik's* editors believed that the police had a new set of civil and political institutions to defend, and they counseled cops to steer clear of fracases between political parties.[41]

Filippov represented those elements of the law that desired the transformation of the police from "brutal, theatrical and dramatic" into "a calm and stable" force operating "with the precision of well-designed machines precisely assembled and made of first-class

35. Joan Neuberger, *Hooliganism: Crime, Culture, and Power in St. Petersburg, 1900–1914* (Berkeley: University of Calif. Press, 1993), chapter 1, emphasizes the connection between the boulevard press and law and order that had begun before 1905.

36. *Vp*, no. 32 (1908): 4.

37. *Vp*, no. 6 (1908): 5–7.

38. *Vp*, no. 29 (1909): 627.

39. Simon Sebag Montefiore, *Young Stalin* (New York: Knopf, 2007), opens with the youthful Georgian thug committing a robbery.

40. V. P. Girchenko, *Daktiloskopiia i ugolnyi rozysk* (Kursk: Tip. Gub. prav., 1914): ii.

41. Ibid., 6; and L. Kosunovich, "V politicheskom vodovorote," *Vp*, no. 27 (1909): 567–69.

material."[42] A. F. Koshko, Filippov's counterpart in Moscow, also held such high standards that Scotland Yard awarded him for the example he set. Moreover, Russian detectives were named the most efficient at a 1913 international congress of criminologists.[43] Detective Koshko contrasts immediately with fellow Muscovite police chief A. A. Reinbot, who dug his hands deep in the pockets of local citizens. Reinbot personified the tug of war between the forces of professionalism and patriarchal paternalism that plagued the police until the autocracy collapsed. Convicted of graft in 1911, Reinbot enjoyed the tsar's favor and did not have to serve out his conviction in prison.[44]

Those who pushed for heightened standards enjoyed institutional support from the legislative Duma that their predecessors had lacked. Lawmakers in this protoparliament and Tsar Nicholas II signed into effect a law that made substantives changes on July 6, 1908.[45] The first step taken toward heightening respect would be to lessen some of the obligations on policemen that turned them essentially into errand boys for procurators and other superiors. In the cities, bachelor policemen lived in barracks, but those with families often tried to rent, which created problems because the law required that they live in the neighborhoods to which they were assigned, areas that they could not always afford.[46] The need for improved education for even the lowest ranks continued throughout *Vestnik*'s years of publication as an issue of immediate editorial concern. "We train all other personnel" who have responsibilities to the public, so why no special courses for these men, who have the most direct contact with it?[47] Not until 1913 would literacy be a requirement, mandated so that police could fill out investigative and arrest protocols.[48]

L. Kosunovich wrote regularly in *Vestnik* on issues relevant to the lower ranks. Envisioning the reform of the police as one aspect of remaking society after the revolution, he invoked the October Manifesto as a welcome affirmation of civil rights. As in "cultured" Western Europe, police protecting citizens' rights would inspire respect. *Vestnik* illustrated the benefits of this more refined force with photos demonstrating the use of martial arts, which promoted self-control over physical brutality when making arrests.[49] Kosunovich made it very clear that the force would have to police itself, as too many used their badges for extortion.[50] He also reminded policemen that confessions gained as a result of beating the suspects often led to acquittals of even the guilty at trial.[51] A telling discussion emerged

42. Thus spake the director of the French Sûreté Yves Guyot in 1887. Quoted in Tom Gunning, "Tracing the Individual Body: Photography, Detectives, and Early Cinema," in *Cinema and the Invention of Modern Life*, ed. Leo Charney and Vanessa R. Schwartz (Berkeley: University of California Press, 1995), 22.

43. Vladimir Ruga and A. Kokorev, *Moskva povsednevnaia: Ocherki gorodsko zhizni nachala XX-ogo veka* (Moscow: OLMA Press, 2006), 256.

44. Thurston, *Liberal City, Conservative State*, 99.

45. *Vp*, no. 30 (1908): 2–3.

46. Ruga and Kokorev, *Moskva povsednevnaia*, 228, 239.

47. Polkovnik Kalmanov, "Blagoe nachinanie," *Vp*, no. 41 (1909): 885–86.

48. Ruga and Kokorev, *Moskva povsednevnaia*, 225.

49. L. Kosunovich, "Svoboda lichnosti i politseiskie aresty," *Vp*, no. 2 (1910): 36–38.

50. Kosunovich referred to the cops' notions of *bezgreshnye dokhody* (innocent income) and *kulachnoe pravo* (right be fisticuffs). *Vp*, no. 28 (1909): 590–93.

51. "Uchastie politsii v proizvodstve predvaritel'nogo sledstviia," nos. 8–12 (1910).

around the question of what is police tact, though one reader joked about the need for tactfulness when escorting home the uproarious drunk.[52]

Street fighting during the revolution exposed the paucity of firearms for the police. In Moscow, for example, the force had fewer than fifteen hundred outdated Smith and Wesson revolvers. As the battles intensified, the city's newly appointed governor-general, F. V. Dubasov, appropriated some Berdan rifles from the military.[53] In Petersburg, Dmitrii Trepov, son of Zasulich's victim, put down the protests with the oft-repeated command, "Don't spare the bullets! Use no blanks!"[54] Arming law enforcers would become a priority, but not without regulations. From 1908 Russian police enjoyed the right to bear arms when "called to restore public order." However, they could fire shots only when "nothing else would stop the disturbances" and after having told the crowd three times, "loudly," to calm down. Every discharge of firearms also required that a protocol be filed immediately.[55] Reforms in 1913 made the state responsible for the purchase of bullets, pricey items that not all cops could have afforded on their own.[56] Omnipresent blurbs in the events of the day sections of newspapers, however, suggests that gun control in imperial Russia was an oxymoron on both sides of the law. An ad in 1909 for a signal gun called "Alarm" (*trevoga*) billed it as "salable to those who do not have a gun permit."[57]

Educated in the modern forensic sciences, the police were to adhere to an objectivity that would serve the citizenry as a whole. This ideal, upon which the corps of judicial investigators had been established, had just as little chance of being fulfilled if the autocracy continued to intervene at will. Lopukhin's own career reflected the tsarist government's manipulation of the law for political purposes. In 1908 Lopukhin, after having been fired in 1905, exposed one of his own *syshchiki*, Evno Azef, as a double agent. Azef had conspired with Socialist Revolutionaries in 1904 in the assassinations of the Minster of Internal Affairs V. K. von Plehve and Grand Duke Sergei. Arrested in January 1909, Lopukhin went to trial in April, charged with having passed along state secrets to the journalist V. L. Burtsev, to whom he had leaked the information about Azef.[58] Although questionable, the accusations were nonetheless written in the letter of the law. Found guilty, though not by a jury, Lopukhin's sentence of five years at hard labor was appealed to the Senate, which reduced his punishment to exile in provincial Krasnodar. His triumphal return in 1912 to a position as vice director of the Siberian

52. *Vp*, no. 19 (1909): 384–86; and no. 42 (1909): 904.

53. Ruga and Kokorev, *Moskva povsednevnaia*, 244–45.

54. Making a pun with the verb *zhalet'*, which can mean "spare," as in the bullets, or pity, the editors of the satirical journal *Bomby* told readers "not to pity those exploiting your labor or trampling on your rights." *Bomby*, no. 1 (1905): 2.

55. N. Volkov, *Zakony o politsii* (Moscow: Pravovedenie, 1910), 146–47.

56. Ruga and Kokorev, *Moskva povsednevnaia*, 260–61. Cops would receive twenty-one bullets for practice, and fifty for service.

57. Advertised in *Rs*, 13 September 1909, no. 210. *Trevoga* means "alarm" with the undercurrent of anxiety rather than a warning signal. Gun shops also sold pistols craftily advertised for hunting game.

58. One rumor floated that the victim in Leshtukov Lane was Azef. *Pg*, 9 October 1909, no. 277.

Trade Bank indicates that the tsarist government had held him criminally responsible for having embarrassed it. Editors of *Vestnik politsii* supported the former Top Cop as best they could.[59]

Two other prominent policemen fell victim to intrigues from the Winter Palace in 1912, both brought down by the politics of the Beilis case. E. F. Mishchuk, Kiev's chief of detectives, and three of his agents went to trial for refusing to investigate the murder of thirteen-year-old Andrei Iushchinskii as the case of a ritual murder of Christians by Jews. Mishchuk had objected that "ritual murders do not take place in the twentieth century," to which the local procurator's office charged that "the chief of detectives cannot be allowed to make up his mind before beginning the investigation."[60] Mishchuk's replacement, Nikolai Krasovskii, suffered the same fate.[61] Moscow's Koshko got called in to review the investigation by Minister of Justice Shcheglovitov. Koshko's conclusion that it "was conducted incorrectly, one-sidedly, and . . . with prejudice" earned the minister's ire but did not cost him his job.[62] This reminds that no matter how competent, Filippov still endured an antimodern presence peering over his shoulder.

### The New Expertise: Reading the Traces Left Behind

The establishment of the eighty-seven new detective divisions around the empire laid the foundation for professionalization. The positive publicity that detectives received raised their profiles, to the annoyance of police chiefs who remained "stepsons" in the Ministry of Internal Affairs. *Vestnik* opened its pages to both sides in the debate, recalling acerbically "that old proverb about two bears in the same den."[63] Kosunovich, describing himself as "one from the old school," protested that the public did not trust these new divisions, whose lawmen lazed around in offices while cops were out on the streets familiarizing themselves with local needs.[64] Filippov responded tartly that Kosunovich should not confuse his men with the fictional behavior of Sherlock Holmes and Nick Carter, "which he obviously reads so greedily." The more than one thousand cases brought to the detectives in their inaugural months reflected public confidence in them. Two underlying issues that emerge in these articles indicate that the heart of the dispute lay in the threat that the new ways posed to the old. Kosunovich, for example, wanted detectives to wear uniforms (*mundiry*) because he believed that the public would respect such a display of status. Filippov countered strenuously that street clothes were much more conducive to investigations.

59. In the numerous articles about this case, the paper tried to put to rest rumors that Lopukhin knew of Azef's involvement with the assassinations. *Vp*, no. 4 (1909): 70.

60. *Sudebnyi dramy* (hereafter *Sd*), no. 9 (1912): 321–48. The defense cited both the Volokhova and Palem cases as examples of shoddy preliminary investigations (321).

61. Ezekiel Leikin, *The Beilis Transcripts: The Anti-Semitic Trial That Shook the World* (Lanham, MD: Jason Aronson, 1993), 11.

62. Charles A. Ruud and Sergei A. Stepanov, *Fontanka 16: The Tsars' Secret Police* (Montreal: McGill-Queen's University Press, 1999), 266.

63. *Vp*, no. 3 (1910): 69.

64. *Vp*, nos. 34, 40 (1908).

Kosunovich also betrayed an anxiety about the new technology, a fear of fingerprinting, on which, as Filippov accurately insisted, the success of reform lay.[65]

Detectives would receive training in new forensic sciences that had the capability to shift an appreciable portion of expert authority away from medical doctors. "Criminalistics" focused on physical evidence rather than confessions and criminological personalities.[66] Before the turn of the century two discoveries in other areas had direct applications for criminalistics. First, by 1900 photography had developed from daguerreotypes to the practicality of the handheld Kodak Brownie. As early as 1891 *Novoe vremia*, never a fan of psychiatric support for the defense, was enthusing about the potential for forensic photography as "the most articulate witness" to a crime.[67] Mug shots had mattered since Lombroso first used them to point out the atavistic features of his born criminals. Forensic photography did more than identify; when the police dressed up their victims, robbers killed during a gun battle, and staged their corpses for the camera, they were dramatizing for the public their control over criminality.[68]

The second breakthrough came as a result of colonial policies when in 1858 William Herschel, a British civil administrator in India, began to test the use of handprints to substitute for signatures in legal documents. Further experimentation by Britain's Francis Galton determined the uniqueness of each individual's fingerprints, which transformed the study of each individual's fingerprints into the science of dactyloscopy. In 1883 France's Alphonse Bertillon created an anthropometric system that measured eleven body parts and facial features of arrestees; the classification of known criminals aided police in capturing recidivists. Adding mug shots and fingerprints to the index cards of Bertillon's measurements allowed law enforcement to compile rogues' galleries. Fingerprints were first used at trial to prove guilt in England in 1902.[69] In Russia, fingerprinting was introduced at a trial in Odessa in 1911 and in Petersburg in 1912.[70]

Criminologist E. F. Burinskii pioneered the Russian shift in forensic expertise away from medicine to the reputedly more objective sciences that dealt with physical traces. His medium was photography, with its presumed capacity to secure factual data. Burinskii first presented evidence in court in 1889 in a case involving the verification of a signature. By 1892 he had persuaded the Ministry of Justice to appoint him officially as a forensic photographer attached to the Petersburg procurator's office, complete with salary, assistant,

65. *Vp*, no. 38 (1908). Another chief of detectives from an unnamed provincial city supported Filippov with examples of local cooperation between police and detectives. *Vp*, no. 42 (1909): 905–6. And another seconded the need for wearing street clothes. *Vp*, no. 45 (1909): 980–82.

66. *Vp*, no. 1 (1907): 4. Articles such as "Torzhestvo daktiliskopii v sude prisiazhnykh," no. 52 (1909): 6–8, became commonplace.

67. *Novoe vremia* (hereafter *Nv*), 21 July and 21 August, 1891, nos. 5528 and 5559.

68. The ever enthusiastic Benjamin marveled at how "photography made it possible for the first time to preserve permanent and unmistakable traces of a human being. The detective story came into being when this most decisive conquest of a person's incognito had been accomplished." Quoted in Gunning, "Tracing the Individual Body," 21.

69. For example, Colin Beavan, *Fingerprints: The Origins of Crime Detection and the Murder Case That Launched Forensic Science* (New York: Hyperion, 2001).

70. I. F. Krylov, *V mire kriminalistiki* (Leningrad: Izd-vo Leningradskogo universiteta, 1980), 42.

and laboratory.[71] Burinskii himself specialized in documents and handwriting. Keen to the controversies that swirled around expertise, the debates among Fuks, Arsen'ev, and others about whether expert testimony constituted science or opinion, Burinskii hoped to single out the objectivity of his new forensics:

> medical expertise answers the question, was the action a crime? and is the accused culpable? only rarely touching the question, did the accused actually commit the crime? The documents expert does not touch the issue of culpability, but asks whether or not a crime was committed, and if so, *did this person do it?*[72]

Known to be politically progressive, Burinskii enjoyed the company of populist writers such as Nikolai Nekrasov and Mikhail Saltykov-Shchedrin.[73] An obituary from 1912 mentioned that Burinskii's reputation had been "dirtied by insinuations," though it did not explain how. The article also praised him for saving many *neschastnye* from hard labor.[74]

Burinskii's work on handwriting pulled him into graphology, the uncertain science of determining personality from handwriting.[75] Differentiating the term *psikhografologiia* from *fiziografologiia*, or psychic from physical graphology, he wrote a history of experimentation with the psyche that dated back to Aristotle. Without dismissing *psikhografologiia* out of hand, he concluded that "personally, I do not think it sufficiently grounded."[76] Both aspects of handwriting analysis played into the Gilevich case. First, Filippov determined the victim to be the missing student Pavel Podlutskii when an uncle brought postcards from the supposedly traveling nephew that were written in an unfamiliar hand. Second, the police supplied the graphologist M. I. Popliakovskii with a photographic facsimile of the killer's penmanship for analysis of his moral characteristics. The neatness and precision of his lettering reflected Gilevich's intelligence, but his style, marked by letters becoming smaller at the end of words, betrayed his "slyness and egoism."[77]

In Burinskii's wake, other criminologists agitated for increased use of photography to seal evidence from crime scenes and corpses and before they deteriorated beyond recovery.[78] In 1896, police took photos of a man's corpse abandoned in a field that were later

---

71. E. F. Burinskii, *Sudebnaia ekspertiza dokumentov* (St. Petersburg: Trud, 1903), 335. Article 29 of the *Ustav O litsakh, sostoiashchikh pri sudebnykh mestakh* establishes the positions. The official photographers were "sworn" in ( *prisiazhenie*), like lawyers and jurors. RGIA, f. 1405, op. 93, d. 2599.

72. Burinskii, *Sudebnaia ekspertiza dokumentov*, 1.

73. A. I. Vinberg, *Rol' ucheniia E. F. Burinskogo v formirovanii otechestvennoi kriminalistiki* (Volgograd: n. p., 1981), 66–67.

74. V. Bernatskii, "Nekrolog," *Vestnik fotografii*, no. 4 (April 1912): 135.

75. The prolific novelist of multiple genres N. D. Aksharumov coauthored with his brother, a medical doctor, *Grafologiia, ili uchenie ob individual'nosti pis'ma, ob otnoshenii pocherki k kharateru* (Riga: Miuller, 1894). The popularity of the subject resulted in a special supplement to *Pg*, no. 1 (1894) that praised the Russian researchers who connected the nerves in the fingers that wrote to the thoughts generated by the brain.

76. Burinskii, *Sudebnaia ekspertiza dokumentov*, 210.

77. *Pl*, 25 December 1909, no. 354. More information on this is the manuscript in the archive of A. Pechinskii; the text, "Pocherk i lichnost'" is available online at http://www.pravo.vuzlib.net/book_z999_page_9.html (accessed January 4, 2010).

78. N. I. Greshishchev, "O sudebno-med. ekspertise v dele ob ubiistbe Komarova," *VOG*, no. 4 (1902): 486.

Fig. 19. Dead bandits posed by police for portraiture in *Vestnik politsii.*

used in the trial, over the vehement objections of the *zashchitnik*, who feared prejudicing the jury.[79] Gilevich's photo had been distributed among *dvorniki*, the most basic point of public interaction. The police reforms of 1908 included granting to official photographers the same rights as other personnel in the procurator's office.[80] Also, the handbooks for judicial investigators began to include sections on how to photograph crime scenes.[81] Kursk's Girchenko taught this new methodology to police personnel.[82] In a regular column in *Vestnik*, "Silent Witnesses," Professor N. D. Sergeevskii instructed his audience in how to read corpses for evidence. His biography reflects how he served *Vestnik*'s editorial policy: a "state councilor with contempt for the liberation movement," he worked part time as a scribe for a local judicial investigator "because he wanted to acquire genuine criminal material."[83]

*Vestnik* provided a primary source for information on the Bertillon system and dactyloscopy. The detective divisions were authorized to be supplied with the necessary

79. "Anna Konovalova," in Nikitin, *Prestupnyi mir*, 120, 132.

80. *UUS*, art. 978. Photographers would be reimbursed for travel to crime scenes.

81. Included in post-1908 editions of P. V. Makalinskii, *Prakticheskoe rukovodstvo dlia sudebnykh sledovatelei, sostoiashchykh pri okruzhnykh sudakh* (Petrograd: M. Merkushev, 1915).

82. The local governor had invited him to give lectures that were then published and distributed for educational purposes. Girchenko, *Daktiloskopiia*, ii.

83. Sergeevskii's premature death in 1909 ended this series. *Vp*, no. 41 (1908): 1.

investigative resources, including photographic equipment, anthropometric measuring devices, and dactyloscopes.[84] In yet another example of ministerial overlap and confusion, funding came from the Ministry of Internal Affairs rather than Justice, and it released a paltry 130,000 rubles for the entire enterprise.[85]

## The Spectacular Corpse

The Gilevich case gave Filippov the opportunity to showcase the investigative prowess of the skilled detective schooled in the new expertise. He turned the body in the bed into a personification of modernity, albeit a putrefying one, when he put it on public display in the morgue at Obukhovskaia Hospital, the head in formaldehyde alongside the body. Filippov had hoped this would help with identification, as though such a thing were possible from the disfigured and rotting remains. He was borrowing from the experience of the Paris morgue, which had only recently closed its doors and windows to the many thousands of voyeurs who had made it one of the city's premier attractions between 1804 and 1907. In 1874 a Russian physician had bemoaned the lack of a comparable institution in St. Petersburg. Citing the unlikely statistic that "eight out of nine bodies are identified there," he lamented that "our autopsies take place in police stations and hospitals. So many bodies remain unidentified because we have no good place to put them on display."[86] *Vestnik* suggested that corpses might be identified more readily if they were dressed and posed in natural positions, such as sitting in an armchair, a tactic used in Paris.[87]

The St. Petersburg facilities had none of the panache of the Paris morgue, which turned the bodies, often costumed, into artifacts for mass consumption. The body from Leshtukhov Lane had been autopsied in the anatomical theater of the Obukhovskaia Hospital, and then laid out naked there in the *pokoinitskaia*, or hospital mortuary. Crowds estimated at up to fifteen thousand "sieged the mortuary." Unlike the masses who had not that long ago taken to the streets, these curiosity seekers formed a new kind of crowd, one that realized "urban experience and modern life through the visual re-presentation" of the victim.[88] If the revolutionary crowds were often characterized by class, this one contained a gendered component made up of the many women who "exited quickly after seeing the body and got sick."[89] On October 10, Filippov ordered that only those with legitimate reasons for thinking that they could recognize the body be permitted in, which reduced the number of visitors from the thousands to the hundreds. The corpse continued to blacken and worms began surfacing ("thus far only a few"), and the smell "infected the entire place."[90]

84. In 1910 the detectives received ministry support for establishing bureaus for fingerprinting. RGIA, f. 1405, op. 531, d. 960.

85. *Vp*, no. 8 (1908): 8–9.

86. Dr. M. N. Shmelev, "Ob ustroistve skudel'ni v Peterburge," *Sbornik sud. med.* 1, no. 2 (1874): 21–23.

87. *Vp*, no. 1 (1909): 8–9.

88. Vanessa R. Schwartz, *Spectacular Realities: Early Mass Culture in Fin de Siècle Paris* (Berkeley: University of California Press, 1998), 202.

89. *Pl*, 8 October 1909, no. 276.

90. *Pl*, 10, 11 October 1909, nos. 278, 279.

The national audience unable to file through the mortuary still had access through photographs, woodcut illustrations, and detailed physical descriptions of the body. This indirect access gave substance to Vanessa Schwartz's argument that as a society becomes more literate, it also becomes more visual, "as word and image generated . . . spectacular realities" that she considers essential to modern urban culture.[91] The editors of *Petersburgskii listok* complained about the unsanitary conditions of the viewing, to which attendants responded positively and "the suspicious liquid was cleaned from the floor."[92] Tapping into the public's fascination with viewing the body, a *Peterburgskaia gazeta* reporter wrote a human interest story about "The Kingdom of Corpses," a detailed description of the gathering and subsequent storage of unidentified bodies by the anatomical institute for "use by science."[93] This was followed up with "The Abode of Death," a description of the institute itself where Gilevich would end up: "there lies one body, baring his teeth, the grimace of death on his face . . . another is twisted into such a fantastical pose that the guard fears trying to straighten him out."[94]

The bodies on display, like the macabre photos of the posed corpses in *Vestnik*, provided a fundamentally democratic invitation to onlookers to participate in the civic discourse of scripting narratives of crime, and many "volunteer Pinkertons" submitted their theories to the police.[95] Defacing the young man in Leshtukov Lane had destroyed the most immediate level of identification, the question of *who*. It also pondered the "whydunit" of crime fiction, why *this* man had died under *those* circumstances.

When Filippov placed the victim's corpse in the public sphere and invited interested onlookers to participate in devising a story of the crime, he accorded it social value. The exhibition of the body, lying naked and headless, integrated it into a larger public phenomenon of displaying the dead as a rhetorical devise to engage the public in what the death had signified. In a previous example from 1885, a young woman shot herself on her wedding night because her parents had made her quit the man she loved and marry another. Her autopsied body lay in the university anatomical theatre, "literally flooded by the public," a sad spark to the debate about forced marriage.[96] Susan Morrissey has documented some of the aesthetics of youthful suicides after 1905, pictured in papers that now had the technology to illustrate their tragic demises; newspapers had long published exemplary suicide notes.[97]

With so little available from which identify the body, the forensic examiners nevertheless did what they could with what they had. Even the pieces cut from the face had been scorched in a frying pan. Consulting the textbook written by professor of forensic sciences N. A. Obolonskii, they agreed that his smooth skin and manicured fingernails

91. Schwartz, *Spectacular Realities*, 3.

92. *Pl*, 9 October 1909, no. 277.

93. A. Bakhtirov, "V tsarstve trypov," *Pg*, 16 October 1909, no. 284.

94. *Pg*, 20 December 1909, no. 348.

95. *Pl*, 28 October 1909, no. 296.

96. The story was reported in *Pl*, 29 January 1885, no. 27.

97. For example, Susan Morrissey, *Suicide and the Body Politic in Imperial Russia* (New York: Cambridge University Press, 2006), 340–42; and Irina Paperno, *Suicide as a Cultural Institution in Dostoevsky's Russia* (Ithaca: Cornell University Press, 1997), chapters 3 and 4.

suggested a member of an intellectual profession.[98] His toes, though, indicated that he wore common, unfashionable shoes.[99] Moreover, the killer had cleverly cut off the ears because their uniqueness facilitated recognition; Gilevich had "what the common people call jugged ears."[100] Polyps found in the nasal cavity might have affected his speech, and his maid had thought his accent either "Polish, Jewish, or Estonian."[101] Stomach contents gave no clues, and blood analysis revealed no signs of poison. Teeth played an especially valuable role. One woman searching for her husband, after fainting from the smell, was persuaded to examine the teeth: the back ones had been filled, unlike her husband's, who was also missing a tooth still in this jaw.[102] The forensic experts made a plaster cast of the teeth and photographed them. A later report that the cast of the teeth had been shown to Gilevich's mother to check for resemblance, while highly doubtful, underscored the captivation with seeking out the "silent witnesses." Medical authorities also had to debunk the notion from popular science that the victim's retina had retained a photographic image of his killer's face.[103]

Perhaps the paranormal could explain what science could not. Petersburg's most powerful medium, Madame Andropova, the wife of an executive at the Noble Bank, claimed to have helped the police solve two murders. For information about the corpse, she had communicated with the soul of a recent suicide, Father Grigorii Gapon, the Orthodox priest who had unwittingly become a political figure when he sparked the 1905 Revolution by leading unarmed workers into an attack near the Winter Palace on Bloody Sunday. Her prediction that the killer had left Russia proved correct, but not that he had sailed to Latin America.[104]

In the face of so much uncertainty, when Konstantin Gilevich identified the body as that of his missing brother, the press at first called him a "student-maniac."[105] Insisting that this was Andrei, Konstantin questioned the police about the twenty thousand rubles his brother was supposed to have on him from the sale of the family estate in Bessarabia, which was the apparent motive for his murder.[106] His demand for the death certificate led to his arrest on suspicion of fraud. Released, Konstantin grew a tail of policemen and reporters who crowded after him on public transport and into restaurants. Rearrested a few days later, after the detectives had determined Andrei to be the killer, Konstantin landed in a holding cell. *Odesskii listok* (The Odessa Sheet) wondered if he could be hypnotized to tell the truth.[107] Never renouncing his original story, the little brother wrote his own chapter in this diabolical drama when, on November 17, he hanged himself in his cell with

98. *Pg*, 14 October 1909, no. 282.

99. *Odesskii listok* (hereafter *Ol*), 18 October 1909, no. 238.

100. *Rs* 13 October 1909, no. 234.

101. *Pl*, 8 October 1909, no. 276.

102. *Pl*, 9 October 1909, no. 277.

103. *Pg*, 6 January 1910, no. 5.

104. Interview in *Pg*, 27 October 1909, no. 295. Another occultist claimed to have foretold Gilevich's capture in Paris. In *Pg*, 17 December 1909, no. 346.

105. *Ol*, 10 October 1909, no. 231.

106. Another brother, Vasilii, asked the police about the money again when he came for his brother's body. The missing money remained the unsolved mystery.

107. *Ol*, 27 October 1909, no. 245.

a towel. The case not yet solved, some people speculated aloud about the possibility of police brutality against this student.[108]

## Urbanizing Russia

Rapid and massive urbanization characterized postreform Russia, as it had Europe in the wake of the industrial revolution. The urban population doubled between 1867 and 1897, the year of the first modern census, from 6.67 to 12.49 million. It doubled yet again in the next two decades; by 1916, 21 percent of the population lived in cities. The population of Petersburg more than tripled, from 491,000 to more than 1.5 million by 1910. Moscow's quadrupled, from 369,000 to 1,481,000. Odessa, the primary port through which exports and imports passed, jumped from a population of 100,000 to over 600,000.[109] Stolypin had touched off a mass migration of peasants in 1906 when he freed them from their collective obligation to pay for the land that the government had sold them as one of the conditions for the emancipation in 1861. By simply cancelling the debt, he opened the floodgates for many of them, especially the men, to escape Karl Marx's "idiocy of rural life." Like these peasants, Gilevich was a migrant, one of the dominant demographic of urban Russia: the young male who moved to a new city.[110]

What the peasant and professional shared in common was the problem that they posed for sociologists. Two of the era's leading figures, Émile Durkheim and Georg Simmel, took up the consequences of social dislocation when modern life cut people adrift from their traditional moorings. Durkheim worried that the resultant anomie contributed to suicide.[111] Simmel, who wrote specifically about city life as a new kind of phenomenon, argued that its stimulating environment had physiological effects. In *The Metropolis and Mental Life* (1903), Simmel seemed to have anticipated Gilevich in his emphasis on the rationality of the successful city dweller, which spoke to Gilevich's mastery of himself and the logic of his plan.[112]

The killer had the foresight to recognize how living in a city offered new modes of experience, what sociologist Louis Wirth later termed "urbanism, or that complex of traits which makes up the characteristic mode of life in cities."[113] Gilevich also fit into Michel de Certeau's later poststructural musings on negotiating urbanism as one of the "practice(s) of everyday life."[114] Another admirer of Baudelaire's *flâneur*, de Certeau found a potential

108. The presence of a priest at the cemetery, despite the suicide, exacerbated doubts. *Rs*, 21 November 1909, no. 268. V. M. Doroshevich, "V lesu," *Rs*, 29 November 1909, no. 274.

109. Michael Hamm, ed., *The City in Late Imperial Russia* (Bloomington: Indiana University Press, 1986), 3.

110. J. William Leasure and Robert A. Lewis, "Internal Migration in Russia in the Late Nineteenth Century," *Slavic Review* 27, no. 3 (1968): 383.

111. Émile Durkheim, *On Suicide*, trans. Robin Buss, intro. Richard Sennett, with notes by Alexander Riley (New York: Penguin Books, 2006).

112. Excerpt from Georg Simmel, *The Metropolis and Mental Life* (1903), republished in *The Nineteenth-Century Visual Culture Reader*, ed. Vanessa R. Schwartz and Jeannene Przyblyski (London : Routledge, 2004), 47–60, 51.

113. Louis Wirth, "Urbanism as a Way of Life," *The American Journal of Sociology* 44, no. 1 (1938): 7. Urbanization, in contrast, simply "denotes the development and extensions of these factors."

114. Michel de Certeau, "Walking the City," in *The Practice of Everyday Life*, trans. Steven Randall (Berkeley: University of California Press, 1984), 91–110.

renegade in the pedestrian who refuses to be bound by the grids mapped out by streets. Challenging the power of the city to structure a rationalized existence within it, the pedestrian strolling at will asserts his or her individual freedom. Gilevich evoked de Certeau's pedestrian, one who resisted the system by manipulating it, presenting an alternative rebel to those who had manned the barricades in Russian streets in 1905.

The daily papers peddled this urbanism, helping their audiences to negotiate the disarray of city life. As Peter Fritzsche has argued about Berlin in 1900, mass-oriented publications, especially newspapers, "constructed a second-hand metropolis which gave a narrative to the concrete one and choreographed its encounters."[115] The news stories tracked the action, taking readers where they could not go themselves. Discussing the crime with each other helped residents to overcome some of the social distances that otherwise separated them, giving the heterogeneous populations a common stock of urban references.

Readers around the empire met the killer personally even before he had been identified. Several men, including the journalist V. N. Lebedev, wrote of encounters with a suspicious "Fedorov," whose advertisement in *Russkoe slovo* for a personal secretary they had answered.[116] The details of these adventures ultimately helped to solve the case. The job promised travel, and Fedorov insisted that his respondents provide him with personal documents for an international passport. As part of the interview, Fedorov set out with Lebedev for a business trip to Nizhnii Novgorod so quickly that he had no time to pack. On board the train, Fedorov switched their destination to Kiev. The new employer's strange behavior included spilling ink on Lebedev's jacket, which he then insisted be exchanged for one of his own. In Kiev, Fedorov demanded that they take in the local baths.[117] Later, in their hotel room, he had tried to entice Lebedev to drink wine that the latter believed had been doctored. Back in Moscow, Fedorov suggested that they hire another assistant, but he never called the reporter again. The puzzling encounters with Fedorov fit the facts as ultimately determined: the murderer had wanted to engage someone of his own build, without identifiable birthmarks, under whose international passport he could travel.

Lebedev's reports sparked memories of other close encounters with the killer from several cities. Gilevich had centered his plan in Moscow, where he began placing his advertisements. Whether or not Gilevich himself was involved, the other suspicious incidents reminded of the dangers of urbanism, of the stranger who instigates a deceptively friendly encounter. One man reported being hired by Gilevich, who poured something in a beer that the man then refused to drink.[118] More ominously, a man resembling Gilevich had paid three months in advance for an apartment in Odessa. Shortly thereafter he telegraphed that he no longer needed it. The landlady found morphine, surgical instruments,

115. Peter Fritzsche, *Reading Berlin 1900* (Cambridge: Harvard University Press, 1996), 1.

116. *Rs*, 14 October 1909, no. 235 ran a story about the ad and a "Mr. X" who had responded. The ad called for "an intelligent man, free from the draft, 24–29," and promised a "good salary." Reprinted in *Ol*, 22 October 1909, no. 241.

117. Konstantin had tried to assure the incredulous police that because he and his brother visited the baths together often, he was completely familiar with his body. *Rs*, 11 October 1909, no. 233.

118. *Pl*, 14 October 1909, no 282.

a hatchet, and prussic acid left behind.[119] An actor answered the ad, but did not follow up because he had just landed a job at the Intimate Theater.[120]

Once Gilevich's face hit the papers, citizens around the empire spotted him erroneously.[121] A mock-up in *Peterburgskaia gazeta* of how he might disguise himself reminded readers that they could not trust their eyes. Gilevich's use of mass transportation made it possible for him to be a disciplined practitioner of urbanism rather than simply a "Petersburg killer." Not only did the train allow him to integrate Moscow, Kiev, Odessa, and Paris into a murder that took place in Petersburg, but he also refused to be locked into the grids formed by the railway, evident in his quick redirection of destinations. Ironically, in liberalism's search for the self-actualizing individual in Russia, few could take center stage more effortlessly than this confidence man extraordinaire, the *flâneur-poseur* marking his territory because he understood how the new systems produced by urbanization functioned, and he exploited them so cold-bloodedly.

Reactionary Russia offered the first plausible post–Konstantin Gilevich identification of the corpse. The murder had taken place against a distinctive political backdrop, the landscape littered with victims of revolutionary violence. A washerwoman from the laundry at the Warsaw train station identified the body as that of her son, Ivan Barkov. She pointed to a spot on the stomach, now blackened with decay, as his birthmark. When doubts arose about this, she impressed Professor Kosorotov to reexamine the spot, which he stated could have been a burned-off birthmark.[122] State councilors rarely do the bidding of laundresses, so presumably Kosorotov actively wanted to participate. Perhaps he believed he could solve the puzzle.

Most important, Barkov's mother had a legitimate motive: the missing Ivan had very recently severed his fractious relationship with the anti-Semitic Union of Russian People. Better known as the Black Hundreds, this political party's history of violence became a matter of national concern when one member hired an unemployed worker to assassinate the Duma deputy M. Ia. Herzenstein outside his Finnish dacha in July 1906. A converted Jew and a member of the constitutionalist Kadet Party, Herzenstein had earned the wrath of the Black Hundreds because of both his ethnicity and vociferous support for increasing the land available for peasant purchase.[123] A potential witness for the prosecution, Barkov had been offered money from the party leader A. I. Dubrovin to leave the city in late August. Disappearing with only twenty-five of the promised hundred rubles, Barkov told his mother that he could not find work, and that party members had threatened his life.[124]

119. *Pg*, 17 October 1909, no. 285.

120. *Ol*, 22 October 1909, no. 241.

121. Someone reported seeing him on a streetcar in Petersburg and asked, "Aren't you dead?" *Gazeta kopeika* (hereafter *Gk*), 12 October 1909, no. 441.

122. *Gk*, 16 October 1909, no. 445. Kosorotov would also perform the autopsy on Gilevich's brain; and as the empire's chief forensic expert, he autopsied the body of Andrei Iushchinskii, the boy reputed to have been killed in Kiev in 1911 as the victim of an alleged Jewish blood libel. The autocracy paid Kosorotov handsomely when he declared the death a ritual murder. Robert Weinberg, "Ritual Murder in Late Imperial Russia: The Trial of Mendel Beilis" (unpublished manuscript).

123. Ascher, *Revolution of 1905*, 167.

124. *Pl*, 15 October 1909, no. 282.

# Преступный Петербургъ

### КЪ УБІЙСТВУ ГИЛЕВИЧА.

#### ГРИМЪ ПРЕСТУПНИКОВЪ

Fig. 20. How Gilevich might have disguised himself.

Murderous politics made a plausible scenario. Socialist revolutionaries employed tactics equally aggressive to those of the Black Hundreds, and could claim partial responsibility for the more than 3,500 tsarist officials either killed or wounded in the first year of the revolution.[125] Blood flowed copiously on both sides of the law.[126] Moreover, the Azef case was still fresh because Lopukhin's double-agent terrorist remained at large. Initially, *Peterburgsksia gazeta* reported that the careful planning involved showed the murder in Leshtukov Lane to be political, but this defied the logic that assassins would want their victim known.[127] G. G. Weber, the civil plaintiff for Herzenstein's wife in the trial of her husband's assassin then underway, told reporters that Barkov had originally agreed to testify, but then recanted.[128] This might be a motive for murder, but after examining photos, Weber said that Barkov bore no resemblance to Gilevich.

The Black Hundreds connection had another link. Duma deputy V. M. Purishkevich, formerly a member of the union and still a prominent reactionary, was from Bessarabia, as was the Gilevich family. Comparing photographs and handwriting proved inconclusive because people saw what they wanted to. Barkov's mother received a letter supposedly from him in Evpatoriia on October 20, but had he written it? Would this illiterate woman even recognize her son's penmanship? Another rumor told of Barkov receiving a job from an engineer, but relatives dismissed Ivan as a "compulsive liar."[129] Finally, on October 23, Barkov returned to Petersburg from Moscow, where he had been working in the office of a salt company. Filippov grew annoyed that despite the dragnet, no officials had recognized him in any of the instances that he had shown his passport.[130] Whether because of ignorance or indifference, the public did not willingly seek out contact with the police if not personally involved. In an even graver affront, the French police initially hesitated to cooperate with Filippov's men because they suspected that the Russian government was attempting to disguise an antitsarist political persona as a monstrous murderer.[131]

Russia's newspaper readers must have been surprised when Gilevich turned up in Paris, because the rumors had sent him south, to Constantinople.[132] A report that Gilevich had disguised himself as a Hindu and boarded an English ship showed that nothing was too fanciful to dim the power of this particular puzzle to inflame imaginations.[133] Filippov himself was reported to have pursued him to Bessarabia, Stavropol, Constantinople, Serbia, and Montenegro, only to return empty-handed. Although it is improbable that Filippov would absent himself

125. Catherine Merridale writes that "between October 1905 and September 1906, 3611 tsarist officials were killed or wounded." *Night of Stone: Death and Memory in Twentieth-Century Russia* (New York: Viking, 2001), 65.

126. S. B. Pavlov, *Opyt pervoi revoliutsii: Rossiia, 1900–1907* (Moscow: Akademicheskii proekt, 2008), especially chapter 8.

127. *Pg*, 6, 12 October 1909, nos. 274, 280.

128. *Pg*, 18 October 1909, no. 284.

129. *Pl*, 15 October 1909, no. 282.

130. *Pl*, 24 October 1909, no. 292.

131. *Pg* had complained that both the French and German papers were both conflating political crimes in Russia with the Gilevich case. *Pg*, 20 December 1909, no. 349.

132. I confess that when following this story I was taken aback when he turned up in Paris, caught so quickly. It inspired my respect for Filippov, who had played the clues sufficiently close to the vest that he did not show his hand to the killer in the French capital, who undoubtedly was following the story more avidly even than I.

133. *Pl*, 2 November 1909, no. 300.

from Petersburg for such a lengthy wild goose chase, he did not correct these stories that led south. When he identified the missing student Podlutskii to be the victim, from postcards sent to his family from Western Europe, he did not share the information with reporters.[134]

The inaccuracies did not impede the narration, because what mattered was plotting a coherent story. South was the logical direction for Gilevich to have traveled, given that he had lived in Bessarabia and Kiev, and his passport under the name "Fedorov" had made him a resident of Stavropol, where his brother Vasilii had lived. Another culturally inspired logic also suggested the South rather than the West: the nature of the crime. In an interview shortly after the discovery, Professor N. A. Vel'iaminov, a surgeon with military experience in Asia, thought it to be the work of bashi-bazouki, irregulars in the Ottoman Army who cut off parts of the faces of their enemies.[135] And there was something inexplicably savage about this killing. More cruel than the death of Alexei Volokhov, found in pieces in his cellar? More cold-blooded than Daria Sokolova bashing in skulls in Gusev Lane? Andrei Gilevich was a professional, not a peasant. The rationale with which he planned and executed this crime fashioned him a new type of barbarian, a modern one.

Mobile murderers make especially attractive protagonists in narratives of urbanism because of their immediate and intrinsically sensational engagement with the popular imagination. The best-known city killer from the turn of the century, Jack the Ripper, can be credited with creating a distinctively urban criminal, one who targeted anonymous victims and wrote to newspapers about his actions. Victims could also be products of urbanism. The young female tourists enticed by Henry Holmes into the torture palace he built in his Chicago hotel in 1893 were women who had come to the big city to enjoy the World's Columbian Exposition.[136] Gilevich had a predecessor in Germany's Rudolph Hennig, who in 1905 murdered a man to acquire his identity. Hennig had promised that for five hundred marks he would find a better job for the domestic waiter, and insisted that he needed the man's references. When the aspirant brought his papers and money, Hennig shot him, stole the papers and money, then attempted a daring escape across the rooftops of Berlin.[137] The Ripper, Hennig, and Gilevich supplied vicarious thrills for those who felt trapped in the urban grid. News about the chase for Henning included a description of his clothing, which prompted some city citizens to dress like him.[138]

## The Stranger among Us

Once identified by name, the considerably more intriguing question arose: who *was* Andrei Gilevich? The press sought to explain his motives and actions. "Avaricious by nature" seemed too facile a characterization, given the nature of his crime. He had a police

134. Not until Gilevich was captured did Filippov inform the press about Podlutskii. *Pl*, 17 December 1909, no. 346.

135. *Pg*, 7 October 1909, no. 275.

136. Erik Larson, *The Devil in the White City: Murder, Magic, and Madness at the Fair That Changed America* (New York: Crown, 2003).

137. Benjamin Hett, *Death in the Tiergarten: Murder and Criminal Justice in the Kaiser's Berlin* (Cambridge: Harvard University Press, 2004), 214. Caught in 1906, Hennig received the death penalty from his jurors.

138. Fritzsche, *Reading Berlin 1900*, 160.

file in Moscow, where he had been indicted for embezzlement in an investment scheme that made clear that he knew how to exploit the workings of capitalism. The details, murky and hyped up for resale, nonetheless piece together a scenario in which Andrei had stolen money from investors in a soap factory. His lawyer's complaints about the money still owed him gave this story a basis in fact, but others sound improbable.[139] Gilevich had supposedly shaken down a member of Petersburg's preeminent Eliseev merchant family, falsely accusing him of theft and threatening to tarnish his reputation by making the accusation public. Nowhere else did the unlikelihood that he owned an automobile appear, but Gilevich was said to have taken his car in for repairs and then driven away from the garage without paying the bill. Managing a seltzer factory in Kiev, which burned down under suspicion of arson, supplied his background in insurance fraud.[140]

The question of his sanity proved difficult to pose because he had orchestrated so rational a plan, which would have disallowed a plea of pathological *affekt*. Mental illness was just that, a sickness, with recognizable symptoms and accepted sources of infection: alcoholism, syphilis, or heredity. Gilevich betrayed no evidence of weakness for either vodka or women, but his suicidal brother pointed to the possibility for hereditary degeneracy. The Gilevich family found itself under public scrutiny. Nothing of note materialized about the deceased father, who left behind a wife, four sons, and a daughter. The information published about them cannot be verified, but the truth about the family members matters less than the background they could supply to explain Andrei's personality. The widow had sold the family estate in Bessarabia and moved with her daughter, Olga, to Moscow. Olga had married a much older landowner "because she had become accustomed to comfortable circumstances," but divorced him after two years.[141] Reporters met Olga when she came from Moscow to verify Konstantin's original identification of the body in the bed, which she could not identify.[142] The mother, suffering a stroke from the accusations against her sons, surrendered no family skeletons.[143]

Of the brothers, the oldest, Nikolai, had a sterling reputation as a military officer. Konstantin had attempted suicide once before, and supposedly complained of headaches from the bullet still lodged in his temple. This farfetched description, highlighted by his plaintive assertion that "it doesn't matter to me, I don't have long to live," portrayed a young man more vulnerable than vile.[144] Two points worked in his favor: even in his suicide note he denied knowledge of Andrei's plot, and taking one's life in a Russian jail could still be met with a certain skepticism. This left brother Vasilii as the best potential for evidence of genetic degeneracy. Once a bureaucrat in the governor's office in Stavropol, Vasilii was now presumed guilty of getting Andrei the false passport under the name "Fedorov." Ominously, the older brother had killed in a duel the man who had exposed his multiple corruptions, and then "strolled away from the site whistling a popular song."[145] Yet

139. *Pl*, 12 October 1909, no. 280.
140. *Ol*, 20 October 1909, no. 239.
141. *Pg*, 16 October 1909, no. 284.
142. *Pl*, 12 October 1909, no. 280.
143. *Pl*, 14 October 1909, no. 282.
144. *Pg*, 13 October 1909, no. 281.
145. *Pg*, 16 October 1909, no. 284.

when the "well-dressed" Vasilii arrived to collect Andrei's body, news about him centered around his anger with the police for Konstantin's suicide. When told to sign the protocol affirming that the body from Paris was indeed his brother's, "his hands shook and his eyes filled with tears." No longer whistling a merry tune, he sobbed with his face in his hands. Unwilling to concede Andrei's guilt, Vasilii raised the specter of yet another man out there, killing and assuming identities.[146]

The question of why haunted, raising the hope that Andrei's head could say something. *Peterburgskaia gazeta* regretted that Russian criminologists did not believe in phrenology, the measuring of the skull to explain mental functions, which it wanted applied to Gilevich. The editors claimed that "in New York courses are taught in it, and for more than thirty years it has helped many thousands of people to understand themselves better." Therefore, if "our distinguished contemporary scientists do not consider its data sufficiently sound" they should at least explain why.[147] The eagerly anticipated autopsy of Gilevich's brain revealed a "monkey furrow" reaching farther and deeper than normal, but many people shared this anomaly. The autopsy results could not dispute that "Gilevich was completely healthy and committed his evil act in full control of his mental reasoning."[148] Ultimately, Gilevich's essential ordinariness generated the most disturbing questions because it could not mark him as different. The *Gazeta kopeika* (The Kopeck Gazette) columnist "The Wanderer" (O. Blotermants) offered a pessimistic appraisal: "Gileviches don't fall from the heavens. They are our flesh and blood, children of these times of troubles and moral collapse." Like too many ordinary Russians, Gilevich did not respect honest work and just wanted fast cash.[149]

Journalism provided only one mode for telling his story. A modern man, Gilevich also became modernism's man. Perhaps the cultural wave inspired by Friedrich Nietzsche's radical critiques of morality and individualism could account for him. In a modernist pseudo-autobiography, *The Killer in Leshtukov Lane*, Boris Ognev turned to the symbolism of the Silver Age of culture then in full flower in Russia.[150] Opening with an epigraph from Leonid Andreev's experimental play *The Life of Man* (1906), in which the unnamed hero challenges Fate to a duel, this rambling booklet, pretentiously peppered with Nietzscheisms to the point of being nonsensical, caricatured a Gilevich of extreme cynicism and egoism. This version showed evidence of Saninism, a cultural phenomenon inspired by the hedonistic antihero created by Mikhail Artsybashev, whose reputation for self-centered decadence survived the censorship that pulled the novel from the shelves quickly after publication in 1907.[151] However poor his prose, Ognev attempted a modernist aesthetic, which would imply an implicit heroism of an individual struggling to find meaning in modern life.

146. Interviewed in *Rs*, 16 December 1909, no. 288, Vasilii also chastised the authorities for their callousness toward his mother. *Pl*, 1 January 1910, no. 1.

147. *Pg*, 22 December 1909, no. 351.

148. *Pg*, 2 January 1910, no. 2.

149. Skitalets, "Pochemu on ubil?," *Gk*, 21 October 1909, no. 450.

150. Boris Ognev, *Ubiitsa v Leshtukovom pereulke v Peterburge* (Moscow: n. p., 1909).

151. Otto Boele, *Erotic Nihilism in Late Imperial Russia: The Case of Mikhail Artsybashev's Sanin* (Madison: University of Wisconsin Press, 2009).

Ognev's engineer-protagonist has three conversations, one with a brother, the second with a prostitute, and the third with skeletons in a graveyard. The sky is black, the clouds grey, the wind sharp, the waves violent, and gloom fills the air. The only color to be seen is shades of red, blood. When his brother seeks "cleanliness of spirit," the engineer assures him that "life is for the strong" and "there is no God." He describes the killing in an "atmosphere filled with miasmas of murderous forces": "blow after blow hit into the soft body, and hot, sticky blood splattered and flowed. I sliced, ripping him like a pestilent crow, tearing pieces from a cold corpse." He tells the prostitute, "I don't know how this happened. I grew up evil. I fell in love with evil." He has a moment of remorse in the cemetery when he grabs a skull, "kisses it and searches in the eye sockets for that spark of tender life." When the scarlet sun rises on his corpse, lying at the edge of a grave, he appears to have been rewarded with death. Although he had mentioned to his brother that he needed money, that plays no motive in this version. Just incomprehensible evil.[152]

In stark contrast, a woman who had known him in childhood, S. A. Anichkova (Baroness Taube), drew Gilevich as a highly sympathetic, multidimensional person in her poignant memoirs of their relationship. Anichkova recalled happy days spent with "Dusia," as his mother called him. Friends from the age of ten, Andrei showed great empathy when he dropped his male buddies to play with her, the lone female, affording her "that equality for which I had long dreamed." Once, when she cut her hand with a cockle shell, "he turned so white that I momentarily forgot about my wound."[153] The irony was palpable: the boy who would become so harrowing with a knife could not stand the sight of blood.

The Andrei of the baroness's memory bore little resemblance to the one who swallowed cyanide in Paris. Although they had lost contact for many years, they reconnected when he was a student at the Technological Institute. She found him much as he was when they had parted, serious, introspective, and devoted to his family, especially his mother and younger brother "Kostik." This ambitious Andrei planned to graduate at the head of his class and then "sprout wings," that is, parlay his engineering degree into an undefined but innovative business. When they met again several years later, though, he had suffered failures and accusations of embezzlement, which he claimed were false. Now she saw the first traces of madness reflected in the "disturbed smile" that crossed his face when he told her that "it seems to me that fate itself has taken up arms against me, and no matter what I do . . . it pushes me from my path, down some dark road that I cannot makeout clearly."

The baroness ends her story with pity for his "accidental victims," the "one who died so tragically," his suicidal brother, and his grieving mother. She reserves particular compassion, though, "as any of us would, for an intelligent and richly talented man whose brain, under adverse conditions, gradually became hypnotized by an obsession, falling into a madness, until, at last, he could spare neither his own life nor that of others."[154] Even the Orthodox Church bemoaned the two lives lost, Gilevich's as well as his victim's.[155]

152. Ognev, *Ubiitsa*, 8–9, 18, 24, 28, 31.

153. S. A. Anichkova (Baronessa Taube), *Prestuplenie ili bezumie?: Vospominaniia ob Andree Gileviche* (St. Petersburg: N. G. Ul', 1910), 4, 6.

154. Ibid., 30, 31.

155. *Prestupnost' chelovekoubiistva i tiazhest' otvetstvennost' za nego* (Tambov: N. I. Berdonosov, 1910), 4.

A turn to the contemporaneous United States will shed light on what this indecipherable Gilevich says about post-1905 Russia. In her study of the crime (she only studies murder) in nineteenth-century America, Karen Halttunen reminds us that it is the narrative that assigns the meaning to the murder.[156] She carefully formulates how writing about the premeditated taking of a life changed over time, moving from cautionary confessional literature that believed human nature in and of itself to be depraved, into tales of Gothic horror that treated the killer as a moral alien.[157] Halttunen's larger objective is to trace the cultural transformation of Puritanism into Enlightenment humanism in the United States, where with encroaching secularization human nature became understood as "intrinsically good, rational, and capable of self-government." Relocating killers beyond the purview of liberal humanism allowed American culture to maintain its enlightened values. In the same vein, it allowed for the popular fascination evident in mass-circulation sensationalism; Americans could treat themselves to the guilty pleasure of reading the sordid details.

It is the disconnects between Halttunen's thesis and the Gilevich story that shed light on Russia. She argued that enlightened humanism rendered violence pornographic in the United States because it imbued pain with a "shock value . . . redefining it as forbidden and therefore obscene."[158] For one thing, Russians did not need the Enlightenment to see killers humanely; they had long sympathized with them as *neschastnye*. Poring over the details of Gilevich's deed, or standing in line to see his victim, might have stimulated pleasure in the audience, but it was neither guilty nor pornographic because pain in Russia was not obscene. The government had made that clear in its response to revolution. The proximity to bloodletting could have provided more catharsis than prurience. Catherine Merridale's observation that "no one is sure exactly how it works, but most people agree that there is some kind of connection between Russia's culture and its history of high mortality" captures some of the difficulty that Westerners have trying to understand Russia from the perspective of the enlightened liberal humanism discussed in Halttunen's study.[159]

In the ensuing years Gilevich's name would reappear, invoked as a shorthand reference for the dark corners of modernity and morality, but he remained a conundrum. Psychiatrist P. A. Ostankov declared him "a typical example of moral insanity," but offered no explanation for how the engineer had fallen ill.[160] Summing up his twenty years as an expert psychiatric witness, A. D. Davydov spoke of the dangers posed by someone whose "internal self cannot distinguish between good and evil, who is morally blind to beauty."[161] Simmel summed up the quandary that Gilevich posed for Russians who recognized the

156. Karen Halttunen, *Murder Most Foul: The Killer and the American Gothic Imagination* (Cambridge: Harvard University Press, 1998), 2.

157. As Halttunen explains, "while Gothic horror made murder unspeakable . . . an endless ritual without moral comprehension . . . Gothic mystery made the crime unknowable . . . resistant to narrative closure" (ibid., 133).

158. Ibid., 4, 88, 69.

159. Merridale, *Night of Stone*, 47.

160. *Pg*, 27 December 1909, no. 355.

161. A. D. Davydov, "K kazuistike vrachebnoi ekspertiy v sudakh," *Vestnik obshchei gigenii, sudebnoi i prakticheskoi meditsiny*, no. 12 (1910): 1605. He connected Gilevich to the "representative of the fair sex, Maria Tarnovskaia," the antiheroine of chapter 6.

modern man in him: "the deepest problems of modern life derive from the claim of the individual to preserve the autonomy and individuality of his existence in the face of over-whelming social forces," which included the pressures exerted by culture and history.[162] Gilevich personified a central paradox of modernity: the alienated individual who inspired the collectivity of the crowd to search him out in all his guises.

## Conclusion

The Gilevich story sparked humor, too. Less than two weeks after the discovery in Leshtukov Lane, before Filippov could boast of having all the threads in his hands, popular satirist Teffi (Nadezhda Buchinskaya) had poked fun at the cacophony of theories stimu-lating street chatter. "Our Pinkertons" played upon the current craze of fast-action crime fiction, her would-be detectives confused over Lombroso, phrenology, and numerous other bits of criminology that had sifted into the popular imagination. After debating whether or not the body in the bed had committed suicide, Teffi's characters finally decide that the police had disfigured a body from the morgue in order to catch a killer. "Why did they need a murderer? . . . You'll have to ask them."[163] In other words, the humorist had not yet bought into Filippov's professionalization. She would hardly have been alone.[164]

The story wound down. In doing so, it branched into other aspects of the modern urban experience. Kuntsevich enjoyed national celebrity for his role in Gilevich's capture in Paris, and was spotted at a premier at the Imperial Theater, chatting up an actress during intermission. On January 16, 1910 *Odesskii listok* turned the story from the killer's into his victim's with the headline, "The Case of the Murder of the Student Podlutskii is Coming to its Natural Conclusion."[165] The Petersburg police put together a photo al-bum of this case, including childhood shots of the unlucky student and the unscrupulous engineer, for another spectacular display in the city's museum of criminality.[166] Their volume enjoyed pride of place alongside pictures of the sexton Il'inskii, who had been beheaded, chopped up, and put in a trunk for delivery at the Warsaw station.[167] Visitors could also take in the museum's anthropological bureau, dedicated to the study of the capital's "criminal world."[168] The physical objects on display made criminality tangible rather than sociological.

Filippov found himself competing for headlines in the boulevard press with Russia's most exciting new cop, Tref, the Doberman pinscher who ruled the nascent K-9 corps with Lady by his side. Among the traces that criminals leave behind is their smell, and police dogs

162. Quoted in Salzani, "The City as Crime Scene," 172.

163. Teffi, "Nashi Pinkertoni," in *Rs*, 15 October 1909, no. 236.

164. Neil Weissman recounts how the problems of old continued, and the divisions were "charged with corruption and excessive use of criminal informers." In "Regular Police," 63.

165. *Ol*, 16 January 1910, no. 12.

166. *Pg*, 6 January 1910, no. 5.

167. City Governor N. V. Kleigel founded the first museum devoted to the St. Petersburg police force in 1900. In 1905, it was moved to a larger building, closer to the city's center, now to be administered by the office of the chief of detectives. *Vp*, no. 3 (1907): 20–22.

168. *Vp*, no. 6 (1908): 15. Samara also publicized its police museum, *Vp*, no. 7 (1909): 129.

Fig. 21. Tref, king of the K-9 corps.

had been a favorite topic in *Vestnik politsii*. Prime Minister Stolypin served as honorary chairman for the Society of Police Dogs.[169] Tref caught killers at a train station, howling at three men in a lineup of workers, who it turned out had taken advantage of the violence in 1905 to revenge themselves upon the station director.[170] The commercial press, too, covered Tref.[171] In prescient irony, however, dog excited the same fear as did the unreformed cops. Bystanders scattered when he turned up to sniff out a murder scene.[172] But Tref also starred in his own adventure stories years before the German shepherd Rin Tin Tin got his.[173]

The success of Russia's modern reforms, however, would be challenged in 1910, when three of its citizens stood trial in Venice for the murder of one of their compatriots in the Italian city. Maria Tarnovskaia might have seemed to be floating in a romantic novel when her prison gondola docked daily at court, jeered and cheered as roundly as any actress on stage. The Tarnovskaia trial, the topic of the next chapter, captured the international imagination as its participants unwittingly helped to write narratives of modern nationalism.

169. RGIA, f. 1284, op. 187, d. 27.

170. *Vp*, no. I (1910): 25–26.

171. *Rs* broke the story in the issue of 20 December 1909, no. 292, and *Pl* followed up in the 28 January 1910, no. 27 issue. There had been talk of putting Tref to work on the Gilevich case. *Rs*, 4 December 1909, no. 278.

172. *Vp*, no. 43 (1909): 947.

173. V. Lebedev, an enthusiast of the canine corps, wrote about "Tref's Adventures" in *Vp*, no. 10 (1910): 279–80.

CHAPTER SIX

# THE "DIVA OF DEATH"

### Maria Tarnovskaia and the Degenerate Slavic Soul

"Yes, I killed him. I killed him for money—and a woman—and I didn't get the
money and I didn't get the woman."
—Walter Neff, "Double Indemnity," 1941

She sat sphinxlike in her cell in the Venetian prison. Drawing a portrait of her for readers
in the popular daily *Odesskii listok*, I. Aleksandrovskii described her as "very tall, long and
thin, in the decadent fashion. Her face and nose are also long, with lusterless, unexpressive
eyes." This inability to read her expression enhanced her mystery: "Her face never changes,
her countenance remains perpetually calm, with no traces of passion or self-reflection.
With such a face, it is impossible to guess her intentions, to know her secret thoughts."[1]
Others concurred with him that "she is no beauty," searching instead for reasons of the
soul to explain how this woman had left a trail of bodies, men willing to kill or be killed
for her, from Kiev to Venice.

It was February 1910. Gilevich had only recently been autopsied and buried. Maria
Tarnovskaia was spending her second year in jail because one hotheaded young lover,
Nikolai Naumov, had shot the man she told him she would marry, Count Pavel Komarovskii, in his Italian villa on September 3, 1907. Tarnovskaia and another lover, Moscow lawyer Donatii Prilukov, were charged with "instigating" Naumov's action, and were
awaiting trial with him. Komarovskii was the third, possibly the fourth, victim that she
had left in her wake, and Naumov the second man to have shot one of Tarnovskaia's
lovers in a fit of jealousy. Tarnovskaia captured headlines from Atlanta to Berlin; a story
spiced this heavily was far more fascinating than fiction.[2] Her motive, like Gilevich's, had
been the hundred-thousand-ruble life insurance policy she had persuaded the widowed
Komarovskii to take out, naming her rather than his young son as his beneficiary. Money
could not compete with sex, though, and such mouthwatering incidents as her putting out
cigarettes on Naumov's torso and carving her initials in his chest pushed aside the policy's

---

1. I. Aleksandrovskii, "Zapiski," *Odesskii listok* (hereafter *Ol*), 21 February 1910, no. 42.

2. The serial novel running in *Peterburgskii listok* (hereafter *Pl*) was, appropriately, Princess Olga Bebutova's
*Sredi zolotom i strastiami: Roman iz sovremennoi Peterburgskoi zhizni* (Among Gold and Passions: A Novel of Contemporary Petersburg Life).

premium as the focal point.[3] As *Russkoe slovo* pointed out, "This is not just a bloody affair, but a dirty one."[4]

The quasi-pornography attracted readers initially, but as the story developed, it turned into a study of competing nationalisms, once Italians and Russians alike came to realize the extent to which their respective self-images as modern states lay at stake. Moreover, the racial discourse so prevalent at the turn of the twentieth century, a by-product of the lethal combination of Darwinism and imperialism, figured prominently in this trial. Pleasant historical memories of the Italian architects who had turned St. Petersburg into the "Venice of the north" in the eighteenth century recalled a bygone era, a past long dead. Now the Italians, who had also reformed their legal system, were prosecuting Russians, setting Beccaria and Lombroso against Dostoevsky and Sechenov. Both nations used the trial and coverage of it to assert different interpretations of criminal culpability, mindful that exercises in rendering justice measured the degree of civilization to which they both aspired.

## Backstory

About 1 a.m. on December 6, 1903, a party of four left Kiev's Grand Hotel. Chattering in French, they had dined in a private room, sending for gypsies from the orchestra to serenade them with guitars. What happened next was unclear because "there were no electric lights, there was only gaslight on the street." One of the men, Vasilii Tarnovskii, went for his carriage. The other, Stefan Borzhevskii, had assisted the women with their coats and was helping Tarnovskii's wife, Maria, into the coach. Suddenly, Tarnovskii shot Borzhevskii in the head, with the words "now it will be better." The women ran back into the hotel screaming for help. Tarnovskii told his driver to take him to a policeman and "tell him I killed someone." Riding past the Noble's Club, the hysterical Tarnovskii saw a friend and stopped. The friend ultimately got Tarnovskii to the police, where he begged to be arrested. Ultimately, he was placed under house arrest at another friend's domicile, and Maria took their two small children to stay with her father. Borzhevskii underwent several operations. Thought to be recovering, he traveled to Yalta, where he died in February from infected bone chips in his brain, his lover Maria Tarnovskaia at his bedside.[5]

Vasilii Tarnovskii stood trial for Borzhevskii's murder in January 1905, two weeks after Bloody Sunday in St. Petersburg. As the citizens of the empire slowly began to gather their political muster for the general strike that would bring Nicholas II to his knees by October, the trial of Vasilii Tarnovskii would seem more a postscript on reckless aristocratic

---

3. A word about sources. I read the Russian newspapers extensively, and some of the international coverage. *Ol* rushed into print a book about the trial, the material taken largely from trial transcripts: L. Evlef and E. Miks, *Delo Tarnovskoi* (Odessa: Tip. "Odesskogo listka," 1910).

4. *Russkoe slovo* (hereafter *Rs*), 25 March 1910, no. 69.

5. The details of this trial are from "Delo V. V. Tarnovskogo," *Sd* 24, no. 3 (1905): 161–222, which included the bill of indictment and much of the stenographic account of the trial. Details contained in this paragraph are from 167. Subsequent page numbers for quotes will be given parenthetically in the text.

rule than the prelude to an international incident. *Sudebnye dramy* covered the tawdry tale in order "to raise a corner of the curtain on the noisy and merry life of these parasites, saturated with perfume and decadence, forever on holiday." The "court ladies" were "in ecstasy" over Vasilii, "concentrating on his every word and devouring him with their eyes" (171). The witness pool consisted largely of servants, waiters, and hotel personnel who supplied delicious details of the lives of the spoiled rich. Tarnovskii's father had hired S. A. Andreevskii, whose career had begun so righteously in 1878 when he had refused to prosecute Vera Zasulich. Such a pricey defense was not necessary when the reluctant procurator himself blamed the victim, Borzhevskii, for "playing upon the delicate feelings of women . . . and the weak will of Tarnovskii." The prosecutor asserted that "for battle with such a powerful destroyer of the family hearth, a man of stronger character was needed than the accused who stands before you." He concluded that "I cannot hide from you that I do not wish to prosecute him." The jurors needed less than a minute to acquit (220).

Their decision might seem a foregone conclusion, given that Vasilii had shot someone whom everyone knew to be his wife's lover. Andreevskii, however, was the only one to describe Tarnovskii as "cuckolded." Even then, he applied the adjective only after "it had become clear that Vasilii would be acquitted, and the air had lightened because that was what everyone wanted." Andreevskii closed with what had become the standard signifier: "Juries don't convict *neschastnye*" (222). Tarnovskii admitted to firing the shot, but swore to having no recollection of having done so, nor of having any desire to kill Borzhevskii. The centerpiece of the trial was less his wife's affair than Tarnovskii's unwillingness to duel. Before his death Borzhevskii had given a statement to the judicial investigator, read aloud at the trial. He had fallen in love with Maria that summer and followed the couple to the Bavarian spa at Kissingen. The lovers met for trysts when Vasilii was away on business. Borzhevskii had heard gossip that Vasilii beat Maria. At a ball less than a week before the fatal dinner party, he witnessed the husband's rudeness to Maria and challenged him to a duel. Vasilii refused. Posthumous testimony about Vasilii's abuse of Maria was also read aloud from Borzhevskii's friend V. A. Stal', "a handsome man with the fine features of an ancient Roman," who had killed himself after the shot and before the trial "because it is my right to do so!" An enigmatic report from Vasilii's trial would figure prominently in Maria's trial: that the divorced Stal', at the hour of his death, had sent a "colossal bouquet of white roses to an unknown woman" (188–89).

How had these three principles ended up together for a convivial evening at the Grand Hotel? Maria, it seemed, wanted the two men to make up, and at supper they had agreed to meet for breakfast the next morning. The question of Vasilii's character arose from his refusal to fight with Borzhevskii. The husband's reasoning was that he wanted to divorce his wife, so therefore her having an affair did not insult his honor. It seemed that all who knew Vasilii thought him "weak-willed" (*slabokharaternyi*). He had wept in the police station, knelt in prayer for Borzhevskii's recovery, and had a medical record of physiological degeneracy, neurasthenia, and heart problems. In addition, his teenage brother had killed himself after falsifying his grades, ashamed that their father would soon discover his transgression.

Significantly, witnesses differentiated between a weak will and cowardice. In 1900, another of his wife's paramours, Pavel Tolstoi, had challenged Tarnovskii to a duel. After declining initially, the two met in Nice, France, where although technically illegal, duels were still fought according to established rules. When Tolstoi cut Vasilii's hand in the sword fight, the doctor in attendance called the fight off. Blood had been drawn, which met the rules of engagement. In a glimpse of what was to come, the French newspaper *Figaro* reported on this duel.

For all the adulterous drama, it was the medical experts who assured Vasilii's acquittal. Much attention had been paid to the details of Vasilii's mental stability at the time he shot, his nerves, loss of memory, and unusually pale skin. Professor Bobrov, in a comparison that would be profound at Maria's trial, spoke for the forensic psychiatrists:

> Abroad, psychiatrists demand specifics about the state of a person's mind only at the very moment of the crime; without that information, they consider the *affekt* to be physiological. The young Russian school teaches us differently. We agree that a person can suffer pathological *affekt* even in the absence of serious mental illness, when there are other circumstances that destroy the person's mental equilibrium, as in this case. (218)

Affirming himself a "student of the Russian school," he declared Vasilii inculpable (218). Had Tarnovskii's wealthy father purchased the prosecution and the experts? Even if he had, what matters is the culturally acceptable frame they applied to Vasilii: a man of absolutely no character, suffering pathological *affekt*.

Maria, "with the profile of a Madonna and the temperament of a Messalina" (161), sat quietly throughout her husband's trial. Vasilii Tarnovskii's life receded from the front pages, replaced by revolution. He and Maria were in the process of getting a divorce, which was difficult but not impossible to accomplish in Orthodox Russia.[6] She had begun her affair with Prilukov, her codefendant in Venice, while consulting with him about the divorce. The narrative of her marriage to Vasilii would be substantively rewritten after Maria went on trial in 1910 when a new lover, Naumov, shot an even newer lover, Komarovskii.

### Death in Venice

Naumov's shot might not have been heard completely around the world, but it made headlines in Western newspapers as the details unraveled.[7] The increasing violence among revolutionaries in Russia had prompted early concerns that this might have been a political assassination. Before dying, though, Komarovskii had explained the romantic element to the Venetian police, who extradited Tarnovskaia and Prilukov from Austria when Naumov implicated them. The evidence that the two had conspired to incite Naumov lay in a series of coded telegrams they sent to each other after she had traveled to provincial Orel, where Naumov lived. She had hoped to use her tearful protest of being forced to marry

---

6. Moreover, a law of 1904 allowed adulterers to remarry. Gregory Freeze, "Matrimonial Sacrament and Profane Stories: Class, Gender, Confession, and the Politics of Divorce in Late Imperial Russia," in *Sacred Stories: Religion and Spirituality in Modern Russia*, ed. Mark D. Steinberg and Heather J. Coleman (Bloomington: Indiana University Press, 2007), 146–78.

7. The story appears in the September 9, 1907 edition of the *Times* of both London and New York.

Fig. 22. Naumov shoots the unsuspecting Komarovskii in his villa.

Komarovskii to trigger him into action. Returning to Vienna, she and Prilukov gave their victims women's names: Naumov was "Bertha" and Komarovskii, "Adele." Maria had put Naumov on a train for Italy and telegraphed Prilukov, "Bertha has the most serious intentions of seeing Adele for the last time." Prilukov then traveled to Venice where, under the name "Zeiffert," he observed what transpired. He then sent an incriminating telegram, signed as Naumov, to Maria from Venice: "You tossed me aside for Komarovskii. I know where he lives. I hate him and will stop this marriage."[8] For his part, Naumov, staying at the luxurious Hotel Danieli, calmly exited Komarovskii's villa in a gondola and took a train to Verona, where he was apprehended several days later.

The story began as an account of the profligate Russian aristocracy, providing yet another example of why they made such unpopular guests in other countries. The three miscreants sat in jail for more than two years as the Italian judiciary put together its case against them. The glacial pace of autocratic response to official Italian requests slowed the process.[9] Naumov's ultrareactionary father had served as governor of Perm Province, which may have retarded efforts. When the case finally came to court, the Italians favored the shootist over his seductress.

8. Evlef and Miks, *Delo Tarnovskoi*, 41–43.
9. *Golos Moskvy*, 2 December 1908.

Despite the fact that he had pulled the trigger, Naumov would never appear as interesting, or as guilty, as the woman with whom he professed to be so deeply in love. The lovesick Lothario Naumov was put forward as the weapon Tarnovskaia had used to kill the wealthy man whom she had persuaded to bequeath her his fortune. Indicted as her accomplice, Prilukov had taken advantage of the national chaos in November 1905 and embezzled from clients before abandoning his own wife and child. Consistently the least sympathetic defendant, Prilukov was also most emblematic of the utter depravity of a situation that came to mean so much more than the sum of its parts. Like Walter Neff, of the pulp potboiler *Double Indemnity*, he had plotted the death of a man who had done him no wrong, for the man's wife and his insurance policy, both of which lay beyond his reach.[10] Running away with Maria, the two lived in Algeria, France, and Austria. Tarnovskaia, with no arrest warrant pending, visited her family in southern Russia, where she made Naumov's acquaintance.

Komarovskii and his first wife had been family friends of the Tarnovskiis when they were a couple. Maria attended his wife's funeral in March 1907, and by August of that year, not only was she engaged to the widower but he had also rewritten his will.[11] In fact, Komarovskii had introduced her to Naumov, since they traveled in the same social circles. The count had welcomed his young acquaintance into his villa, and was stunned when the hothead fired at him five times. "My friend, why do you want to kill me?" he had implored. "You must not marry Maria!" came the reply. Clinging to life for several days, the wounded Komarovskii reportedly sent telegrams begging Tarnovskaia to come. In vain.[12]

### Publicity as a Twentieth-Century Phenomenon

The facts of the case and the profiles of the defendants do not require further commentary on why this case attracted so much press. A story with this level of captivation encouraged the media to continue to improve some of the technologies that were facilitating the scope and style of news coverage. The major Russian papers dispatched special correspondents to Venice. The two that gave the most extended coverage were *Odesskii listok*, given the prominence of the accused in southern Russia, and Moscow's nationally circulated *Russkoe slovo*. European newspapers that boasted countrywide circulations because of their attention to human interest stories also gave extensive coverage: Germany's *Berliner Tageblatt* (Berlin Daily), then in its heyday under editor Theodor Wolff; London's premier tabloid, the *Daily Mail*, the brainchild of Alfred Harmsworth; Austria's liberal bourgeois *Neue Freie Presse* (New Free Press), edited by Moriz Benedikt; and France's *Matin* (Morning),

10. This story by James M. Cain appeared first in *Liberty* magazine in 1935, to be filmed in 1944 by Billy Wilder for Paramount Pictures.

11. B. Minskii from the Moscow daily *Utro Rossii* interviewed the sister of Komarovskii's first wife, who had died of blood poisoning. Remembering Maria from their school days, she reported that Tarnovskaia was "already a monster of vice and cruelty" who organized orgies and persuaded her admirers to drink poison. *Utro Rossii*, 20 March 1910, no. 65.

12. Evlef and Miks, *Delo Tarnovskoi*, 11–12.

one of the world's largest newspapers, with a circulation of seven hundred thousand.[13] The Italian newspaper of record was *Corriere della Sera* (Evening Courier), published in Milan, which today remains an important national public voice.

The newspapers used woodcut illustrations, and the occasional blurred photograph, but the best visuals came from the movie cameras rolling outside the courtroom, fledgling newsreels capturing the comings and goings of the participants for projection onto the screen.[14] Although the term "paparazzi" had not yet been coined,[15] the behavior patterns were developing that contributed to the evolution of celebrity:

> Italian reporters and photographers, armed with cameras, go up to the cage in which the accused sit and, taking aim, they wait for when the object to be photographed turns around or bends his or her head, then click goes the shutter! The photographers toss their heads back proudly, as if they've achieved god knows what great and glorious accomplishment.[16]

Thus did this profane trio behind bars in Venice make its mark on twentieth-century mass communications.

Exploiting the colorful characters for their exotica as Russian nobility was an obvious marketing strategy for the Italian press. The stakes, however, lay in more than the sale of newspapers. The presiding magistrate was Angelo Fusinato, whose brother Guido was a leading jurist, a member of parliament, and had represented Italy in 1907 at the Second Hague Peace Conference. Fusinato was reported to have set aside one-third of the courtroom for the correspondents from all corners of the globe. Prime Minister Luigi Luzzatti also had a brother at court, one of Prilukov's defense attorneys. Each defendant had five lawyers, testament to the widespread coverage that landed their names in print.[17] The international guests who visited the courtroom included the modernist writer Gabriele d'Annunzio,[18] political "Young Turks" on diplomatic assignment from the crumbling Ottoman Empire, and members of the entourage of former President Theodore Roosevelt, then in Paris speaking on "Citizenship in a Republic."

Transported picturesquely in prison gondolas, the accused finally came to trial in February 1910.[19] A fourth defendant, Tarnovskaia's Swiss maid, Elisa Perrier, made lackluster copy because her life hid no scandals. Maria's list of conquests had been expanded to include Petia Tarnovskii, her husband's younger brother, who was now

13. *Berliner Tageblatt*, *Neue Freie Presse*, and *Matin* all fell victim to fascism.

14. *Kinematograf*, 1 April 1910, no. 2, advertised "Protsess Tarnovskoi v Venetsii," promising scenes from the court and of the gondolas.

15. Federico Fellini is credited with coining the word, which invokes the sound of mosquitos buzzing annoyingly around their prey, when he named the news photographer "Paparazzo" in *La Dolce Vita* (1960).

16. Judge Fusinato warned photographers that he would not allow them to disrespect anyone by shoving their cameras in people's faces. *Rs*, 26, 28 February 1910, nos. 46, 48.

17. *Russkii vestnik* (hereafter *Rv*) noted the high quality of the lawyers involved. *Rv*, 6 May 1910, no. 102.

18. D'Annunzio was reported to be writing a play based on the trial. *Rul'*, 24 May 1910.

19. March in Italy, which used the Gregorian calendar.

Fig. 23. Tarnovskaia arrives at court in her prison gondola.

reputed to have killed himself over her rather than because of his academic failure. Stal's suicide had been rewritten with her as his motive, the mysterious beneficiary of the white roses. In some of the more outrageous rumors decorating the trial, Stal' had left a note begging Maria to visit his corpse in the morgue, and she had taken Naumov to his grave in order to show him the lengths to which other men had been willing to go for her.[20]

Even the Russian press initially preferred Naumov's naïveté to the chill Maria was radiating from her cell. Her seduction of Komarovskii so soon after the death of his first wife could only come across as exceptionally callous. *Odesskii listok* compared her to "Gilevich, an abscess on the social body," although unlike his, "no pity can be found for her victims."[21] The youthful Naumov fancied himself a poet, and contributed occasionally to his local right-wing newspaper *Orelskaia rech'* (The Orel Speech). *Odesskii listok* published a poem that this would-be Baudelaire had written, redolent with the first whiff of the scandal:

> Queen Indal had one among her countless slaves
> of white Europeans.
> She didn't love him,
> But capriciously gave herself to him occasionally.
> He, loving her, knew very well that one day she would
> Tire of this caprice and kill her slave,

20. *Rs*, 5 March 1910, no. 52.
21. Ivan Chuzhanov, "Tarnovskaia i obshchestvo," *Ol*, 24 February, no. 44.

But this anticipation of death, this fear,
Only made his love sweeter. He was happy.

The Odessa paper filled columns with prurient *faits divers*, overdrawing her affairs in Kiev. The suicidal Stal' "recognized her spiritual poverty . . . but still he could not stop himself from seeing her, to feel her presence, to smell her perfume, to poison himself with the venom of her amusing conversation."[22] Maria was a vamp before the term was coined, an exotic female predator.[23]

*Russkoe slovo*, in contrast, had dispatched one of its premier journalists, war correspondent Vasilii Ivanovich Nemirovich-Danchenko, who had known Komarovskii from the latter's service in the Russo-Japanese War. Having visited his villa, the writer recalled how the count, popular in Venetian society, had shocked his social circle with his involvement with Maria so soon after his dear wife's death. Nemirovich-Danchenko's description of Maria's most striking attribute, her long, willowy body that towered over the count's, struck a psychological visual.

Despite his obvious sympathy for Komarovskii, this seasoned correspondent identified an immediate problem with the Italian coverage. He brought attention to the fact that Komarovskii had not died of the shot, but of the peritonitis that he developed following a botched operation to remove the bullet. Nemirovich-Danchenko faulted "the Italian Sherlock Holmes," the investigator who had cracked the case, for the lengthy interrogation of his badly wounded friend.[24] Criticizing the Italians' excessive theatricality, he wondered why it had taken the case more than two years to come to trial, noting that their newspaper exaggerated the defendants' aristocratic titles.[25]

Nemirovich-Danchenko turned the tide of the Russian coverage with his objection to the Italian courtroom's presentation of the crime as essentially Slavic. Mikhail Pervukhin, the *Russkoe slovo* reporter assigned to the trial, lamented that "it's not just our revolutionaries but also we Russians who are unpopular in Europe."[26] *Odesskii listok* carried a story that set up the nationalist points of contention as they related to justice: in Italy, "men who kill their wives or mistresses are always acquitted, but the opposite, never!" Italians and Russians began to argue over where the trial should be held; it had become clear that local cultural norms would dictate how the case would be prosecuted and how the jury would levy its decision. The Italian position that "Russia must know that Italy is the country of Beccaria and Lombroso. It does not judge as other countries do; Italy judges evenhand-

22. *Ol*, 20 February 1910, no. 41.

23. The term "vamp" is attributed to Theda Bara's character in the film *A Fool There Was* (1915), when she lures a happily married family man to his self-destruction. The female vampire must be dated to Lucy Westenra, whom Count Dracula turned into one in Bram Stoker's 1897 novel. Lucy must be destroyed by the men who loved her, a mirror opposite of Tarnovskaia.

24. The historical enmity between Catholicism and Orthodoxy rarely came up at this trial, but the hospital in which Komarovskii died as a result of an operation later deemed unnecessary was criticized for the excessive influence of clerics. *Rs*, 17 March 1910, no. 62.

25. V. I. Nemirovich-Danchenko, "Venetsiankii volokita," *Rs*, 18 February 1910, no. 39.

26. *Rs*, 19 February 1910, no. 40.

edly, after deep thought" captured the essence of the exasperation felt on both sides.[27] Nationalist emotions brought substantive cultural and political differences to the fore.

## Italian Expertise

Professor Bobrov, testifying on Vasilii Tarnovskii's behalf in 1905, had pointed out that the Russian views of pathological will and criminal behavior differed from Western views. These differences surfaced sharply in the Venetian trial of Tarnovskii's wife. To convict Tarnovskaia, the Italian prosecution had to prove that she had successfully transformed Naumov into her lethal weapon when they were not even in the same country at the time. The two Italian psychiatrists who dominated the proceedings were the nation's most prominent: Leonardo Bianchi (1848–1927) and Enrico Morselli (1852–1929). Bianchi, professor of nervous and mental diseases at the Royal University of Naples, was the leading Italian neuropsychiatrist of the era. His textbook *Foundations of Mental Health* went through three editions and was translated into English. Appointed minister of education in 1905, though his tenure lasted only one year, he expanded the teaching of experimental psychology at universities and was elected to the Senate in 1919.[28]

One of Lombroso's most impassioned apostles, Morselli had begun his career studying under the master in Turin, moving to the University of Genoa in 1889.[29] Something of a psychiatric polymath, Morselli pioneered in research into the psychological reasons for suicides even before Durkheim made self-murder essential to sociology.[30] Morselli had always been interested in psychiatry's two sides, the scientific-medical and the philosophical, and the list of psychologists who engaged with his ideas, not uncritically, included William James, Maria Montessori, and Sigmund Freud.[31]

Morselli drew largely from his mentor's *The Criminal Woman, the Prostitute, and the Normal Woman* (1893), which distinguished female from male criminals according to anthropological criteria.[32] Natural rather than social, women commit different crimes, and for different reasons, than do men. Lombroso located female criminality in prostitution, which

27. *Ol*, 4 April 1910, no. 77. Professor Luigi Bianchi made the exclamation.

28. Dr. G. C. Ferrari, "Progress of Psychiatry in Italy," *Journal of Mental Science* 52 (1906): 398.

29. Giancarlo Gramaglia, "Notes sur la psychanalyse italienne entre les deux guerres, 1915–1945," *Revue internationale d'histoire de la psychanalyse* 5 (1992): 129–42.

30. Morselli published *Suicidio: Saggio di statist ica morale comparata* (Milan: Dumolard, 1879), almost two decades before Durkheim's more influential work appeared.

31. William James reviewed Morselli politely but negatively; the review is reprinted in *Essays in Psychical Research*, intro. Robert A. McDermott (Cambridge: Harvard University Press, 1986), 182–83. See also Maria Montessori, *Pedagogical Anthropology*, trans. Frederic Taber Cooper (New York: Frederick A. Stokes, 1913), 21–23; and Sigmund Freud, *Letters of Sigmund Freud, 1873–1939*, ed. Ernst L. Freud, trans. Tania and James Stern (London: Hogarth, 1960), 365.

32. In a remarkable coincidence of names, it had been the Russian doctor Praskov'ia Tarnovskaia who had collected the detailed physical information from Russian female prostitutes that Lombroso needed for this research.

he considered a deeply atavistic category of social relations.[33] He defined prostitution as female sexual behavior that deviated from the norm of heterosexual monogamy, the pillar that upheld civilized social relations. Tarnovskaia therefore conformed to his philosophy that "the primitive woman was rarely a murderess; but she was always a prostitute."[34] Moreover, because "a full type [the female offender] is more terrible than the male," Tarnovskaia's sex made her especially dangerous. Lombroso's theory that the female "dominates weaker people, sometimes through suggestion, sometimes through force," underscored for Italians why Tarnovskaia was the truly guilty party.[35] Morselli told Corriere della Sera that "her [Tarnovskaia's] character is a mixture of masculine and feminine traits, a contrast that strengthens her hysterical neurosis."[36] Lombroso himself was reported to have called Tarnovskaia "the most remarkable criminal of modern times," because "her methods show an absolute mastery of masculine sentiment, passion, and covetousness."[37]

Race rather than gender, though, lay at the heart of the political implications of Lombroso's research. Daniel Pick has argued persuasively that, for all the attention given to his ideas about individual "born criminals," Lombroso developed his criminological theories as a reaction to his profound concern with the southern Italians following the unification of the peninsula in the 1860s. Post-*Risorgimento* Italy presented a "particular crisis," reflected in the stark differences in health and cultural development between the populations in the north and south, which called for "new forms of political and social representation." Single-minded in his desire to contribute to the transformation of unified Italy into a modern nation-state, Lombroso "saw himself as a progressive, bringing science, more specifically evolutionary biology and physical anthropology, to bear upon Italy's 'backwardness.'"[38] He founded criminal anthropology to explain the deviance of southerners as atavism, which could account for how the two populaces were related yet unequal. David Horn furthered this line of thought, pointing out that "Lombroso's anthropology sought, among other things, to trace historical shifts in the nature of crime and criminality, to locate Italy in relation to other—more uniformly modern—nations in Europe."[39] When Lombroso theorized that "a stagnant aristocracy, like the criminal population, was anathema to the interests of the modern rationalist state," he added the issue of social estate, now being formulated as class, a progressive indicator of industrialization.[40] The

33. Lombroso wrote, "Prostitution was especially widespread in early time, which clearly confirms that modesty and matrimony are a late product of evolution." Cesare Lombroso and Guglielmo Ferrero, *Criminal Woman, the Prostitute, and the Normal Woman*, transl. and intro. by Nicole Hahn Rafter and Mary Gibson (Durham: Duke University Press, 2004), 102. In their introduction, Rafter and Gibson point to his conclusion that "white European women no longer desire sexual intercourse except for procreation, the defining act of womanhood" (21).

34. David G. Horn, *The Criminal Body: Lombroso and the Anatomy of Deviance* (New York: Routledge, 2003), 54.

35. Lombroso, *Criminal Woman*, 183, 192.

36. Quoted in *Ol*, 18 March 1910, no. 63.

37. *The New York Times* quoted Lombroso on March 13, 1910, five months after his death.

38. Daniel Pick, "The Faces of Anarchy: Lombroso and the Politics of Criminal Science in Post-Unification Italy," *History Workshop Journal* 20:10 (1986): 65.

39. Horn, *Criminal Body*, 33.

40. Pick, "Faces of Anarchy," 64.

analytical triumvirate of race, class, and gender could not be disentangled from one another throughout the trial, but race proved the most damning. Being Slavic degenerated them all.

At the turn of the twentieth century, as anthropologist George Stocking has pointed out, the concept of "race" was heavily influenced by a neo-Lamarckism that blended cultural with genetic origins.[41] Race, in this formulation, results from an "indestructible stock of ideas, traditions, sentiments, modes of thought, an unconscious inheritance from their ancestors." Not only physical characteristics demarcate races, but also "their mental and, above all, their moral characteristics, the slow growth and accumulation of centuries of toil and conflict."[42] Establishing a hierarchy of races developed quite naturally in the context of Darwinian evolutionism, combined with the social theory that viewed "differences between human races . . . in terms of their places on a temporal evolutionary continuum of physical and cultural development."[43] Morselli stated explicitly that "we cannot judge the people of this nation (Russia) by our criteria. Italy has such a rich history of civilization that it is impossible to compare Russia to it. Only recently have Russians begun to enter into Western civilization, mixing it with Eastern."[44] When the Italian prosecution described the three Russian defendants as "barbarians dressed as Europeans,"[45] it was reaffirming a dichotomy between the progressive West and atavistic, autocratic Russia.

Tarnovskaia and Naumov represented the types that modern Italy had rid itself of, theoretically.[46] Before marrying into the Ukrainian nobility, Tarnovskaia had been the daughter of Count O'Rourke, whose great-grandfather had moved from Ireland early in the eighteenth century. The Italian psychiatrists went so ludicrously far as to link her Irish lineage back to "Bloody" Mary, Queen of Scots (r. 1542–1567). The fathers of both Tarnovskaia and Naumov attended the trial, and their aggrieved faces and aristocratic bearing made good copy. *Russkie vedomosti*, a Moscow-based newspaper with a liberal slant, sarcastically pitied the two parents; as representatives of anti-Semitic southwestern Russia, they had to listen to Jewish and socialist lawyers air their families' dirtiest laundry.[47]

It was not enough simply to say that the Russian nobility behaved badly. Bianchi and Morselli had to discredit both the country and the social estate as they made their argument for Italian superiority. As psychiatrists, they had to able to explain how Tarnovskaia, from abroad, had been able to compel Naumov to take such drastic action. This fit the prosecutorial agenda that made Tarnovskaia legally responsible because she had subjected

41. George W. Stocking, Jr., "The Turn-of-the-Century Concept of Race," *Modernism/Modernity* 1, no. 1 (1994): 10.

42. Ibid., 4. Stocking is quoting Henry Cabot Lodge, speaking to the Senate in favor of restrictive immigration reform in 1896. Such restrictions were not passed until the Johnson–Reed Act of 1924, which was aimed in part at the same areas of southern Italy that so bothered Lombroso.

43. Stocking, "Turn-of-the-Century Concept of Race," 12.

44. *Ol*, 4 April 1910, no. 77.

45. *Rs*, April 16, 1910, no. 87.

46. Max Nordau dedicated *Degeneration* (1892) to Lombroso; the book presented a blistering critique of contemporaneous European high cultures.

47. *Rv*, 6 May 1910, no, 102.

the weak-willed Naumov to her much stronger will. A headline from *Petersburgskii listok* summed up the stakes: "Murder! Jealousy or Hypnotism?"[48] Bekhterev joined Morselli among the many others internationally who had given the imprimatur of science to hypnotism, perceived to be a deeper threat than jealousy.[49] Komarovskii's mother swore that Tarnovskaia had cast "special looks" her son's way. Even the prison director found that "Naumov exhibits an especially weak degree of opposition . . . possibly from hypnotism."[50]

The Italians found Russians more susceptible to such suggestion than they were. Bianchi considered "the Venetian tragedy is a direct reflection of the Russian lifestyle." For him, the Russo-Japanese War and "the bloody events that followed it," the 1905 Revolution, had stripped life of its value and contributed to a rise in suicide and collective hypnotic behavior. Stretching speciously back to the Middle Ages, he cited the Children's Crusade of 1212 as an analogue to the "psychic epidemic" currently underway in Russia. "In a country that moves toward civilization through a long period of human hecatomb, general stagnation, and melancholia, there is a pull toward suicide," he continued, reinforcing what the *Russkie vedomosti* correspondent referred to snidely as an Italian "nostalgia for suicide."[51] Bianchi further aggravated Russians with his assurance that "European scientists are studying Russian life and looking for a scientific explanation for this."[52]

The key to legal culpability lay in convincing jurors that Tarnovskaia had subjected Naumov to her will with malicious intent. Two other prominent psychiatrists also testified on this point, local forensic psychiatrist Luigi Cappelletti, and Ernesto Belmondo, like Morselli from the Genoa school.[53] Cappelletti gave a three-hour speech on how Naumov's physiological centers had been weakened both by heredity and head traumas, evidence of how "he falls under the influence of another's will to such an extent that he loses any independence. He acted in such a state when he killed Komarovskii, and therefore scientifically he is not responsible." Belmondo enlightened the audience at the trial about masochism, which Naumov suffered, and explained why he willingly put his body under the sadist Tarnovskaia's cigarettes. Belmondo began reading aloud from the biography of Leopold von Sacher-Masoch, the author of the concept. When the presiding judge interrupted with a question of relevance, Belmondo responded that Sacher-Masoch's mother was Russian, and "there are many masochists in Russia, especially among well-born men."[54]

For Bianchi, Naumov was "not a killer by nature." But when "she hypnotized him, the youthful passion he felt for her destroyed his free will. He found himself unconscious,

48. *Pl*, 5 April 1910, no. 93.

49. V. M. Bekhterev, *Gipnos, vnushenie, i psikho-terapiia* (St. Petersburg: Tip. Khodozh. pechati, 1911); and *Bred gipnoticheskogo ocharovaniia* (St. Petersburg: "Ia trei," 1913). Morselli published *Il magnetismo animale, la fascinazione e gli stati ipnotici* (Torino: Roux e Favale), 1886.

50. *Rs*, 24 March 1910, no. 68; and *Ol*, 14 March 1910, no. 60.

51. *Rv*, 13 April 1910, no. 84.

52. *Pl*, 4 April 1910, no. 93.

53. Paolo Francesco Peloso, "Psychiatry in Genoa," *History of Psychiatry* 15, no. 1 (2004): 27–43.

54. *Rs*, 1 April 1910, no. 74. From Galicia, Sacher-Masoch was a Russophile who enjoyed a broad following in the tsarist empire from the 1870s. Alexander Etkind, "Is There Pleasure in Suffering?: Contexts of Desire from Masoch to Kuzmin," in *Eros and Pornography in Russian Culture*, ed. Marcus Levitt and A. L. Topokov (Moscow: Ladomir, 1999), 288–99.

under the power of his beloved, a hypnosis much more powerful than that produced by a specialist." This spell maintained its hold over him, Bianchi argued, as a result of the mood swings that her telegrams had generated, driving him back and forth between joy and despair, exacerbated by his loneliness in Venice. Remarkably, after shooting Komarovskii, "consciousness returned to him and he was liberated from this idée fixe," which explained his postshooting rational behavior. In prison Naumov expressed remorse, telling Bianchi that "even if they acquit me I will always have a stone on my conscience because I killed someone who was my friend." Bianchi, himself the director of a mental hospital, spoke with authority when assuring jurors that Naumov had acted "with a darkened consciousness, absent his own will," and posed no threat to society.[55]

Morselli insisted that "we often find among the Russian aristocracy moral insanity, or something like this illness." However, the experts looked at only Tarnovskaia's family, never Naumov's, despite the obvious obstructionism to modernity put up by political reactionaries. Writing that "O'Rourke is an ancient family and therefore must have a tendency to fall, a tendency to degeneracy," he mused that this clan's closets likely sheltered many more mentally ill members. He doomed Maria from conception, when "the coming together of the Irish in her father and the Slavic in her mother led to complete degeneration."[56] Morselli decided that "only the lower classes in Russia are spiritually healthy, with fresh strength and energy."[57] That could not have sat well with even most liberal Russians.

Tarnovskaia's lone champion in the Italian courtroom was Luigi Bossi, prominent in both gynecology and psychiatry, who had already engaged in professional battle with Morselli over the sources of female hysteria. A natural for Tarnovskaia, Bossi had built his reputation around "an eccentric theory on the uterine rather than the cerebral origin of mental illness in women."[58] Interviewed outside the courtroom, Bossi informed reporters that Tarnovskaia "is suffering from a sickness that often results in either suicide or crime, and this lessens her culpability." Treating her in her cell, Bossi argued that from childhood she had suffered "a female illness that distorted her psyche," which was "in full flower at the time of the count's murder." Because "this malady is not well known, and therefore requires all the efforts of the experts," he joined with Count O'Rourke in appealing to doctors who had treated her in Russia to come to Venice on her behalf.[59] The audience laughed so uproariously at his testimony that the judge threatened to close the proceedings to the public.[60]

Bossi found degeneracy inherited from both parents, though he stressed the physical damage that her body had endured from childhood: in addition to getting hit on the head with a swing after falling from it, she had suffered typhus, and a bite from a rabid dog, for

55. *Ol*, 4 April 1910, no. 77.

56. *Pl*, 5 April 1910, no. 94.

57. *Ol*, 4 April 1910, no. 77

58. Peloso, "Psychiatry in Genoa," 35–36.

59. A Professor Lipinskii, who had treated Tarnovskaia for insomnia in 1905, argued that Bekhterev was wrong, but this was David against the Goliath of psychiatric circles. Lipinskii traveled to Venice in hopes of testifying, but was not called. *Ol*, 27 February 1910, no. 47.

60. *Rs*, 24 February 1910, no. 44.

which she was treated with a medicine that "as is well known, sometimes brings paralysis with it." Her continued use of cocaine and ether further injured her organism. Ultimately, though, he could allow that "it is enough to say that she was a member of the Russian aristocracy, as the upper classes in Russia are famous for their vices." He joined his opinion with the others on "the difficulties in judging the psyche of the Slavic soul, often mysterious and not understood by Western Europeans."[61]

This racialization of the defendants, especially Morselli's, set off the firestorm in the Russian press. *Russkie vedomosti* hired as a correspondent the novelist and journalist Mikhail Osorgin (Il'in), who had left Russia for Italy after spending a few months in jail during the 1905 Revolution. Osorgin, also from Perm Province, did not publicize any political problems he might have had with the Naumovs. His self-imposed exile, though, did not sway him to favor the Italian over the Russian position. He zeroed in on how Morselli played the race card, noting how the Italian criminologist referred repeatedly to the particularity of the Slavic race, presenting both Naumov and Prilukov as "typical specimens of Slavic illnesses, both alcoholics," though no evidence supported this clichéd contention.[62]

Morselli had turned to Russian fiction for gendered explanations of Maria's behavior, complaining that "unfortunately, we know Slavic women very poorly, only from the novels of Tolstoy and Turgenev . . . we do not know the extent to which the Russian aristocratic woman is inclined to neurosis and psychosis, because *War and Peace* has only recently been translated into Italian." He continued, "Tarnovskaia approached this crime in the grip of a partial anaesthetization of moral feelings, a condition widely spread among Russian women." The prosecutor also cited the novels of Charles Flaubert and the Goncourt brothers as proper sources for understanding female hysteria, forgivably distinct from degeneracy, as direct evidence that Tarnovskaia did not suffer it.[63]

Osorgin puzzled, "What does that have to do with the Slavic races? For us it is especially vexing that the Italians are convinced that the anaesthetization of moral feelings in Russian women is commonplace." He asked indignantly, "In what novel was he so struck by the uniquely immoral Russian woman? Liza in *A Nest of Gentry*? Elena in *On the Eve*?," two of Ivan Turgenev's honorable but ill-starred heroines. He added, "if one is talking about race, then the racial characteristics of the Latins has provided much material for French belles lettres." He mused that "if it is genuinely possible to draw conclusions about a people from novels, then the Italian genius D'Annunzio has in recent years been occupied with a search for the positive in sexual relations between family members." That had not prompted Russian psychiatrists to speak of the "anaesthetization of moral feelings in the Latin race."[64]

Annoyed that Morselli had drawn his "strictly scientific" conclusions after having learned about Russian life from French novels, Pervukhin lambasted the Italians. "Good lord, what have you not heard about this unhappy *anima slava*, this ill-fated 'Russian

61. *Rs*, 2 April 1910, no. 75.

62. *Rv*, 13 April 1910, no. 84.

63. *Rs*, 17 April 1910, no. 88.

64. *Rv*, 13 April 1910, no. 84. Sergei Iablonskii complained about the Italian's "illiteracy" with regard to Russian fiction, as they compared the accused very inappropriately to Raskolnikov. *Rs*, 9 May 1910, no. 105.

psychology?'" he queried. Morselli's classification of Russia as an Asiatic country, deeply mystic, was especially galling because "this son of Italy" ignored the local flagellants. Italy was a country "where even today they replay the infamous 'miracle of San Gennaro' annually, where even now the masses are wildly fanatical and take part in theatrical processions born during the Middle Ages, when thousands upon thousands were infected with a collective hysteria." Angry about Belmondo's position that "Russian men are extraordinarily attracted to masochism, and its women to sadism," he regretted that these "groundless accusations against Russia have no possibilities of appeal." He concluded sarcastically, "now let's talk about *anima latina*. There are no murders in Italy. Naples is the most moral city in the world, where there are no hooligans, no rogues."[65] The correspondent for *Petersburgskii listok* noted the nationalism that divided opinion: "in Russia, no one labors under the illusion that any of these three defendants have especially fragile souls; they are ordinary criminals, with nothing 'Slavic' in their psychology."[66] *Russkoe slovo* columnist Sergei Iablonskii found that "sexual perversion is the equalizer in the civilized world."[67]

Russian writers understood correctly that the stakes ran deeper than nationalist insults. The Tarnovskaia trial had given Lombroso's disciples a forum to present their "new forms of political and social representation," moving now from the national to the international stage. Politically, atavistic and autocratic Russia measured poorly against their modern, unified Italy. The potent subtext of competitive nationalisms endowed the trial with implications that had martial relevance, as the European continent lurched toward war. The political agenda of modern, democratic Italy depended on the rejection of that same weakness in males that had earned Vasilii Tarnovskii his acquittal.[68] Within a year of Maria's trial, Italians would be involved in their first international military campaign since unification, fighting the Ottoman Empire for the colonization of present-day Libya. Noteworthy as an antecedent to World War I, including the first use of airplanes in combat, the Italo-Turkish War of 1911 made an aggressive show of force not long after this trial.

Equally significant is the direction toward race that the Italian men of science moved. Their prejudice against Slavs indicated their belief in racial hierarchies, hardly an uncommon position.[69] The Italian experts testifying at Tarnovskaia's trial were contributing to a "modern rethinking of society and the social" at the turn of the century, enlisting "social facts . . . in new kinds of political and technical projects."[70] Even though they disagreed

65. *Rs*, 8 April 1910, no. 80.

66. *Pl*, 4 May 1910, no. 120.

67. *Rs*, 9 May 1910, no. 105.

68. In the lead-up to the war, Italians, like Germans, worried that their aristocratic officers were too effeminate and needed to be replaced with a bourgeois "hardened masculinity." Jason Crouthamel, "Male Sexuality and Psychological Trauma: Soldiers and Sexual Disorder in World War I and Weimar Germany," *Journal of the History of Sexuality* 17, no. 1 (2008): 64.

69. As Laura Goering pointed out, at the turn of the century, for "Europeans who viewed neurasthenia.. as a sign of degeneration. the inferior Slavs and the degenerate Jews were the prime candidates." Laura Goering, ""Russian Nervousness": Neurasthenia and National Identity in Nineteenth-Century Russia," *Medical History* 47, no. 1 (2003): 34.

70. David Horn, *Social Bodies: Science, Reproduction, and Italian Modernity* (Princeton: Princeton University Press, 1994), 6–7.

over the physiological origins of Tarnovskaia's degeneracy, Morselli and Bossi would both become proponents of eugenics. Bossi's insistence on the sexual origins of her illness did not occlude ideas about race, and his participation in the Great War led him to argue for the racial inferiority of the Germans.[71] Bianchi, too, advocated eugenics.

As they prepared for war, the Italians needed trustworthy friends. Much that came out in the Tarnovskaia trial evidenced that this did not include Russia. In London, a European capital that made a more attractive ally, the funeral of King Edward VII coincided with the end of the Tarnovskaia trial. The full regalia of the British military on parade overwhelmed the vulgar trio in Venice, camouflaging the stress fractures that would appear in the future alliance between constitutional monarchy and autocracy.[72]

## Rescripting Messalina

When her husband had shot her lover in 1903, the Russians viewed Tarnovskaia as an arrogant adulteress, akin to the promiscuous Roman empress Messalina. Once the Italians had decided that she was the personification of atavistic Russia, the Russians needed to rehabilitate her in order to reclaim their identity. The years the Italians had spent compiling the case was cynically dismissed as "deductive" by Russians, because "the investigators had already made up their minds about Tarnovskaia and Prilukov, they only had to gather facts that would support their conclusions."[73] Presiding Judge Fusinato also inspired prejudice against her: "His voice is calm, confident, authoritative . . . he speaks as if recounting the contents of a novel: You, Signora Tarnovskaia, you were a scandalously unfaithful woman. Witnesses say that you brought lovers into your husband's home."[74]

Stories of the taunting that greeted the gondolas each morning, shouts directed at her as "cursed by God!" and cries of "down with the murderess!," contrasted with the murmurings that Naumov was a "poor young man." The Venetians' antagonism toward her juxtaposed with the Russians' sympathy:

There, on the canal, still lit by the dying rays of the spring sun, there, on the shore, on the bridge—the same crowd is there, renting gondolas by the hour, filled with "lovers of justice." The minute that the gondola carrying her appears, they threaten with their fists. . . . What a sharp contrast with a Russian crowd, accompanying the party of those already considered condemned . . . these people cry out, "neschastnye"![75]

71. Peloso, "Psychiatry in Genoa," 46.

72. Michael Hughes looks at cultural issues, though not Tarnovskaia, in "Searching for the Soul of Russia: British Perceptions of Russia during the First World War," *Twentieth Century British History* 20, no. 2 (2009): 198–226. See also Keith Neilson, *Britain and the Last Tsar: British Policy and Russia, 1894–1917* (New York: Oxford University Press, 1995).

73. Evlef and Miks, *Delo Tarnovskoi*, 47.

74. *Rs*, 28 February 1910, no. 48. The *New York Times* correspondent covering the trial reported, though, that "Fusinato came gradually under her spell, and was kinder and more considerate of her feelings as the trial progressed" (21 May 1910).

75. *Rs*, 28 February 1910, no. 48.

Yet for Tarnovskaia to become sympathetic, her biography required serious revisionism. On the same page that *Odesskii listok* carried a blurb that at age fourteen Maria had paid a maid to watch her copulating with a fireman, the paper let Tarnovskaia speak for herself.[76] The newspaper began publishing notes that she purportedly wrote in her cell. The origin of these notebooks was never confirmed, but it was presumed that she handed them to Bossi, the gynecologist permitted to visit her. These notes were republished as serialized booklets, sold for eight kopecks. Authenticity was at best a secondary issue; these autobiographical outpourings provided the basis for a fundamentally fresh perspective on the embattled Tarnovskaia. Much of this information was repeated when Tarnovskaia was called to the stand in March, but it had been circulated as a private confession before her public testimony.

Tarnovskaia's musings gave her the space to demonstrate remorse, and to explain how she had become a person capable of evil. Instead of denying her depravity, she blamed her husband for having debauched her youthful naïveté. The formerly weak-willed Vasilii metamorphosed into quite a different character once *she* was the one on trial. The posthumous testimonies of Borzhevskii and Stal' came belatedly to fruition. The blushing seventeen-year-old bride was abandoned on her honeymoon, and then forced to participate in orgies with the others whom her husband brought to their marital bed. "Every day I learned a new form of vice," she wrote. One of her husband's mistresses "told me that phrase, which to this day I cannot forget . . . 'when you enter the hall, where a large gathering is waiting for you, you must try to hold your mouth in an unchanging smile; never show your internal suffering, either moral or physical; please everyone, without exception, men and women.'" She rewrote the Borzhevskii affair when she testified that, on informing her husband that other men were falling in love with her, he had responded with indifference, not jealousy.[77]

Then she turned on Prilukov. "Machiavellian," he appeared "always a mysterious person: serious, cold, positive, able to manipulate everyone. . . . I remember his words: 'the essence of life is this: to be able to overcome all obstacles by whatever means.'" Now she was the one with no strength of character: "Eternally indecisive and weak, unable to restrain myself, I felt my head spinning, I was going out of my mind . . . I lived in genuine terror." Professing a dubious maternal instinct, she claimed that "my life, with the exception of a few moments, was always very sad. I was under the constant threat of losing my son." Explaining the stoicism that made her appear callous, she wrote: "if people only knew how much pain and suffering is hidden behind my mask of indifference! Only now do I see that my trial is founded on the despicability and revenge of people who were close to me, and now pour out slanderous fabrications. If I could show all the tears that I have shed, if I could describe all the bitterness that I am enduring . . . purity in love was forbidden to me."[78]

While her autobiography circulated, Naumov was called to the stand. His defense lay entirely in his protestations that she had spellbound him, and he sniveled of hoping for a telegram from her calling off the murder. Traces on his body of the initials she had carved

76. *Ol*, 21 February 1910, no. 42.
77. Ibid.
78. *Ol*, 22 February 1910, no. 43.

into it lent plausibility to some of his protestations. *Rech'* (Speech), the official newspaper of Russia's liberal Kadet political party, criticized Naumov most severely. Emphasizing the "theatricality" of his confession, the journalist covering the trial considered his performance "talented but insincere." He asked rhetorically, "can a Russian honestly master, and so quickly, the number of pompous phrases, . . . the very tone of the old melodramas?" Naumov spoke to the jury "with a deliberate quiver in his voice: the male audience sighed, the females wiped their eyes and noses with lace handkerchiefs." Contempt dripped from this journalist's pen, but he recognized that "the show was staged brilliantly in the spirit of Italian psychology."[79]

The Russian reporters at liberal newspapers would predictably be annoyed to find a homicidal monarchist presented as a model Russian. But Naumov also had medicine on his side. Two head traumas suffered in his youth, a swimming accident, and a collision with a billiard table increased the neurological susceptibility of his brain.[80] As the trial began, Naumov received unofficial but prestigious support from Bekhterev, who was interviewed in the influential *Novoe vremia*. The third edition of Bekhterev's *Suggestion and Its Role in Social Life* (ca. 1897) had just appeared, a study of a variety of pathological epidemics that looked at collective rather than individual behaviors. Without having observed her personally, Bekhterev considered Tarnovskaia to be "imperious, with poorly developed ethics," who "selected weak people, enslaved their wills, and transformed them into the obedient weapons of her intentions." The "neuropathological" Naumov found himself completely subordinate to her suggestion (*vnyshenie*).[81]

Bekhterev's *Suggestion* fell in line with the Italians' views of collective hysterias. However, he did not speak out after Russian favor had switched from the gunman to the seductress. Remarkably, Russia's psychiatric community remained silent, even though many had expressed ideas similar to Bianchi's about the negative effects of the revolution on the nation's mental health.[82] Historian Jacqueline Friedlander found that most Russian psychiatrists "thought that the events of 1905 had a very real emotional impact, and that, as a result of this emotional intensity, some people who were either active participants or bystanders caught up in these events did become mentally ill."[83] The physician D. N. Zhbankov wrote a series of widely circulated articles on revolutionary violence, citing "the panic and terror that had paralyzed both the reason and power of many people."[84]

79. The article from *Rech'* was reprinted in *Ol*, 28 February 1910, no. 48.

80. *Rs*, 14 March 1910, no. 60.

81. V. M. Bekhterev, *Vnushenie i ego rol' v obshchestvennoi zhizni* (St. Petersburg: K. L. Rikkera, 1908). The English translation is *Suggestion and Its Role in Social Life*, ed. Lloyd H. Strickland, trans. Tzvetanka Dobreva-Martinova (New Brunswick: Transaction Publishers, 1998). Bekhterev cites Bianchi's work on the susceptibility of crowds to suggestion (176). The quotes are from the reprinted interview in *Ol*, 2 February 1910, no, 45.

82. Pavel Kovalevskii had reviewed both Bianchi and Morselli positively in the book review section of *Arkhiv* 7, no. 1 (1886): 120; and Petrov had used Morselli's work in his explanation of Pozdnyshev's pathological *affekt*.

83. Jacqueline Friedlander, "Psychiatrists and Crisis in Russia, 1880–1917" (PhD diss., University of California-Berkeley, 2007), 293.

84. Daniel Beer, *Renovating Russia: The Human Sciences and the Fate of Liberal Modernity, 1880–1930* (Ithaca: Cornell University Press, 2008), 160.

Russian psychiatrists had themselves become politicized following 1905, which was evident at their national congress held just prior to the Tarnovskaia trial at which they voted to support female suffrage. Hardly a psychiatric issue, but as Bekhterev had pointed out in his opening address, "Scientific papers can be read in any specialized assembly, but only at congresses can social questions be decided."[85] Ironically, at their January congress, the distinctive character traits of various nationalities had been a discussion topic.[86] Moreover, Russian professionals enjoyed better relations with Lombroso's criminal anthropology than was evident in their avoidance of Tarnovskaia. Lombroso had died less than a year earlier, which had inspired a respectful response in Russia.[87] Prominent middlebrow man of letters P. D. Boborykin praised him for directing criminology toward the study of the person, and welcomed Guglielmo Ferrero, coauthor of *The Criminal Woman*, to Russia because "it is time for us to enhance our cultural ties with representatives of the Italian intelligentsia."[88] That they steered clear of Tarnovskaia suggests that, recognizing the political implications of the Italian argument, they would not betray their own modern nationalist sensibilities by agreeing with it.

Perhaps Russians could extend some generosity of spirit to the young Lochinvar with the hot head and the weak will. He was, after all, a man in love. Little could be found for the lawyer who had abandoned his family and embezzled from clients. The crowds at the gondolas met Prilukov's with "funereal silence."[89] Only two friends made the trip to Venice to persuade the court that he had been an outstanding citizen before falling under Tarnovskaia's spell. His strongest defense was evidence of at least one of the three suicide attempts he claimed. Prilukov tried to show that he himself had no "inclinations to greed, violence, or intrigues," but rather "was completely subject to her will, and suffered nervous disorders."[90] A former partner in his law office, V. G. Mankovskii, testified that Prilukov had been a model husband before meeting Tarnovskaia, but the reason that the partner had been called to court was to remind jurors that Prilukov was a thief.[91] Osorgin found Prilukov "the most tragic figure at the trial" because he had fallen the furthest from grace.[92] Judge Fusinato ordered him to eat more because his gaunt appearance reflected poorly on his jailors.[93]

---

85. Bekhterev was responding to the complaint of the delegate Dr. N. A. Sokol'skii that "science has become secondary." *Pg*, 5 January 1910, no. 4.

86. *Rs*, 6 January 1910, no. 4. For example, one paper asked, "Who doesn't know of the mental and physical strength of the English?"

87. The prominent Moscow psychiatrist N. N. Bazhenov organized a testimonial for Lombroso at the university. *Rs*, 24 October 1909, no. 244.

88. Boborykin discussed how he had been introduced to Lombroso by an enthusiastic Russian psychiatrist, but would only give the initial "D." I suspect this was Dmitrii Dril', who began his career supportive of Lombroso but later soured on the notion of the "born criminal." *Rs*, 9, 24 October 1909, nos. 231, 244.

89. *Rs*, 28 February 1910, no. 48.

90. Evlef and Miks, *Delo Tarnovskoi*, 46–47.

91. *Rs*, 20 March 1910, no. 65.

92. *Rv*, 17 March 1910, no. 62.

93. *Rs*, 26 February 1910, no. 46.

# "ENCHANTRESS" BEWITCHES ALL AT MURDER TRIAL.

### Even the Judge Is Not Proof Against the Fascinations of the Countess Tarnovsky in Venice's Sensational Case.

Fig. 24. Tarnovskaia bewitches them all.

Tarnovskaia finally took the stand. First, she had to account for conduct that was morally questionable by any standard, even if not all that had been printed out her was true. Her testimony followed the narrative of her recently published memoirs. She established Vasilii as the degenerate who drove her to other men, from whom she sought only affection. Sniffling that she was a "timid" woman, she "nursed the most serious intentions of marrying Komarovskii and restoring her reputation in society." Aligning herself with fan-favorite Naumov,[94] she admitted that "she was honestly taken with Naumov, and loved him for his goodness, his valor, his knightly character," which had "reminded her of Borzhevskii." As she continued, "there would have been no scandal if not for Prilukov's diabolical evil."[95] Court and audience alike were puzzled by her insistent denial at having written the packet of twenty-seven love letters to Prilukov submitted as evidence, because the handwriting experts identified her penmanship.[96]

### *Odesskii listok* Surveys the Public

*Odesskii listok* took the lead in asking Russians about their beleaguered heroine. The editors posed the question of her culpability to the local criminologist E. Nemirovskii. Noting that "the characters of the main actors in the drama belong to the pen of a great

---

94. The Italian women were reported to be infatuated with Naumov, tossing flowers and "almost weeping." *Rs*, 14 March 1910, no. 60.

95. *Rs,* 3 March 1910, no. 50.

96. *Ol*, 28 March 1910, no. 71; and 4 April 1910, no. 77.

artist," he wondered aloud, "Are they criminals or insane? Do they deserve punishment or compassion?" Admitting that the border between "vice and psychosis" was very thin, Nemirovskii found that "the harsh regime of the foreign prison does not offer the best results" and predicted that "soon Tarnovskaia will fall into complete psychological collapse, which will turn into a slow capital punishment."[97]

More ambitiously, the paper's editors evidenced a combination of imagination and acumen when they solicited readers' responses to the Tarnovskaia affair. French sociologist Gabriel Tarde had written in 1898 that "the machine age, since the invention of printing, has brought to life an entirely new kind of public, which has grown unceasingly, and of which the indefinite extension is one of the most distinguishing traits of our period."[98] By inviting readers to participate in a proto public-opinion survey, the editors helped to transform their audience into an identifiable and participatory public, not unlike the crowds who viewed what remained of Gilevich's victim. The lack of science-based random sampling in their solicitation did not make the responses any less useful for purposes of public engagement.

The specific set of questions asked is worth repeating here because they make plain the interest in the relationship between psychology and behavior, the impact of social circumstances looming large. In addition, the editors left questions open-ended to invite further discussion. Pointedly, Tarnovskaia was the only defendant in whom they solicited interest. The question of external influences on her free will dominated:

1. Is Tarnovskaia a criminal or a victim? If a victim, primarily of what?

    A. Heredity?
    B. Upbringing (family, school)?
    C. The conditions of her indecent married life and the fashionable social circles she frequented?

2. Is Tarnovskaia psychologically and physiologically normal? If not, how in your opinion does her abnormality express itself?
3. What was the primary motive for her actions?
4. Would you consider betrayal by your spouse as sufficient to justify a betrayal on your part?
5. What can be said in her defense?
6. Do you believe in the possibility that she can be morally rejuvenated? Under what conditions?
7. If you were on the jury, would you convict or acquit her?
8. Do you personally know such women as Tarnovskaia? What role do they play in their social groups?

The editors also requested that the respondents provide personal data that would permit them to look for correlations between background and attitude: sex, age, marital status,

97. *Ol*, 16 March 1910, no. 61.
98. Quoted in Gregory Shaya, "Mayhem for Moderns: The Culture of Sensationalism in France, c. 1900 (PhD diss., University of Michigan, 2000), 15.

education, and occupation.[99] They reported one hundred responses, which they considered significant, given that "skeptics said that nothing would come of this survey because the Russian public is lazy, stationary, passive. Not so!"[100]

The editors began with a swipe at Lombroso. Given that two-thirds of their respondents were female, they challenged his presumption that women "write less than men . . . as a consequence of less development of the graphic centers." Their explanation for the preponderance of female responses reflected the cultural sexism that made the "court ladies" so prominent. Their caveat rang familiar: "Believe me, I do not want to insult women, but who more than they can gain an understanding of the affairs and entanglements of other families? Who, besides women, are interested in the sins not only of those close to them but also those whom they are likely never even to meet?" In this same vein, the editors considered the male respondents "objective and principled." The women were more likely to have designated themselves simply "middle class" (*srednoe obshchestvo*), 69 percent to 45 percent of men. Unsurprisingly, men listed a "higher education" at an advantage of 31 to 8 percent. The most significant difference between the sex-based answers came on question eight, when 80 percent of the men claimed to be personally acquainted with a type such as Tarnovskaia. Only 67 percent of the women knew such a type. Uniformity came in one category: all of the doctors, who numbered "more than ten," deemed her "sick," a "victim."[101]

The editors selected for publication the most provocative answers. Noting with the caution of social scientists that "it is risky to try to extrapolate from these conclusions explanations of the characteristics of modern society," they published answers that reveal a society engaged with contemporary issues and eager to express their thoughts. Responses ranged from the general to the very specific. One respondent claimed to have studied with Tarnovskaia in secondary school, and described her as "outstanding only for her weak intellectual development and as a teller of lewd tales." She pointed out that "Maria cannot claim innocence with regard to her husband because she knew every well then what kind of man Vasiuka Tarnovskii was . . . everyone knew he had the French disease (syphilis)." A professor from the juridical faculty of an unnamed university opined that "there is no criminal who would not also be a victim of circumstances in which he was born and lived. We are all to a greater or lesser degree victims of these circumstances."[102] One man quipped, "She's a victim of heredity. That is, she wanted to inherit after Komarovskii's death." Another set the sentiment that "Tarnovskaia is one of the victims of that circle from which she came. As a juror, I would render this verdict: guilty, but deserves amelioration."[103]

Because the questions asked solely about Tarnovskaia, a gendered element is expected. Readers responded ardently to issues of sexual equality. A majority of both sexes rejected

99. *Ol*, 3 March 1910, no. 50.

100. *Ol*, 12 March 1910, no. 58.

101. The results were published in the newspaper, beginning with *Ol*, 12 March 1910, no. 58. They were further analyzed by V. A. Sorokin and published as a booklet, *Prestupnitsa-li Tarnovskaia?* (Odessa: M. Prishchelov, 1910).

102. *Ol*, 12 March 1910, no. 58.

103. Ibid.

the justification in the question, "does betrayal by one spouse exonerate betrayal by the other?" but 25 percent of the women and 20 percent of the men approved. Some commentators incriminated the female of the species, and a few chastised Tarnovskaia on the basis of her sex in particular. The more commonly expressed sentiment was that life can be precarious for women in a man's world. Not surprisingly, women evidence more sympathy than men. A husband and wife split their opinion: he called her a criminal motivated by greed, but she countered that Tarnovskaia was a victim of her family's degeneracy.[104] Another woman claimed that "she lived her life as 95 percent of men live theirs," whereas a man wrote that he "would gladly put out cigarettes in her odious body." A man who thought that "society is healthier without the idiots who would kill themselves over her," confessed that his wife found this harsh. And although some women believed that as a mother Tarnovskaia should have held herself to a higher standard, another young mother celebrated: "I adore Tarnovskaia! Let her avenge all the abandoned and damned women! Let her use these means that she enjoys, as a woman, to exert her power over men!"[105]

The most spirited response came not from the survey, but from a maid who sent in her monthly salary, ten rubles, to assure publication. The editors returned the money and printed her words:

> Only men are judging her. I would be interested to see what would happen if judges, lawyers, and jurors were women. . . . The only thing I find her guilty of is that she did not do enough to destroy the lives of those swine. I think the court should be grateful to her, in the name of all Russians, because she liberated us from such procreators and fathers, such garbage as Naumov, Komarovskii, and Prilukov.[106]

A lawyer voiced the opposite view, echoing Foitnitskii that:

> A woman is an instigator by nature. A woman is the soul of crime, and the man carries it out physically. I agree with the French opinion that in every crime you must look for the woman. History tells of many criminal plots, not all of them enacted, in which a woman played an important role, standing in the shadows when the crime was discovered. Thanks to the knightly attitude of her male accomplice, or to the "absence of evidence of her participation" she walks free.[107]

## Tarnovskaia and the Challenge of the "New" Woman

Maria Tarnovskaia found her sexual identity destabilized, deployed by others in a variety of self-interested positions. She personified a paradox that launched coverage of the trial beyond the confines of the packed Venetian courthouse and into the morass of

---

104. *Ol*, 21 March 1910, no. 66.
105. *Ol*, 2 April 1910, no. 75.
106. Ibid.
107. *Ol*, 12 March 1910, no. 58,

modernity: did she better represent the modern "new" woman, or the decaying one of the old world? The answer to that question split along national-cultural-sexual lines.

Where the Italian professional males defined her as decadent because they needed to condemn the weakness of Italy's own aristocratic past, France's New Women celebrated her independence and sexual openness. Specifically, they made the trial about gender rather than race or social estate. In her study of these women in fin de siècle France, Mary Louise Roberts characterizes them as subversives, who "consciously or not . . . exploited (the) volatility of gender norms, undermining convention by imagining new seditious aims for old female roles."[108] The French newspaper *Matin*, jaundiced if not quite "yellow," splashed *La Comtesse Fatale* (the deadly countess) on its front pages.[109] Where *Odesskii listok* had turned to readers, *Matin* interviewed contemporaneously popular French female stage stars and writers to get the women's angle. New Women themselves, in that they put themselves out in the public eye, they expressed a solidarity with Tarnovskaia.[110] Translated and reprinted in the Russian press, this forum allowed Tarnovskaia to transcend the banality of her actions, transformed once again by others into what they needed from her. No loftier star than Sarah Bernhardt, at age sixty-four, still performing on stage, and now on the movie screen, sided with the "deadly countess": "I pity Tarnovskaia with my whole soul, because she never found in life a lover more worthy than those whom she had. Under the circumstances of her life, she had only two choices: kill or be killed."[111]

The writer Daniel Lesueur (pen name of Jeanne Lapauze), "who occupies a top spot in French belles lettres" and received the Legion of Honor in 1900, responded that "Tarnovskaia struck my imagination as a novelist and my feelings as a woman. She is that femme fatale whom we are trying to create in our works, and here life has given her to us in reality." Lesueur was herself a feminist, with an attraction for Nietzschean possibilities to create a *surfemme*, a female *Ubermensch*, but her primary fascination with Tarnovskaia lay in the latter's ability to exercise power over men: "It seems to me that in human beings there are secret forces that slip away from psychologists' skills . . . I sense a magnetic influence, a physical power emanating from our moral being." She connected Tarnovskaia's secrets to those of electricity, which, as she explained, complemented testimony about her hypnotic influences.[112]

Best-selling author Marcelle Tinayre,[113] another outspoken feminist, whose novel *La rebelle* (1906) told the quasi-autobiographical story of a female journalist who ultimately chooses marriage over a professional career, mulled over Tarnovskaia: "An entire legend

---

108. Mary Louise Roberts, *Disruptive Acts: The New Woman in Fin-de-Siècle France* (Chicago: University of Chicago Press, 2002), 244.

109. *Matin*, 2 March 1910, no. 9500.

110. *Matin*, 7 March 1910, no. 9505.

111. These interviews were reprinted in translation for Russian audiences in *Pl*, 26 February 1910, no. 56; and *Ol*, 28 February 1910, no. 48. These newspapers occasionally translated other stories from *Matin* about the case.

112. *Ol*, 28 February 1910, no. 48; Daniel Lesueur, *Nietzscheenne* (Paris: Plon-Nourrit, 1908).

113. On Tinayre, see Roberts, *Disruptive Acts*, 45–46; Margot Irvine, "Marcelle Tinayre's *Notes d'une voyageuse en Turquie*: Creating Solidarity among Women," in *A "Belle Epoque"?: Women in French Society and Culture, 1890–1914*, ed. Diana Holmes and Carrie Tarr (New York: Berghahn Books, 2006), 295–306.

has already been created around her name, but I know from personal experience how necessary it is to be wary of legends. They say that the beauty of this woman is powerful, equal to her fatal charms." Tinayre, though, offered the opinion that what created those charms was "the weakness of men. This Naumov is far from a true Romeo, because committing this murder is not evidence of love." As she pointed out, Naumov "could declare his love by assuming all responsibility for the crime. With tears in his eyes he accused the woman, 'It was she, not I!' . . . this is not a man in love. It's not even a man."[114]

Berthe Badoux, one of the leading actresses of Paris's fashionable *Théâtre du Gymnase*, opined that "this romantic story carries us back to the past, to the era of violent passions. Yet still, all this happened recently, all the characters exist in real life. . . . we look on her with interest, as great material for an actress." Badoux captured the melodramatic essence of the courtroom, that "the Tarnovskaia trial is like a bad play, but one with superlative roles."[115] Although Italy's New Women were not solicited for their opinions in the popular press, one of them, Anna Vivanti, proved equal to the task of re-creating the narrative arc of Tarnovskaia's engrossing life. Born in London in 1865 to an Italian father and German mother, Vivanti wrote poems, novels, and at times sang on the operatic stage, in addition to penning a biography of legendary Italian actress Eleonora Duse.[116] The polyglot Vivanti visited Tarnovskaia after the trial when she was incarcerated at the Trani prison in Puglia. She wrote one semifictional autobiography of Tarnovskaia in French in 1912, which was translated immediately into Russian, and then into English in 1915.[117] Following the account from Tarnovskaia's serialized autobiography, Vivanti turned her into Christianity's most beloved tragic heroine, Mary Magdalene. Victimized by the men in her life, Tarnovkaia truly loved her debauched, indifferent husband, and saw Prilukov as a "scorpion." Vivanti's penitent heroine planned to use Komarovskii's life insurance to repay Prilukov's clients and give the rest to the poor.[118]

The European feminists declaring their support for Tarnovskaia represented a particularly politicized New Woman, one whose primary objective lay in establishing equality of opportunity between the sexes.[119] Paradoxically, Tarnovskaia was by no means one of them. A second type of New Woman had also appeared on the world stage, the femme fatale, or *rokovaia zhenshchina*, to use the Russian.[120] This "fatal female"

114. *Pl*, 26 February 1910, no. 56; and *Ol*, 28 February 1910, no. 48.

115. Ibid.

116. For added intrigue, Vivanti's husband, John Chartres, was a member of British intelligence and sat at the Irish desk. Brian P. Murphy, *John Chartres: Mystery Man of the Treaty* (Dublin: Irish Academic Press, 1995).

117. Anna Vivanti, *Roman Marii Tarnovskoi* (Kiev: Tip. Gazeti Poslednye novosti, 1912). Another pirated translation of the Vivanti biography also appeared in 1912, *Memuary M. Tarnovskoi*, published in Kiev by Samoobrazovanie. Bossi wrote the introduction to Vivanti's book, accentuating "his life work to investigate the relation in women between criminal impulse and morbid physical condition" (vii).

118. Vivanti, *Roman Marii Tarnovskoi*, 140.

119. Sarah Grand coined the term "New Woman" in 1894, "in reference to women who were entering higher education and new areas of employment." Rebecca Stott, *The Fabrication of the Late Victorian Femme Fatale: The Kiss of Death* (New York: Palgrave Macmillan, 1996), 12.

120. The *Chicago Daily Tribune* echoed the Italian fears, calling her a "succubus [that] typifies the acme of modern degenerate feminism" and "the product of worn out civilization" (April 25, 1910).

embodied the male angst about the changing relationship between the sexes. Born in turn-of-the-century high art, she found herself staged most powerfully by Oscar Wilde in his play *Salomé* (1891), the New Testament story of the young woman who demanded the head of John the Baptist as her reward for performing the erotic dance of the seven veils.[121] Androgynous, she was as aggressively male in her behavior as she was excessively female in her appearance, as Bekhterev, Lombroso, and Morselli had characterized Tarnovskaia.[122] A predator, like the black widow and the vampire who devour their partners after sex, the femme fatale surfaced as the self-destructive sexual fantasy of the fin de siècle male forced to grapple not only with social change but also with developments in psychology that made him susceptible to instincts and environments over which he had no control. Like Tarnovskaia, the femme fatale was often racialized, another of the dangers in the culture of imperialism that was about to launch Italy into war in Tripolitania.[123] When the Italian press wrote of this "Slavic tragedy," it was casting the tsarist empire as a degenerate, predatory female.

Vlas Doroshevich of *Russkoe slovo*, Russia's leading newspaper columnist, looked only at the superficiality of calling her a femme fatale. He portrayed her more of an aspirant toward the social equality that France's New Women spoke about, not the vampire that she was. In a column reprinted in other newspapers entitled *Rokovaia zhenshchina*, he observed that Tarnovskaia was on trial for actions that others had taken. Commenting sarcastically that it would make as much sense to blame Halley's comet, which was at the time making one of its periodic close orbits around the earth, he kept the discussion focused on gender, but shifted the accusations away from Tarnovskaia toward the men involved. Contemptuous of how they blamed her for their problems, he noted the incongruity that because of their love for her she was on trial. He rejected Naumov's claims of being hypnotized, and mocked Prilukov: "Let's stand together at the insurance company and declare our feelings and, God willing, a notary will crown our love!"[124]

Nemirovich-Danchenko gave Tarnovskaia the last word by writing a column in her voice, in which she spoke about male hypocrisy. He began in praise of her behavior, especially when contrasted with that of the Venetian "court ladies," with "their matted, unkempt hair plastered to their unappealing, sweaty brows." The journalist admired in particular what others had disliked, Tarnovskaia's stoicism as she "endured all the blows inflicted by the procurator, and her 'yesterday' lovers." On the stand Maria had blamed her husband and Prilukov, but now Nemirovich-Danchenko had turned her into victim of her gendered environment. His Tarnovskaia used the men to explain rather than to excuse her actions: "I am not waiting for acquittal, not expecting it. There is court. The law. The murder happened. I alone am guilty." The crusader in him took over, as he continued to put words in her mouth: "Gentlemen of the court, remember your childhoods, in school,

121. Patrick Bade, *Femme Fatale: Images of Evil and Fascinating Women* (New York: Mayflower Books, 1970), 6. *Ol* reported that the French press had compared her to "the cruel 'Salomé' depicted by Wilde." *Ol*, 31 March 1910, no. 73.

122. Bade, *Femme Fatale*, 39.

123. Stott, *Fabrication*, especially 36–37.

124. V. M. Doroshevich, "Rokovaia zhenshchina," *Rs*, 21 February 1910, no. 42.

the cadet corps, in Junker uniforms, did you not lie to girls? . . . Why do you demand that I be cleaner, stronger, more moral than you?[125]

The "gifted and objectionable" journalist Vasilii Rozanov appreciated the predatory New Woman, but primarily because he disliked the monotony he found inherent in liberalism.[126] A member of Moscow's eclectic Religious-Philosophical Society and a bitter critic of positivism, Rozanov was one of the most controversial representatives of Russia's Silver Age, then in full cultural swing. Obsessed with race, sexuality, and modernity, he was a natural to offer his view of the affair, about which he wrote under the pseudonym "V. Varvarin" in *Russkoe slovo*.[127] Where the Italians had racialized the story as "Slavic," Rozanov had found a distinctively cultural Russianness about it. Morselli had grounded Russian women in Turgenev's heroines, but Rozanov turned to Dostoevsky. Opening with a quote from the procurator's indictment of Mitia in *The Brothers Karamazov* that "our fatal troika is moving headlong, maybe to destruction . . . at an insane gallop," he observed that "these words can't help but remind of the telegrams arriving from Vienna." He invited readers to "remember Nastasia Filipovna in *The Idiot*; no reader can decide if she's insane or not, but no one doubts that she's abnormal," like Tarnovskaia.[128]

Rozanov, who often self-identified as female, spoke comfortably as Tarnovskaia: "I ran into three men. Before meeting me they were 'honorable, quiet, and hardworking,' like every juror, like the psychiatrists, doctors, and judges, all judging me." In the fin de siècle dichotomy between Apollonian rationale and Dionysian indulgence made popular by Nietzsche, Rozanov's Tarnovskaia embraced the latter: "It's simple: we're beautiful, and not only in our body are we entertaining. Men go out of their minds over us, in ways that they don't for their wives." Rozanov, though, was talking about sex, not social inequity. His Tarnovskaia asks, "What are you judging Naumov for? Because he freed himself from the chains of the governor's chancellery and suddenly ran after me? Or that because of me Prilukov tossed aside civil trials?" Rozanov reminded readers how Tarnovskaia's victims celebrated "exactly as Pushkin had: death exchanged for an hour of sweetness . . . don't forget that the mortally wounded Komarovskii asked first, 'has Tarnovskaia been informed?' " Rozanov concluded, "In calm, reasonable, and truly too philistine Europe, the 'Tarnovskaia Affair' raised old memories." He preferred "not to be judged by philistine-jurors, but by passionate romantics."[129] Russia would be spared the bourgeois future that Rozanov found so distasteful. Italy, in contrast, wanted those old memories expunged.

The Russian preference for Tarnovskaia had been prompted by the nature of the Italian attack on her, but the end result had forced a number of liberal Russians to speak out in favor of this degenerate vampire. Rozanov had a point, and the liberals did not have all the answers. A five-act play about the trial written by "Prince Myshkin" succeeded

125. V. I. Nemirovich-Danchenko, "Poslednoe slovo," *Rs*, 12 March 1910, no. 57.

126. Laura Engelstein, *Keys to Happiness: Sex and the Search for Modernity in Fin-de-Siècle Russia* (Ithaca: Cornell University Press, 1992), 12. Engelstein devotes chapter 8 to his "patriarchal eroticism."

127. Rozanov took this pseudonym from his wife's name, Varvara. Vera Proskurina, "Vasilii Rozanov's Erotic Mythology," in Levitt and Topokov, *Eros and Pornography*, 282.

128. *Rs*, 5 March 1910, no. 52.

129. Ibid.

at Russifying her character by giving her attributes of both New Women. Although the drama ends with two professor-experts observing that "the legend of the *rokovaia zhenshchina* has disappeared, and what remains is confidence in the stupidity of men," the source of her fatalism rested in her pursuit of her desires.[130] It took an inept and anonymous playwright to articulate the paradox, as Rita Felski pointed out, of "the relationship between modern discourses of sexuality and the emancipation of women." As Felski further argued, "desire [is] constitutive of our modern sense of subjectivity as such." At the turn of the twentieth century, acknowledging the status of women as "desiring subjects" conferred "upon them a form of symbolic citizenship."[131] Still, Tarnovskaia made a very poor role model for the subjective citizen. Just as Gilevich had made a highly problematic self-actuating individual, so did Tarnovskaia lack the politically correct credentials desirable for liberalism's New Woman. What was liberal Russia to do?

## Conclusion

The verdicts came in as anticipated: Perrier was acquitted, but the other three were convicted of some degree of guilt, their sentences lessened because Komarovskii had died from peritonitis. Naumov received the lightest, three years and one month. Tarnovskaia's eight years more than doubled that. Prilukov, the "living corpse" who had seemed peripheral to the trial, was handed the harshest punishment, ten years, guilty in essence of being so detestable. The Venetian police had fire hoses ready to dampen prospective rioters, but only a few fights broke out between Naumov's fans and those Tarnovskaia had been able to muster by the end of the trial. Leaving the courtroom, Naumov kissed her hand, to cheers. Then the curtain came down on this woeful comic opera.

Prilukov returned into his jail cell, but Naumov walked away on the basis of "time served." The men disappeared into history, but not so Tarnovskaia. Months later the *Washington Post* reported her "good time in Venice prison" with "jailers her slaves" and smoking smuggled cigarettes.[132] In 1913 she was mistakenly reported to have hanged herself in a railroad station, still grabbing headlines as the "deadly countess."[133] The outbreak of the First World War made Russia's decadent nobility unbearably trite, and Tarnovskaia was released from Trani. Her historical trail then ran cold, though she died where so many other European refugees ended up, in Argentina, in 1949.

A second biography of her appeared in German in 1962.[134] Written by Hans Habe, the most common of the pen names used by Jewish-Hungarian journalist Janos Békessy,

130. *Ubiistvo pod gipnozom*, 2nd ed. (St. Petersburg: Teatral'naia novinka, 1910), 36.

131. Rita Felski, *The Gender of Modernity* (Cambridge: Harvard University Press, 1995), 181–82. She refers to Lawrence Birken's *Consuming Desire: Sexual Science and the Emergence of a Culture of Abundance, 1871–1914* (Ithaca: Cornell University Press, 1988) on desire and subjectivity.

132. *Washington Post*, 22 January 1911.

133. *New York Times*, 18 August 1913.

134. Hans Habe, *Die Tarnowska* (Vienna: Verlag Kurt Desch, 1962), translated into English by Catherine Hutter as *Countess Tarnovska* (London: George C. Harrap, 1963).

this novelization uses Tarnovskaia to ponder the possibilities of Christian redemption. A tragic coincidence connected Habe and Tarnovskaia: his seventeen-year-old daughter was brutally stabbed to death, her body found "in the thick underbrush of Mulholland Drive" in Los Angeles on January 2, 1969.[135] That summer the Charles Manson family went on its killing spree in a neighborhood not far from this address, which led to the conjecture that Marina had been their first victim. Manson, like Tarnovskaia, did not commit the murders himself, but was convicted for his ability to bend others to his violent will. This roundabout connection between Tarnovskaia and Manson is located where it belongs, in the sphere of speculation, publicity, and sensational trials that capture widespread public attention. Maria Tarnovskaia was a small-minded woman who found others like herself with whom to pervert sex, drugs, and money. There was nothing historically significant about this behavior, but, specific as it was to a time and place, it fired into contemporaneous debates about other issues that elevated the status of a few profane Russians well beyond what their sordid lives merited.

135. The murder, with a photograph of the young Marina Elizabeth, made the front page of the *Los Angeles Times* that day. *The New York Times* and other national newspapers also covered this story.

CHAPTER SEVEN

# CRIME FICTION STEPS INTO ACTION

"I've been as bad an influence on American literature as anyone I can think of."
—Dashiell Hammett, the author who, as James Ellroy put it,
"gave murder back to the people who actually committed it."

Suddenly we heard a nervous knock at the door.

"Come in!" cried Putilin.

In the doorway stood the senior agent on duty, pale and quivering.

"Sir, there has been a horrible crime," he said.

"What's going on?" Putilin asked anxiously.

"We have just been informed that in three different areas of the city three corpses
have been found."

"What's so terrible about that, my friend?" smiled Putilin.

"You didn't let me finish, sir. All three bodies have been found without their heads."

"What? Without their heads?" Putilin jumped up.

"Yes. Their heads have all been cut off. Judging by the freshness of their blood, the
heads were cut off very recently and, evidently, not from corpses but from live people."

Putilin winced. I did not feel so well.[1]

Thus begins "Eleven Headless Corpses," starring a fictional Petersburg chief of detectives
I. D. Putilin, who borrowed nothing more than his name from the real Putilin. Written
by Roman Dobryi (R. L. Andropov) and published during the interrevolutionary years,
1907–1917, these stories circulated when the memories of street violence were still fresh
in readers' minds. The second writer to fictionalize Putilin, Dobryi created a very different
Putilin than had M. V. Shevliakov, who began ghost writing for the retired detective in the
1890s, when Putilin needed the money to pay off debts. Sadly, the detective's premature
death from influenza in 1893 kept from him both the financial benefits and the knowledge

---

1. "Odinnadtsat' trupov bez golovy," in *Russkii syshchik I. D. Putilin*, 2 vols. (Moscow: TERRA, Knizhnaia
lavka—RTR, 1997), 2:226–44.

that he had become Russia's first detective to star in hero-centered pulp fiction.[2] More accurately, he was the only one.[3]

Putilin and Shevliakov had sorted through notes from the retired detective's investigations, newspaper clippings, and stenographic accounts of subsequent trials, repackaging his life into sketches. Shevliakov's story "The Human Satan," its title scarier than the perpetrator, begins:

> Early on the morning of 25 November a cop on the beat at Semenovskii Square found the corpse of an unknown man, lying in the snow face down, his hands tied to his body. Investigating further, the police doctor and other local officials observed that his neck had been tied with a so-called "hangman's noose" made of thick twine. In the victim's pocket they found a pack of grease-stained cards and a few needles. A more careful examination of the corpse showed that the middle finger on his right hand had been pricked several times, obviously from the needles.

Putilin deduces that the cuts on the victim's fingers identify him as a tailor, information that has no bearing on the solution. Three weeks later, a second body is found with a hangman's noose. Putilin sends his *syshchiki* undercover to eavesdrop on patrons in *traktiry*. One overhears a conversation at the Peking (the hangout where the laundress accused in the Gusev Lane deaths had established her alibi of drunkenness), which leads them to the killer, a common criminal who strangles his victims before robbing them. Ultimately the Petersburg police depend upon a confession from one of the title character's henchman to capture him.[4] So much for deduction.

Both authors wrote under the shadow of Arthur Conan Doyle, whose influence could be found in superficial borrowings. Shevliakov dubbed Putilin the "Russian Sherlock Holmes," and his stories fit neatly into the turn-of-the-century transition from moralistic crime fictions to action-oriented serials. Dobryi gave his detective a physician as a sidekick-cum-narrator, Ivan Nikolaevich. Dobryi's doctor Ivan Nikolaevich, though, is not the "intermediary between the reader and the dramatic action" that makes Watson so critical to the narrative structure of the Holmes stories.[5] Ivan Nikolaevich plays the foil for the detective: "Putilin was always a great positivist, but I, despite the fact that I am a doctor by profession, am inclined to allow that, as Hamlet said to Horatio, 'There are more things in heaven and earth than are dreamt of in your philosophy.'"[6]

What strikes straightaway in comparing Shevliakov's with Dobryi's personifications of Putilin is the latter's descriptions of excessively horrifying crimes. The opening passage from "Eleven Headless Corpses" taps straight into fear:

2. Ivan Putilin, *Russkii Sherlok Kholms: Zapiski nachal'nika Sankt-Peterburgskogo syska* (Moscow: Eksmo Press, 2001), 4–10. The quote is from *Russkii syshchik*, 1:264.

3. The former chief of Kharkov detectives V. V. Lange wrote memoirs, *Prestupnyi mir: Moi vospominaniia ob Odesse i Kharkove* (Odessa: L. Nitche, 1906), but he did not then star in action fiction.

4. "Chelovek-satan," in Ivan Putilin, 258–64.

5. Pierre Nordon, *Conan Doyle: A Biography*, trans. Frances Partridge (New York: Holt, Rinehart and Winston, 1967), 268.

6. "Tainy okhtinskogo kladbishcha," *Russkii syshchik*, 2:264.

I must tell you that for the past two years there have been exceptionally brutal, bloody incidents. . . . Sometimes Putilin would send for me at night: "My friend, I need your help. Can you tell me, in your opinion, how long this person lived after the wounds were inflicted? I must know."

A "panic grips Petersburg," understandably, as headless bodies pile up in the streets, to be laid out in a makeshift morgue, the severed heads beside them, available for viewing to the interested public.[7] It is not clear whether this story appeared before or after Gilevich perpetrated his analogous deed on a significantly smaller but real-life scale, though the parallels are obvious. Putilin, confident that the killer will want to admire his handiwork, watches as a veiled woman adjusts one of the heads.[8] Tracking her, he discovers her to be Grunia, the leader of the cutthroat gang determined to make *his* head their twelfth. Putilin evades this fate, and when the jury exiles her to Siberia, she taunts them that escape from there will be easy.

The contrast between Shevliakov and Dobryi, writing ostensibly about the same person and their work separated by only a few years, brings into focus the heightened sensationalism in crime fiction after 1905, giving insight into some of the revolution's cultural repercussions. Two visions of Russia emerge. One is as fast paced as modernity itself, offering outlines, albeit dimly lit, of a future built on the detective's world of law-and-order stability. Stimulating courage and confidence, the stories of this genre tapped into the violence of revolution and offered a way forward, suggesting a future installment.

The other vision, however, draws from stories that feature a crime but do not resolve it. No resolution means that no order is restored, no one is punished, and no closure that can make sense of the crime. Thus the audience finds itself mired in a perpetual present, that is, in a space without the security of a usable past, one that had been disrupted by the crime. Being stuck in the present lessens enthusiasm about the possibilities that lie in the future.[9] This crime fiction drew from the fatalism that characterizes much of Russian culture, undercutting the potential for liberalism's self-actualizing individual. Thus this genre supplied both causes and effects of postrevolutionary instability.

Dobryi's Putilin differed from Shevliakov's because his Russia did too. Cities were growing too quickly for civic leaders to manage them. Economic growth put more money in more pockets and encouraged commercialism. Russians of all social strata enjoyed varying degrees of political self-confidence from the gains made by taking to the streets in political demonstrations in 1905. For many, though, confidence had been shaken by the limits of their success and the government's brutal reprisal. As a result, new kinds

7. In "Odinnadtsat' trupov," 230, Ivan Nikolaevich described the bodies in detail; they are eerily reminiscent of "The Kingdom of Corpses" from the Gilevich case: "What a terrible sight! It froze the soul. Eight headless, naked corpses lay close to one another. They were all strong, healthy male bodies, deformed by the struggles they suffered in death."

8. The scene at the morgue reminds of interest in Gilevich's victim: "Who wasn't there, in this motley ribbon of public, stretching out continuously, uninterruptedly. It was a lively kaleidoscope of the most diverse Petersburg types, beginning with the beggars and ending with the fashionable ladies dressed to the nines." "Odinnadtsat' trupov," 230.

9. Anders Stephanson, "A Conversation with Fredric Jameson regarding Postmodernism," *Social Text*, no. 17 (1987): 41.

Fig. 25. Roman Dobryi's Putilin series:
*Forty Years among Murderers and Thieves.*

of audiences were taking shape, whose tastes and interests were amplified by the pace of change. The burgeoning urban middle strata, from bureaucrats to workers, consumed them, but a significant portion of the audience was teenage, the generation that would reach adulthood during the years of war and revolution.[10]

Russians followed readers in other industrializing nations when they began purchasing crisp, cheap, and exciting crime fiction. One visual affect came directly from the media of the 1905 Revolution, the satirical journals that flourished when the censorship lost much of its authority.[11] Many of these journals splashed color on their covers, the red of the blood in the streets.[12] Visuals played an even more influential role when projected onto canvas, as narrative cinema became technologically and culturally feasible after 1908; in the Russian context, this coincided with the postrevolutionary ethos that balanced precariously between promise and defeat. Distinguished by its sensationalism, this commercial literature stimulated bodily sensations. Like the heroes and villains, readers would break out

---

10. Students in Kiev formed a "Society of Readers of Holmes and Pinkerton." A. I. Reitblat, *Ot Bovy k Balmontu: i drugie raboty po istoricheskoi sotsiologii russkoi literatury* (Moscow: Novoe literaturnoe obozrenie, 2009), 299, 305. Boris Dralyuk writes of the poets Alexander Blok and Sergei Esenin, who loved these adventures. "Pinkertonovshchina, 1907–1934: The Cultural Reception of 'Western' Detective Serials in Pre-Revolutionary Russia and the Soviet Union" (PhD diss., University of California at Los Angeles, 2011), 25–26, 32.

11. Dobryi also contributed to the 1905 satirical journal Burelom.

12. Oleg Minin, "The Value of the Liberated Word: The Russian Satirical Press of 1905 and the Theory of Cultural Production," *Russian Review* 70, no. 2 (2011): 220.

in a cold sweat, freeze with terror, feel their heartbeats quicken and their skin prickle with goose bumps.[13] Everywhere decried by critics for its appeal to base emotional instincts at the expense of superior reason, this fiction was imbued with political power precisely because it struck emotional chords.

Following anthropologists and sociologists, historians have begun to include emotions in the larger cultural context for analyzing social and political change.[14] Looking back at the crime fiction analyzed in chapter four, the dominant emotion of empathy with the killer complemented, even helped to engender, the high percentage of acquittals. Pathological *affekt* became acceptable as a factor mitigating culpability, a byproduct of *The Kreutzer Sonata*. After 1905, the action-fiction intensified sensations, helping to generate "a specific manner of apprehending the world."[15] Consuming the action-fiction must be understood as a social practice, that is, a way in which individual readers connect to the larger society. "Organized by stories and images," crime fiction on page and screen provided its audiences with "experience(s) inseparable from the culturally situated language and gestures in which it is conveyed."[16] The social practice of enjoying crime fiction was not itself new, but after 1905 the narratives had been affected by events and the audiences had expanded considerably.


## Putilin to Pinkerton

Published posthumously in a series of eighteen booklets that enjoyed a combined circulation of at least 383,000,[17] Putilin's escapades did not circulate abroad in translation, just as Shkliarevskii's had not in the 1870s. This lack of transnational appeal underscores the cultural particularity of the Russian genre. The initial collection of Putilin's stories appeared in 1898 in *From the Realm of Adventures*.[18] Shevliakov's recounting of Putilin's first major case, the murder in Gusev Lane, makes good use of the newspaper reports from the crime scenes, and it tells of the case that Putilin put together for the prosecution rather than from the trial. Daria Sokolova finds herself remade from head to toe in "The Bloody Beauty's Dastardly Deed."[19]

Like news reports and bills of indictments, crimes scenes were often splattered with blood and brains in Shevliakov's stories. His descriptions of the suspects illustrate

13. When asked why he read these stories, one student responded, "terror grips me, and I am filled with dread." V. Soroka, "Nat Pinkterton i detskaia literatura," *Russkaia shkola*, no. 1 (1910): 51.

14. Jan Plamper credited "the new genres like crime novels that allowed for the production of fear in readers," a contributing factor to what he refers to as a "new permissibility of fear." In "Fear: Soldiers and Emotion in Early Twentieth-Century Russian Military Psychology," *Slavic Review* 68, no. 2 (2009): 263.

15. Jean Paul Sarte, quoted in Sara Ahmed, *The Cultural Politics of Emotion* (New York Routledge, 2004), 5.

16. Mark D. Steinberg, "Melancholy and Modernity: Emotions and Social Life in Russia between the Revolutions," *Journal of Social History* 41, no. 4 (2008): 815.

17. Jeffrey Brooks, *When Russia Learned to Read: Literacy and Popular Literature, 1861–1917* (Evanston: Northwestern University Press, 2003), 146.

18. *Iz oblasti prikliuchenii: Po rasskazam byvshogo nachal'nika Sankt-Peterburgskii sysknoi politsii I. D. Putilina* (St. Petersburg: Demakov, 1898).

19. "Strashnoe delo krovavoi krasavitsy," in *Ivan Putilin*, 233–50.

Lombroso's influence: "The *dvornik* made a negative impression on me immediately. Pock-marked, with high cheekbones, and sharp, crossed eyes, he struck me as a sly rogue."[20] His clever *syshchik* finds Daria when overhearing a conversation about a soldier's wife who had returned the previous year to her village with surprising wealth. Bluffed into confessing in 1867, the unschooled peasant woman now turns into a dynamic force capable of matching wits with Putilin. No pockmarked prostitute she, but a "healthy beauty, with even, white teeth," who fought with "unusual strength, not female."[21] Her physiology explained how she evaded him for so long.

Shevliakov's stories make plain the influence of the factual memoirs written by the judicial investigators in the 1870s. Observing that "sometimes I think that not even doctors and priests, our most intimate witnesses, have heard as many secrets or uncovered the hidden as have I," his Putilin wrote sympathetically about murderers who had been "seduced" by the circumstances of poverty to kill for money on the spur of the moment. Characteristically, they repent their crimes. As he ruminated, "an hour earlier this person did not know that he would . . . slash or strangle, and then wander confusedly . . . unable to forget."[22] Like the emergent psychiatrist trying to put together the pieces of the mind, the professional detective was learning that the mind was also one of the pieces of the puzzle of the crime he had to solve.[23]

Dobryi's Putilin, on the other hand, speaks directly to the anxieties left from the terror that had roamed the streets during the revolution. "The Petersburg Jack the Ripper" opens with Ivan Nikolaevich being awakened to conduct the forensic examination of a young woman found disemboweled in a house where no one knew her:

> On the stone floor of the vestibule lay the corpse of a young woman completely nude. A cross had been carved on her stomach, and her internal organs were spilling out. . . .
>
> "What is this? What's going on?" I turned to my colleague, the police doctor.
>
> "Well, not a caesarian section. We doctors perform that operation more carefully," he joked.
>
> I did not think that amusing and glanced at Putilin.[24]

In "Petersburg Ripper," the policeman in charge arrests the *dvornik* when he cannot explain a wound in his hand, and a search of his quarters turns up a diamond ring. Putilin, though, is more interested in the other residents of the house, especially the engineer who had not moved out when the other frightened residents had left. Someone new moves in, a gentleman with sideburns[25] who flirts with the engineer's maid, Masha. Readers familiar

---

20. Ibid, 236.

21. Ibid., 249.

22. "Soblaznennye," *Russkii syshchik*, 1:120–28.

23. Sigmund Freud enjoyed detective fiction, "fully aware of the analogies between psychoanalytic investigation and detective work." Peter Brooks, *Reading for the Plot: Design and Intention in Narrative* (New York: A. A. Knopf, 1984), 270.

24. "Peterburgskii Dzhek-potroshitel'," *Russkii syshchik*, 2:103.

25. Putilin was famous for his sideburns.

with the formula recognize the engineer to be the killer, and Putilin the flirt. Gaining access via Masha to the engineer's rooms, Putilin learns that he had been betrayed by his wife and vowed to take his revenge on other unfaithful women, such as the victim, whom he had seduced into coming home with him. A young woman in Putilin's employ entraps the killer; this female detective, familiar from serial fiction, improved on women's factual professional options. Pathological *affekt* now a clinical illness, Putilin assures the crazed killer that, because the latter has obviously suffered a nervous collapse, he will testify on his behalf. The jury dispatches him to a hospital rather than to hard labor.[26]

Other crime fiction that negotiated the transition included "The Clandestine Murder and Robbery of a Millionaire Merchant." A booklet from 1906, it showcased cooperation between the police and the lower classes that contradicted much of what could be seen on the streets. A doorman is found knocked unconscious, the millionaire merchant inside, "his head beaten in, swimming in a pool of blood." Unlike the misfortunate *dvornik* in Gusev Lane in 1867, this one is a chief witness rather than a suspect. The "experienced police were grateful to accept (his) services, and did not spare any of the state's money to send him around" in search of the culprits, who had stayed in Moscow and rented rooms on notorious Tverskaia Street. No less able than a detective to don disguises, the *dvornik* passes as an educated man, eventually recognizing one gunman's voice at a masquerade. The jury sends the killer and his confederate to hard labor, but that was not punishment enough, and they were shot trying to escape: "thus did the just Lord punish these men, forsaken by God and with no mercy in their hearts, for killing an innocent man."[27]

True crime could be simplified for five kopecks. A case from 1901 that had merited thirteen pages as the story "Family Drama" in the collection *The Criminal World and Its Defenders* was shortened into a booklet and rewritten to emphasize violent death over motive:[28] "The Murder of the Merchant's Wife in the Courtyard" (1905) now told the simple story of a jealous husband who shot his wife for flirting with the *dvornik*.[29] "The Contemporary Conscience," a "dramatic scene" performed on the Petersburg stage in 1907, took imagery from Pushkin's "Queen of Spades": A man sees a ghost while playing cards. He confesses to his wife that he is being haunted by his guilty conscience, that five years ago he discovered a passenger with a stuffed wallet sleeping in his train car and killed him for the money. This version takes a contemporary twist when it turns out that the victim had not died. Carrying more money than the killer had taken, he lied to the insurance company in order to collect the full amount as stolen.[30] Portentous of Gilevich.

One particularly emotional story merited retelling across time and genre. "She Killed Her Fiancé, or Crazy with Love" (1907) began as a true crime in nineteenth-century

26. "Peterburgskii Dzhek-potroshitel'," 103–15.

27. V. Moskevich, "Taunstvennoe ubiistvo i ograblenie kuptsa-millionera" (Moscow: Filatov, 1906).

28. "Semeinaia drama," in N. V. Nikitin, *Prestupnyi mir i ego zashchitniki* (St. Petersburg: Trud, 1902), 27–40.

29. M. Zotov, *Ubiistvo Ligovskoi kupchikhi v dvornitskoi* (St. Peterburg: Odnobishchev, 1905). This was the "Kashin affair" from 1901. Zashchitnik Karabchevskii got secured his acquittal. "Delo Nikolaia Kashina," N. P. Karabchevskii. *Rechi.* 1882–1912. 2nd ed. (Supplemented with five speeches) (St. Petersburg: Trud, 1902), 468.

30. A. E. Zarin, *Sovremennaia sovest'* (St. Petersburg: Busel', 1907).

Nizhnii Novgorod, moved to the stage in *The Merchant Osipov's Murderous Daughter* (1894), and was now a short story. In a tragic clash between the old ways and the new, a merchant's daughter accidentally kills the clerk whom she loves, after her patriarchal father had promised her to someone else.[31] In the 1907 version, her father's decision drives the girl insane. Audiences now find her "throwing herself on the floor, tearing out her hair, and banging her head against the table." Escaping the nurse assigned to guard her, she stabs the hapless clerk while swearing to him her eternal love.[32] The conflict between past and present still unresolved, the tragedy was made into a movie in 1913. Now *The Merchant Bashkirov's Daughter* suffers rape by the peasant who helped her and knows her secret. She does him in by liquoring him up and setting fire to the *traktir* in which he has passed out.[33]

Borrowing a pre-1905 scenario and rewriting it in more horrific detail cost another young woman her head in the public baths in 1909. Now, her father's corpse hung above hers, "his eyes popping out of their orbits, his tongue hanging out by its full length." In "The Terrible Drama in the Moscow Baths," the killer leaves a note pinned to the father's corpse, so this time the investigator can solve the crime. The dead man was a Jewish moneylender who had pressured the killer's wife, in debt to him, to commit a robbery. Her subsequent guilt drove her to slit their daughter's throat before hanging herself. As the note pinned to the victim explained, their ghosts had haunted the killer, urging vengeance. The defense turned to the Talmud: "An eye for an eye." Acquittal.[34]

The master of pulp A.E. Zarin wrote much and across genres. "The Story of One Investigation" (1909) opens with the body of a moneylender found in a park, his head chopped opened, a pocket ripped off suspiciously. The main characters read about it appropriately in the boulevard *Peterburgskaia gazeta*. Treading the line between public and private, detective A.R. Patmosov, "well built and with an intelligent face . . . takes up cases when asked by private individuals, and the police often turn to him for their most difficult cases." The father of the young man arrested by the official investigator comes to Patmosov with Putilin's business card, and the detective nabs the real killer, a portrait painter in love with a married woman being blackmailed by the victim. The torn pocket held letters from the wife to the painter in which she confides that she cannot cheat on her kindly husband, despite her feelings for the artist. All's morally well, so it ends well: the jury mitigates the murderer's sentence, the elderly husband dies of natural causes, and the couple lives happily in exile in Irkutsk.[35]

The prolific Khristofor Shukhmin, who disappeared from the pages of literary history as quickly as his fiction did from the memory of its readers, tried recreating Western-style detective fiction in serial form around the character of a detective Zubarev. Insisting upon authenticity, Shukhmin claimed that the stories were notes from real cases that had been

31. P.I. Felonoz, "Ubiitsa kupecheskaia doch' Osipova" (Moscow: n. p., 1894).

32. "Ubiistvo nevestoi svoego zhenikha, ili sumashestvie ot liubvi" (Moscow: Maksimov, 1907), 11.

33. *Doch' kuptsa Bashkirova*, dir. Nikolai Larin, 1913. Released by Milestone Film & Video, 1992.

34. *Strashnaia drama v Moskovskikh baniakh* (Moscow: Maksimov, 1909). I thank Ethan Pollack for bringing me this story.

35. A.E. Zarin, *Istoriia odnogo syska* (St. Petersburg: Pushkinskaia skoropechatnia, 1909). This was part of a series, "the best criminal novels, trials, and memoirs."

sold to him in 1907 by a relative of Zubarev's. Privileging the investigation itself, in the story "In the Networks of Thieves and Robbers," Zubarev used his powers of deduction to identify the wrongdoers from dust and spots that went unnoticed to the unpracticed eye. His ability to disguise himself being equally laudatory, he returned a merchant's kidnaped family to the merchant before any ransom was paid.[36] When the Great War broke out Shukhmin replaced Zubarev with action hero "The Brave Cossack Kuz'ma Kriuchkov." Shukhmin's idea that soldiers would replace detectives as action heroes, however, proved ill-founded.[37]


## The Americans to the Rescue!

For readers who had no interest in shades of gray, American crime fighters came to Russia to pump up the action in black and white. Nor is there any equivocation about the exotic American electric chair, which ends many of these adventures, even though Russians were by and large emphatically against the death penalty. These foreign detectives, especially Nat Pinkerton and Nick Carter, must be included as an aspect of the Russian genre because of their singular popularity with Russian readers. Significantly different from super sleuth Sherlock Holmes, the Americans came from a tradition that understood detectives to be more visceral than cerebral, and to use guns and fists where Holmes and Gaboriau had specialized in quiet observation. This genre had shoved aside Poe's Dupin in favor of Allan Pinkerton, the man who had founded the first detective agency in Chicago in 1852. The Pinkertons branched out from solving train robberies to spying for the Union during the Civil War, and then became a quasi-paramilitary force in the fight against organized labor. Like Putilin, Pinkerton employed ghostwriters to aggrandize his life in such stories as "The Mississippi Outlaws and the Detective" (1879). A second edition of his "The Molly Maguires and the Detectives" (1877), about his battle with radical Irish workers on strike in the Pennsylvania coalmines, appeared ironically in 1905.[38]

It was not, however, the strikebreaking Pinkerton who captured the imaginations of readers at the turn of the twentieth century. Nat, a private "consulting" detective, starred as the most popular of the hero-centered action booklets that were selling reportedly by the millions in Russia in 1908.[39] The creation of German pulp writers who cashed in on

36. Khristofor Shukhmin, "V setiakh vorov i grabitelei: Razskas po zapiskam syshchika Zubareva" (Moscow: A. S. Balashov, 1914).

37. A legitimate war hero in 1914, Kriuchkov found himself transformed into a semi-fictional character whose exploits were embellished for pleasurable patriotism. Hubertus F. Jahn, *Patriotic Culture in Russia during World War I* (Ithaca: Cornell University Press, 1995), 24, 158.

38. "Amerikanskii Sherlok Kholms," an obituary for the recently deceased Robert Pinkerton, Allan's son, points out that Pinkertons helped "arch-millionaires" during strikes, when they went under cover as workers. In *Vestnik politsii* (hereafter *Vp*), no. 6 (1908): 22–23. "Kto takoi Nat Pinkerton?," a story in *Vestnik politsii*, no. 5 (1910): 152–53, reprinted from *Novoe vremia* (hereafter *Nv*), reports that he "directed a supragovernmental organ of American millionaires that destroyed trade unions," and was not the author of the serials.

39. Reitblat, *Ot Bovy*, 302, estimates that in 1908, 624 serials were published, with a combined circulation of ten million. Boris Dralyuk has compiled the numbers from *Knizhnaia letopis'* for 1907–1909, which supports Reitblat's figures. I thank him for making them available to me.

the popular interest in such Americana as Nick Carter, Buffalo Bill, and Philadelphia's own trigger-happy Ethel King, Nat's name may well have come from the Pinkerton "National" Detective Agency.[40] Authorship of this pulp is impossible to identify with certitude, and the serials that circulated in Russia included translations as well as the borrowing of the formula and colorful covers by Russian authors. Aided by his hardheaded German-American sidekick, Bob Ruland, Nat enjoys episodic adventures in Berlin and Hamburg, though his primary locale is American cities.[41] German hacks also created their own version of the French gentleman thief Arsène Lupin in the character of Lord Lister, who stole from the rich for the poor.[42] Their culturally specific twists in plot and character identify some of these installments as written by Russians, but the phenomenon did not depend on native authors.[43]

Nat and his cohorts burst onto the Russian scene so quickly that cultural elites complained about a *Pinkertonovshchina*, a wave of serial detectives bleaching high ideals out of the brains of young readers. The audience extended well beyond school children, as even *Vestnik politsii*'s editors recognized their readers' taste for Pinkerton.[44] The popularity of the serials began a steady decline after 1909, but then reprints began appearing in 1913. Circulations rose again during the war years and into the early Soviet era, though not to the previous highs.[45] As Boris Dralyuk has argued about these periodicals, their "reliably formulaic serials . . . answered . . . psychological demands conditioned by a society in turmoil."[46] Despite their appellation as "detectives," these protagonists were hardly ratiocinative figures who privileged the logic of the investigative process. The interrevolutionary *Pinkertonovshchina* was a phenomenon that affected Russian crime fiction most by what Nat and Nick do not do: they do not puzzle out complex crimes. Despite literary critic Kornei Chukovsky's invectives against the serials, several pedagogues praised the detectives' personality traits and bemoaned the paucity of characters worth emulating in Russia's

40. Ronald A. Fullerton, "Toward a Commercial Popular Culture in Germany: The Development of Pamphlet Fiction, 1871–1914," *Journal of Social History* 12, no. 4 (1979): 499.

41. One teacher noted that students could identify American cities during their geography lessons because of their familiarity with these heroes, and heroines. V. Soroka, "Nat Pinkterton i detskaia literatura," "*Russkaia shkola*," no. 2 (1910): 77.

42. Referring to himself as both "The Great Stranger" (*velikii neznakomets*) and "The Threat to the Police" (*groza politsii*), Lord Lister also at times signed himself "Raffles," the name of a fictional gentleman thief created by Conan Doyle's brother-in-law, E. W. Hornung.

43. The back jacket of one of the Nick Carter pamphlets, published by the firm Razvlechenie in 1908, warned readers to watch out for imitations: "ours cost seven kopecks and are forty-eight pages, and theirs are five kopecks and thirty-two pages." Ironically, the publisher of this crime fiction had an office on Leshtukov Lane, the address where Gilevich lived as "Fedorov."

44. When the new detective divisions were opened following the 1908 reform, a writer for *Vestnik politsii*, with tongue in cheek, advised the new recruits not to turn to Nick Carter as a role model. He listed some of the thirty articles Nick always had with him, from disguises to bombs. F. A. Medvedev, "O mode Pinkertona, Kartera, i Kholmsa," *Vp*, no. 36 (1909) 767–69.

45. Dralyuk, "Pinkertonovshchina, 1907–1934," chapter 4, "The Persistence of Pinkertons." Publication figures from Knizhnaia letopis' chart the return of the action heroes, in lower numbers.

46. Boris Dralyuk, "As Many Street Cops as Corners: Displacing 1905 in the Pinkertons," *Russian History* 38, no. 2 (2011): 173–74.

Fig. 26. Ethel King vanquishes the criminal fortune-teller.

children's literature. They appreciated how the serials taught that an assertive personality can conquer modern life.[47]

Despite the difficulties in trying to discover who exactly wrote these stories,[48] they follow an identifiable formula that separates them not only from Holmes but also from Putilin. Crimes are committed, yes, and many a murder. But the function of the fictional transgression is to give the heroes, and occasionally the heroines, the opportunity to extricate themselves from life-threatening situations, and especially to travel at high speeds on modern modes of transportation.

In "The Criminals' Conspiracy," Nat found himself in danger. "The situation was desperate; anyone else would have considered himself a goner, but not Pinkerton!" The criminals prepare to shoot him on the count of three, "but I will go on two!" he cries, and tosses a grenade from his pocket.[49] In "Arrest in the Clouds," Pinkerton takes an express train from Chicago to New York, but gets off in Cleveland because he sees a hot air balloon take off in the direction of Richmond with a man being hanged by the guide wire. He fulfills the promise of the title by getting himself into the gondola of the scoundrels' balloon outside of Atlanta.[50] In "The Victim of the Metro," Nat is on the train when it hits an old man who had tried to hire him the day before.[51] "Battle on the Hanging Bridge" opens with a man tossed from the Brooklyn Bridge landing on a barge passing underneath. The victim, a millionaire who is suspicious that his wife meets her lover on the bridge, lives long enough to give clues that get turned over to Pinkerton. "Othello" inspired this adventure: the killer's accomplice had given the husband one of his wife's handkerchiefs, lying to him that she had dropped it in a tryst with a man on the bridge. Again Pinkerton enacts the story's title. His opponent jumps off and the body is never recovered, which provides a setup for a future encounter.[52] The Iago of this version lands in Sing Sing, where he dies of tuberculosis.[53]

Shadings in plot and character in several adventures suggest Russian authors. In "Among the Anarchists," the chief of the New York police asks Nat to protect a Russian *sanovnik* (dignitary) sailing incognito into Hoboken, planning a secret trip to Washington, D.C., to meet with the unnamed American president. Nat disguises himself as the *sanovnik* to mislead the anarchists in New York, while the real one takes the express train

47. Kornei Chukovsky's diatribe, *Nat Pinkerton i sovremennaia literatura: Kuda my prishli?* (Moscow: n. p., 1910), became the classic Russian response to the dangers of sensational culture. Educators, including Soroka, found more positives. A. Suvorovskii, "Nat Pinkerton v detskom pominanii," *Vestnik vospitaniia*, no. 1 (1909): 157–63; N. Vergin, "Literatura syska v otsenke uchenikov srednykh klassov gimnazii," *Pedagogicheskii sbornik* (October 1909): 288–302; and Soroka, "Nat Pinktterton," no. 1: 38–63 and no. 2: 60–78.

48. Dralyuk, "Pinkertonovshchina, 1907–1934," chapter 3, discusses a few of the Russian authors, including sports writer N. N. Breshko-Breshkovskii, and probably future Socialist Realist author Valentin Kataev, who likely wrote some of these serials.

49. "Zagovor prestupnikov: Pinkerton v bol'shoi opasnost'," in *Nat Pinkerton, korol' syshchikov* (Moscow: GELEOS, 2006), 33, 37.

50. "Arest v oblakakh," in *Nat Pinkerton*, 71–105.

51. "Zhertva metropolitena," in *Nat Pinkerton*, 106–42.

52. "Bor'ba na visiachem mostu," in *Nat Pinkerton*, 177–211.

53. Chukovsky rejoiced when he found a prisoner who had died of tuberculosis rather than electrocution, probably Lord Stonefel'd from "Bor'ba na visiachem mostu." *Nat Pinkerton*, 50.

to D.C. Nat and Bob, who has put on blackface to play the *sanovnik*'s servant, end up in a rowboat with a bomb, from which they jump before it explodes. In the water, Nat finds his knife and cuts their bonds, getting them to the American capital in time to crash a dinner party at the White House. The denouement smacks of Russia when the chief anarchist, sentenced to fifteen years, commits suicide.[54]

Another story that intimates Russian authorship, "Legran, the King of Adventurists," uses ruses found in Putilin stories. For example, the villains hide in a hotel room's secret closet, as in Shevliakov's "Insane Vengeance,"[55] and a woman behaves suspiciously at the morgue, like Grunia in "Eleven Headless Corpses."[56] One of Nat's most remarkable American adventures tells a story that reads like Russia recovering from 1905. "The Scourge of Redston" ends with a vigilante lynch mob stringing up the corrupt police inspector and his crony after Pinkerton, shocked by official corruption, has exposed them.[57]

Pinkerton's escapades pale next to Nick Carter's. Appearing first in 1886 in "The Old Detective's Pupil," a dime novel written by American John Russell Coryell, Carter races tirelessly around the United States.[58] The original American Nick, always fictitious, faced Russian nihilists early in his career, and almost found himself married to their "tiger chief" Princess Olga; the publisher forced her to imbibe poison in order to keep Nick celibate.[59]

Russians devoured Nick. In 1908, when the San Francisco public "loses confidence in the police because of the growing number of white men killed by yellow ones," Nick takes on corrupt cops, Shanghai Jim, and a gang of "slant-eyed devils" in "The Brotherhood of Death."[60] "Where is Dr. Kvartz, the most evil and dangerous man of his time?" begins "The Dead Witness." Kvartz was supposed to have been hanged in a Kansas City jail on Christmas night, but a hurricane blew in and his prison uniform was discovered in the Missouri River near Jefferson City. Only Nick believes correctly that the villain has survived. Aided by the last surviving member of the Jesse James gang, Kvartz kills his benefactor for the cash remaining from their bank heists. Kvartz subsequently breaks his vile companion, Zanoni, out of prison, where she sits for having murdered her sister. With his trusted crew of Patsy, Dick, and the Japanese lad Ten-Itsi, Nick captures the deadly duo. The adventure ends with Carter doubting that he has seen the last of these two, who never found prison much of an impediment.[61]

When someone starts heaving the bodies of strangled engineers from speeding trains in "Steam Engine No. 13," the railroad company in St. Paul hires Nick. Solving the case, he escapes being buried alive in the coal car and then gassed in his hotel room before ending up on the cowcatcher of another locomotive, "lurching from side to side," chasing the

54. "Sredi anarkhistov," no. 112 (St. Petersburg: Razvlechenie, 1908).

55. "Bezumnaia mest'," *Russkii syshchik*, 1:42–71.

56. "Legran, korol' avantiuristov," vyp. 115 (St. Petersburg: Razvlechenie, 1908).

57. "Bich Redstona," Nat Pinkerton, 143–76.

58. Nick Carter starred in the highly profitable world of pulp fiction published by Street & Smith. Quentin Reynolds, *The Fiction Factory; or, From Pulp Row to Quality Street* (New York: Random House, 1955), 61–68.

59. Love for an American transformed Princess Olga's revolutionary politics (ibid., 66–67).

60. "Bratstvo smerti," vyp. 25 (St. Petersburg: Razvlechenie, 1908).

61. "Mertvoi sviditel'," vyp. 25 (St. Petersburg: Razvlechenie, 1908).

Fig. 27. Nat Pinkerton and Bob Ruland "Among the Anarchists," written by an unknown author.

Fig. 28. Nick Carter in hot pursuit of Engine no. 13.

engine in the title. The killer, powering No. 13, has escaped from an insane asylum, and "as Nick drew closer to him, he grew wild, his bloodshot eyes shining with a predatory ferocity. Thick drops of sweat rolled down his face, blackened with coal dust."[62]

Another popular German imported detective offered adventures in modernity and endings that evaded simple capture. Theo von Blankensee, a pen name for Mattias Blank, created the detective Luther Frank, hero of *Murder on the Northern Express*. The Blank/von Blankensee translations were part of a crime-fiction series, *Dramas of Life*, produced by commercial publishing giant I.D. Sytin, and included Russian authors. Presumably, like Adolphe Belot, Blank would have seen Russian authors take liberties with his works. Blank himself also wrote stories featuring Sherlock Holmes accompanied by Harry Taxon, a young man with no apparent skills in either medicine or narration, but ample muscle. Appearing first in Russian in 1908, *Northern Express* went through at least three other editions.[63] The express train of the title is carrying passengers across a muddled geography that included the Canadian cities of Montreal, Derbyshire, Buffalo, and Quebec. The body of a young beauty is found wrapped up in a blanket in the observation car, stabbed through the neck with a knife lying nearby. Circumstances dictated that one of the passengers must be the killer, and happenstance had put detective Luther Frank of the New York police headquarters on board the express.[64] Frank begins the investigation, only to be replaced by the Montreal police inspector, who questions Frank's ability to follow the clues.

Blankensee litters his story with red herrings, and the Montreal inspector assigned to the case fishes for every one of them: secret identities, faked addresses, and the inheritance of a family fortune when the victim's father dies of grief. Inspector Marshall, a "sickly, downcast figure with a narrow chest and long neck, upon which bobbled a large head," contrasts sharply with Frank, who "from long years of experience could distinguish the truth from a lie."[65] The lesson to be learned is how not to content oneself with the obvious. Frank succeeded because of his mastery of modern media, from the streetcar to the newspaper. Willing to be led astray rather than surrender to the obvious, he discovered that the victim had been having an affair with a married man, Marshall's primary suspect. Frank, who initially did not *cherchez la femme* because he doubted that a woman would be physically able to commit this crime, exposed the wronged wife as the true culprit. The question of culpability sounded a Russian note when the murderess takes her own life, leaving a confession in her diary that her husband had driven her to kill because of his many infidelities.[66]

---

62. "Paravoz #13," vyp. 9 (St. Petersburg: Razvlechenie, 1908).

63. Matias Blank, *Ubiistvo na severnom ekpresse* (Moscow: I.D. Sytin, 1916). The first edition came out in ten thousand copies. *Knizhnaia letopis'*, no. 34 (1908): 1.

64. Matthias Blank's detective Frank first appeared in the play *Erlebnisse des Detektiv Frank* in 1908, and then later in installments, "Erlebnisse des Detektiv Frank," 1–5, 1910. As Eugene Sawyer and others took over writing Nick Carter, so did O.E. Ehrenfreund write more Detektiv Frank stories, 1916–1918. Pulp and Adventure Heroes website: http://www.reocities.com/jjnevins/pulpsg.html (accessed September 24, 2010).

65. Blank, *Ubiistvo*, 13.

66. Luther Frank finds himself on a train from Monaco to Genoa with two bank robbers in *Razgrom banka v Monako* (Ekaterinburg: Ekateringorskoe pechatnoe delo, n.d.). A Kiev publisher also produced *Razgrom* in 1909, at three thousand copies. *Knizhnaia letopis'*, no. 43 (1909): 2.

*Voice of Blood* (1909), also by Blankensee, took readers into the labyrinth of primordial human instincts that link crime fiction with the occult, mysteries that lie beyond the explanatory power of reason. The novel begins one February night, as Simon Mandl' explains his theory about "the voice of blood" in criminal investigations to his good friend Richard fon-Forster. Mandl' believes that a "person connected to the crime, for example, a blood relative of the victim, can scent the criminal, even when there is no other basis for suspicion." Returning home through a thick fog, fon-Forster senses that a figure leaving his house is his cousin Robert Shteinlein. Brushing this off as a hallucination, he finds his father murdered when he arrives home. The police chief arrests an obvious suspect, a vagrant who had sneaked into the house for warmth on the night of the murder. Besides, Shteinlein can prove his presence elsewhere. Yet fon-Forster, disturbed that an innocent man might be punished, cannot allow his reason to dictate to his senses. In a series of feats he breaks Shteinlein's alibi and uncovers his illegal gambling operation. Cornered, the cousin puts a bullet in his heart, "escaping the judgment of humans, to settle his account in the other court."[67]

Sytin's series also included *The Female Detective*, featuring the ingenious American Harriet Bolton-Reid, who begins tracking the murderer of her best friend in New York, ultimately capturing him in a Dallas *traktir*, where she has disguised her identity behind an Indian headdress.[68] Other titles capitalized on crime tinted by heightened emotions: *A Terrible Vengeance, The Day I Took My Revenge, The Fatal Desire*; and by modern transportation, *In the Automobile*.

## Sherlockology

"By a man's finger-nails, by his coat-sleeve, by his boots, by his trouser knees, by the callosities of his forefinger and thumb, by his expression, by his shirt-cuffs—by each of these things a man's calling is plainly revealed."[69] These words, spoken by Dr. Watson to his friend the consulting detective Sherlock Holmes in "A Study in Scarlet," published in the *Beeton's Christmas Annual* in 1887, launched the career of history's most famous sleuth. The logical precision with which Holmes followed clues and his copious use of disguises has made the London detective a favorite in multiple media.[70] Always more popular in Russia than Putilin, Conan Doyle's character assumed a variety of personalities.[71] *Sherlock Holmes*, a play "according to the novel by Conan Doyle" was performed by Petersburg's Nezlobin

67. Teo fon-Blankensee, *Golos krovi: Ugolovnyi roman* (Moscow: I.D. Sytin, 1909), 6, 24, 101. The first edition circulated at seven thousand copies. *Knizhnaia letopis'*, no. 44 (1908): 2.

68. "Zhenshchina-Syshchik" (1916) has been republished in S. A. Afanas'ev, *Nat Pinkerton. Zhenshchina-Syshchik. Nik Karter* (Moscow: Vneshiberink, 1992), 193–235.

69. Arthur Conan Doyle, *A Study in Scarlet*, intro. Anne Perry, notes James Danly (New York: Modern Library, 2003), 20.

70. The most recent film versions star Robert Downey, Jr. as Holmes and Jude Law as Watson, action figures appropriate to the American cinema. BBC television updated the two in a miniseries that began in 2010, Watson now a veteran of Iraq rather than colonial India and blogs his adventures with Sherlock.

71. The Holmes stories, translated by G. A. Charskii, were in their third edition in 1908. An ad for "Biblioteka ugovol'nykh romanov" in 1909 offered Putilin's work for free to all who purchased the twelve-volume set of Sherlock Holmes, at two rubles per volume. *Vp*, no. 1 (1909).

Theater Company in 1906.[72] Transplanted from London fog and Victorian ethics, on the Russian stage Sherlock finds himself reduced to an action figure. Matching wits with the evil "Moriani," this Sherlock resorts to gunplay, which Conan Doyle's brainy Brit rarely needed.[73] Sherlock also made an appearance in a satirical journal, exposing a woman who was passing as Maksim Gorkii's wife to be instead Leonid Andreev's.[74]

Holmes and Watson traveled to Russia in a series of stories co-authored by P. Nikitin and P. Orlovets.[75] Their Sherlock had acquired his fluency in the language and fascination with the culture by renting a room with board from Russian emigrants during the two years that he lived in Buenos Aires.[76] When Sherlock introduces himself to a bailiff, the man laughs because his own son was almost expelled from the gymnasium for reading Holmes rather than Russia's literary classics.[77] In "The Secret of the Nizhnii Novgorod Storehouse," Holmes realizes that the villains have been projecting films onto a canvas to fool terrified clerks, who believe the images to be ghosts. He notes that although "cinematography had already appeared on God's earth, it was not yet widely known in Russia."[78] Something of a Siberiaphile, Holmes tracks down "Hunters of Live People" in the taiga, a gang that slaughters sport hunters and gold miners for their wares.[79] Action subsumes detection when Holmes warns his own ragtag troop of miners that "we don't have the power to arrest them, which means that it will be necessary to destroy them . . . of course it would be better to take them alive, but . . . that is unlikely." Then, he "shouldered his rifle, and a loud shot rang out in the quiet night."[80] The Russian Holmes might solve every crime, but he does not capture every criminal.

Holmes's trademark logic opened him to burlesques that made his rationale excessive, and his disguises became caricatures. Middlebrow playwright G. G. Ge penned the two-act comedy *The Crime of Sherlock Holmes* (1911), in which Sherlock appears as a female correspondent for the European press, but he is identifiable as an American because he touches all the objects in a room, and who but an American would do that? In the guise of a redheaded sailor, he romances a woman "with the face of an orangutan." Lestrade, the inspector from Scotland Yard whose incompetence makes Holmes's superior skills necessary, appears as a slapstick figure.[81]

72. I read a working copy of the Nezlobin production, written by V. V. Protopopov.

73. The ex-prizefighter "Gentleman" Jim Corbett took a faux-Holmes on the American circuit. In *The Burglar and the Lady*, the boxer plays the detective's assistant, named Raffles. Amnon Kabatchnik, *Sherlock Holmes on the Stage: A Chronological Encyclopedia of Plays Featuring the Great Detective* (Lanham, MD: Scarecrow Press, 2008), 47–51.

74. *Moi pulemet*, no. 3 (1906): 2.

75. Some of these have been republished in P. Nikitin and P. Orlovets, *Sherlok Kholms v Rossii* (Moscow: EKSMO, 2002).

76. "Taina Nizhegorodskogo glavnogo doma," in Nikitin and Orlovets, *Sherlok Kholms v Rossii*, 12.

77. "Okhotniki na zhivykh liudei," in Nikitin and Orlovets, *Sherlok Kholms v Rossii*, 254.

78. "Taina," in Nikitin and Orlovets, *Sherlok Kholms v Rossii*, 31. Nat also used a movie camera to catch a killer in "Kinematograf v poli oblichutelia" (St. Petersburg: Tip. pervoi trudovoi artel', n.d.).

79. "Okhotniki na zhivykh liudei," in Nikitin and Orlovets, *Sherlok Kholms v Rossii*, 243–80.

80. Ibid., 279.

81. Grigorii Grigorevich Ge, "Prestuplenie Sherlok Kholmsa," in his collected plays, vol. 2 (St Petersburg: Zhizn', 1911), 143–71. Ge also transformed George du Maurier's sensation *Trilby* for *Teatr i iskusstvo* in 1897.

Fig. 29. P. Nikitin's *On the Trail of the Criminal: Sherlock Holmes, Resurrected in Russia.*

In *Sherlock Holmes: A Day in the Life of the Great Detective*, a one-act play written for the cabarets of the early twentieth century, author M. Linskii satirized his famous powers of deduction. The victim who had been chopped to pieces, pronounces Holmes, could not have committed suicide. Discovering heavy boots and a false beard discarded in his apartment, Holmes deduces that a man has been there, because a woman would have dressed differently. One scene scoffs at Holmes's famous hobby: disguised as a musician, he plays a violin so touchingly that the villain who hears him breaks into tears and promises to mend his ways. How does Holmes solve this murder? He reads about it in the newspaper![82]

Another Sherlock who devoted himself to cracking cases in Russian popular literature was authored by "Not Doyle." This Sherlock ends up in a balloon and solves a case that involves Canadian railroad stock. The "Not Doyle" touch shows itself when rain rather than Holmes brings down the balloon, and of the two men who forged the stock, one commits suicide and the other escapes to France, where he lives happily ever after on his ill-gotten gains.[83]

Putilin's ghostwriter Shevliakov also tried his pen at Sherlock Holmes, his British detective strikingly formalist in contrast to his kindhearted Russian one. In a five-act play from 1909, he put the famous detective up against Arsène Lupin, who also enjoyed a Russian audience on page and screen.[84] Lupin has been accused of a murder that he did not commit, and Holmes is summoned from London to track him down. Shevliakov's Holmes constantly asserts himself as a representative of the law, which can only add to the audience's preference for Lupin, whom they know to be innocent. When the two confront each other at the climax, Holmes challenges Lupin, asking, "What would happen to society if crimes went unpunished? Did you ever think of that? We would all become the helpless booty of villains and swindlers." The thief counters that he will continue his ways "until that time when society finally learns to understand human need."[85] Felonious do-gooder Lord Lister, too, bested Sherlock in one encounter when he broke up a ring of white slave traders.[86]

Imitation may well be the sincerest form of flattery, but it is also affected by a cultural specificity that uses emulation to say something about the imitator. Conan Doyle created a character with such identifiable attributes that he lent himself to caricature, and there is nothing uniquely Russian about satirizing Sherlock Holmes.[87] Motive, the *why*, also

82. M. Linskii, Sherlok Kholms: *Odin den' v zhizni znamenitnogo detektiva* (St. Petersburg: Sh. Bussel', 1912). The cover states that this vaudeville is "a publication of the theatrical publication in the capitals, *Teatral'nye novinki*, and has been performed in such theaters as Bi-Ba-Bo, Blue Eye, Green Parrot, and in Odessa's Theater of Miniatures."

83. Not Doil', *Sherlok Kholms: Novye prikliucheniia* (St. Petersburg: Buze i Lassman, 1908). Harry Taxon accompanied Holmes, so they might have been translations from von Blankensee.

84. Russia's police must have enjoyed him, as Lupin appeared in *Vp.* "Arest Aresena Liupena," no. 10 (1908): 21–24; and the novel of his adventures "813" began serialization in no. 13 (1910).

85. M. Shevliakov and G. Fedorovich, *Pokhozhdeniia Arsena Liupena i Sherlok Kholmsa* (Moscow: Teatral'naia biblioteka A.A. Solovevoi, 1909). Said to be "translated from the French." Although there was a French play with this title, this play's plot differed considerably. Amnon Kabatchnik, "Arsène Lupin vs. Sherlock Holmes," *Sherlock Holmes on the Stage*, 52–53.

86. *Belye rabyni* (Moscow: Razvlechenie, n.d.).

87. The very British W.S. Gilbert wrote a comic opera, *A Sensation Novel in Three Volumes*, that burlesqued the Holmes phenomenon.

Fig. 30. Lord Lister rescues the white slaves.

engaged Holmes in his search for the *who*, but the Russian lampoons made his logic an obsessive trait that is secondary in their own crime fiction. This suggests that Russians consider such deduction a British characteristic, as it also highlights their own cultural preference for the "whydunit."

A comparison of two stories featuring Holmes and the fictional Putilin reveals that they have much in common, but the differences say more. Dobryi's "The Poisoning of a Millionaire Heiress" mirrors Conan Doyle's "The Speckled Band." In both, a young woman, due to inherit a fortune and living in the house of an older guardian who stands to collect if she dies, is threatened by an inexplicable illness. In Dobryi's version, she is already bedridden, and in Conan Doyle's, her twin sister has died mysteriously. The answer to both mysteries lies in India. Deadly flowers from there are poisoning Putilin's millionaire heiress, and Holmes's "speckled band" is a poisonous swamp adder who killed one twin and now, when released in her bedroom by their nefarious stepfather, threatens the other. Putilin finds his answer in a dream, Holmes in his knowledge of empire and herpetology. The Russian's wicked uncle takes his own life after the heiress's fiancé refuses to press charges. Holmes sends the snake back to its master, whom it bites and kills. Putilin, like Holmes, undertook "the task of reconstructing a full and authoritative narrative of the crime,"[88] but they diverge on critical points, especially the function of logic and the legitimacy of suicide as a means to avoid prosecution.

Holmes's status as a detective for hire rather than a representative of the police gives him a malleability when reading the letter of the law, but this must not be confused with taking the law into his own hands.[89] Dobryi's Putilin also behaves at times like a private detective.[90] However fully rounded Conan Doyle's character, however clever his deductions and intriguing his use of cocaine, the endurance of Holmes's popularity in Russia as elsewhere requires a fuller explanation. Appearing at the turn of the twentieth century, his modern methods made order out of chaos, defending the bourgeois values and imperialism that prevented the sun from setting on the British Empire.[91]

Entering domestic situations made vulnerable by the commission of a crime, he gained the confidence of the principle characters through his objectivity and competence, and then left, returning to his status as outsider without making any further demands.[92] Michael Chabon pointed out that

88. Karen Halttunen, *Murder Most Foul: The Killer and the American Gothic Imagination* (Cambridge, MA: Harvard University Press, 1998), 132.

89. For a list of cases in which he skirts the letter of the law, see Jens Jenson, "Sherlock Holmes and Justice," in *Scandinavia and Sherlock Holmes*, ed. Bjarne Nielsen (New York: Baker Street Irregulars, 2006), 41–48.

90. "Potselui bronzovoi devy," in *Russkii syshchik*, 2:116–33.

91. The literature on Holmes and empire includes: Susan Cannon Harris, "Pathological Possibilities: Contagion and Empire in Doyle's Sherlock Holmes Stories," *Victorian Literature and Culture* 31, no. 2 (2003): 447–66; Catherine Wynne, *The Colonial Conan Doyle: British Imperialism, Irish Nationalism, and the Gothic* (Westport, CT: Greenwood Press, 2002); and Joseph A. Kestner, *Sherlock's Men: Masculinity, Conan Doyle, and Cultural History* (Burlington, VT: Ashgate, 2003).

92. As W.H. Auden noted, the detective's function "is to restore the state of grace" to a community disturbed by a murder. "The Guilty Vicarage, Notes on the Detective Story by an Addict," *The Complete Works of W.H. Auden: Prose*, Volume 2, 1939–1948, ed. Edward Mendelson (Princeton: Princeton University Press, 2002), 267. This essay appeared first in the May issue of *Harper's Magazine*, 1947.

it has become commonplace to view the Holmes tales, and the detective story tradition that they engendered, as fundamentally conservative. In this reading the detective, while technically independent of the law, is in truth the dedicated agent of the prevailing social order—a static, hierarchical structure, in which murder is an aberration.[93]

Upon unpacking the case of the "Cardboard Box," Holmes queries, "What is the meaning of it, Watson? What object is served by this circle of misery and violence and fear? It must tend to some end, or else our universe is ruled by chance, which is unthinkable."[94]

This observation points to an epistemological difference between the role of the detective in Russian and Western fiction. As Warren Spanos argued, "the detective story has its source in the comforting certainty that an acute 'eye,' private or otherwise, can solve the crime . . . by inferring causal relationships between clues." In doing so, his actions replicate the construction of "the well-made positivistic universe."[95] Sherlockology contributed to "public acceptance of authority . . . not because of wholesale endorsement of power," but rather because Sherlock Holmes personified an authority "consistent with milder liberal principles."[96]

Russian detective stories did not simply end differently. More to the point, they offered a counternarrative that rejected the closure found in Sherlockology.[97] Putilin and the other fictional detectives dealt with crime as the actions of individuals pushed beyond the bounds of their humanity. Ambiguity was their hallmark. Writing about these issues, the authors demonstrated that they shared their readers' aspirations for stability and justice. On the other hand, by rejecting a law-and-order closure, they evidenced their hesitation to embrace the desirability of restoring the "prevailing social order." This became even more apparent on the movie screens beginning to go up around the empire.

93. Michael Chabon, "The Game's Afoot," *New York Review of Books* (February 24, 2005), http://www.nybooks.com/search/?q=michael+chabon&origin=magazine&page=2 (accessed November 12, 2010).

94. The story "The Adventure of the Cardboard Box" appeared in the January issue of *The Strand Magazine* (1893). Todd Herzog makes an analogous argument about the rejection of logic among authors of crime fiction in Weimar Germany, connecting it to the rise of modernism: "It is precisely this commitment to logic and causality in classical detective fiction that attracted the attention of German modernists who sought to disrupts such assumptions." In his *Crime Stories: Criminalistic Fantasy and the Culture of Crisis in Weimar Germany* (New York: Berghahn Books, 2009), 15.

95. Quoted in Patricia Linton, "The Detective Novel as a Resistant Text," in *Multicultural Detective Fiction: Murder from the "Other" Side,* ed. Adrienne Johnson Gosselin (New York: Garland Publishing, 1999), 20.

96. Caroline Reitz, *Detecting the Nation: Fictions of Detection and The Imperial Venture* (Columbus: Ohio State University Press, 2004), 67.

97. In her study of the Native American detectives in Linda Hogan's *Mean Spirit*, Patricia Linton makes the point that for them, "the cultural need for a solution means that whatever provides a solution is accepted as knowledge." In other words, like the Russians, they reverse Western ideas of crime solving to their own cultural ends, and in doing so subvert the letter-of-the-law legal system. Linton, "Detective Novel," 26. To explain the absence of an authentic Russian "classical detective," A. I. Reitblat cited the absence of private property, a developed culture of rule of law, a culture that privileges logic, and a highly educated reading public. I do not disagree, but I take greater interest in the detectives that Russian writers did produce. Reitblat, *Ot Bovy,* 306

The *Pinkertonovshchina* complemented the movie serials becoming increasingly popular, and it might be that the films supplanted the colorful paperbacks by attracting the time and money that would otherwise have been spent on them.[98] Statistics show film attendance on the rise as detective serials decline, although several students confessed to losing interest in Pinkerton because they grew bored with his ease at solving crimes.[99] Certainly the screen grabbed the popular imagination. *Peterburgskie kinemoteatry* (Petersburg Movie Theaters) exulted in 1912, "who would have said five or six years ago that the best places along Nevskii would be the movie theaters?" Thanks to the entrepreneurial Alekseev brothers, "there does not seem to be a single building from the Nikolaev Station to the Anichkin Bridge that doesn't have one of their theaters." The lowest paying positions in law enforcement, beat cops, were losing personnel to movie-house managers.[100] Ticket sales in 1913 numbered 108 million.[101]

Its sheer visuality makes the cinema an intrinsically sensational medium. A sumptuous set made a feast for the eyes, and increasingly sophisticated tracking devices allowed cameras to assimilate viewers into the intimate lives of the on-screen characters by seeing through their eyes. The connection between the consumption of popular cinema and its effects on the behavior of those consumers cannot be drawn with a straight line, but as Graeme Turner writes, "understanding a movie is not essentially an aesthetic practice, it is a social practice which mobilizes the full range of meaning systems within the culture."[102] And crime films sold: in the Russian films produced in 1912, crimes of greed and vengeance dominated the plots of seventy-six out of every hundred movies. Criminal gangs appeared in almost one-third of the films.[103] In 1915 two men who savagely murdered the women they had picked up that evening claimed that the movies had incited their behavior, though their jury did not forgive them.[104]

The emergence of the cinema marked one of modernity's most fundamentally transformative capabilities. Combining the imagination of fiction with the veracity of the photograph, the cinema circulated a performance that was simultaneously fixed and fluid. Movies

98. Information about the movies comes from a variety sources: Veniamin Vishnevskii's authoritative *Khudozhestvennye fil'my dorevoliutsionnoi Rossii* (Moscow: Goskinoizdat, 1945); Yuri Tsivian, Paolo Cherchi Usai, Lorenzo Codelli, Carlo Monanaro, and David Robinson, eds., *Silent Witnesses: Russian Films 1908–1919* (London: British Film Institute, 1989); and librettos published in the St. Petersburg periodical *Gazeta kinematografov, 1910–1914.* I viewed a number of films at both the Library of Congress and Moscow's film archive in Belye stol'by.

99. N. Vergin, "Literatura syska," 295–97; Soroka, "Nat Pinkterton," no. 2: 69, reported that one respondent preferred Putilin because it took him longer to solve cases; and in Suvorovskii, "Nat Pinkerton," 162, a girl admitted wanting to read of him failing to solve a case.

100. *Peterburgskie kinemoteatry*, no. 3 (1912).

101. Denise J. Youngblood, *Russian War Films: On the Cinema Front, 1914–2005* (Lawrence: University Press of Kansas, 2007), 11.

102. Graeme Turner, *Film as Social Practice*, 3rd ed. (New York: Routledge, 1999), 206.

103. A.A. Chernyshev, *Russkaia dooktiabrskaia kinozhurnalistika* (Moscow: Izd-vo Moskovskogo universiteta, 1987), 67.

104. "V zhurnalakh i gazetakh," *Pegas*, no. 1 (November 1915): 73.

created new audiences at the same time that they were engendering a fundamentally new way of perceiving the world.[105] For a variety of reasons, Russian studios did not begin the mass production of native films until 1912.[106] Production increased significantly after the outbreak of war in 1914; the number of studios jumped from eighteen to forty-seven by 1916.[107] By this time, "the audience for cinema outnumbered the total audience for all other forms of entertainment in the towns and cities of the Russian empire."[108] Because of the increased production during World War One, I extend my chronology in this chapter beyond 1914. Moreover, the war was insignificant on screen.[109] Crime fiction, on the other hand, developed some its most intriguing characters in movie serials.

Russians entered movie theaters already grounded in culturally affective associations between crime and punishment, between violent death and justice. Whether they preferred Nat or newspaper coverage of crime, they were constantly negotiating the correspondences in the courtroom as well as in literature. Moviemakers turned to forensic psychiatry, drawing from the "belief in the reign of dark, latent desires over the human will."[110] The Russian cinema borrowed tropes of death from the other crime fictions, both intentional murder and suicide. In the final reel, as in the last chapter, conflicts ended without a clear resolution to the problem that caused them in the first place.

This ambivalence was reinforced by the peculiar nature of Russia's film censorship. Whereas in the West moral reformers tried to influence content because they feared its potential for noxious influences on the lower classes,[111] in Russia the Holy Synod of the Orthodox Church was in charge, even though the Ministry of Internal Affairs housed the censorship of literature. Rather than evaluating the messages to be mediated, the church determined the medium itself to be inherently depraved. Therefore, the censors' task became "to prevent good messages from being spoiled by a bad medium."[112] For example, they forbade shots of anything Orthodox, which meant that Russian films are unnaturally secular. Yet they tolerated the egregious sin of suicide, so long as characters were not

105. In Miriam Hansen's oft-quoted observation, "the emergence of cinema spectatorship is profoundly intertwined with the transformation of the public sphere." *Babel and Babylon: Spectatorship in American Silent Film* (Cambridge: Harvard University Press, 1991), 2.

106. Russian theaters imported most films, primarily from the French Pathé Brothers and Denmark's Nordisk Films.

107. S.S. Ginzburg, *Kinematografiia dorevoliutsionnoi Rossii* (Moscow: Iskusstvo, 1963), 159.

108. Richard Taylor and Ian Christi, eds., *The Film Factory: Russian and Soviet Cinema in Documents, 1896–1939* (Cambridge: Harvard University Press, 1988), 21.

109. About the films produced, Denise Youngblood wrote that "from August 1, 1914 to the end of the year, nearly half (50 of 103) concerned the war, but two years later, in 1916, the figure was only 13 out of 500." In *Russian War Films*, 13. The reader looks in vain for fifty titles throughout the wars years in Vishnevskii, *Khudozhestvennye fil'my*.

110. Ginzburg, *Kinematografiia*, 380.

111. Robert A. Armour, "Effects of Censorship Pressure on the New York Nickelodeon Market, 1907–1909," *Film History* 4, no. 2 (1990): 113–21; Gilbert Geis, "Film Censorship in Norway," *The Quarterly of Film Radio and Television* 8, no. 3 (1954): 290–301; Samantha Barbas, "The Political Spectator: Censorship, Protest, and the Moviegoing Experience, 1912–1922," *Film History* 11, no. 2 (1999): 217–29.

112. Yuri Tsivian, "Censure Bans on Religious Subjects in Russian films," in Roland Cosandey, André Gaudreault, and Tom Gunning, *Une Invention du diable?: Cinéma des premiers temps et religion* (Sainte-Foy: Presses Université Laval, 1992), 79.

filmed shooting themselves in the head. In the United States, the Christian clergy took the lead and joined with civic leaders to force the closure of movie houses considered to be showing immoral films.[113] Ultimately, the Catholic Church pressed for the creation of a censorship board that would control the message; for example, mandating that filmmakers show that "crime does not pay."[114]

The first two narrative films produced by Russian studios, both in 1908, were plotted around the violent murder of a woman by her jealous lover. The men who made these films would come to dominate the industry from opposite ends. Alexander Drankov, of whom it was said that without his studio "the elements would not rage and monarchs would not meet,"[115] did for the movies what Nat Pinkerton had accomplished for pulp fiction; he did not waste time with a realistic plot when his audience did not demand one. Alexander Khanzhonkov, in contrast, aspired to make the motion picture an artistic medium, and some of the mature productions from his studio are prerevolutionary Russia's most opulent films.

Russia's inaugural moving pictures traded in acceptable, even romantic levels of emotional violence associated with groups who lived beyond the law of the state. Drankov's *Stenka Razin*, based loosely on a song about the popular peasant brigand from the seventeenth century, ends with the title character drowning his Persian mistress because he believes the lies of his crew that she has been unfaithful. Khanzhonkov's *Drama in a Gypsy Camp* ends with the death of another innocent woman, this one by her husband's knife. More telling yet about the symbolic use of death for its own sake is the spin producer Khanzhonkov put on his 1910 ecranization of the poem "Peddlars" (*Korobeinki*), written by populist Nikolai Nekrasov in 1861. In the poem, flirtatious peasants hide in the rye from prying eyes, but Khanzhonkov changes the ending so that now the hero gets murdered for his profits. No one is brought to justice.

*The Secret of House No. 5* (1912), one of the precious few films from the era available in its entirety, featured overview shots that made the spectators omniscient, seeing more, hence knowing more, than did the characters. The cameraman also used point-of-view shots that allowed the audience to see through the eyes of on-screen characters. Reviewed as "grippingly interesting to watch,"[116] *House No. 5* demonstrates how the innovative cinema could utilize trick photography from its nightclub days. The film opens with a count and a famous courtesan at a restaurant, a gypsy dancing madly in the background. The intertitle reads "Intolerable Luxury." The audience looks with the courtesan's eyes at a handsome young man and feels her attraction. He shows her an unpaid promissory note, and their glance to the count indicates him to be the object of a plan. The two engage him with the story of a mysterious house where a portrait of a woman comes to life and tortures to death anyone who tries to spend the night there. The count accepts their bet that he cannot survive.

113. Hansen, *Babel and Babylon*, 63; and Peter Kobel, *Silent Movies: The Birth of Film and the Triumph of Movie Culture* (New York: Little, Brown, 2007).

114. Thomas Doherty, *Hollywood's Censor: Joseph I. Breen and the Production Code Administration* (New York: Columbia University Press, 2007). In stark contrast to prerevolutionary Russia, "suicide, as a solution of problems in the development of screen drama, is to be discouraged as morally questionable and as bad theater—unless absolutely necessary for the development of the plot" (355).

115. Quoted in Tsivian et al., *Silent Witnesses*, 556.

116. Ibid., 158.

That night, the portrait comes to life as the courtesan steps out of it. The lover, who has disguised himself as a *dvornik*, shoots the count in the back. They take money from the corpse and replace it with a faked suicide note: "I could not bear the expectation of the horror." The director did not pose the question of how the count might have shot himself in the back.

Titles themselves suggest contents: *Orgy of Blood* (1911), *In Pursuit of Sensations* (1911), *Over the Corpses to Happiness* (1915).[117] These movies imparted something of the French Grand Guignol, the notorious Parisian theater founded in 1897 that specialized in short plays about horrific events, presented without didactic moralizing. Gothic elements return the attention to the crime, rendering the investigation irrelevant. *The Treasure of Prince Skalon* (1911), ominously subtitled *A Criminal Drama from Moscow Life*, told a Poe-like story of a prince sealing his wife and her lover, a lackey, in the larder before they could do the same to him. Morbid sensibilities colored romance and tapped into the fashionable fear of live burials.[118] *Midnight at the Cemetery* (1909), written and directed by Vasilii Goncharov at the Khanzhonkov Studio, was remade in 1911 by rising directorial talent Iakov Protazanov as *Nailed Down*. A fiancé has promised his deceased sweetheart that he would hammer the nail she gave him into her coffin. Accidentally affixing his coat to the casket, which catches as he turns to leave, the sensation that she is pulling him back strikes him dead.[119] Drankov studios copied the plot in *The Cabinet of Death* (1914), directed by one of prerevolutionary Russia's cinematic luminaries, Evgenii Bauer, before he bolted to the more prestigious, and better funded, Khanzhonkov Studios. These sickly romances, though filmed with Gothic overtones, lack the generic element that makes gothic literature relevant: a secret from the past that has a direct bearing on the present. These movies served up horror for its own shocking sake.

Criminological forays into hereditary degeneracy and the unconscious will also played on the silver screen. In *The Scourge of Heredity* (1911), the son of an alcoholic is not permitted to marry the boss's daughter until he proves his sobriety.[120] After their marriage, however, his genes get the better of him and in a fit of insane jealousy he kills a man with whom his innocent wife is speaking. The wife brings their child to court to beg for leniency, but the killer dies in a paroxysm before the judge delivers his ruling. This rhetorical device of the guilty dying before judgment is handed down appears in other media and is consonant with the theme found in fact as well as fiction of refusing to turn one's fate over to the state.[121]

In *Five Emeralds* (1912), two strangers on a train begin chatting. The woman shows the man a brooch with five emeralds. He drifts off to sleep. Awakening, he draws the blinds to find the woman strangled, scratches on his hands, and the brooch in his pocket. He

117. The movies complemented such fiction as *Waves of Blood* (Moscow: Nashe slovo, 1911); "Chertov Bridge, or The Horrific, Bloody Crime"; and "The Victims of Living Corpses" (St. Petersburg: N.I. Kholmushin, 1911).

118. Joanna Bourke, *Fear: A Cultural History* (Emeryville, CA: Shoemaker Hoard, 2006), 34–41, discusses this pervasive fear in the United States at the turn of the twentieth century.

119. The libretto is in *Gazeta kinematogrofov*, no. 24 (1913).

120. The libretto is in *Gazeta kinematogrofov*, no. 18 (1911).

121. Sokolova's *Song is Sung* ended thus, and it also appears in "cruel romances," a uniquely Russian genre about love turned sour. In "Untitled No. 46," *Russkii zhestokii romans* (Moscow: Gos. tsentr russkogo folklora, 1994), the action takes place in a courtroom, the accused woman dying on the stand immediately before the judge was to read her verdict.

suffers no compunctions about selling the emeralds for personal wealth, but remains curious about what happened that night on the train. Not even the hypnotist he hires can help him to regain his memory. Like the protagonist in *Scourge*, he did not commit murder of his own volition, and neither does the law render judgment.

The solitary Russian who always got his man, or woman, appeared in the Drankov production *The Adventures of I. D. Putilin, the Renowned Head of the Petrograd C.I.D.* (1915), alternatively titled *Phantoms from the Past* and *On the Murderer's Trail*. Based on Shevliakov's "Insane Vengeance," it recounted how a married couple slit the throat of the man who had raped the wife in her youth.[122] Only one of the three original reels remains, but it provides sufficient substance to illustrate how the camera let viewers witness events, like the detective, as "private eyes."

Shevliakov's story begins with a dead man in a hotel room; the movie opens with his murder. The audience watches a couple drinking champagne and sees the woman drop powder into the man's glass. She leaves, marking the door with chalk for the obsessed husband, who enters and furiously stabs the unconscious libertine. He returns home and hides the knife in a potted palm. The audience views the clues in a close-up of bloody fingerprints on a champagne bottle. Intertitles explain "Putilin in the Search for Masha," though in the original story this character carried the euphonious moniker "Sonka the Hussar" for her ability to slam vodka like a soldier. Putilin, "Hot on the Trail," disguises himself as a worker to romance Masha, before throwing her in jail until she agrees to help him. On the street she spots "The Fateful Photo" of the man who had hired her to seduce the victim. Putilin, still in disguise, enters a *traktir* and flirts with a woman, pouring her rounds, while tossing out the contents of the glasses he pours for himself (a maneuver also used in "Petersburg Jack the Ripper"). The woman turns out to be the killer's maid, and after she passes out he searches the apartment and finds the weapon in the potted palm. Arrest would be as uncinematic as it would be un-Russian; Putilin leaves a note: "I was here," signed "the Sokolov you killed." After an indeterminate passage of time, Putilin returns dressed as the victim, fake beard and all, waving the knife. The missing reel deprives of us knowing how the killer reacted.

The undisputed master of the genre, Drankov, added the ingredient of celebrity when he starred popular operatic tenor Dmitrii Smirnov in *The Secret of Loge A* (1915), filmed on location at Smirnov's estate.[123] Enough remains to realize that Drankov's primary ambition was to show off his handsome singer as a man of action unconstrained by a coherent storyline. The reviewer for the film journal *Pegas* (Pegasus) advised that "it's best to say nothing of the plot," a sentiment shared by screenwriter L. Nikulin.[124] Smirnov's fans get to see him in costume backstage, goggled behind the wheel of a sports car, and posing in Roman regalia for a "Nietzschean" artist who tries to poison him for no clear reason. The intrepid tenor instead forces the painter to drink the wine he had tainted.

Drankov did not simply satisfy audiences, he created them. He produced a film series, *Dark Moscow*, epitomized by the movie *The Sensational Murder of Countess X* (1915). Where he excelled in the production of crime fiction, though, was in serializing adventures that starred

122. "Bezumnaia mest'" *Russkii syshchik*, 1:42–71.

123. Opera superstar Fedor Shaliapin recreated his role as Tsar Ivan the Terrible in the opera *Pskovitianka* for film in 1915, believing that a gramophone of his baritone would suffice. He received a phenomenal twenty-five thousand rubles, but the movie flopped. Jay Leyda, *Kino* (Princeton: Princeton University Press, 1973), 77–78.

124. Tsivian et al., *Silent Witnesses*, 298.

an identifiable character, and he put the frantic pace of the action-fiction on screen. France's Eclair Studio had pioneered in serials, introducing Zigomar, a gypsy crime lord born in pulp, in 1911.[125] Heir to Rocambole, Zigomar was joined by popular thief Arsène Lupin and Fantômas, the "Lord of Evil," both of whom moved easily from graphic serials to the nascent cinema.[126] To be sure, detectives Nick Carter and Nat Pinkerton also chased criminals through French serials, and in *Zigomar against Nick Carter* (1912), the gypsy readily outsmarts the detective. Some of these movies played in Russia, as did several starring Sherlock Holmes.

Russian viewers generally preferred villains to heroes in cinematic serial action. The appeal of an outlaw, someone undermining the state's authority at every opportunity, requires no further explanation when writing about tsarist Russia. Indeed, Russia had an extensive popular culture peopled by bandits.[127] Models for fiction came from fact. Vaska Churkin, a factory worker who lived on vodka and violence, terrorized parts of Moscow Province in the 1880s and found himself so celebrated in a newspaper serial that the government ordered his publisher to kill him off.[128] Drankov resurrected Churkin in 1915, billing him as "the Russian Fantômas." Unfortunately, not enough remains for meaningful reconstruction, but the last installment was entitled "The Death of Churkin."

These serialized adventures are about sensational crime rather than murder per se, and it is never quite clear how many bodies are lying around after a blaze of bullets. Another Russian who had captivated the attentions of newspaper readers in the 1880s and returned in a film serial was Sofiia Bliuvshtein, known as "light-fingered Sonka" for her ability to pick a pocket. After escaping one incarceration by seducing her jailor, Sonka landed on the Russian prison island of Sakhalin, where a photograph of her in chains was turned into a postcard that kept her legend in circulation.[129] In 1903 she found herself a heroine in M. D. Klefortov's film *Light-fingered Sonka*, who at trial claimed the highly contrived motivation to "steal not for myself, but for those who suffer."[130]

Drankov put her on screen in a six-part serial starring Nina Gofman, the first installment of which was released in 1914 and continued through 1915. "Light-fingered Sonka" allowed viewers to experience the spectrum of urban Russia, made all the more perceptible because so much was shot on outdoor locations. When she undressed (partially) before climbing into bed, she punctuated the voyeurism of the audience. Our "Rocambole in skirts" flirted with a well-dressed gentleman in a park, perhaps a bit too much because at some point she ends up pregnant, like the Sonka on Sakhalin. Or could the father of her child have been the man who kept pouring her alcohol on a set that evoked the familiar interior of "furnished rooms"? She avenged herself after sobering up by stealing from him, then setting the rooms ablaze. Serialized Sonka took her viewers into a courtroom and then to a mental institution, where she had eluded jail by feigning madness. Still using fire as a *modus operandi*, firebug Sonka escapes the asylum by burning it down. However, a

125. Richard Abel, *The Ciné Goes to Town: French Cinema, 1896–1914* (Berkeley: University of California Press, 1994), 358–59.

126. Maurice Leblanc created Lupin in 1905, Pierre Souvestre and Marcel Allain added Fantômas in 1911.

127. Jeffrey Brooks writes extensively about this in *When Russia Learned to Read*, chapter 5.

128. Brooks, *When Russia Learned to Read*, 124. The "real" Churkin had been exiled to Siberia.

129. *Pl*, 14 July 1886, no. 188.

130. Quoted in Brooks, *When Russia Learned to Read*, 204.

salary dispute with Drankov sent Gofman to the minor Kinolenta production company to continue the Sonka story, which was met with decidedly less enthusiasm by audiences. The last installment, *Sonka's Encounter with Rocambole* (1916), ended with the "old, sick, and freezing" Sonka's death. Little wonder that "interest had begun to wane."[131]

The most cynical of Russia's criminal protagonists appeared in the serial *Sashka, the Seminarian* (1915), produced by the Ermol'ev Studio. Billing him as the "Russian Rocambole" unnecessarily undercuts Sashka's individuality. As history would reveal, the young Joseph Djughashvili had begun studying in a seminary before turning to a life of crime as "Koba," naming himself after a Georgian outlaw, before turning to politics as "Stalin." Enough remains of serial Sashka to appreciate the seminarian's natural aggressiveness. In one scene, he pretends to beat his girlfriend so that a passerby will come to her aid; Sashka then follows the Good Samaritan back to his room and pulls a pistol on him. Nor does Sashka always bother with cleverness to disguise himself, as when he takes a *dvornik*'s clothes at gunpoint. His female accomplice, dressed as a nurse in a hospital to which Sashka has been taken, chloroforms a doctor and steals his smock for her lover. This serial's cinematography is in some shots mindful of Maurice Tourneur's more sophisticated *Alias Jimmy Valentine*, also from 1915. Scenes of a bank robbery spotlight the bars that separate tellers from their customers, foreshadowing a jail cell. And just as Fantômas and Jimmy outwit the detectives who keep them running, so Sashka gets the better of Seleznev, the sleuth on his trail. An essential difference, however, outweighs the similarities: Jimmy reforms, Sashka does not.[132]

Another telling difference between the French and Russian crime serials appears in the timing of their productions. Fantômas vanished from the French cinema after the outbreak of the First World War, and the director who had brought him to the screen, Louis Feuillade, was decorated for his military service. Both Zigomar and Arsène Lupin left the French screen in wartime. Russian producers, though, filmed the gentleman thief's *Latest Adventures* (1918), and *The Lively Fantomas* (1915) and *Rokambol'* (1917) also enjoyed Russian embodiments.[133] The expanded themes of criminality, in the glaring paucity of heroic war-related dramas, bespeaks a critical absence of public opinion that the war made suitable entertainment. Nor did either home or battlefront provide a background against which other social and cultural themes were projected. If Russian audiences craved tragic endings, the battlefield offered a superfluity of them.

## Murder in Mind

Drankov held the premium on action-oriented murder, but Khanzhonkov mastered the psychological reasoning that motivated this crime on-screen. Khanzhonkov paced his movies slowly, highlighting a characteristic of Russian movies to devote camera time to

131. Tsivian et al., *Silent Witnesses*, 296.

132. *Alias Jimmy Valentine* was based on the short story "A Retrieved Reformation" by O. Henry, which had also been staged as a play by Paul Armstrong.

133. The Russian Lupin's serial ends with the common cultural trope of arson. Lecoq showed up from a Russian studio in *Lecoq in Old Age* (1916).

characters' internal conflicts, the emphasis again on "whydunit."[134] Russia's foundational psychological murder, *Crime and Punishment*, was filmed three times, never with audience approval. The third version (1914) was a gramophone movie, that is, it had to be accompanied by a recording of the actors speaking. Tolstoy's *Kreutzer Sonata* fared better. Filmed twice, in 1911 and 1914, the first, written and directed by Petr Chardynin, who also starred as Pozdnyshev, was particularly noteworthy for the film debut of future matinee idol Ivan Mozzhukhin as the violinist accused of being the wife's lover. A review of the second version praised it as emblematic of the uniquely Russian cinema that "leaves foreign productions far behind. We mean the psychological element."[135]

The first film in the Russian Golden Series, a conscious attempt to attract a middle-class audience with a sophisticated product, was *Corpse No. 1346* (1911).[136] The hero is a doctor whose hand becomes infected in a struggle with a crazed bystander when performing an emergency surgery. This costs him his career and drives him to drink, which pushes his wife to another man. He makes new friends at the *traktir* and joins them to rob a postal sleigh, but the medical man still inside him returns when the driver is wounded in the stickup. His violent collaborators shoot him, and his body is catalogued in the morgue under the movie's title.

Fascination with death was an aspect of the broadly European fin de siècle culture that Khanzhonkov brought to the screen in a series of movies about murder. His oeuvre connected film audiences with the themes and aesthetics of Russia's artistic Silver Age, the cultural avant-garde steeped in the decadence and degeneration that corresponded easily to the psychological aspects of crime fiction. In *Life in Death* (1914), the main protagonist kills his sweetheart in order to embalm her to maintain her beauty for eternity. Scripted by the Symbolist poet Valeri Briusov, *Life* was heavily freighted with images designed to move the audience to contemplate the overarching ideal of a beautiful death.[137] This would seem to justify murder on aesthetic grounds, as Thomas De Quincey had imagined, but the fin de siècle fascination had ominous political undertones. *Evil Night* (1914), a psychological drama directed by Bauer, once again allows Mozzhukhin to kill someone, this time a friend who had seduced his fiancée and driven her to suicide.[138] More than showing an act of vengeance, *Evil Night* serves up the easy recourse to murder as way to end problems without resolving them.

What about killing someone who holds secrets that could ruin a life? In *Shadows of Sin* (1915), megastar Vera Karalli murders to extricate herself from scandal.[139] Years earlier she had seduced her impressionable tutor and then refused to marry him. Time passes, to find her happily married, with a younger brother working as a judicial investigator. The tutor comes back into her life, now intimate with a circus rider, which locates him outside the circle of bourgeois respectability evident from the scenes of her domestic life. He had kept her photograph and letters, with which he threatens blackmail. She steals away to retrieve the evidence, but he catches her in the act. As they struggle, she discovers that a whip conceals a

134. Ginzburg, *Kinematografiia*, 310–13; and Tsivian et al., *Silent Witnesses*, 30–32.
135. Tsivian et al., *Silent Witnesses*, 226.
136. The libretto is in *Gazeta kinematografov*, no. 3 (1912).
137. Vishnevskii, *Khudozhestvennye fil'my*. 40.
138. Ibid.
139. Ibid., 80.

knife in the handle, with which she stabs him. Karalli's brother investigates the crime, accusing the rider. In one scene he furtively hands his sister what looks like a hat pin, presumably found at the scene, and that implicates her. Karalli staggers out into the winter evening, clad only in her nightgown. When a maid discovers her missing, she rouses the household. They find her frozen corpse.[140] The brother opens her clenched fist, which holds the pin.

Leaving only traces, two other films can but remind of the popularity of the genre. Khanzhonkov and Bauer collaborated with respected screenwriter Nikandr Turkin in a failed attempt at combining criminal sensationalism with social commentary in *The Murder of the Ballerina Plamenovaia* (1915). Their efforts to "ennoble and raise this lowly genre" returned "no noteworthy results."[141] On a positive note, *The Public Prosecutor* (1917), subtitled *For a Debt* and *The Voice of Conscience*, was noted as one of illustrious director Iakov Protazonov's "most successful films."[142]

A common alternative to killing someone else to settle a score was to turn a gun on oneself, and suicide became a not uncommon form of premeditated death in the Russian cinema.[143] Self-murder played a significant thematic role in late imperial cinema, when the jury of one's peers was replaced by that of one's self. Suicide functioned as a "perceived (if contested) means to affirm and defend the sanctity of life—not life itself, but life infused with justice, truth, and value."[144] *Liulia Bek* (1914), described as a "psychological drama about love and self-sacrifice,"[145] made literal that sacrifice of the self. Written by Anna Mar, who penned "typical psychological dramas on the eve of the revolution,"[146] the title character is a café singer in search of happiness, which lies beyond her reach. She meets a young man who is prepared to abandon his fiancée for her, but she cannot accept his love.

*Chrysanthemums* (1914) introduced Karalli, a ballerina from the Bolshoi who often played one on screen, as in this film.[147] In love with the cad Mozzhukhin, she cannot support him in the lifestyle he prefers, so he abandons her for a wealthy widow. Preparing for performance, she peeks out from behind the curtains and spots the two in the audience. He has sent her his signature bouquet of chrysanthemums, which she alternately kisses and crushes, as she would him. In an action Karalli would repeat in other films, she drinks from a vial of poison right before going on stage, so that she will die in front of her audience. In the final scene, Mozzhukhin scatters the title-flowers in her memory, recompense without penance.

The Russian cinema famously required "tragic endings" because, as one critic noted, local audiences "stubbornly refuse to accept" that "all's well that end's well."[148] This unnamed

<hr>

140. Yuri Tsivian, "Censure Bans on Religious Subjects in Russian films," discusses self-freezing as "visually acceptable to the censorship . . . a characteristically Russian suicide" (78).

141. Vishnevskii, *Khudozhestvennye fil'my.* 81.

142. Ibid., 136.

143. Tsivian has noted that on camera suicides could shoot themselves in the heart but not the head ("Censure Bans," 78–79).

144. Susan Morrissey, *Suicide and the Body Politic in Imperial Russia* (Cambridge: Cambridge University Press, 2006), 349.

145. Vishnevskii, *Khudozhestvennye fil'my.* 43.

146. Ibid., 115. This description refers to *Smerch liubovnyi* (Storm of Love), directed by Bauer and staring some of the biggest names: Vera Karalli, Vitol'd Polonskii, and Ivan Perestiani.

147. Vishnevskii, *Khudozhestvennye fil'my.* 51.

148. Yuri Tsivian, "Some Preparatory Remarks on Russian Cinema," in *Silent Witnesses*, 24.

writer for *Kinogazeta* was responding to complaints that Russian movies ended without the Western commonplace of bringing the film's narrative to closure in the final reel. Just as some students tired of the detective serials because of the certainty of success. Given the same plot, a Western movie would end happily with order being restored, the guilty punished, or at least a *deus ex machina* to resolve the problem posed by the plot. In 1913 when Georges Méliès put a gypsy woman on the French screen in *The Gypsy's Warning*, she is abandoned rather than killed by her lover, as in Khanzhonkov's film. Moreover, Méliès's cad gets his comeuppance when his new, and racially white, fiancée leaves him because of his shameful conduct.

Perhaps the most explicit contrast between Russian and Western cultural views of the importance of the maintenance of law and order can be in Protazanov's 1914 remake of D. W. Griffith's *The Lonely Villa* (1909), a cinematic celebration of technology: when thieves break into a family's villa, the wife telephones her husband, who drives back from the city and rescues her. In Protazanov's *Drama on the Telephone*, the husband fails to return in time. The final reel of a Russian film offered the same predictability as its Western counterpart; viewers knew better than to expect that narrative threads would be woven together into a moral or a smile. Like the fictional investigator from the 1870s who could not bring himself to arrest the guilty son of the woman he idealizes, or the investigator who never discovered whose head had been found in the baths, Russian film characters did not follow a narrative arc built so that the last scene would make sense of the first.

## Conclusion

Russians successfully pressed their autocracy for political concessions in 1905, but the price they paid in cruel recriminations turned out to be rather steep for their limited profits. Attempts to recover from and adapt to the postrevolutionary situation can be found in crime fiction, which aided audiences by its repetition of familiar themes, while at the same time informed them of ways in which their world had changed. The most salient new characteristic of the postrevolutionary genre lay in its sensationalism, in its stimulation of the senses both physical and psychological. The action fiction of post-1905 Russia circulated images of terror as it also tapped into frustration about the limits that remained over the expression of personal autonomy.

The emotion that predominates, though, is fatalism. A philosophy grounded in the notion that all that has happened must have happened as it did, fatalism seems to force its followers to resign themselves to their inability to take action that could affect their future. In this understanding, it complements the Christian tenet of "God's will be done," which resulted in political criticisms of Orthodoxy for denying the notion of agency to its practitioners.[149] Orthodoxy might have instilled this aspect of fatalism, but it also encouraged

---

149. The radicalized worker Semen Kanatchikov summarized the views of many Russians before the revolution: "Each of us had his own assessment of the harmfulness of religion. At that time I viewed religion as a fabrication contrived by priests, which prevented people from growing intellectually and workers in particular from creating the heavenly kingdom here on earth." *A Radical Worker in Tsarist Russia: The Autobiography of Semën Ivanovich Kanatchikov*, trans. and ed. by Reginald E. Zelnik (Stanford: Stanford University Press, 1986), 58–59.

mercy and forgiveness, which rely upon free will. Putting aside religion, concentrating instead on the explanatory powers of fatalism as a philosophy, we can discern how it constructs a framework for understanding "who we are . . . what happens to us and how what happens fits into the larger scheme of things."[150] Most important, fatalism focuses on the "significance of the outcome rather than the causal path that brought it about."[151] Take, for example, the film *Shadows of Sin*. The outcome is Karalli freezing herself to death. The cause of her doing so was that she had killed a man. Serving up her own punishment, she takes fate into her own hands. Moreover, director Chardynin frames her far more sympathetically than he does the man who was her victim twice over, thereby undermining the importance of cause because someone like her victim might as well have deserved to die.[152]

This focus on the outcome, as opposed to the chain of causes and effects, distinguishes fatalism substantively from the determinism espoused by Bekhterev and other forensic psychiatrists. They focused on causality to argue that their intervention could change the circumstances that had led to deviant behavior. Fatalism differs just as much from free will, whose proponents sought to find the self-actuating individual. The creators of crime fiction substituted *fate* for *cause*, and because the significance lies in the outcome, the formulaic ending that reified the lack of a law-and-order solution had political resonance. Russia's crime fiction reveals an attitude toward the oppressive government that can be characterized as passive-aggressive: passive to the degree that it did not confront representatives of the state directly, and aggressive not only in its villainous heroes, but more subtly in its use of murder to make political commentary, permitting even sociopathic killers to evade punishment by the state. Crime that captured the imagination without the need to capture the criminal reflected the significantly low level of commitment to Russia's dysfunctional system of law and order.

Sashka the Seminarian stands out as an exemplar of the anger of those who felt cheated by the revolution's limited results. Not intimidated by the state, he does not hesitate to use force to take what he wants. He knows that "violence is the key to the rule of power . . . the cheapest and quickest dramatic demonstration of who can and who cannot get away with what against whom,"[153] a lesson learned well from the retributive autocracy. No *neschastnyi* he. Quite the contrary.

Putilin and Sashka were Russian originals. That similarities can be found between them and Western cops and robbers simply locates Russia within the panorama of European responses to the modern technological changes that caught societies and politics up in their shifting gears. Russians killed each other, steeped in the fatalism that allowed a life to end without satisfactorily answering the question that Shkliarevskii had posed a generation earlier: What prompted the murder?

150. Robert C. Solomon, "On Fate and Fatalism," *Philosophy East and West* 53, no. 4 (2003): 448.

151. Ibid., 438, 443–44.

152. As Robert C. Solomon argues, "fatalism has little to do with determinism. There need be no specifiable causal chain." In "Nietzsche on Fatalism and 'Free Will,'" *Journal of Nietzsche Studies* 23, no. 1 (2002): 66.

153. Sarah Eschholz and Jana Bufkin, "Crime in the Movies: Investigating the Efficacy of Measures of Both Sex and Gender for Predicting Violence," *Sociological Forum* 16, no. 4 (2001): 660.

CHAPTER EIGHT

# TRUE CRIME AND THE TROUBLED
# GENDERING OF MODERNITY

"The future historian will be justified in writing a treatise on the part played
by criminal sensationalism in clogging the minds of Europeans on the eve of
the war."

—Grand Duke Alexander Mikhailovich, 1931

"We continue our coverage of the story, as told to us by that hundred-mouthed goddess,
Gossip, reporting now the details of the last moments before the murder. . . . Not for a
minute did she suspect that two killers stood before her, that she had been sentenced to
death. She turned to Dolmatov, smiling, and asked him to sit while she called a friend to
join them. Something whistled through the air and hit with a dull thud. Baron Geismar had
landed the first blow on the back of their victim's head. His spiral bludgeon whistled again
and again. The stupefied victim staggered, but stayed on her feet. Dolmatov came up from
behind to aid the assailant. Facing her, he put one hand over her mouth to muffle any cries,
grabbing her throat with the other. The victim sank to the floor, pulling Dolmatov down
with her. His face was so close to hers that they looked each other in the eye. Still squeezing
Time's throat, Dolmatov cried out to Geismar, 'The axe! The axe!' The baron rushed into
the hall to retrieve it from Dolmatov's coat pocket. The victim was still alive. They had to
hurry. Someone could come in at any moment. . . . Later, after the killers had disappeared
and people had come to take her to the hospital, she was able to mutter, 'I don't understand.'
Dying, she had no idea why she had been so brutally murdered. The doctors found fifteen
bone fragments of various shapes and sizes, and her left temple had been cracked open."[1]

Gilevich and Tarnovskaia had certainly set the bar high for sensational murder, and A. A.
Dolmatov and Baron V. V. Geismar cleared it. In January 1913, these two young aristocrats
from prominent families beat to death Marianna Time, the wife of the Russian director of
craftsmen of the International Society of Sleeping Cars. They wanted her diamond earrings,
which they did not find in their frantic search of her bedroom, even though the jewelry lay
in an unlocked case beside her bed. The only valuable trophy they came away with was the
wedding ring that Dolmatov had wrenched from the dying woman's finger. Yet another

---

1. *Peterburgskaia listok* (hereafter *Pl*), 25 May 1913, no. 141.

case solved by chief of detectives Filippov with the aid of his assistants Marshlak and Kuntsevich, this one starred a nobility so debauched that they lent credence to the Italians' accusations that Russia's degenerate aristocracy was holding the empire back. The Russian jury recognized the depravity of these men's actions and dispatched the man with the axe to seventeen years hard labor and his younger confederate with the bludgeon to fifteen.[2]

This final chapter, however, does not concern itself with class conflict, even as this homicidal pair metaphorically led the Russian nobility toward extinction. Dolmatov's and Geismar's social status contributed to the appeal of the story, but this chapter places them at the peak of the explosion of sensationalism that colored the waning years of the autocracy. The murders analyzed in this chapter referenced each other, and were ballyhooed enough to be recalled twenty years later by a grand duke living in Parisian exile. Alexander Mikhailovich, however, had misrecognized the sensational reportage of them as mindless escapism, as a retreat from the serious matter of the approaching war. A pattern emerges from those deaths that merited the most extensive coverage, when men killing women with whom they were intimate flashed most brightly in the headlines.

No surprise that sex sold, but the political stakes ran much deeper; the empire's most talked about murders raised questions about normative gendered behaviors. Gender has long been recognized as one of the fundamental ways in which "actors manipulate, interpret, legitimize, and reproduce the patterns . . . that order their social world."[3] Labeling behaviors according to gendered norms is one way in which society assimilates the individual. Modernity had ushered in new forms of social relations between sexes, and it was identified positively in the West with a rational, bourgeois masculinity capable of breaking with the past's inhibiting structures.[4] Despite having pressured for substantive changes in 1905, Russians were still struggling within the patriarchal system that structured both society and politics. Russian men killed their women for many reasons, for a diamond ring as easily as for a broken heart. But the motives for their actions, and the public response to them, revealed some of the ways in which modernity was affecting gendered norms in post-1905 Russia. This affect on gendered norms had political implications to the extent that it reflected first a repudiation of patriarchy, and second, it did not suggest that bourgeois liberalism provided a preferable alternative.


## True Crime and the Modern Mass Media

"Don't forget, we live in the age of stenography!" warned the assistant lawyer A.B. Vroblevskii in 1913.[5] Marking a moment that would later be felt so acutely by users of the

---

2. A story about the case began: "Even before the trial, public opinion had convicted them, without mercy or pity." *Ubiistvo Time: Sudebnyi otchet* (St. Petersburg: Viktoriia, 1913), 3.

3. Sherry B. Ortner, "Theory in Anthropology since the Sixties," *Comparative Studies in Society and History* 26, no. I (1984): 145.

4. Marshall Berman, *All That Is Solid Melts into Air: The Experience of Modernity* (New York: Simon & Schuster, 1982). Berman's work has been criticized for its male centeredness, but as Rita Felski pointed out in her greatly nuanced study of the gendering of modernity, "The identification of masculinity is not, of course, simply an invention of contemporary theorists." IIn her *The Gender of Modernity* (Cambridge: Harvard University Press, 1995), 16.

5. A.B. Vroblevskii, *Sport ili pravosudie?: Tainstvennoe izcheznovinie 40 svidetelei iz dela Prasolova* (Iaroslavl': E.F. Vakhrameev, 1913), 10.

Internet's social networks, Vroblevskii was cautioning that modern technology had powers to fix the spoken word in time and space. He himself had authored a critical account of the trial of wife killer Vasilii Prasolov (discussed below), one of a growing number of books about factual cases. The print media, booming from the easing of censorship and the increases in literacy and disposable income, peddled true crime in new forms. The accused themselves were more frequently taking pen in hand either to protest their innocence or confess their guilt.

Mapping "that vague and shifting region between real and fictional reality where mass belief resides," Mark Seltzer underscores the role of the reporting of the mass media from the scene of the crime to create what he terms the "pathological public sphere."[6] The editors of *Peterburgskii listok* had credited gossip as their source for their recapitulation of the last few moments of Marianna Time's life, a tacit acknowledgment of the mixture of media. Tarnovskaia's serialized confession, despite the liberties taken with facticity, nonetheless had a truth value that helped to engender the sympathy that the seductress needed badly. Another serial, F.S. Znakomyi's *Where is the Truth?: A Story from Contemporary Life*, competed directly with the action fiction, advertising as it did "twenty-four pages and an illustrated cover for each installment." Based on the murder of psychiatrist Max Shenfel'd by his patient Genrikh fon Rautenfel'd at a clinic in Riga in July 1912, the author promised facts compiled from a "multiple of newspapers and other documents."[7] The increasing intertextuality of true crime helped to shape the evolving discourse of murder. Also a natural topic for the cinema, true crime turned the courtroom into a camera-ready social theater. Gilevich and Tarnovskaia both made it into the movies. Theater owners in Kiev, where Tarnovskaia's husband still lived, petitioned the Holy Synod to be allowed to show scenes of her burning Naumov with cigarettes, without success.[8] The film version of the Gilevich case gives hints of cinematic possibilities for embellishment. *The Scalped Corpse* (1915), a "criminal chronicle based on the trial of the notorious engineer and adventurer Gilevich," was considerably less horrific than the photographs published in the papers. The scattered reels that remain make evident that the film version bore no resemblance to the crime committed in those furnished rooms.[9] This Gilevich has a gang and a girlfriend, and some undecipherable business with musical instruments—a piano and a bass. The engineer who stalked his prey in 1909 depended on his ability to remain anonymous in an urban environment. In the film he dons a selection of disguises, fake facial hair and costumes that allow him to evade the detective pursuing him, though the two do engage once in fisticuffs. The on-screen Gilevich packs a pistol and borrowed no more from the factual one than his macabre deed for the title.

Unfortunately, little else of true-crime celluloid remains for viewing. Vasilii Goncharov, who would become an important screenwriter, directed his first film, *Drama in Moscow*, in 1909, an "incredibly unsuccessful attempt to make a film about a shocking trial" that

6. Mark Seltzer, "Murder/Media/Modernity," *Canadian Review of American Studies* 38, no. 1 (2008): 11.

7. F.S. Znakomyi's *Gde pravda?: Povest' iz sovremennoi zhizni* (Riga: Sol'ntse, 1913), which sold for five kopecks. V. Rozanov wrote about this murder in *Nv*, 21 July 1912, no. 13065, and Bekhterev attended the funeral.

8. *Gazeta kinematografov*, no. 29 (1913): 1.

9. When I watched what remains of this film in the Moscow film archives in 2003, the projectionist asked me if I *really* wanted to watch a film with such a gruesome title. I assured her that I did.

Fig. 31. The patient Genrikh fon Rautenfel'd kills the psychiatrist Max Shenfe'ld.

was banned after its first showing for unexplained reasons.[10] *The Merchant Bashkirov's Daughter* (1913), the film version of the Nizhnii Novgorod drama about the young woman who accidentally killed the man she loves after her patriarchal father had selected a different fiancé for her, featured close-ups that intensified her suffering and an inferno at the end, when she sets fire to the *traktir* in which she has barricaded the peasant who raped her. Tying technology to the ritual that gave defendants the final say, *The Last Word of the Accused* was filmed twice, in 1912 and 1916. Released as a gramophone movie, the film was accompanied by a recording in a rudimentary attempt at talkies. *The Volotina Case*, about the "noisiest trial" from Kiev, appeared in 1915 and was remade two years later. *Plevako Defended Her* (1916) was based on the Kachka trial. In 1917 Drankov put on screen two of the best publicized cases of the prewar years, *The Memoirs of Countess Maria Tarnovskaia*, based on Anna Vivanti's novel, and *The Count Roniker Case*, about the trial of an aristocrat in Warsaw accused of killing his teenage brother-in-law in order to increase his wife's inheritance.

The publisher of *Why I Killed: The Confession of the Convicted Evitskii, Consumed by Passion* (1914), wrote in the introduction that "not so long ago the public turned to literature as the mirror of life as they searched for answers. Now they turn to the courts, the primary source for material from real life."[11] Koni despaired at this. Writing in 1914, he cited the "unhealthy curiosity of the crowd for sensational details." Like the highbrow critics of the yellow journalism war that had been waged in New York between Joseph Pulitzer and William Randolph Hearst, he deplored that "the era of the press had begun," and that "people often stood defenseless against insinuations in the press." For him, the attraction to sensationalism

---

10. Veniamin Vishnevskii, *Khudozhestvennye fil'my dorevoliutsionnoi Rossii* (Moscow: Goskinoizdat, 1945), 9.

11. *Pochemu ia ubil: Ispoved' osuzhdennogo. Vo vlasti strasti. Protsess Evitskogo* (St. Petersburg: Sh. Bussel', 1914), 3. This was the first offering from the projected new series, the "Library of Criminal Trials."

could be found in "mental lethargy." Quoting Pushkin, he agreed that too many of his fellow countrymen were simply "lazy, lacking curiosity."[12] Quite the opposite was true; Koni just did not believe that what "enquiring minds wanted to know"[13] merited making the effort.

## "Murder . . . Has Been Going on Too Long for It to Be News"

Detective novelist Raymond Chandler's ironic comment on the non-newsworthiness of one person taking the life of another emphasizes what a common occurrence the crime has always been. Therefore, when it becomes a story, as opposed to just another item in the paper, the murder in question must be about more than death. The Gilevich and Tarnovskaia stories had obvious reach, but why the interest in Vasilii Prasolov, who killed his estranged wife Zina at Moscow's tony Strel'na restaurant in the wee dawn hours of October 9, 1911? True, she was drinking brandy with the wealthy furrier D. M. Rogatkin-Ezhikov, but a man shooting his adulterous wife in public was not new. An unnamed publisher pointed out that "in its essential details this one does not stand out from many analogous ones." So why, "in the endless list of recent criminal trials, has not one attracted such exceptional and intense public attention as the murder of Zinaida Ivanovna Prasolova"?[14] Love. Sex. Adultery. Celebrities. A cornucopia of emotions in this one.

Vasilii Prasolov did not go to trial until January 1913, and it lasted a deliciously long ten days. He had spent several months under observation in a mental ward, where the psychiatrists declared him mentally stable at the moment of the murder. He had, however, tried to hang himself in his jail cell, his second suicide attempt. Because culpability rather than guilt was in question, the verdict would hang on the jurors' assessment of Vasilii's character, and witnesses on both sides hurled so many insinuations that neither side could establish credibility. His *zashchitniki*, V. M. Bobrishchev-Pushkin and N. N. Izmailov, eschewed the usual gambit of implicating the victim in her own murder. In his closing argument, Izmailov said, "I will not for a minute touch the good name of the deceased," adding assiduously that "I will defend her better than the procurator did."[15] Rather ingenuously Bobrishchev-Pushkin declared, "I will say nothing judgmental about Zinaida Ivanovna out of pity for the defendant, whose love for her has not dimmed, and also because of my deep respect for her memory."[16] Deference for Zina worked to secure Vasilii's acquittal.

12. A.F. Koni, "Predislovie" to Grigorii Avetovich Dzhanshiev, *Sbornik statei* (Moscow: Riabushinskii, 1914), 6–7. Despite his general enthusiasm for jurors, in 1905 Koni had expressed concern about the influence of newspapers, and objected to sending press crimes to juries because "there is always something in the wind that will influence jurors."

13. This was the longtime advertising for the supermarket tabloid *National Enquirer*.

14. In addition to the widespread coverage in the national press, transcripts of the first trial were published: *Delo ob ubiistve Zinaidy Ivanovny Prasolovoi* (n.p., 1913); and *Delo V. V. Prasolova: Polnyi otchet* (Moscow: K.L. Men'shov, 1913). The speeches by the procurator and civil plaintiff in the second trial were published in *Ubiistvo Z. I. Prasolovoi: Novoe v dele Prasolovoi* (Moscow: P.P. Riabushinskii, 1914). The person who wrote the commentary signed only as "the publisher," which connects this publication back to Nikolai Riabushinkii, whose friendship with Zina was raised at trial to question her morals.

15. *Delo V. V. Prasolova: Polnyi otchet* (Moscow: K.L. Men'shov, 1913), 158. Hereafter, *Polnyi otchet*.

16. Ibid., 177.

"Человѣческіе ==
== Документы"

Библіотека сенсаціонныхъ процессовъ

Дѣло
Прасолова

З. И. Прасолова.    В. В. Прасоловъ.

Контора
Изданій
А. Л. Будо.
Москва

Цѣна
25
Коп.

Fig. 32. The Prasolov affair, from the *Library of Sensational Crimes.*

What made this trial unusual was the degree of personal detail revealed as both sides delved into the Prasolovs' troubled relationship. It put Moscow's "golden youth," slang for the rich and irresponsible, on exhibition. Vasilii Tarnovskii's 1905 trial for killing his wife's lover played like a prelude to this one, the mass media all the more sophisticated now, and public appetites all the more voracious. The Prasolovs had met while still in secondary school, she one year older than he. Zina belonged to the prosperous merchant Dennitsin family and had studied voice at the conservatory. Vasilii had graduated from Moscow University, continued his education briefly in France, and worked as the representative of a Parisian firm in Moscow. They had a daughter, whose tragic death in September 1910 from an unnamed illness opened up competing accusations of indifference: Zina had gone to the theater the night her baby girl had undergone an operation, and Vasilii did not attend her funeral, protesting later to have been too distraught.

Zina's family, to no surprise, vilified him on the stand. Zina's sister Maria, who had also been in the Rogatkin-Ezhikov party at the Strel'na, testified that Vasilii had propositioned her during Zina's pregnancy. Her brother Nikolai, a singer, intimated a very different sort of sexuality, casting suspicions on the nature of Vasilii's relationship with his Armenian friend Alexander (Sasha) Konzhuntsev: "Vasilii patted his cheek, practically sitting in his lap, and stroked his hair." Another hostile witness remembered "Vasia" on "Sashenka's" knees, raising his hand to his lips to be kissed. Vasia was also snidely accused of having made soup for Sashen'ka, surely a fey gesture. In predictable contrast, Vasilii's family spoke mostly of his depression and his devotion to Zina. His mother, however, could not resist mentioning Zina's poor housekeeping and lack of maternal affections.[17]

The available facts constructed a deeply flawed marriage. The Prasolovs had separated a year before the ruinous rendezvous in the restaurant. Adultery offered one legal option for divorce, yet even the most casual observer of Russian society could see that marital unfaithfulness was seldom considered sufficiently serious to end a marriage.[18] Zina had taken up the fashionable feat of expressing jealousy by throwing acid at Vasilii in a fit over his relationship with Sophia Frumson, a singer at the popular Aquarium nightclub.[19] His collar had protected most of his face, though he was hospitalized briefly. A year before the murder, the police had been called when Frumson attacked Vasilii, also at the Strel'na. In addition, Frumson had thrown such a scandal at a skating rink that the story made it into the daily papers. Then Zina came to appreciate Frumson's outbursts, and shortly before the murder the two women dined publicly at the Saburov Bouffe. On the stand, Frumson told the procurator that "it's difficult for me to say anything bad about her."[20]

17. Ibid., 36, 91, 41. As Bobrishchev-Pushkin pointed out (181), homosexuality was illegal in Russia, so if the prosecution believed Konzhuntsev to be one, why was he not arrested?

18. Barbara Engel, *Breaking the Ties that Bound: The Politics of Marital Strife in Late Imperial Russia* (Ithaca: Cornell University Press, 2011), 212, notes that men were considerably more likely than women to mention adultery in their petitions; women needed additional transgressions because infidelity was commonplace.

19. The most exciting of Russia's *vitrioleuses* was the daughter of a major general. In 1909 Vera fon Vik, who had fallen on hard times, badly disfigured the face of the current mistress of the man she loved. Vera published her confession, asking that she be convicted, a request that her jury denied her. V.F. fon Vik, *Zapiski podsudimoi* (St. Petersburg: Smolinskii, 1914).

20. *Polnyi otchet*, 55.

# ДИКАЯ СЦЕНА ВЪ ОКРУЖНОМЪ СУДѢ.

Fig. 33. Throwing acid, another popular sensational crime.

For Zina's part, after Vasilii had moved out, the soon-to-be-infamous I.K. Arenson began paying her rent, and then found her a new apartment. Describing himself now as her fiancé, Arenson had a key, which he swore he used only to take care of the flat when Zina was in Kislevodsk with another sister, Sophia. Telegrams to Zina from both Arenson and her sister Maria muddy this idyllic relationship. He signs, "I kiss you passionately," and Maria complains that he refuses to pay the rent until Zina returns.[21] It was evident that Arenson was on its way to becoming a household name when a lawyer named Aronson working the Count Roniker trial in Warsaw asked reporters not to confuse him with "the Prasolov Arenson."[22] "Arenson" became the byword for the summoning of witnesses who had no knowledge of the crime itself, but could instead supply salacious information about the personal relationships among the cast of characters.[23]

An ideal topic for the silver screen, the story went quickly into film, *In Moscow's Golden Spiderweb*, a pun on the phrase "golden youth." Even before production began, theaters were displaying photographs of the principals.[24] The Prasolov family successfully petitioned the Moscow police to forbid showing the movie in their neighborhood.[25] The celebrity status

21. Ibid., 132–33.

22. *Pl*, 22 December 1913, no. 295.

23. Arenson refused to testify at court, but his statement from the preliminary investigation was read aloud. *Polnyi otchet*, 48–51.

24. *Obozrenie kinematografov, sketing-ringov i teatrov*, 10 February 1912, no. 238.

25. V.P. Mikhailov, *Rasskazy o kinematografe staroi Moskvy* (Moscow: Materik, 2003), 245.

of several witnesses stirred the already excitable public. Nikolai Riabushinskii, the black sheep of an extremely prominent merchant family, was also at the Strel'na that night.[26] His brother Pavel was one of Moscow's leading citizens, the publisher of the Moscow daily *Utro Rossii* (Russia's Morning), and cofounder of the Progressist political party, which represented the interests of economically liberal industrialists and bankers such as himself. His less responsible brother published the Symbolist journal *Zolotoe runo* (The Golden Fleece), which had infamously sponsored a competition in 1907 for the best depiction of the Devil.[27] Nikolai and Zina were acquainted, and she had died in his car as he rushed her to the hospital. Nikolai answered on the stand about inviting Zina to his notorious villa, the Black Swan.

Even more intriguing, Zina had become involved with opera star Dmitrii Smirnov, an acquaintance she had made when still married to Vasilii. The self-righteous tenor testified that he had run into Zina by accident several times on tours of southern Russia, in the spa areas of Kislevodsk and Yalta. He admitted that they were very friendly, but not lovers, and he swore that he had tried to reconcile her with Vasilii.[28] Telegrams from Smirnov, however, intimate a far more intimate relationship. All were signed "Dimochka." The one sent from Yalta to her in Nizhnii Novgorod, where she went annually with family members to the national fair, captured their relationship in brief: "Terribly boring write more often I sent you two letters and await yours. I have many invitations to perform in October how's your health I hope no unpleasantness everything worries me I kiss you madly."[29]

Domestic dystopia lay at the heart of this case. Throughout the trial Vasilii insisted that he had forgiven Zina, that he still loved his wife and dreamed only of getting back together with her and raising a family. Konzhuntsev submitted letters that Vasilii had written to him when on business in Odessa and Constantinople during the separation from Zina, in which Vasilli confided that "you are the only person to whom I can bare my soul."[30] Opening himself up thus lent credence to Vasilii's insistence that he wanted to maintain his relationship with Zina:

> I am suffering again from dark melancholia and depression. I can't get control of myself without feeling sad. Why sad, you ask? Because my happiness is destroyed. . . . My friend here Shestov gave me the same advice that you did, to not meet with Zinaida Ivanovna again and to forget the past. . . . He's married and has two daughters, and says that as long as I travel alone, I will have my wife in my heart and be pulled toward Moscow. But with whom can I travel? Certainly not Sophia Vladimirovna [Frumson], even though she loves me deliriously. . . . Living alone would be unbearable. I would commit suicide.

26. A year earlier Nikolai Riabushinskii had been found guilty of slandering the restaurant's manager, R. L. Ritter, who also testified at the Prasolov trial. *Moskovskii listok* (hereafter *Ml*), 6 May 1910, no. 102.

27. Riabushinskii found no contestant worthy. John E. Bowlt, "Through the Glass Darkly: Images of Decadence in Early Twentieth-Century Russian Art," *Journal of Contemporary History* 17, no. I (1982): 99.

28. For example, they spoke to each other in the familiar *ty*, which he explained is "what we do in theatrical circles." *Polnyi otchet*, 94.

29. Ibid., 130.

30. A. S. Konzhuntsev gave Vasilii's letters to the defense; they were republished in *Polnyi otchet*, 120–30.

Vasilii also wrote ominously of having accidentally shot his palm: "I was loading the revolver and have no idea how it fired."[31]

Neither spouse could claim fidelity, but was her betrayal worse than his? Zina's father had hired two civil plaintiffs to rescue her reputation. Her defense included love letters, published in the press, that she had written during their courtship. In one she wrote with titillating frankness about her sexuality:

> I asked you to leave, but you didn't, why, why did you stay when I repeatedly told you to go, when we were both in such an agitated state, and you know perfectly well how difficult it is to control yourself, and you've told me more than once that you won't answer for yourself, and I've told you that I can't for myself either. Now I understand completely why you said it was good that the policeman interrupted, because all would have ended very badly, but why did this have to happen, that our love turned into some sort of animal instinct?[32]

The couple had sexual relations first in a private room in Moscow's popular Hermitage pleasure gardens in 1907, before their marriage.

Zina showed herself to be a New Woman of the same type that Tarnovskaia had been, open to her passions and unwilling to settle into married life. She had a literary cohort, Mania El'tsova, the heroine of the most popular novel of the day, Anastasia Verbitskaia's *Keys to Happiness*.[33] The controversial Mania enjoyed multiple lovers, a child out of wedlock, and the drive for artistic freedom that Zina felt when she spoke of her desire for a singing career. Mania represented the sexualized New Woman in a racial reversal: her most supportive lover, Mark Shteinbakh, was a wealthy Jew. Like Zina, Mania died young, though by her own hand. Mania's openness met with a backlash from critics, but her popularity attested to the reality that the subject was open for debate. Both sides at the Prasolov trial recognized the implicit connection between Zina and Mania. Civil plaintiff A.R. Lednitskii reported that Vasilii "had at least one of the keys to her happiness in his hands, but he mocked her desires." *Zashchitnik* Izmailov referred to Arenson's key as "not to her apartment but to her happiness, stolen by him for his own debased happiness."[34] Acquitting Vasilii did not translate directly into convicting Zina.

The audience at court greeted Vasilii's verdict with applause. The cinematic quality of the trial inspired an editorial in the newspaper *Kinematograph* (Cinematography). The journalist Nikolai Pasmurov reminded his readers of the difference between listening attentively to every detail and only reading newspaper articles. He reported that attacks on Vasilii's character had backfired because sitting before them was "a man, not a creature from hell." Judging the person outweighed judging the crime, "and it was impossible in that atmosphere to send someone to hard labor." He concluded, "let him go with his conscience and suffer the consequences of the murder he committed."[35] Shades of Dostoevsky!

31. Ibid., 128, 125.
32. The civil plaintiff put her letters in evidence; they were republished in *Polnyi otchet*, 101–20.
33. The novel was written in five volumes, 1908–1913, and became the most heralded movie of 1913.
34. *Polnyi otchet*, 149, 164.
35. N. Pasmurov, "Prasolovshchina," *Kinematograf*, no. 29, 1913.

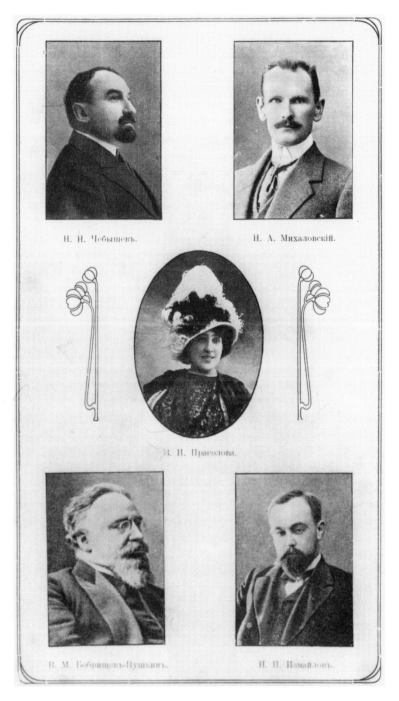

Fig. 34. Zina Prasolova, surrounded by lawyers, none of whom incriminated her.

The procurator D. V. Novitskii, pressed by Zina's father, appealed Vasilii's acquittal on the technicality that the defense had not obeyed article 557 of the code, which required an explanation of the reasoning behind their selection of witnesses. The Senate agreed that too much extraneous material had been presented, by the prosecution as well, and ordered a change of venue for the retrial to provincial Iaroslavl'. More than half of the first set of witnesses was not summoned to that city, where the charges against Vasilii were dropped from "premeditated" to "in a fit of anger" with its lesser sentence. Iaroslavl' lawyer Vroblevskii got hauled into court for criticizing the prosecution; he questioned whether the first trial had been *Sport or Justice?*[36] The second proceedings proved anticlimactic. Zina's father did not appear because her sister Sophia, known to snort cocaine, had just committed suicide. Her brother Sergei was also in trouble with the law.[37] The new venue meant nothing to the jurors, who overrode the expert psychiatrists and concluded that Vasilii had shot her in a moment of pathological *affekt*. The judge released him to his parents.[38]

The question remains: why did this trial engage public interest to such a surprising degree? Levels of sensationalism account for what landed it on the front page, but what kept it there? Procurator N. N. Chebyshev noted that "not even the inventor of the telegraph attracted as much attention in his life as the public has given to this wife killer."[39] The answer lies in the themes brought out at trial that raised issues of gendered behavior after 1905. For all the attention brought to Zina's sexual liaisons, the spotlight had shined more brightly on Vasilii. What sort of man was he?

Political responsibility had become a masculine attribute by 1913, and one that differed substantively from the preceding patriarchal relationships that had kept men as well as women subordinated. Without exaggerating the democratic structure of Russia's Duma, in which representation was weighted in favor of conservative, landowning males, its representatives still depended on elections. Members took the initiative by drafting and debating legislation on a national scale. Physical strength gave one measure of a man, but the successful liberal, industrialized democrat needed mental fortitude to understand choices and make decisions.[40] The publisher and industrialist Pavel Riabushinskii was such a man, in contrast to his brother Nikolai. The demand for a sober accounting of one's actions applied to the domestic as well as the national economy. When Vasilii Prasolov shot his errant wife, he showed the same woeful lack of character that had allowed Vasilii Tarnovskii to kill his wife's lover when the latter was unaware and unarmed. The homicidal husband who pulled the trigger on his wife because she refused to build a nest for him had become a familiar character in the pre-1905 courtroom.[41] The political situation had changed, but had masculinity as well?

36. The word "sport" referred specifically to the procurator's closing words, "Say in your verdict that the sports that these people play must not include spilling the blood of women!" *Polnyi otchet*, 145.

37. *Russkoe slovo* (hereafter *Rs*), 26 September 1913, no. 272.

38. Vroblevskii, *Sport ili pravosudie?*, 10. The author later helped to write the Soviet criminal code in the 1920s.

39. Quoted in *Polnyi otchet*, 1.

40. Peter N. Stearns writes about the impact of modernity on notions of manhood in *Be a Man!: Males in Modern Society* (New York: Holmes & Meier, 1979), especially chapter 5.

41. For example, acquittals ended two such cases: "Na romanicheskoi pochve," *Sd* 15, no. 12 (1902): 383–85; and "Istoriia odnogo braka," *Sd* 22, no. 8 (1904): 145–236.

At the turn of the twentieth century, codes of honor in even the most liberal democracies, despite their legal statutes, offered Vasilii some form of defense for having taken the most drastic measures to protect his name. Vasilii, though, had shot his wife rather than her lover(s), and then broken down in tears. The bill of indictment had tried to give him a backbone when it charged that he had handed his revolver to an onlooker with the words "I did what I came here to do," but the witness to whom he gave the gun swore that he had said no such thing.[42] The procurator tried to portray a Vasilii already so debauched that he had no honor. Zina was his victim twice over; first he had taken her happiness, and then her life. Procurator Novitskii argued that "he was obligated to tell the men with his wife that . . . a bloody duel must decide the fate of each of us."[43] The prosecution played up heavily the suspicions about his relationship with Konzhuntsev, and his sexuality was further feminized by talk that he wore silk underwear and a gold bracelet.[44] The civil plaintiff Lebnitskii, whose obligation lay with Zina, spoke of the new era's equality between the sexes, charging Vasilii with behaving like a medieval patriarch.[45] The second civil plaintiff M. F. Khodasevich gave him no quarter: "he already stinks like a three-day-old corpse."[46]

*Zashchitniki* Izmailov and Bobrishchev-Pushkin would earn their money by tacking the course, familiar from the Palem trial, of persuading jurors that their own common sense about human nature was superior to that of court-appointed psychiatrists. Bobrishchev-Pushkin made quick work of the experts, dismissing them as "clinicians, not forensic psychiatrists" because none had cited pathological *affekt*. Specifically, the *zashchitniki* used the descriptions of his actions from other patrons at the Strel'na to illustrate that Vasilii had suffered this affliction. Sidestepping an assault on Zina's character, they pointed the finger instead at the predatory Arenson, "the fiancé on the installment plan," who had ruined both Prasolovs.[47]

How to justify, though, that Vasilii had shot Zina rather than Arenson? Izmailov legitimized Vasilii as a *neschastnyi* without using the word: "Melancholy (*toska*) made his heart ache, and when a Russian man finds himself in this situation, he drinks. And Prasolov drank, melancholy flooding his heart." The indictment had included Vasilii's alcohol and drug consumption on the night in question, delineated by Bobrishchev-Pushkin: "after drinking champagne mixed with porter, then cognac, he maintained a sober countenance by poisoning himself with cocaine." When Vasilii saw Zina and her party, he needed more cognac for the courage to approach her. Yet the defense did not consider Vasilii to be intoxicated because he had not blacked out. "She was free, but he was not. He had not ripped from his breast the love that inflamed his soul. . . . Blood pounded in his head. Everything went dim. A light flashed and the terrible deed was done."[48]

42. *Polnyi otchet*, 21.
43. Ibid., 142–43.
44. Ibid., 1.
45. Ibid., 153. Engel, *Breaking the Ties*, 168–71, points to increasing criticism of "despotic" husbands.
46. *Polnyi otchet*, 155.
47. Ibid., 175–76. Bobrishchev-Pushkin ridiculed the psychiatrists, sniping that "they would find a mother who had just thrown her baby out of the window sane because she had logically fed the child first."
48. Ibid., 170, 186, 187.

Izmailov and Bobrishchev-Pushkin wrote a successful narrative consonant with Russian notions of jury justice. This begs the question, however, of why Russian public opinion found weakness acceptable in masculine behavior, especially at a moment when it could be anticipated that grit was needed. A deputy to the First Duma, V. V. Nedonoskov, raised the question of the proper behavior of politicians when he emptied a pistol into his lover, Kleopatra Georgievna Zheleznova, in the spa town of Kislevodsk in July 1907. Elected from Ural'sk and a member of the leftist Labor Party (*Trudovik*), the assistant lawyer Nedonoskov pleaded innocent on the grounds that he could not remember the incident.[49] Eight of the council of ten psychiatrists who had observed him in the mental hospital concluded that he had been suffering from pathological *affekt* when he shot Zheleznova. Nedonoskov went to trial three times between 1909 and 1911, until the superior court stopped listening to prosecutorial appeals. The prosecution claimed that his election to the Duma proved his sanity, but the defense pointed to numerous physiological indications of hereditary degeneracy, especially on the left side of his face, better developed than the right, and with the telltale Darwinian bumps in his skull. The prominent psychiatrists Chechott and Vl. P. Serbskii testified for the defense.[50]

Significant parallels between Nedonoskov's case and the Prasolov trial that followed it point to an instability in gender relations that privileged the emotional male who could not control his impulses. Nedonoskov could not marry Zheleznova because both already had spouses whom they had quit years earlier. Zheleznova also had a five-year-old daughter, Tunus'ka, not by her husband. None of this bothered Nedonoskov, who dreamed only of the day when she would get a divorce and they could legalize what he saw already as their family. "Klera," as he called her, did not share his fantasy. She liked money and men, in that order. The two were not together as a couple in Kislevodsk that July, and alcohol played no part in the shooting. On the contrary, Nedonoskov had followed her and a young man into a kumis shop, where he sat across from their table, growing increasingly disturbed as he watched them drink the healthful mare's milk. Following the two outside, he asked to speak to her. He wanted to be able to drop by her apartment and visit the child, "Tinochka." She agreed, with the qualification that he leave by the girl's bedtime. When Klera walked away, Nedonoskov's mind went blank. Eyewitnesses saw him start firing, still pulling the trigger after all the bullets were spent, an action already determined by forensic psychiatrists as a sign of pathological *affekt*.[51] A passerby grabbed a walking stick from someone in the crowd and began hitting him. The student with Zheleznova pulled a knife. Nedonoskov claimed to have regained consciousness befuddled about why he was under attack.

49. One of the more than two hundred deputies who signed the Vyborg Manifesto in July 1906 to protest the tsar's dissolution of the First Duma, Nedonoskov was prohibited from standing for election to the Second Duma.

50. *Sudebnye dramy* published as a separate monograph a complete coverage of the trial in 1911, with a supplement that included Nedonoskov's diaries and information about the multiple appeals. The journal then serialized an abbreviated version in the monthly issues in 1912. *Ubiistvo K. G. Zheleznovoi* (Moscow: A. I. Snegirev, 1911).

51. Serbskii argued that "someone suffering physiological (as opposed to pathological) *affekt* would not have fired an empty revolver." *Ubiistvo K. G. Zheleznovoi*, supplement, 100–101.

As in the Prasolov case, private correspondence found its way into print. In addition to letters, Nedonoskov kept jailhouse diaries. Tears splashed on almost every page: "On days when it's raining, it's as if the clouds are weeping with me." He tries to hold back when Tunus'ka visits him in jail because "she does not like to see me cry," but "weakness conquered me, I could not fight it, my heart burst and I began to sob." Nedonoskov had landed in trouble with his Labor Party after having "lent" Klera funds collected for the central committee that she had failed to repay. But even when he writes of Klera's desire for material goods, "I blame myself. I so loved her appearance, I chose fine dresses, and without me she would not have bought anything. . . . I defined her style." Page after page speaks of his obsession: "I break out in a cold sweat at the thought that these torments will never, ever end . . . 'Klera is no more!' is the nail drilled into my brain."[52]

Remorse still needed pathological *affekt* for forgiveness. I. A. Evitskii took his confession to the public, satisfying more with shock value than self-reproach. On an October night in 1912, he had shot his mistress, the mother of their six-year-old son, Boris, and sat in the bedroom with her corpse for several hours. From a wealthy noble family in Ekaterinskaia Province, Evitskii had "traded a successful military career for failure in commerce."[53] His family fortune exhausted at the roulette tables in Monte Carlo, he married into a wealthy merchant family, to "the kind of Russian woman who will be faithful to the grave of her first love, but who has no sexual feelings."[54] He had met his victim when she worked in one of his garment factories, a "Carmen, in both beauty and personality."[55] Although he protested that he had tried to hide their relationship from his wife and friends, it seems unlikely that no one noticed when "Duda" appeared "in the rotunda of a fashionable Petersburg restaurant wearing nothing but high heels and a diamond necklace."[56]

*Peterburgskii listok* rightly headlined this saga "In the Slough of Passion." Much of the trial covered their sex life: orgies at the Villa Rodé, blind musicians hired to play for them in the restaurant's private rooms, accusations of necrophilia and incest, a bout with syphilis—testimony delivered disappointingly behind closed doors. Evitskii's name had already been recorded in police blotters; an arrest for scandalous behavior at the Tivoli and another for forging his wife's signature to promissory notes. Why, though, had he killed his Duda (Zenovia Sorochinskaia)? Because she had asked him for twenty-five rubles as a dowry to marry someone else. He told jurors, "I was not jealous, I was insulted." Acquiescing to having fired, he pled not guilty to murder.[57] The well-established psychiatrists Chechott and Pavel Rozenbakh declared him sane at the moment when he shot her, evidenced by his calm afterward just sitting by her bed. Nor did the doctors diagnose Evitskii as an alcoholic, despite his staggering consumption of liquor, or as an hereditary degenerate, even after his descriptions of his father taking lascivious license with serf girls.[58] Convicted of

52. Ibid., 20, 15, 7, 88–89.
53. *Pl*, 15 December 1913, no. 344.
54. *Pochemu ia ubil*, 49.
55. *Pl*, 17 December 1913, no. 346.
56. Ibid.
57. *Russkii vestnik* (hereafter *Rv*), 18 December 1913, no. 291.
58. Evitskii denied that he suffered alcoholism, because he never drank when alone. *Pochemu ia ubil*, 50.

killing her "in a fit of anger," he got six years at hard labor. Trying to explain his obsession with Duda, even though she "slit open live birds with her bare hands, skinned frogs to fish for lobster, and consciously poisoned dogs and cats,"[59] Evitskii echoed the excesses of the Putilin stories in which heads were chopped off live men.


### The Intertextual Vasilii Prasolov

The neurasthenic male, whom Vasilii Prasolov personified, had years ago become "a hero in our belles lettres, interpreted by experts at court, written about in journal articles, separate monographs, and public lectures given on him."[60] Likewise, the popularity of the social melodramas performed in the courtroom could surpass those on the legitimate stage.[61] Variations on the character of the tearful killer appeared in film to such an extent that common characteristics take shape, giving the story of a weak man and his unfaithful partner generic properties. By identifying the crossovers in themes and characters in the transformation from true to cinematic crime, we can see some of the "ways in which [Russian] culture [made] sense of itself."[62] Two glossy films that postdated Vasilii's trial, both directed by Evgenii Bauer for the Khanzhonkov Studio, have characters that impersonate the principals in the Prasolov case. *Children of the Age* (1914) and *Child of the Big City* (1914), as is evident from their titles, address what Vasilii and Zina were, the "children" of the new century, with its greatly enhanced possibilities for commercialized consumption. *Children of the Age* enters film history as the first starring vehicle for Vera Kholodnaia, on her way to becoming Russia's most iridescent leading lady. Her "Mary" suffered Zina's most prevalent character flaws. Married to a bank clerk, and with a small child, Mary found herself attracted to the sweet life. *Children* takes a sexually violent turn when her husband's boss, a wealthy businessman with hints of Arenson, drives Mary into the woods in his big black automobile and rapes her. Unnerved at first, she later decides that he is preferable to her husband the clerk. Unlike Vasilii, this husband kills himself rather than his unfaithful wife.[63]

The plotline of *Child of the Big City* centered on the same comment that Vasilii had made to a friend accompanying him that fateful night in the Strel'na, that the contemporary woman "cannot build the family hearth" and offer the cozy life that he so craved.[64] In this film the bourgeois hero plucks a seamstress from a life of poverty because, doubting that the modern woman can offer happiness, he seeks a simple girl. The seamstress quickly acquires expensive tastes, and when she rejects his plea to live only "for each other," he

59. Ibid., 86.

60. A. A. Iakovlov, "Neskol'ko sluchaev neurastenii s preobladeniem iavlenii so storony psikhiki," *Arkhiv psikhiatrii* 9, no. 1 (1887): 1–25.

61. Theater owners in Petersburg complained of a drop in ticket sales during the trial of another brother-in-law, in addition to Roniker, accused of poisoning for an inheritance. *Delo ob otravlenii V. D. Buturlina* (Moscow: Sudebnye dramy, 1911), 7.

62. Graeme Turner, *Film as Social Practice*, 3rd ed. (New York: Routledge, 1999), 3.

63. *Deti veka*, directed by Evgenii Bauer (Moscow: Khanzhonkov, 1914).

64. *Polnyi otchet*, 20.

shoots himself outside the apartment they once shared. The movie ends with her stepping blithely over his corpse, hailing a cab for Maxim's (a.k.a., the Strel'na).[65]

The difference between the two Vasilii characters killing themselves rather than the Zina characters does not contradict the cultural readings as much as it might appear to at first blush. These movies traded in the corruptibility of New Women such as Zina. But the suicidal men paralleled Vasilii in their weaknesses. Vasilii had made two attempts on his own life and had never presented himself as a defender against the poachers, Arenson and Smirnov. He wept copiously at court, begging to be excused when his mother took the stand.[66] His letters supported the testimony from character witnesses about his emotional frailties. In crucial ways, Vasilii's behavior reflected that of the film heroes created by Russia's most popular male movie star, Ivan Mozzhukhin. Famous for his tears, not his bravado, Mozzhukhin paralleled Prasolov with hysterics that led to murder.

The neurotic male who kills the female objective of his idée fixe brings to mind Tolstoy's *Kreutzer Sonata*, but with crucial differences: Pozdnyshev obsesses over sex and suspects an infidelity that did not occur. The obsessive, murderous male played well on-screen, best under the Bauer touch. *Daydreams* (1915) features a protagonist who, mourning the deceased wife whose braid he keeps as a fetish, spots her double on the street. The second woman pays with her life for the man's fixation on her.[67] A painter obsessed with death chokes the life out of the ballerina who is posing for him in *The Dying Swan* (1916). He cannot bear to see her express emotions that he cannot control. The ballerina smiles happily when she finds true love, but the painter wants only melancholy from her.[68] These movies end before the law intervenes, both closing with shots of the men and their victims, which left open-ended the question of what form justice would take for their homicidal protagonists.

*Do You Remember?* (1914) rewrites *The Kreutzer Sonata* and gives agency to the wife. Starring Mozzhukhin, again as a violinist, this time he acts on his desire for another man's wife, played by ballerina Karalli. Their mutual attraction ends in adultery.[69] This version of the threat posed by a sensual musician ends in the aggrieved husband's suicide rather than the death of the seducible spouse. She returns to him, too late, a quiet reminder that many Russian husbands do not give themselves time or opportunity to calculate their options. That so many of these cinematic protagonists, like Russian defendants, chose to resolve their problems with violent death, either their own or the females who disappointed them,

65. *Ditia bol'shogo goroda*, directed by Evgenii Bauer (Moscow: Khanzhonkov, 1914). VHS (New York: Milestone Film & Video, 1992).

66. Not required to testify, Vasilii nonetheless wanted to explain what had happened, "speaking quietly, agitated, and weeping at times." *Polnyi otchet*, 12.

67. *Grezy*, directed by Evgenii Bauer (Moscow: Khanzhonkov, 1915). VHS (New York: Milestone Film & Video, 1992).

68. *Umirayushchii lebed*, directed by Evgenii Bauer (Moscow: Khanzhonkov, 1917). DVD (Chatsworth, CA: Image Entertainment, 2003).

69. *Ty pomnish' li?*, directed by Petr Chardynin (Moscow: Khanzhonkov, 1914). The libretto is translated in James von Geldern and Louise McReynolds, trans. and eds., *Entertaining Tsarist Russia: An Anthology of Popular Urban Cultural Sources in Late Imperial Russia* (Bloomington: Indiana University Press, 1998), 339–41.

encouraged the fatalistic emotions that worked against accepting responsibility, a characteristic necessary for the successful bourgeois male.[70]

## The Ladies in the Morgue

If in the movies the men turned the revolvers on themselves, in reality it was the women they killed, despite their own suicidal thoughts. Two acquittals and one reduced charge later, it is tempting to essentialize the male jurors as protectors of Russian manhood from the ominous New Woman. As we have seen, however, juries tended to express a more refined sense of justice than simple sexism. Zina, Klera, and Duda had all been sexually unfaithful, but none was shot primarily for this reason, though the interest in the deaths of sexually active women offered them up for "erotic contemplation."[71] To understand attitudes toward the New Woman better, we return to Marianna Time, whose savage death opened this chapter. Her killers ended up working the mines in Siberia because they had crossed a boundary no Russian jury would permit; they had murdered for money.[72] Still, this married woman had spent the night with a young man while her husband was away on business. We must revisit the scene of that crime.

All who knew her agreed that Marianna was frivolous, but not even her husband Kazimir criticized her conduct. She had enjoyed nightlife after her marriage as much as she had before it, and she had a son, not Kazimir's, though he had adopted the boy. On the afternoon of January 9 she had met two young men as they caught each others' reflections in a department store window on Nevskii Prospect. Presenting themselves as French, a language they both spoke easily, the two took in a movie with Marianna. The next evening the trio dined at the Vienna restaurant on Gogol Street, a favorite hangout for local literati. The list of pleasure spots on the itinerary for their three-day relationship included the Crystal Palace, Villa Rodé, and the Taberen tavern. The first night Geismar had returned alone to the France Hotel on the Fontanka Canal where the two men shared a room. Dolmatov accompanied Time to her apartment on Furshtatskaia Street, a reasonably comfortable address close to the city's center. He had hoped to seduce her and steal the earrings that had drawn him to her on the street. Alas, her husband was at home. Dolmatov introduced himself as the engineer Paul Gerard, from Paris, and handed Kazimir a business card before taking his leave. Her husband left the next morning on business, and Marianna made plans for the evening with her newfound friends. This time Dolmatov spent the night, but claimed to have slept on the divan. The next morning he returned to the France Hotel, empty-handed.[73]

---

70. George Mosse described "modern" masculinity as it emerged in the West in the nineteenth century as "middle class sensibilities ... a 'quiet strength' that did not conflict with virtues such as fair play, harmony, and order, which an undue display of power must not disrupt." *The Image of Man: The Creation of Modern Masculinity* (New York: Oxford University Press, 1996), 15.

71. Patricia Cohen, *The Murder of Helen Jewett* (New York: Vintage, 1999), 21.

72. *Ubiistvo Time*, 85. The prosecutor reminded the courtroom that these two were not "Raskolnikov, begging forgiveness" (83).

73. At court, the testimony about the night he spent with her was heard behind closed doors, affirming the unlikelihood that he had made his bed on the couch.

Both men were in dreadful financial straits, deeply in debt and cut off by parents weary of bailing them out. Their bill at the France had not been paid in months. Dolmatov owed six hundred rubles; the promissory note was coming due in a few days and his creditor was threatening to create a scandal for his father, a state councilor in the Ministry of Foreign Affairs. The two decided that their last, best chance was to kill Time and steal the earrings, so they returned to her apartment that afternoon and prepared for another night on the town. Geismar had agreed beforehand to hit her with his bludgeon, and Dolmatov had brought a small hatchet purchased for other reasons. Anxious and hesitant, neither wanted to begin. But once Geismar delivered the first blow, they burst into a frenzy and added the axe, though still she cried out. Geismar ran into the bedroom, returning with two pillows to muffle her wheezing and to hide her face. In their panic, they could not find the earrings, and had to exit quickly before the maid walked in. Dolmatov put on the coat with the seal-skin collar and matching hat that people would remember seeing on one of the men with Marianna. Geismar wore a distinctive bowler. The doorman watched them leave, but saw nothing suspicious in young men leaving the Time flat. The maid, who had heard nothing from the kitchen, found her soon after they left. This pernicious pair even had to borrow money from a *dvornik* for the cab they had taken from her apartment.

Rumors swirled for the first weeks: had women dressed as men revenged themselves on this lady of easy virtue? Filippov's first step was to find out if any of the missing jewelry had been pawned, and the ring turned up at a shop where it had been hocked by a respectable blond man wearing a sealskin collar and hat.[74] He had given the jeweler his card, which read V. O. Iankovskii; the man lived in Tashkent and had no connection to the crime. The killer's collection of business cards bespoke a man with entrée into society. Agents staked out at her funeral spotted a blond man, but he whisked himself away in an automobile.[75] Filippov discovered that two young men had signed a note for a longstanding bill at the France Hotel, and then left the city promptly after the murder. Dolmatov and Geismar had not used aliases at the France because they had needed their family names to get credit at the hotel.

The detective acquired handwriting samples and photographs that witnesses identified as the men out with Marianna. Dolmatov had left a bloody fingerprint on the hatchet, and although the killers had tossed other incriminating evidence into the Fontanka, they kept the suits they had been wearing without cleaning off all the splashes of blood. They escaped by train to the estate of a close friend of Dolmatov's uncle, Captain Iu. A. Tinzee, who knew nothing of their criminal activities. Filippov dispatched Marshlak and special investigator P. A. Aleksandrov to set a trap for them at the Preobrazhenskaia train station, close to the estate. To lure them away from the house, Marshlak sent an unsigned telegram that they were to come to Pskov, where Geismar's mother lived. Nabbed at the ticket window, the two were found to be packing pistols. The setup at the station prevented either suicides or a shootout.[76]

74. *Gazeta kopeika* (hereafter *Gk*), fanned the flames of scandal, reporting that it had been returned and then stolen once again from her body in the morgue. *Gk*, 18 January 1913, no. 1618.

75. *Pl*, 17, 18 January 1913, nos. 16, 17.

76. *Pl*, a great fan of the detective bureau, detailed the trap, beginning in the 7 February 1913, no. 37 issue, the story running for several days.

Both from prominent families, Geismar's mother was Dolmatov's godmother. Well educated despite being so lazy that they did not finish their university degrees, Geismar worked at the State Bank and Dolmatov had a position in his father's ministry. At least they *had* been employed thus, until they stopped showing up for work in the months leading up to the murder. An oily character named "Ollo" lurked in the background as someone who took advantage of the young men's weak wills. Geismar and Dolmatov had gambled and partied their way through 1912, including a month in Paris where Dolmatov had followed French nightclub performer Kleo Kristof and picked up Paul Gerard's business card. His connections at various embassies got them back to Petersburg, where the New Year found them desperate. When captured, they told several versions of Time's accidental death before admitting the truth. Their parents bundled them off quickly for psychiatric evaluation, to no avail.

The trial began in May and lasted five days. The lucky ones who managed to score tickets could thrill to the details of two men who had absolutely wasted privileged lives. Photos from the crime scene had been leaked to the press, and A. S. Zarudnyi, Geismar's *zashchitnik*, objected that they had prejudiced the public; the defendants' own lives were sufficiently prejudicial in and of themselves. Published descriptions could not help the case either: "Dolmatov has red splotches on his face from nerves. You would never think to look at him that he's so popular with the ladies. His lifestyle has left its mark on him, and he looks ten years older than his age."[77] The nation's top forensic specialist, Kosorotov, performed the autopsy. Describing the defensive wounds on her arms, he stressed how she had fought back. Never assuming responsibility for their own lives, the only regret they showed for Marianna's death lay in their having gotten caught. Geismar, whose father had died in his boyhood, worried about the shame he would bring on his mother. His love for her did not prevent him from pilfering and pawning her things. With Ollo, this trio had plotted to murder Geismar's wealthy aunt, but never put the plan in action.

Parents testified to a series of illnesses, dating back to childhood, that they hoped could reduce their sons' culpability. Dolmatov's father told a sad story of ruin from an immature indiscretion. In his youth, the boy had been corrupted by an older woman (Time was also older than he) and contracted syphilis. Despite successful treatment with 606, a tonic familiar to his audience from the ubiquitous advertisements that promised to cure this most horrifying disease, his father nonetheless forbade him to marry the decent young woman to whom he was engaged. That grave disappointment had sent him over the edge. His mother collapsed on the stand after testifying through her sobs that her son "had no character at all."[78]

Whereas Dolmatov was an "ordinary neurasthenic," Geismar had hereditary pathologies from his father's diseased brain to a suicidal uncle and grandmother. The doctors found in him physiological evidence of degeneration: asymmetrical ear canals, chest, facial features, and poor reflexes. But this would not be a case in which a *zashchitnik* could take the noose from around one and place it on the other's neck. The court psychiatrist, Professor Karpinskii, theorized that the men functioned together as two halves of a whole. A letter from Dolmatov to Geismar encapsulated their relationship: "You and I aren't very outgoing, and we

77. *Pl*, 11 February 1913, no. 41.

78. *Ubiistvo Time*, 66.

Fig. 35. Dolmatov and Geismar taken into court under guard.

hang out with scoundrels, so we must prize our friendship!" Neither defendant would speak a last word. It took the jurors twenty-five minutes to convict them both, with no leniency. Partners to the bitter end, they embraced and kissed each other upon hearing the verdict.[79]

Time's husband had hired a civil plaintiff, but neither side was prepared to smear the reputation of someone who had died as Marianna had. That she was by ethnicity Polish and by confession Catholic did not generate prejudice against Time in print. Letters read in court (but not reproduced) suggested that she "was not completely frivolous, and was deeply respected by her friends."[80] Marianna had aspired to a life on the stage, and *Peterburgskii listok* interviewed a director who had worked with her at the small, private Iavorskii theater, where she had landed a few bit parts. Speaking Polish and French fluently, in addition to Russian, she took the stage name "Gromova" and worked to rid herself of her Polish accent. Accepting that she would always play only minor roles, she left the theater. The director told a final story about their relationship, probably apocryphal, and very empathetic. He had run into her recently, and they discussed their mutual interest in the occult. She showed him the lifeline on her left hand, which a palm reader had told her indicated that her life would end bloodily. He calmed her down, and she replied that "it's better to die quickly, without illness or suffering." He ended, "she died suddenly, but the scoundrels made her suffer."[81]

What could not be forgiven was their motive. As *Petersburgskii listok* reported, "The police asked them the value of what they had stolen. Approximately two hundred rubles. So for the sake of that paltry sum two intelligent people, occupying top spots in the social

79. Ibid., 68–69, 74, 75, 91.

80. Kazimir Time was awarded a token ruble on their conviction. Ibid., 84.

81. N. R-skii, "M. L. Time (Gromova) kak aktrisa," *Pl*, 19 January 1913, no. 18. *Pl*'s serial novel then running was by the high priestess of the occult Vera Kryzhanovskaia.

and business registers, committed this shocking murder."[82] In *Russoke slovo*, satirist Teffi wrote that in contemporary life, when a woman invites a young man to her home, she needs to think about his cash appraisal of her.[83] Teffi's gallows humor, like several news stories, connected Dolmatov and Geismar to another sensational trial from 1913. Albert Greichunas, a skating-rink instructor, went to trial in March for killing the "Queen of Diamonds," Maria Tolstinskaia, also for her jewelry.[84]

The sobriquet "queen of diamonds" came from a popular operetta written by the "Russian Offenbach" V.P. Valentinov in 1908.[85] Tat'iana, the title character, sings popular romances as she reigns over the concert hall. She has affairs with an aging capitalist and a young Neapolitan tenor, who wants to duel the capitalist. Tat'iana spares the tenor by going off with the rich man "to pursue wealth and find a place where there are no tears," saving his physical life at the sacrifice of her spiritual one. In the Prasolov affair, Frumson had been referred to occasionally as the "queen of diamonds," as were other female performers.

Maria Tolstinskaia performed herself at Petersburg's most fashionable skating rink on the Field of Mars, near the Winter Palace. Like Zina, the daughter of a wealthy merchant, she also, as did Marianna and Klera, gave birth to a child out of wedlock. The father of Tolstinskaia's daughter Tamara was a Nubian, no less.[86] She came nightly to the rink, "sparkling in her diamonds and multicolored precious stones," seeking that place where tears did not flow. Greichunas, the handsome instructor from Riga, caught her fancy. His job constantly placed other women in his arms, and together they glided across the ice. Popular instructors such as he reputedly could earn "a thousand rubles by giving private lessons."[87] Maria would come to the Field of Mars and throw scandals, until he agreed to quit his job and let her keep him, an *alfons*, the Russian slang for gigolo. With shades of Olga Palem and Kandinskii, and of the queen in the operetta, an older man was in turn keeping Tolstinskaia.

The press took imaginative advantage of the concurrent trial of Greichunas and the interrogations of Dolmatov and Geismar by making them acquaintances from the rink. *Petersburgskii listok* hypothesized that Time herself had become flirtatiously involved with Dolmatov, which, when combined with the rumor that jealous women had murdered Time, turned the long-dead Tolstinskaia into a suspect.[88] The press also made Geismar into a cousin of the covetous Count Roniker, on trial in Warsaw. These farfetched connections could be dizzying, but they reinforced the hold that these specific murder trials had on the popular imagination.

Greichunas had no aristocratic pedigree. He claimed to have killed Maria accidentally, choking her during a fight. Frightened, he had grabbed up some of her jewelry for the money he needed to escape, but was captured at the Prussian border. Defended by former procurator F. A. Vol'kenshtein, Greichunas received six years at hard labor, guilty

82. *Pl*, 7 February 1913, no. 37.

83. Quoted in *Protsess Prasolova i ubiistvo Time* (Berlin: Verlag von Heinrich Caspari, 1913), 82.

84. The Library of Sensational Trials reported on this case in ten-kopeck serials. *Ubiistvo Tolstinskoi* (St. Petersburg: Viktoriia, 1913). I could find only the first one.

85. The operetta is translated in von Geldern and McReynolds, *Entertaining Tsarist Russia*, 198–202.

86. *Ubiistvo Tolstinskoi*, 5.

87. *Pl*, 5 March 1913, no. 62.

88. Ibid.

Fig. 36. Albert Greichunas, homicidal roller-rink Romeo.

of having strangled her in a fit of anger rather than by premeditating her death. The paid-for lover whose employment at the skating rink projected a provocative sexual presence, Greichunas differed distinctively from the other male murderers, who had been weakened by desire and disappointment. Yet with all the press's murmuring about her exotic lifestyle, Tolstinskaia came across less as *his* victim than as someone betrayed by her own desires.[89] Asserting her sexuality linked her to Zina, Klera, and Mania Eltsova. Their desires did not debauch these women, did not push them to murder or theft. On the contrary, like Maria Tarnovskaia, desire made them modern, subjective individuals.

Zina, Klera, Duda, Maria, and Marianna lying in the morgue present a grim view of the realities of sexual equality. Moreover, their corpses reify the vulnerability of the sexualized New Woman. But these five ladies do not foreclose on hope. The sensational narratives of their lives, flouted in the press and the courtroom, were written to invoke sympathy rather than condescension. Did they, however, create problems for the other brand of New Women, the feminists who privileged suffrage over sexuality, equality over excess? Feminist, and future Bolshevik, Alexandra Kollontai tried to answer that question in a review of New Women steppin' out in fiction. Kollontai worried about the difficulties of "tossing aside that which has been ingrained in us for decades," the self-abnegation that women internalized, thereby keeping themselves dependent. Kollontai was writing about women with stiffer moral fiber than our deceased heroines, but her observation that they were no longer throwing acid on each other, but rather "finding a common language," in fact describes a scene that probably would have raised her own feminist eyebrows: Zina and Frumson at the Bouffe.[90]

89. *Ubiistvo Tolstinskoi*, 14.
90. Alexandra Kollontai, "Novaia zhenshchina," *Sovremennyi mir*, no. 9 (1913): 161–62, 167.

Russians did not obligate their New Women to choose between their politics and their sexuality. Encouragement for women striking out on their own accentuated the real victories that women were scoring in the waning years of the autocracy. In 1911, for example, women received the right to take the state exams and earn a university degree. At least one female *zashchitnik*, a Miss Fleishitz, appeared in court in 1909, defending a man accused of stealing billiard balls. The irate procurator forced a mistrial by storming out, but she enjoyed on principle the support of prominent jurists Tagantsev, Foinitskii, and Karabchevskii.[91] Legislation in 1913 that would have allowed women to serve both as barristers and jurors, however, failed to pass the State Council. Still, by 1914 wives no longer needed official permission from husbands to secure their internal passports.[92] Russian feminists looked at prostitutes almost as exploited sisters, and organized to help young women vulnerable to the industrial economy.[93] The emergence of the assertive female can be traced through the representations of the murderous merchant's daughter from Nizhnii Novgorod. In 1894, on stage, she found herself in prison and her father unforgiving. Twenty years later, still victimized by men, she could now take her revenge on-screen when she burns her rapist to death.

Marianna Time cheerfully picking up men on the street while Vasilii Prasolov floods the courtroom with his tears marks a distinct reversal of Western gender roles, she the *flâneur* and he the hysteric. What these two shared in common was the lack of control over their emotions. Social theorists, like historians, have made self-control central to the emergence of "modern" personalities, articulated by the omnipresent Michel Foucault as the "interiorization" of feelings.[94] Sociologist Norbert Elias made emotional control central to the "civilizing process," which he connected to state formation and the decrease in "the threat of weapons and physical force."[95] The tsarist state, however, continued to assert its "monopoly of the legitimate use of physical force," to cite another German sociologist, Max Weber, in ways that might have been lawful, but were not always perceived to be just.[96] Like a despotic patriarch, the autocracy continued to claim this control. Therefore neither Russia's obsessive men nor its desiring women felt any need to discipline themselves.

Returning to the theory that notions of gender are malleable to the manipulation of the actors within the system that fashions them, we can offer a culturally inspired interpretation of what it meant that a substantive swathe of Russian public opinion sanctioned Vasilii's and Marianna's behaviors. This absence of self-control belies the emergence of

91. Technically, the code did not specify that women could not be lawyers, as it did that female doctors could not perform forensic duties or testify as experts. *Rs*, 7 November 1909, no. 256.

92. Wayne Dowler, *Russia in 1913* (DeKalb: Northern Illinois University Press, 2010), 143–45.

93. Rochelle Goldberg Ruthchild, *Equality and Revolution: Women's Rights in the Russian Empire, 1905–1917* (Pittsburgh: University of Pittsburgh Press, 2010), 175–81.

94. Michel Foucault, *Discipline and Punish: The Birth of the Prison*, trans. Alan Sheridan (New York: Vintage Books, 1995), 238. See also Catherine A. Lutz, "Engendered Emotion: Gender, Power, and the Rhetoric of Emotional Control in American Discourse," in *Language and the Politics of Emotion*, ed. Catherine A. Lutz and Lila Abu-Lughod (New York: Cambridge University Press, 1990), 72–73.

95. Norbert Elias, *The Civilizing Process: Sociogenetic and Psychogenetic Investigations*, trans. Edmund Jepbcott, ed. Eric Dunning, Johan Goudsblom, and Stephen Mennell (Cambridge: Blackwell, 2000), 157.

96. Max Weber, "Politics as a Vocation," *From Max Weber: Essays in Sociology*, trans. and ed. H.H. Gerth and C. Wright Mills (New York: Oxford University Press, 1946), 78.

a modern individual recognizable by Western standards. To limit my examples to the murders mentioned in this chapter, we can see that the women did not die because they were sexually unfaithful, but rather because they would not remain pinned down in a monogamous relationship or provide a domestic refuge around the hearth, requisites that even Lombroso saw as necessary for social stability in the modern world. The murderous men, in contrast, expressed a deep desire for domesticity, to the point of expressing great love for the women's children even when not biologically theirs.

Russia's patriarchal social and political system found itself under attack in these murder trials. The women's rejection of patriarchy is self-evident; they needed neither husbands for themselves nor fathers for their children. The men demonstrated a plaintive appeal for becoming patriarchs in some form themselves. But the state hindered their maturity by restricting their access to the public sphere, an action that affected even the ineffable Geismar and Dolmatov. When the men turned to their private lives, their women, too, denied them passage into an adulthood "equated with responsibility for wife and children."[97] Acquitting the hysterical Vasiliis of murder feminized them, in the sense that like women they were "not quite adults and therefore not responsible themselves."[98] To worry, as Koni and the grand duke had, about the burst of sensationalism at the turn of the twentieth century was to mistake the form for the content. The value of using sensational murder trials to mark the gendered contours of social and political change comes into sharper focus when viewed from the comparative perspective. And so do some of the fundamental distinctions between Russia and the West.


## Masculinity on Trial in the West

The yellow journalism wars had abated in New York when the first "murder of the century" took place in the rooftop restaurant of Madison Square Garden on June 25, 1906. The victim, Stanford White, was coincidentally the architect who had designed the building.[99] Harry Thaw, scion of a wealthy Pittsburgh family, shot White in the head for having despoiled his wife years earlier, before his marriage to her. A rare beauty, Mrs. Thaw, née Evelyn Nesbit, had danced as one of the "Florodora girls" in the hit Broadway show, and had posed for advertising artist Charles Dana Gibson as one of his "Girls." Having caught the eye of notorious philanderer White, she willingly became his mistress. Her leaving White and marrying Thaw in April 1905 did not bother the "benevolent vampire," who had moved on to other young women. Thaw, reputedly a sadist with a taste for cocaine, could not let go of his obsession with White for having taken his wife's virginity. Evelyn's testimony about the red velvet swing in White's love nest set the scandalous tone. Substitute witnesses from the industrialist Andrew Carnegie family for the Riabushinskiis, actor

97. Sherry B. Ortner, "The Virgin and the State," *Feminist Studies* 4, no. 3 (1978): 29.

98. Ruth Harris, *Murders and Madness: Medicine, Law, and Society in the Fin De Siècle* (Oxford: Clarendon Press, 1989), 234.

99. The Moorish-inspired structure that White designed, however, was at 26 Street and Madison Avenue, and is not today's "Garden," the sports arena at 50 Street and Eighth Avenue.

John Barrymore for Smirnov, and Thaw's trial bears a striking similarity to Prasolov's.[100] But the difference between the victims is crucial; Harry shot Stanford because he believed that White had dishonored him; Vasilii shot Zina despite the other men. Admittedly, both had been drinking, but their motives reflected substantively different attitudes toward domesticity.

The question of Thaw's state of mind popped up immediately because the American courts had developed a tradition of using the insanity plea to acquit men who obeyed the unwritten law that allowed them to use violence against men who threatened their home life, hence their good names.[101] New York's authorities found Thaw sane, but his friends, not surprisingly, said the opposite. Close chum Burr MacIntosh, who had seen him the evening of the murder, reported that "I have been with him a great deal as of late—almost every day. He has not been himself. I believe he is crazy."[102] The *Times* noted that "the stumbling block in the way of the insanity theory is Thaw himself. The young man persistently refuses to show any signs of mental disorder."[103]

The famed California attorney Delphin Delmas defended Thaw, twisting the insanity plea brilliantly:

> Let me call the "insanity" of Thaw "Dementia Americana." It is the species of insanity that makes every American man believe his home to be sacred; that is the species of insanity which makes him believe the honor of his daughter is sacred; that is the species of insanity which makes him believe the honor of his wife is sacred; that is the species of insanity which makes him believe that whosoever invades his home, that whosoever stains the virtue of his threshold, has violated the highest of human laws and must appeal to the mercy of God, if mercy there be for him anywhere in the universe.

After asserting deceptively that "I shall rely on no such unstable thing as the supposed unwritten law," he made his case on the fatherless Evelyn's testimony about White's seduction. Turning to the Bible, as trial attorneys were wont to, he asked, "have ye forgotten the words of Jehovah, when upon the return from Egypt, He said: 'Ye shall not afflict a fatherless child. I will surely heal that cry, and I will kill you with the sword.'"[104] In other words, Harry had been doing the Lord's work.

100. Paula Uruburu, *American Eve: Evelyn Nesbit, Stanford White, the Birth of the "It" Girl, and the Crime of the Century* (New York: Riverhead Books, 2008). A less lubricious Evelyn Nesbit plays a lead role in E. Doctorow's *Ragtime* (1975).

101. Dawn Keetley, "From Anger to Jealousy: Explaining Domestic Homicide in Antebellum America," *Journal of Social History* 42. no. 2 (2008): 269–97; Robert M. Ireland, "The Libertine Must Die: Sexual Dishonor and the Unwritten Law in the Nineteenth-Century United States," *Journal of Social History* 23, no. 1 (1989): 27–44; Hendrik Hartog, "Lawyering, Husbands' Rights, and 'the Unwritten Law' in Nineteenth-Century America," *Journal of American History* 84, no. 1 (June 1997): 67–96; and Martha Merrill Umphrey, "The Dialogics of Legal Meaning: Spectacular Trials, the Unwritten Law, and Narratives of Criminal Responsibility," *Law and Society Review* 33, no. 2 (1999): 393–423.

102. *New York Times*, June 27, 1906.

103. *New York Times*, June 28, 1906.

104. Delmas's closing argument is available online: http://www.law.umkc.edu/faculty/projects/ftrials/thaw/delmassummation.html (accessed January 28, 2011).

Fig. 37. Murderers killing more frequently in public places.

Like Prasolov, Thaw went to trial twice, his first trial ending when the jurors could not reach a unanimous verdict. At the second, in January 1908, they agreed with his defense and dispatched him to the Matteawan Hospital for the Criminally Insane. Thaw predicted at the train station, "I am confident that my stay at Matteawan will be for a short period of time only."[105] He was released in 1915.

A murder in London had transnational appeal in January 1910 when another wife disappeared and a fileted body was found buried in the basement of her house several weeks later. Hawley Crippen had told their friends and neighbors that his wife Cora had left for California, where, as he later informed them, she had died. By mid-February Crippen had moved his secretary, and mistress, Ethel Le Neve into their home. When Cora's suspicious friends finally persuaded the police to investigate, Crippen and Le Neve set sail for Canada under assumed names, she cross-dressed as his son. Exploring the basement turned up the ribboned remains of a corpse, which prompted a manhunt for the fugitives. The Marconi telegraph itself made headlines by transmitting information ship-to-shore that facilitated their capture. Small wonder that this case became so infamous that Madame Tussaud's heirs displayed a wax effigy of the mild-mannered murderer in her celebrated museum after he was hanged in November 1910.

105. *New York Times*, 2 February 1908.

In her study of the Crippen case, Julie Early contrasts the portrayals of the two women in his life to explore how the public understood him. She finds the "most remarkable feature of the case (to be) the transformation of Crippen from the vicious mad-dog killer . . . to the principled, honorable and beleaguered little man whose necessary execution was met with rueful regret." Cora was cast in terms of "sluttish vulgarity," the opposite of Ethel's "dutiful innocence." On trial with Crippen, Ethel skated around what might be considered a negative, her decade-long affair with the married Crippen, which had resulted in at least one miscarriage. Cora, however, had performed in music halls as "Belle Elmore," her reputation further vilified by a neighbor's description of her failings as a housekeeper. Ethel became the "quiet, ladylike, unassuming typewriter, always to time, neat in appearance, methodical, obedient."[106] Why would not the slender, bespectacled, unassuming doctor want to replace his harridan with a homemaker?

Reluctantly, Crippen's jury sent him to the gallows. Their verdict falls in line with Martin Wiener's tracing of how British law courts began to privilege personal responsibility over violence as a characteristic of Victorian masculinity.[107] Prosecutor Sir Travers Humphreys waxed morosely that "in another country he would I feel sure have been given the benefit of 'extenuating circumstances.'"[108] This was not a case of Russian journalists defending compassion for the mentally unstable Tarnovskaia, but a British magistrate regretting that English rule of law could not forgive a man for murdering his shrewish wife. Besides, the Russian hesitancy to convict when the public had sided with the defendant could have assumed the moral high ground when, a century later, DNA results revealed the corpse in the coal cellar, the most direct evidence against Crippen, to be that of a man.[109]

In Paris, just weeks before the declaration of war in 1914, Henriette Caillaux, wife of the ex-premier Joseph Caillaux, shot and killed Gaston Calmette, editor of the rightist newspaper *Le Figaro*. The people involved were guaranteed to stir the crowd, and her motive derived from the growing power of the press. Calmette had just published love letters written to Henriette by "Ton Jo" (Your Joey) thirteen years earlier, when both were married to other spouses. Edward Berenson has argued persuasively that the public discourse of this case centered around the politics of divorce, considered by conservatives to be a greater threat to the welfare of the nation than murder.[110] Linked to the republican liberalism that was eroding France's bourgeois family, divorce was a weapon that feminists used to subvert the male head of the household.

106. Julie English Early, "A New Man for a New Century: Dr. Crippen and the Principles of Masculinity," in *Disorder in the Courts: Trials and Sexual Conflict at the Turn of the Century*, ed. George Robb and Nancy Erber (New York: New York University Press, 1999), 210, 213, 222.

107. Martin J. Wiener, *Men of Blood: Violence, Manliness, and Criminal Justice in Victorian England* (New York: Cambridge University Press, 2004). He argues that "ever more firmly reiterated principles of strict personal responsibility and the intolerability of violent behavior . . . gained in power and determining verdicts and ultimate dispositions" (270).

108. Early, "New Man," 212.

109. Roger Graef, "Desperate Police 'Framed' Dr. Hawley Crippen for Wife's Murder," *The Sunday Times*, June 29, 2008. That the body parts in the cellar did not belong to Cora does not mean that Hawley did not kill her.

110. Edward Berenson, "The Politics of Divorce in France of the Belle Epoque: The Case of Joseph and Henriette Caillaux," *American Historical Review* 93, no. 1 (February 1988): 31–55.

Joseph Caillaux had protested that he had divorced his first wife for Henriette for many of the same reasons that Hawley Crippen had substituted Ethel for Cora. Berthe was too aggressively a New Woman, and a man needed a wife who was "soft, quiet, and retiring," someone who would not smash the frail egos of a masculinity defeated by the Prussians in 1871. Joseph considered that Berthe shared too many of the "quintessentially masculine qualities 'overdeveloped' in himself."[111] The second Mme Caillaux, a divorcée, diverted the judges' attention to her honor, besmirched by Calmette when he published intimacies about her. Henriette claimed one of France's most popular defenses, that hers had been a crime of passion.[112] She exited the courtroom a free woman.[113]

What can we make of the fact that the only one of our front-page heroines not to end up in the morgue was the one who put a man there? The first conclusion is obvious: At the turn of the twentieth century, public spaces could be dangerous places for women. Those who died did so because they desired the independence to be out on their own, on the arm of the escort of their choice. Significantly, however, the media through which their lives were returned to the public sphere returned their voices as well. The headlines, the movies, the pamphlets—all produced to excite the most intense sensations—connected the women's desires with those of their audiences. The ladies in the morgue, and wherever Cora Crippen ended up, displayed the limits of modernity. These limits referenced not only equality between the sexes, but also the normative structure of the stable, nuclear family headed by a rational man. The men who put them there claimed to want the latter, but killing when they failed to secure the patriarchal norm was a fatalistic gesture that confirmed their inability to head such a household.

For all the changes implemented by the Great Reforms and after the 1905 Revolution, and in part as a result of them, emotions had run amok in tsarist Russia by 1914. Men were suffering pathological *affekt*, and women were indulging their sexualities. Gratification rather than restraint reigned in personal behavior. As Laura Engelstein has argued, "the pre–World War I crisis of the Russian elites . . . expressed itself partly in a preoccupation with sexual pleasure and disorder," which intensified after 1905. And, she elaborates, "on the subject of sex. . . . No matter how diverting the pretext, politics was never far behind."[114] These tempestuous trials echoed her point.

## Conclusion

"The gypsies cried, the glasses clinked, and the Rumanian violinists, clad in red, hypnotized inebriated men and women into a daring attempt to explore the depths of vice," wrote Grand Duke Alexander Mikhailovich, brother-in-law and cousin of Tsar

---

111. Berenson, "The Politics of Divorce," 35.

112. Harris, *Murder and Madness*, chapter 6, "Female Crimes of Passion," 208–42.

113. The information about this widely heralded court case comes primarily from Edward Berenson, *The Trial of Madame Caillaux* (Berkeley: University of California Press, 1992).

114. Laura Engelstein, *The Keys to Happiness: Sex and the Search for Modernity in Fin-de-siècle Russia* (Ithaca: Cornell University Press, 1992), 6, 420.

Nicholas II. Segueing into the Prasolov case, as he remembered it, "the young man . . . fired at her three times through the pocket of his tuxedo." He seemed grateful that "had it not been for the war, the nation would have been treated once more to the nauseating details of the Prasoloff [sic] case."[115] The intervening years clouded the grand duke's memory; he recalled Marianna Time as "an accomplished actress," and that Gilevich had been captured in a Monte Carlo casino. The factual errors do not undermine the essence of his argument: the public greed for the sensational had led to "the suicide of a continent."[116] This Russian aristocrat, who kept an apartment in Paris, also mentions with distaste the trial of Madame Caillaux. That the Caillaux verdict came in the day that Austria declared war on Serbia marks an historical coincidence that he thought almost foreordained.

So much change was flooding the Continent, sailing across the English Channel and the Atlantic Ocean, that social critics in 1913 were anticipating the deluge that began on July 28, 1914. "Money, women, and blood—the three primary elements of Russian life, and symptoms that the end of it is near," wrote an anonymous journalist in a commentary on the combined Prasolov and Time cases, subtitled "The Nightmares of Russian Life." The primary sites of debauchery (razgul) included Moscow's two most notorious restaurants, the Strel'na and the Iar, and, of course, the ubiquitous skating rink. Referring to the Prasolov affair as "the tumor in Russian life," he adds details from the murders of Time and the "Queen of Diamonds" as evidence that "the horrors in Russian life are not ending." He offered a political explanation: "Russia, after the failure of the heroic revolution, now throws itself into the other extreme."[117]

This writer might well have included the galas celebrating the tercentenary of the Romanov dynasty as one of the spectacles of 1913, illustrating another extreme. Playing dress up as the first Romanov, Nicholas II indulged in his own personal fantasies. Richard Wortman pointed out that "the festivities of 1913 convinced him of his role in the national myth . . . and assured him of the triumph of his mission to restore personal autocracy."[118] Like Dolmatov and Geismar, he overspent, squandering the considerable political capital that an autocrat accrues. And like the ladies lying in the morgue, he was murdered, another victim of his own failed patriarchy.

115. Aleksandr Mikhailovich, Grand Duke of Russia, *Once a Grand Duke* (New York: Farrar & Rinehart, 1932), 254–55.

116. Ibid., 259.

117. *Protsess Prasolova i ubiistvo Time*, 5, 84, 61.

118. Richard S. Wortman, *Scenarios of Power: Myth and Ceremony in Russian Monarchy*, 2 vols. (Princeton: Princeton University Press, 1995), I: 528.

# CONCLUSION

"It is not funny that a man should be killed, but it is sometimes funny that he should be killed for so little, and that his death should be the coin of what we call civilization."

—Raymond Chandler, *The Simple Art of Murder*, 1950

"Seconds passed . . . Rasputin had already reached the gates when I stopped, bit my left hand as hard as I could to make myself concentrate, and with one shot (the third one), hit him in the back. He stopped and this time, taking careful aim from the same spot, I fired for the fourth time. I apparently hit him in the head, for he keeled over face first in the snow, his head twitching. I ran up to him and kicked him in the temple with all my might. He lay there, his arms stretched out in front of him, clawing at the snow as if he were trying to crawl forward on his belly. But he could no longer move and only gnashed and gritted his teeth."[1]

Thus did Vladimir Purishkevich, devout monarchist and leader of the reactionary Black Hundreds, flip the coin of Russian civilization in 1916 and murder the Mad Monk whom he believed to be the puppeteer manipulating the strings of Nicholas II's ministers, the men responsible for the devastation the country was suffering in the world war.[2] This same Purishkevich had at one point been thought to be implicated in the Gilevich case. His co-conspirators that night of December 16 included Prince Felix Iusupov, who was married to the tsar's niece and whose St. Petersburg mansion served as the scene of the crime; Grand Duke Dmitrii Pavlovich, cousin to the tsar; Lieutenant S. M. Sukhotin, from the Preobrazhenskii Regiment and a friend to Iusupov; and Dr. Lazavert, Purishkevich's colleague from his work with wounded soldiers on a hospital train. Disguised as Iusupov's chauffeur, Lazavert drove to collect the monk for the evening. He had slipped potassium cyanide into wine that Rasputin had proceeded to drink; sinisterly, it produced

1. V. M. Purishkevich, *The Murder of Rasputin*, ed. and intro. Michael E. Shaw, trans. Bella Costello (Ann Arbor: Ardis, 1985), 148.

2. Purishkevich gave an animated speech in the Duma to this effect in November 1916. Quoted in Robert Alexander, *Rasputin's Daughter* (New York: Penguin, 2006), 147.

no ill effects.[3] When the body was finally recovered from the canal three days later, it made headline news around the world: "HINT THAT NOBLES KILLED RASPUTIN STIRS PETROGRAD: GOSSIP ALLEGES A PLOT," read the special cable to *The New York Times*.[4]

Rasputin's assassins believed that ridding the Winter Palace of this baleful influence would appease public opinion, grown increasingly restless at the autocracy's inability to manage either the battlefield or the home front. In taking this action, they revealed how they had misconstrued a very modern political problem, the rupture between government and public opinion, as simply an issue of personality. When the public forced the feckless tsar to abdicate a month later, the impromptu Provisional Government went through several incarnations before being thrown out by the Bolsheviks scarcely two months shy of the anniversary of Rasputin's death. Tsarist Russia's failure to evolve into a rule-of-law state, a *Rechtsstaat*, has provided a ready rationalization for the Bolsheviks' assumption of dictatorial powers. Indeed, the obduracy of the autocracy has offered such a logical accounting for this failure that other aspects of legality have been overlooked, especially the ways in which the public understood and applied the law code.

Writing in the progressive *Russkie vedomosti* in 1913, Sergei Ordynskii identified how verdicts reveal the ways in which legal statutes remain open to interpretation, underscoring how the rule of law is itself malleable, subject to local values. Observing that "if historians found only the law codes and the verdicts in archives," he argued that "this would furnish sufficient material for them to reconstruct not only both state and society of a given era, but also to identify the gyrations of internal politics and the chief moments of contention between the government and the people."[5] He astutely differentiated the objectivity of the law code from the subjective issues that emerged from the legal debates in the adversarial courtroom. The high-minded reformers of the 1860s had objectivity in mind when they sought to guarantee that the accused had someone in court who would oversee the righteous application of the code. When Prince Urusov scripted a narrative of piety for the illiterate Mavra Volokhova, whose husband was found in pieces in their cellar, he invested personalities, environment, and circumstances with explanatory powers that surpassed the rational reading of the letter of the law. Public participation in justice, represented by the jurors who collected money for Volokhova after they acquitted her, provides an understanding of the rule of law that focuses on popular justice, not a *Rechtsstaat*.

The autocracy's potential for arbitrary treatment, coupled with its refusal to guarantee personal inviolability, favored the personality on trial because everyone at court lay vulnerable to the capricious state. In many cases the prosecution found itself arguing from the position of rule of law, as when Olga Palem ran from the hotel room having just fired two rounds from the pistol in hand. Yet whether the killer was Palem or Raskolnikov, the audience

---

3. The most recent comprehensive work on the infamous monk is Edvard Radzinsky, *The Rasputin File* (Norwell, MA: Anchor, 2001).

4. The headline ran in the *New York Times* on January 3, 1917, a date that reflected the combined use of different calendars and the time taken to discover the identity of the corpse.

5. This New Year's editorial was reprinted in *Obshchestvennoe nastroenie i glavnye sobytiia goda* (Moscow: *Russkie vedomosti*, 1913), 38.

recognized that the circumstances in which the act was committed could overwhelm the strictures of the legal code. Under those conditions, the code posed a greater problem than the solution it offered to the crime of murder; to have sent Palem to prison would have justified Sasha Dovnar's treatment of her and trivialized her biologically determined mental instability. Juries subverted the liberal potential inherent in the rule of law when they disconnected the crime against the individual from punishment by the state. The illiberal state, with its predatory perspective on politics, had forced their hand. Yet when we break the state down into its personal components, we discover many powerful senators and ministers of justice who continued to want the independent juries, even when jurors tempered their own insistence upon following the letter of the law. Autocracy held all Russians in check.

Russia's legal culture was also influenced by the confession to which most citizens belonged, Orthodoxy, just as, for example, Puritanism affected American jurisprudence.[6] The civil and criminal laws that had evolved from church canon law reflected values that also adapted over time to subjective life. Almost everyone who has written about any aspect of Russia's reformed courts mentions the constant deployment of religious images, beginning with the oath that subordinated all aspects of the case to "the life-giving cross" and the "day of his terrible judgment." Theologian Georges Florovsky articulated the fundamentals of the Orthodox personality, which he contrasted to the liberal subject: "psychology based on the concept of temptation, inner struggle with the passions, conversion and decision, was a deeper psychology than that which would deal with the fixed character."[7] To show tearful regret, as Vasilii Prasolov had done, was to allow the transgressor to be judged by God, not man. And when the psychiatrists modernized the disclaimer of intentionality through the diagnosis of pathological *affekt*, secular public opinion could judge in tune with the religious.

No evidence persuades that people in Russia were more deeply religious than in other societies, and their cultural values drew from a variety of media, not simply the Sunday sermon. Crime fiction's distinctive cultural cast also privileged temptation and inner struggle. The greater interest in the *why* over the *who* can easily be essentialized as the Russian distrust of heartless reason's effort to explain away articles of faith, exemplified by Dostoevsky's rantings against the legal system, both in his fiction and his *Diary of a Writer*. But the greater importance of the *why*, coupled with the failure to arrest the *who*, had a specific political resonance in late imperial Russia. Fictional judicial investigators whose authors did not permit them to solve crimes undercut official competence. This generic convention suggests a low-level political subversion, a cultural obstinacy that worked against respect for the prosecution. When killers took their own lives rather than submit to the state, as Isabella did in *The Song is Sung*, they were asserting themselves against it. Post-1905 action fiction, noteworthy for its criminal protagonists, showed a newfound assertiveness that did not bode well for chief of detectives Filippov, despite his sincerity in trying to professionalize the suspect institution in which he served.

---

6. In addition to Karen Halttunen, *Murder Most Foul: The Killer and the American Gothic Imagination* (Cambridge, MA: Harvard University Press, 1998), see Richard J. Ross, "The Career of Puritan Jurisprudence," *Law and History Review* 26, no. 2 (2008): 227–58.

7. Georges Florovsky, "The Problem of Old Russian Culture," *Slavic Review* 21, no. 1 (1962): 10.

Was Russia moving toward a liberal rule of law after 1905, only to be derailed by a war that stretched governance beyond the breaking point? The problems ran much deeper than the proverbial clock of history running out of time. Writing in 1909, in the *Vekhi* (Landmarks) symposium of formerly leftist intellectuals, the legal scholar Bogdan Kistiakovskii berated the intelligentsia because "of all cultural values, law is the one it relegated furthest to the background." Even though "one would think that the Russian intelligentsia has reason enough to be concerned with personal rights," Kistiakovskii detailed its historical disregard for legal theory.[8] His keen insights notwithstanding, in essence Kistiakovskii was telling Russians to stop just reading Sherlock Holmes and start writing him. But Russians, lacking the social and political structure in which a Holmes could operate efficiently, produced instead their Putilins. Would Kistiakovskii have argued to convict Vasilii Prasolov? Surely he would have objected to the unwritten law that kept Harry Thaw from prison. A more balanced approach to thinking about the failure of rule of law in Tsarist Russia would register the irony that Russian juries enjoyed more interpretive leeway than did their Western counterparts.

Still, they could not persuade their government to safeguard their person. The fatalism that had long characterized Russian culture, from highbrow personal reflections to lowbrow shoot-outs, was deeply ingrained in its legal culture. This fatalism lacked the mechanism of cause and effect that allows for human intervention and the possibility of changing the circumstances and producing a favorable outcome. To the contrary, it invoked feelings of helplessness that were channeled into a variety of emotions, from rage to suicidal depression. Moreover, it stunted the emotional maturity of many Russians, who experienced Fate as the state's enforced limits on their personal autonomy. This use of force, psychological as well as physical, turned many Russians to their expansive legal culture for clues about how to negotiate their relationship to the autocracy. From serving on juries to watching "Sashka," they dug out a space in which to pitch battles, but neither side found a place where they could arbitrate a peaceful resolution. After 1905, the electoral Duma challenged the autocracy, but neither enjoyed absolute power or popularity.

The culture of fatalism contributed to a deeply felt personalization of criminality, one with implications for Russia's modernity. The shift that historians have long noted, from the criminal action to the person who committed the crime, had been orchestrated by the emergence of professional disciplines. Professionalization throughout the nineteenth century contributed to both the rise of the modern state and the liberalism that characterized it: modern because it functioned according to rational, impersonal negotiations; liberal because professionals developed specialized knowledge that they took an oath to deploy ethically and equitably. Confronted with murder, criminologists sought physiological, environmental, and sociological explanations for behavior that resulted in violent death, and they directed attention to the personality of the accused. Novelists and attorneys on both sides in the adversarial courtroom did the same. Urusov and Karabchevskii were as literary as Dostoevsky and Tolstoy in their creation of characters. Harriet Murav has posited that

---

8. *Vekhi (Landmarks): A Collection of Articles about the Russian Intelligentsia*, trans. and ed. Marshall S. Shatz and Judith E. Zimmerman, foreword Marc Raeff (Armonk, NY: M.E. Sharpe, 1994), 91, 96.

"both the law and the literary work are actively engaged with the foundational narratives that a culture tells itself."[9] Russia's foundational narrative told of its moral superiority as a merciful community. One storyline, though, dating from the pre-Petrine era, depended on a powerful tsar transcending self-interest in order to protect that community. After the Great Reforms this thread could no longer stitch the plot together.

Tellingly, Russians gave killers as well as their victims voice and agency. Powerless in the public sphere, why would defendants not also be so in their private world, unable to control their emotions, much less their volition? The frequent recourse to taking a human life in both fact and fiction suggested that many Russians saw a failure such as the Prasolov marriage not simply a as personal matter, but also as one implicated in social and political structures not worth saving. When the French criminologist Alexandre Lacassagne opined that societies get the criminals they deserve, he was referring to the cultural specificity of crime and punishment. Modernity, too, bears the particulars of the society undergoing it. The historian Carol Gluck has reversed Lacassagne's equation to note that "not every country gets the modernity it wants or deserves."[10] I paraphrase Tolstoy and add that "all happy countries are alike; each modern country is modern in its own way." Many Russians who had experienced modernity by way of sensational murder trials understood its liabilities as well as its benefits, but they had lacked the opportunities, and some of them the will, to resolve the problems played out in court. Happy to see Nicholas go, they did not anticipate the commensurate loss of the right to read Zina's letters aloud, or to dispatch Vasilii home to his parents. Not simple escapism, as Koni and the grand prince worried, taking actions such as these permitted Russians to participate in the adjudication of law and order. Murder trials, intrinsically interesting because of the nature of the crime, provided a popular site where the public could challenge the state on issues of political relevance. The Bolsheviks shuttered that site, and after 1917 a "Soviet" murder differed culturally as well as politically from one "most Russian."[11] The change was perhaps lost on the corpse, but not in the courts. Mavra had lost her Prince.

9. Harriet Murav, *Russia's Legal Fictions* (Ann Arbor: University of Michigan Press, 1998), 4.

10. Carol Gluck, "The End of Elsewhere: Writing Modernity Now," *American Historical Review* 116, no. 3 (2011), 676.

11. Moreover, the sociological pendulum in the Bolshevik criminal code of 1922 swung back from the criminal to the crime. A. Zhilenko, "Evoliutsiia poniatiia umen'shennoi vmeniaemosti," *Pravo i zhizn'*, nos. 5–6 (1924): 37–45.

# INDEX

Acquittals, 7, 23, 27, 29, 33, 38, 46, 48, 78, 81, 83, 94, 96, 99, 103, 110, 132, 137, 173, 208, 239, 244, 251. See also *neschastnye*

Alcohol and murderous behavior, 2, 62–63, 73, 106, 247

Alexander I, Tsar, 16

Alexander II, Tsar, 2, 7, 16, 21, 85

Alexander III, Tsar, 7, 10, 107, 136

Andreevskii, S. A., 45, 51n, 80, 173

Appeals, 18, 22, 25, 37n, 43, 47, 51, 59, 67, 72, 80n, 87n, 88, 95, 98, 103, 111, 151, 245, 248

Arsen'ev, K. K., 34, 36–37, 52, 106

Attorneys, defense: Andreevskii, S. A., 45, 51n, 80, 173; Arsen'ev, K. K., 34, 36–37, 52, 106; critique of, 42–45; Karabchevskii, N. P. 50–52, 64, 77–76, 80, 105, 111, 258, 268; Plevako, F. N., 37–40, 66, 73, 74; Spasovich, V. D., 9n, 37–42, 85, 95, 105, 134; Urusov, Prince A. I., 15, 34–37, 48, 73, 266. *See also names of individual attorneys*

Attorneys, prosecutorial (procurators): Bobrishchev-Pushkin, A. V., 44, 52, 65, 88, 110; Gromnitskii, M. F., 15, 21n, 23, 27, 32; Obninskii, P. N., 23, 44, 69, 73; Vol'kenshtein, F. A., 44–45, 256. *See also names of individual attorneys*

Azef Affair, 151, 163

Balinskii, I. M., 48, 52, 55

Bar Association, 7, 38, 42–43, 61

Bartenev, A. M., 73

Bauer, Evgenii, 227, 231–32, 250–51

Beccaria, Cesare, 3, 17, 179

Befani, Pola, 72

Beilis Case, 51, 110–11, 152, 161n

Bekhterev, V. M., 65, 76–77, 80, 183, 189–90, 197, 234, 237n

Bekker, Sarra: murder of, 47, 48n, 78; and the judicial significance of her case, 52

Bellin, E. F., 66–69

Benjamin, Walter, 13, 144–45, 153n

Bernhardt, Sarah, 195

Blank, Mattias, 216–17

Bludov, D. N., 9n, 16, 29, 85

Bobrishchev-Pushkin, A. V., 44, 52, 65, 88, 110

Botkin, I. Ia., 136–37

Broadsheets, 138–39

Catherine the Great, Tsarina, 16, 104

Censorship, 4, 37, 38n, 93, 136, 146, 166, 204, 225–26, 237

Chechott, O. A., 48, 52, 248, 249

Chizh', V. F., 64

Civil plaintiff, 31, 48, 80, 163, 244, 247, 255

Code of Criminal Procedure, 2, 86

Collins, Wilkie, 115

Confessions, 2, 9, 24, 43, 104, 117, 120–22, 126–27, 130–32, 140, 150, 153, 168, 188–89, 216, 237

*Court Ladies*, 8, 90, 131, 173, 197

Court system: adversarial, 2, 3, 8, 10, 17, 32, 42, 45, 48, 55, 70, 115, 133–34, 266; inquisitorial, 2, 8, 16–17, 29–30, 39, 43, 48, 53, 138; structure of the, 18

Crime fiction: in China, 115; in England, 13, 115–16 (*see also* Sherlock Holmes); in France, 117, 129, and French criminals (Fantômas, 229–30, Lupin, Arsène, 210, 220, 229–30, Rocambole, 116, 229–30); generic properties of, 10, 114–17, 123, 125–27, 129, 140, 157, 222, 233, 267; and melodramatic mode, 129, 131; at the movies, 224–33, 237, *Light-fingered Sonka*, 229–30, *Sashka the Seminarian*, 230, 243; theatrical versions of, 127–31; in the United States, 13, 117 (*see also* Poe, Edgar Allan)

"Crimes of Passion," 19, 98, 145, 183, 196, 238, 263

Crippen, Hawley, 261–62

Darwin, Charles, 52, 56, 172, 182, 248

Degeneracy theory, 9, 62, 75–77, 165–66, 173, 183–85, 227, 254

Dmitrieva, Vera, and Colonel Kostrubo-Karitskii, N. N., 37–40

Dobryi, Roman (R. L. Andropov), 201–6, 222

Dolmatov A. A., and Baron Geismar, V. V., 254–55

Doroshevich, Vlas, 197

Dostoevsky, F. M., 13, 24, 118; *The Brothers Karamazov*, 90, 104, 133–34, 198; *Crime and Punishment*, 10, 24, 113–14, 117, 120, 231, 252n; *A Writer's Diary*, 41–42, 119–20

Dovnar, Alexander, 79–80

Drankov, Alexander, 226–30, 238

Dril', Dmitrii, 61–63, 65, 190n

Duma, 11, 143, 150, 161, 246, 248, 268

*Dvorniki*, 1, 21, 48, 90, 131, 155, 206, 207, 227, 230, 253

Dzhanshiev, G. A., 43, 89, 92, 105–7

Elias, Norbert, 258

Elizabeth I, Tsarina, 28

Engelstein, Laura, 6, 263

Evitskii, I. A., 238–39

Fatalism, 167, 199, 203, 227, 233–34, 268

Felski, Rita, 199, 236n

Filippov, V. G., 141–43, 149, 152, 156, 163, 236, 253

Foinitskii, Ivan, 23, 44, 106, 258

Forensics, 8, 158; and fingerprints, 153, 228, 253; and handwriting, 154, 163, 191; and photography, 149, 153–57, 163; professionalization of, 54–55, 66–69; psychiatric, 47–52, 174

Foucault, Michel, 9n, 13, 140, 258

Free will, 13, 56, 57, 61, 68, 72, 77, 111, 183, 189, 192, 234

Fuks, Viktor, 47, 86, 88, 93, 97–99, 107, 127

Gaboriau, Émile, 116, 121, 127; and *L'affaire Lerouge*, 116, 127

Gender, as a determinate issue, 8, 11, 100, 106n, 131, 156, 181, 185, 193–99, 236, 246, 258. See also *New Woman; Masculinity*

Gilevich, Andrei: and his crime, iii, 141–42, 148, 203, 237; and his symbolic function, 144, 168

Gogol, Nikolai, 16, 18, 41, 120

Gorskii, Vitol'd, 74

Great Reforms, 2, 3, 6, 44, 46, 110, 263, 269

Greichunas, Albert, 256

Gromnitskii, M. F., 15, 21n, 23, 27, 32

Halttunen, Karen, 168

Hypnotism, 51, 68, 69n, 135, 158, 167, 183–84, 189, 195, 197, 228, 263

Iablonskii, Sergei, 77, 185n, 186

Insanity Plea, 19, 21; and *affect*, 58, 61, 73n, 136–38, 174, 204, 207, 246–49, 263, 267; in England, 57; and Elizaveta Semenova, 47–52, 62, 64, 75, 81n; in France, 57; in Protopopov case, 58–59; in the United States, 260

Intertextuality, 119, 137, 237, 250

Jack the Ripper, 4, 66, 164, 206

Judicial investigators, 10, 21–26, 53; fictional, 122–28, 231

Judicial mistakes, 104–5, 132, 135

Judicial Reform of 1864, 2, 7, 16–19, 84

Jury, 2, 8, 9, 13; in England, 83, 91, 96, 99, 109, 262; fictional, 131–36; in France, 83–84, 91, 98, 109; in Germany, 91, 109; and *law finding* vs. *fact finding*, 97–98; reforms of, 88, 106–8; social profile of, 86–89; in the United States, 82–83, 96–97, 99–100

Kachka, Praskovia, 69–72, 75, 131, and film of trial, 238

Kara, Alexander, 31, 74–75

Karabchevskii, N. P., 50–52, 64, 77–76, 80, 105, 111, 258, 268
Karalli, Vera, 231–34, 251
Katkov, M. N., 82, 93, 118
*Keys to Happiness, The,* 244, 257
Khanzhonkov, Alexander, 226–27, 230–33, 250
Kholodnaia, Vera, 250
Kistiakovskii, Bogdan, 268
Komarovskii, Pavel, 171, 174–76
Koni, A. F., 27–28, 40n, 44, 61, 81, 89, 93–94, 97, 110, 238–39
Kosorotov, D. K. 161, 254
Kovalevskii, P. I, 61–62, 64–65, 136–37, 189n

Lacenaire, Pierre François, 13, 116
Lombroso, Cesare, 63–64, 135, 153, 179–81, 186, 190, 193

Maksimenko, Alexandra, 66–67
Manasein, N. A., 108
Masculinity, 181, 236, 246, 248, 256–58, 264; in the comparative perspective, 259–63
*Merchant Bashkirov's Daughter,* 130, 208, 238, 258
Ministers of Justice: Manasein, N. A., 108; Murav'ev, N. V., 47, 108; Nabokov, D. N., 47, 108; Pahlen, K. I., 2, 23; Panin, V. N., 5, 107; Shcheglovitov, I. G., 23, 81, 110–11, 152; Zamiatin, D. M., 16. *See also names of individual Ministers of Justice*
Mironovich, I. I., 47–52, 64
Mittermaier, Karl, 17, 43, 55, 77n, 83–84
M'Naghten Rule, 57
Modernism, 166–67, 223n
Modernity, 3, 69, 168–69, 203, 216, 222, 258, 266, 269
Morgue, 156–57, 203
Morrissey, Susan, 131, 157
Morselli, Enrico, 137, 180–87, 198
Mozzhukhin, Ivan, 231–32, 251
Murav'ev, N. V., 47, 108
Murder, legal definition of, 19–20, 40

Nabokov, D. N., 47, 108
Nedonoskov, V. V., 247–49
Nekliudov, N. A., 35, 47, 95, 101, 105, 119
Nemirovich-Danchenko, V. I., 179, 197
*Neschastnye,* 9, 62n, 76, 85, 93, 100, 108, 110, 111, 117, 147, 154, 168, 173, 187, 234, 247
*New Woman,* 194–99, 244, 251–52, 257–58, 263
*Newgate novels,* 13, 115
Newspapers: *Gazeta kopeika,* 116; *Golos,* 4, 8, 41, 119; *Novoe vremia,* 48n, 78, 81; *Odesskii listok,* 158, 169, 171, 176, 178–79, 188, 191–94; *Peterburgskaia gazeta,* 8n, 47, 141, 157, 161–63, 166, 208; *Peterburgskii listok,* 4, 6, 118, 127, 132, 157, 183, 186, 237, 249, 255–56; *Russkie vedomosti,* 42, 182, 266; *Russkoe slovo,* 77, 142, 160, 172, 176, 179, 197–98, 256; *Sudebnyi vestnik,* 4, 26; *Vestnik politsii,* 146–50, 152, 155–56
Nicholas I, Tsar, 11, 16, 21, 92, 111
Nicholas II, Tsar, 143, 150, 264–65
Nietzsche, Friedrich, 166, 195, 198, 228

Obninskii, P. N., 23, 44, 69, 73
Orlov, V. V. 72–73
Orthodoxy, 8, 9, 40, 56, 59–62, 66, 72, 92, 100–101, 120, 134, 136–37, 162, 167, 233, 267; and film censorship, 225

Pahlen, K. I., 2, 23
Palem, Olga, 79–82, 131, 256, 266; and significance of trial, 98, 109–11, 152n, 267
Panin, V. N., 5, 107
Panov, S. A., 124, 125, 127
Patenko, F. A., 66–69
Peter the Great, Tsar, 16, 34, 53
*Pinkertonovshchina,* 210, 222, 224; fictional detectives in (Ethel King, 210; Lord Lister, 209, 220–21; Nat Pinkerton, 209, 212–14; Nick Carter, 209, 213–16, 229)
Plevako, F. N., 37–40, 66, 73, 74
Pobedonostsev, K. P., 82, 90
Podlutskii, Pavel, 154, 164, 169
Poe, Edgar Allan, 13, 116–17, 144, 227
Poison, 20, 21, 36n, 64n, 66–67, 121, 123–24, 126, 130, 158, 213, 221, 228, 232, 250
Police, 10, 26–29; Director A. A. Lopukhin of, 29, 146, 151, 163; reforms of, 146–52, 207
Pozdnyshev, Vasia, 134–38, 140, 189, 231, 251
Prasolov, Vasilii: and his crime, 239; and his masculinity, 246–47, 250, 251n, 258–59; and his trial, 240–46
Prasolova, Zinaida, 239–46; in film, 250–51
Public opinion, 191–94, 237–39, 264. *See also* sensationalism
Public sphere, 4, 72, 157, 225, 259, 263, 269; and *"pathological"* public sphere, 6, 237; vs. private "bourgeois" sphere, 145
Purishkevich, V. M., 163, 265
Putilin, I. D., 2, 10, 27, 28, 147, 201–3, 205–8, 222–23, 228, 250, 268

Racialism, 181–82, 184–87, 197, 233, 244
Raskolnikov, Rodion, 10, 24, 113–14, 117, 120,
    133, 137, 185n, 252n, 266
Revolution of 1905, 11, 20, 39, 83, 142–43, 149,
    151, 158, 163, 170, 172, 176, 183, 189, 203–5,
    213, 233, 236, 263, 267–68
Riabushinskii brothers: Nikolai, 223, 243n; Pavel,
    223, 246
Rodensky, Lisa, 120
Rozanov, Vasilii, 198
Rule of Law, 7, 9, 16, 41, 93, 262, 266–68
Russo-Japanese War, 179, 183
Rybakovskaia, Aleksandra, 34, 52, 100n

Satirical journals, 29, 49, 146, 151n, 204, 218
Sechenev, I. M., 56–57, 59, 70, 118
Sensationalism, 3–4, 6, 10–11, 52, 66, 76, 89, 104,
    118, 121, 138, 140, 147, 164, 168, 200, 203–5,
    224, 227–29, 233, 235–36, 238, 242, 246,
    256–59, 263–64, 269
Shcheglovitov, I. G., 23, 81, 110–11, 152
Shcherbachev, A. N., 73
Sherlock Holmes, 10, 28, 115–16, 147, 152, 179,
    216–23, 229, 268
Shevliakov, M. V., 201–3, 205–6, 213, 220, 228
Shkliarevskii, Alexander, 121–24, 132
Silver Age, 166, 231
Skadovskii, Lev, 76–77
Skitskii brothers, 46
Smirnov, Dmitrii, 228, 243
Smith, Roger, 53, 57, 60
Sokolov, Alexander, 127, 131
Sokolova, Alexandra, 126
Sokolova, Daria, 2, 12, 27, 164; fictionalized, 205
Sorochinskaia, Zenovia, 249
Sorokin, I. M., 48, 52
Spasovich, V. D., 9n, 37–42, 85, 95, 105, 134
Steinberg, Mark, 3n, 13n
Stolypin, P. A., 142, 146, 159, 170
Subjectivity, 9, 11, 45, 52, 56, 75, 118, 199, 257, 266
Sudebnye dramy, 75, 103–4, 146, 173
Suicide, 70, 121, 125, 130–31, 157–59, 165, 173,
    178, 213, 220, 222, 225, 232, 239, 243, 246,
    251
Syshchiki, 28–29, 202, 206

Tagantsev, N. S., 47, 60, 64, 75–76, 81, 105, 258
Tarnovskaia, Maria, 168n, 170; and her crime, 171,
    174–76; film version of, 238; French women
    supporting, 195–96; public opinion about,
    191–94; and her trial, 189–90, 199
Tarnovskii, Vasilii, 172–74

Teffi (Nadezhda Lokhvitskaya), 169, 256
Thaw, Harry, 259–60
Time, Marianna, 235, 237, 252–58, 264
Tolstinskaia, Maria, 256
Tolstoi, Dmitrii, 3, 27
Tolstoy, Lev, Kreutzer Sonata, 134–38, 251;
    Resurrection, 135–36
Trepovs, Dmitrii, 151; Fedor, 9, 27, 93
Trials for murder: Bartenev, A. M., 73; Dmitrieva,
    Vera, and Colonel Kostrubo-Karitskii, N. N.,
    37–40; Dolmatov A. A., and Baron Geismar,
    V. V., 254–55; Evitskii, I. A., 238–39; Gorskii,
    Vitol'd, 74; Greichunas, Albert, 256; Kachka,
    Praskovia, 70–72, 238; Kara, Alexander, 31,
    74–75; Maksimenko, Alexandra, 66–67;
    Mironovich, I. I., 47–52, 64; Nedonoskov, V. V.,
    247–49; Orlov, V. V. 72–73; Palem, Olga,
    79–82; Prasolov, Vasilii, 240–46; Rybakovskaia,
    Aleksandra, 34, 52, 100n; Shcherbachev, A. N.,
    73; Skadovskii, Lev, 76–77; Skitskii brothers,
    46; Sokolova, Daria, 2, 12; Tarnovskaia, Maria,
    189–90, 199; Tarnovskii, Vasilii, 172–74;
    Volokhova, Mavra, 15, 32–33; Zasadkovich,
    Matvei, 45–46. See also individual names

Urbanization, 6, 144–45, 156–57, 159–60, 164
Urusov, Prince A. I., 15, 34–37, 48, 73, 266

Verdicts, splintering, 30, 67, 94
Victims: Befani, Pola, 72; Bekker, Sarra, 47–49,
    52, 78; Dovnar, Alexander, 79–80; Komarovskii,
    Pavel, 171, 174–76; Podlutskii, Pavel, 154, 164,
    169; Prasolova, Zinaida, 239–45; Sorochinskaia,
    Zenovia, 249; Time, Marianna, 235, 237,
    252–58, 264; Tolstinskaia, Maria, 256;
    Visnovskaia, Maria, 73; Zheleznova, Kleopatra,
    248. See also individual victims
Visnovskaia, Maria, 73
Vladimirov, L. E., 43, 61–63, 84, 91, 108
Vol'kenshtein, F. A., 44–45, 256
Volokhova, Mavra, 15, 27, 31–33, 37, 101, 269
Votiak Case, 51, 68

Wiltenburg, Joy, 13
Wortman, Richard, 7, 16, 85n, 264

Zamiatin, D. M., 16
Zasadkovich, Matvei, 45–46
Zashchitniki. See Attorneys, defense
Zasulich, Vera, 9, 45, 92–94; and trial compared to
    United States v. Battiste ruling, 97, 173
Zheleznova, Kleopatra, 248